Series Editors: Yvonne Rydin and Andrew Thornley

The context in which planning operates has changed dramatically in recent years. Economic processes have become increasingly globalized and economic fortunes have fluctuated. Administrations in various countries have not only changed, but old ideologies have been swept away and new ones have tentatively emerged. A new environmental agenda has prioritized the goal of sustainable development, requiring continued action at international, national and local levels.

Cities are today faced with new pressures for economic competitiveness, greater accountability and participation, improved quality of life for citizens, and global environmental responsibilities. These pressures are often contradictory, and create difficult dilemmas for policy-makers, especially in the context of fiscal austerity.

In these changing circumstances, planners, from many backgrounds, in many different organizations, have come to re-evaluate their work. They have to engage with actors in government, the private sector and non-governmental organizations in discussions over the role of planning in relation to the environment and cities. The intention of the Planning, Environment, Cities series is to explore the changing nature of planning and contribute to the debate about its future.

This series is aimed primarily at students and practitioners of planning and such related professions as estate management, housing and architecture, as well as those in politics, public and social administration, geography and urban studies. It comprises both general texts and books designed to make a more particular contribution, in both cases characterized by: an international approach; extensive use of case studies; and emphasis on contemporary relevance and the application of theory to advance planning practice.

planning · environment · cities

Series Editors: Yvonne Rydin and Andrew Thornley

Planning, Environment, Cities
Series Standing Order ISBN 978–0–333–71703–5 hardback
Series Standing Order ISBN 978–0–333–69346–9 paperback
(*outside North America only*)

You can receive future titles in this series as they are published. To place a standing order please contact your
bookseller or, in the case of difficulty, write to us at the address below with your name and address, the title
of the series and one of the ISBNs quoted above: Customer Services Department, Macmillan Distribution Ltd,
Houndmills, Basingstoke, Hampshire, RG21 6XS, UK.

Sustainable Cities
Governing for Urban Innovation

Simon Joss

First published 2015 by
PALGRAVE

Palgrave in the UK is an imprint of Macmillan Publishers Limited,
registered in England, company number 785998, of 4 Crinan Street,
London, N1 9XW.

Palgrave Macmillan in the US is a division of St Martin's Press LLC,
175 Fifth Avenue, New York, NY 10010.

Palgrave is a global imprint of the above companies
and is represented throughout the world.

Palgrave® and Macmillan® are registered trademarks in the United States,
the United Kingdom, Europe and other countries.

ISBN 978-1-137-00636-3   hardback
ISBN 978-1-137-00635-6   paperback

This book is printed on paper suitable for recycling and made from fully
managed and sustained forest sources. Logging, pulping and manufacturing
processes are expected to conform to the environmental regulations of the
country of origin.

A catalogue record for this book is available from the British Library.

A catalog record for this book is available from the Library of Congress.

Printed in China

Contents

List of Illustrative Material

Figures

Tables

Boxes

Illustrations

Preface

Do we need a new way of thinking about the sustainable city? Are there some questions which tend to be overlooked in current debates? Should the challenge of sustainable urban development perhaps be framed differently?

The answer to these questions may well be 'yes', as this book seeks to argue. This recognizes that, while the aspirational goal of urban sustainability may already be very well established, its realization can seem further away than ever. The problem is not so much that our collective enthusiasm for sustainable cities has weakened over time. If anything, the evidence suggests that the opposite is true: growing interest can be witnessed globally, from a string of high-level international policy declarations to a multitude of national innovation programmes, and from iconic international urban projects by leading architects and developers to a myriad of local initiatives championed by diverse groups of planners, innovators and activists. This growing interest is readily explained by the confluence of several major trends that mark out the twenty-first century as the 'urban age', not least unprecedented rates of urbanization especially across the developing world, and the significant contribution of cities and towns to global climate change and other environmental pressures. Like sustainability itself, then, the city has become ever more central to our assumptions about what the future will, or should, look like.

What remains less easily explained and agreed upon is what exactly the sustainable city entails; that is, how the relationship between social equity, economic development and environmental regeneration should be articulated and applied to various urban scales and settings. Just as perplexing, the question of how to go about planning, implementing and governing sustainable urban development all too often eludes easy explanation, in theory as much as in practice. Hence, while there appears to be a broad consensus – at least at policy level – on the need for sustainable cities and concomitant urgency for action, the emergent discourse equally makes clear the need for detailed research and probing inquiry into the principles, dimensions, processes, as well as outcomes, of the sustainable city. The challenge here is not so much to become better at observing and emulating apparent 'best practice', but rather to pose the right questions about this ongoing global process of experimentation. We have, it seems, only begun to formulate these questions.

This book contributes to this discussion by opening up the sustainable city to critical examination and offering new knowledge about this fascinating yet in many ways challenging contemporary phenomenon. The aim is to provoke fresh and critical thinking, focusing on questions of the sustainable city that are frequently left untouched and unanswered in mainstream debate, but which, it is suggested, may well be key to understanding this intriguing proposition. The main approach chosen here centres upon the sustainable city understood as both an innovation and related governance process. Thus, the phenomenon is not analysed against an absolute, fixed notion or goal of sustainable urban development, nor primarily in technical terms. Rather, it relates to the processes by which ideas about, and strategies for, urban sustainability materialize, are taken up in policy, translated into plans, and subsequently implemented in practice. The particular benefit of the innovation perspective lies in its interest in understanding how new and, as such, typically unorthodox and occasionally radical ideas and practices emerge within experimental niches – which is one way of viewing sustainable city initiatives – from where they seek to challenge and ultimately replace existing, mainstream (unsustainable) economic activity and urban development. This prompts important questions about the conditions necessary for such 'niche development' and, in doing so, points to the critical interaction between sustainable city initiatives and their wider policy and regulatory contexts. Furthermore, the innovation perspective suggests a long-term trajectory, whereby sustainable urban development consists of evolving processes stretching across time, during which the development path may adapt significantly owing to, say, new scientific insights, technological advances, or changing policy and social priorities.

The governance perspective complements the innovation perspective; it does so by focusing on the processes of institutional steering and co-ordination as well as networking among often heterogeneous groups of public and private, local as well as international, actors. This perspective, then, is helpful for considering the influence of strategic policy discourses and policy making on sustainable city initiatives, and it can be used to analyse the decision-making processes and dynamics involved in sustainable urban development.

Importantly, in doing so, it allows for critical engagement with questions about the social and political conditioning at work within the sustainable city and how this shapes related processes and outcomes. This acknowledges that urban sustainability is not a value-free, apolitical proposition and practice but, instead, that it is imbued with essential questions of political strategies, policy priorities and social interests.

Applied in tandem, the innovation and governance perspectives form an overarching framework guiding the analyses. This framework allows the book not only to examine various pertinent aspects of sustainable cities, but also, crucially, to reflect on, and take issue with, some of the mainstream discourses on the topic. In particular, the book critically engages with what is arguably a prevailing contemporary view of the sustainable city as a quasi self-steering, adaptive system. This view has arisen from the powerful combination of three dominant strands of thinking: first, the conceptualization of the sustainable city as part-ecological, part-technological system, according to which the city behaves akin to an organism or machine; second, the emphasis on sustainable urban development as a largely self-governing process driven in no small part by economic priorities and business interests; and third, the focus on advanced technical information and knowledge guiding frameworks and methodologies for implementing urban sustainability. Altogether, this dominant stance arguably neglects important questions about political interests and power, social voice and public accountability. In response, the book explores these questions throughout, and in the concluding chapter identifies possible criteria for considering the sustainable city as a more pluralistic public governance process.

The book is structured in such a way as to make it possible to read the chapters separately, and in no particular order, as self-contained essays. Nevertheless, there is a logical progression built into the book: following the initial overview, in Chapter 1, the second chapter discusses the key debates informing the overarching theoretical framework; this is then used as basis for the analyses in the subsequent chapters. A broad, historical perspective on the genesis of sustainable city policy discourses is presented in Chapter 3, culminating in the discussion of key contemporary policy debates and how these influence recent concepts and practices of urban sustainability. This is followed in Chapter 4 by a detailed empirical analysis of various practical eco-city programmes and initiatives that have emerged across global regions since the early 2000s. Building on this comprehensive survey, Chapter 5 delves more deeply into the question of (new) governance for urban sustainability, based on two detailed case studies which highlight complex interrelationships between sustainable city initiatives and their wider urban policy contexts. This is followed in Chapter 6 with a discussion of the emerging role of international frameworks for sustainable cities in both facilitating innovation and steering governance processes; here, three different types of framework are analysed and compared, suggesting a common tension at work between defining global standards of urban sustainability and situating these within particular local settings. Chapter 7 addresses the role of knowledge in the sustainable city, and especially how certain forms of knowledge influence both the theory and practice of urban sustainability and how, in turn, the sustainable city produces and privileges certain kinds of knowledge; this again points to the essential if problematic aspect of governance process. The concluding Chapter 8 brings together the various analytical perspectives developed throughout the book; in doing so, it critically reflects on key issues of innovation and governance and seeks to articulate a more pluralistic public governance stance in response to the perceived shortcomings of recent debates about, and developments in, sustainable cities.

SIMON JOSS

Acknowledgements

This book has been in the making for a couple of years; the research underlying it for many more still. It has come about as a result of several precious partnerships, exchange visits and galvanizing discussions; and I am grateful to colleagues and friends who over the years have provided much inspiration and encouragement. A special acknowledgement must go to Robert Kargon and Arthur Molella. Their pioneering work on techno-cities prompted my foray into eco-city research, and the resulting partnership between our organizations has been the main catalyst for our International Eco-Cities Initiative. I am indebted to both of them, and grateful for their friendship.

Over the years, I have had the pleasure of engaging in joint research activities with colleagues from around the world. An important milestone was the research seminar series 'The Governance of Eco-City Innovation', followed by the Bellagio conference 'Developing International Standards and Policy for Eco-Cities', and lately the research network 'Tomorrow's City Today: An International Comparison of Eco-City Frameworks'. I should particularly like to acknowledge the contributions made by (in alphabetical order): John Barry, Hugh Barton, Jutta Berns-Mumbi, Vatsal Bhatt, Federico Caprotti, I-Chun Catherine Chang, Federico Cugurullo, Martin de Jong, Tu Lan Do, Shanfeng Dong, Katarina Eckerberg, Anders Franzen, Lars Frederiksen, Cate Harris, Peter Head, Anna Hult, Morris Low, Bernhard Müller, Alice Owen, Luis A. Paredes, William Rees, Sue Riddlestone, Mark Roseland, Yvonne Rydin, Debashis Sen, Sofia T. Shwayri, Buhm Soon Park, Hiroaki Suzuki, Hongxing Xie, and Li Yu.

Closer to home, I have benefited from the encouragement and support of colleagues at the University of Westminster. Special thanks are due to Nick Bailey, Dan Greenwood, Liza Griffin, Tassilo Herrschel, Patricia Hogwood, Amanda Machin, Alan Morrison, Peter Newman, Malcolm Rigg, Fred Steward, and last but not least Daniel Tomozeiu, whose dedication and professionalism have made all the difference. I have also drawn much inspiration from the engagement with my doctoral students Rob Cowley, Njogu Morgan and Martin Stumpler. A very special acknowledgement must go to Rob Cowley, who has supported my work on this book with quite superb editorial and research assistantship and has contributed much stimulating intellectual discussion to the International Eco-Cities Initiative.

The research informing this book would not have been possible without the generous support from several funding bodies. I am particularly indebted to Professor Lord Bhikhu Parekh and Dr Chandrakant Shroff, whose Nirman Foundation provided all-important seed funding. Subsequent grants came from the Economic and Social Research Council, the Rockefeller Foundation, and the Leverhulme Trust, all of which are gratefully acknowledged.

I should like to thank the editorial team at Palgrave, and in particular Stephen Wenham for his professional guidance, and Yvonne Rydin, who as series co-editor offered invaluable advice and encouragement. Many thanks also go to the anonymous reviewers for their constructive comments and suggestions for improving the book.

Most of all, I am grateful to my family, and especially to Paul for your love and support.

SIMON JOSS

Chapter 1

Sustainability and the City?

CHAPTER OVERVIEW

The 'sustainable city' is a seemingly simple and alluring proposition, which holds the promise of reducing cities' negative impact on the local and global environment while concurrently making urban areas more attractive and convenient as places in which to work and live. A closer look, however, reveals a picture many times more complex: urban sustainability has multiple dimensions, each of them elaborate and co-existing in intricate relationships, often causing tension. Conceptually as well as analytically, the sustainable city can be difficult to define and delineate, as it crosses disciplinary boundaries, mixes normative assumptions with empirical observations, and is closely shaped by specific geographical, cultural and political contingencies. This opening chapter begins to unravel this expansive, captivating phenomenon, by considering key sustainable city dimensions and identifying underlying challenges confronting the study and practice of urban sustainability.

Introducing the sustainable city

'Welcome to Eco-City. No fuel bills, no traffic jams, no pollution. Move in 2009.' With these headline-grabbing words, the cover of the December 2008 issue of *BBC Focus* magazine heralded the arrival of a brand-new generation of sustainable cities (see Illustration 1.1; *BBC Focus*, 2008). The main feature article explains that 'the pressure cities are putting on the planet's resources is huge … In response, cities all over the world are setting themselves high targets to reduce carbon emissions and produce clean energy. But if they don't succeed, there is another option: building new eco-cities entirely from scratch' (Taylor, 2008: 45). The magazine features two exemplars of this 'city of tomorrow': Dongtan, a model eco-city planned for opening in 2010 near Shanghai in China; and Masdar, proclaimed by its developers as the world's first fully 'zero-

1

Illustration 1.1

Cover page of *BBC Focus* magazine, issue 197 (December 2008).

carbon' and 'zero-waste' city, to be located on the outskirts of Abu Dhabi in the Arab Emirates.

In practice, since the first phase of Masdar's development was unveiled under the glare of the global media in 2010, the original overall completion date of 2016 has been pushed back to the early 2020s, reportedly due to the global recession, and some of its early ambitions have been scaled down. For its part, construction of Dongtan Eco-City was halted in 2008 and the project postponed indefinitely due to a combination of funding and political problems at local level. 'Move in 2009', therefore, appears to have been somewhat premature. Nevertheless, the *BBC Focus* magazine hit on a trend – namely, the rise to international prominence of the sustainable city among policy-makers, urban planners, architects, engineers and environmental specialists. Although, as a concept and practical experiment, the sustainable city has a longer history behind it – and its underlying ideas can be traced back over several decades if not a century or more – it is largely since the turn of the new millennium that its profile has risen globally and its policy resonance has become increasingly ubiquitous. As a consequence, the last decade or so has seen a myriad of variously labelled 'eco-city', 'sustainable city', 'low-carbon city', 'resilient city' and 'smart city' initiatives spring up across global regions.

Three examples (which are discussed in more detail in Chapters 2 and 4) illustrate this trend. In China – notwithstanding the particular difficulties afflicting Dongtan – the number of eco-cities under development by 2010 was estimated to be over one hundred according to an authoritative report by the World Bank (2009: ii); to this, more recent separate 'low-carbon city' and 'smart city' initiatives have been added. It appears, therefore, that within a short period of time the Chinese national and municipal authorities have come to embrace the sustainable city enthusiastically. In France, in 2008 the government launched a two-fold national initiative to encourage investment and innovation in sustainable urban development: one, ÉcoCité, is aimed at larger cities; the other, ÉcoQuartier, is focused on medium-sized towns and cities. To date, close to 50 cities have signed up to this initiative, being implemented by national agencies and municipal authorities working in concert. In India, following an earlier eco-city initiative (2002–7) spearheaded by one government ministry with a focus on 'retrofitting' six ancient pilgrim cities, other ministries have more recently launched a 'solar cities' initiative (working with 60 cities to reduce conventional energy use by at least ten per cent within five years), a 'near-zero energy satellite towns' programme, and the construction of four new eco-cities along the newly designated Delhi–Mumbai Corridor. To these examples of national developments can be added a growing number of international networks and platforms promoting urban sustainability, such as the C40 Cities Climate Leadership Group founded in 2005 and currently including 63 major cities, and the World Bank's Eco2 Cities initiative which, since its launch in 2009, has been mainly active across Asia. Overall, then, the last decade or so has seen the emergence of the sustainable city as a practical phenomenon at an unprecedented rate and on a global scale.

'Sustainable city' is a simple and appealing proposition, or so it seems, that easily resonates in policy and public discourse, and effortlessly travels across national and cultural borders. A city that reduces energy consumption, protects the environment, promotes urban density, eases traffic congestion, lessens urban heat island effects, champions urban agriculture, recycles waste, provides clean water, expands parkland, creates 'walkable' neighbourhoods, generates local employment, supports human health and well-being, celebrates civic engagement, and enhances efficient information management – in short, the sustainable city – is an ideal and goal to which most people will feel happy to subscribe. And yet, presenting the sustainable city as a long wish list of normative ideals and as utopian vision risks trying to be 'all things to all people' and deferring the sustainable city to some indeterminate future. The challenge, then, consists of generating detailed, sophisticated and contextualized knowledge and understanding – building on the critical analysis of present conditions – concerning specific aspects of, and requirements for, the sustainable city. It further consists of moving beyond normative thinking – essential though that may be – to developing, testing and finally implementing the sustainable city in practice. The many urban sustainability initiatives, both small and large, that have mushroomed globally in recent decades collectively represent efforts to generate such knowledge and engage in innovation.

As such, the sustainable city may be usefully conceptualized as an evolving, experimental process, rather than as a fixed entity or specific outcome. Not surprisingly, this process leaves many questions still to be fully answered, and frequently throws up new issues along the way. How should different sustainable development aspects – reducing greenhouse gas emissions, supporting economic growth, improving social conditions – be brought to bear on the city in a way that is mutually reinforcing? What is the appropriate scale at which sustainable urban development should be directed: the neighbourhood, the city, even the city-region? Should the focus of sustainable urbanism rest more on the 'retrofitting' of existing building stock and infrastructure, or instead – as the *BBC Focus* magazine essay seems to suggest – on new urban developments? Should the focus be more on technological innovation, or perhaps on changing people's behaviour? Who should take a lead in developing urban sustainability strategies: national governments, international organizations, cities themselves? What are appropriate mechanisms for planning, co-ordinating, financing and monitoring urban sustainability action? What is the prospect for global standards for sustainable urban development, and how would these be reconciled with local priorities and requirements? And, not least, how do we know whether urban sustainability measures actually work? These and many more questions and issues give an indication of the richness and complexity presented by the sustainable city as a both conceptual and practical endeavour. They also give a good indication of the difficulties and challenges involved in systematically analysing this phenomenon, as well as the creative potential for figuring out answers and developing solutions.

The sustainable city as process

This book aims to contribute to the ongoing task of generating knowledge and stimulating debate about the contemporary sustainable city. It does so by presenting a comprehensive overview, and in-depth discussion, of recent evolutions in urban sustainability policy and practice; and it places the current phenomenon of the sustainable city in a wider historical context, considering the legacy of earlier discourses and how these have been recast in response to recent trends. The book draws on key conceptual perspectives on sustainable urban development and seeks to expand these further; and it discusses numerous examples and case studies of sustainable city initiatives analysed through empirical research.

As a multidisciplinary field of study, the sustainable city calls upon several research disciplines; these each conceptualize urban sustainability in certain ways and pursue particular empirical interests, rooted in their respective theoretical and methodological traditions. For example, environmental scientists have begun to analyse the city in terms of material flows – the input and throughput of energy, water and building materials, and the outputs of waste and pollutants – as a way of assessing, and ultimately improving the efficiency of, energy and material flow cycles of cities (see e.g. Pulselli et al., 2004; Kennedy et al., 2007; Weisz and Steinberger, 2010; Zhang et al., 2010). Similarly, but with more of a technological slant, engineers and technologists increasingly conceptualize the city as an 'urban operating system', whereby diverse data concerning urban infrastructure and services – such as traffic flows, energy consumption and water requirements – can be digitally captured and monitored in real time and controlled centrally with the help of information and communication technologies (for an overview, see e.g. Hollands, 2008; Caragliu et al., 2011; Chourabi et al., 2012). Here again, the premise is that such an integrated, networked system approach – often dubbed 'smart city' – improves the efficiency of urban infrastructure and services management which, in turn, should improve cities' sustainability performance. These system approaches add new dimensions to the more established focus on 'green buildings' widely promoted by the architectural and design professions (see e.g. Curwell et al., 1999; Yudelson, 2008; EPA, 2013; Kibert, 2013). The 'green building' agenda is also concerned with energy efficiency, sustainable material use and waste reduction, but mainly in relation to developing new, and retrofitting existing, buildings and building complexes. Unlike the system approaches, it typically also incorporates socio-economic, cultural and aesthetic concerns, such as how to design for 'mixed-use' developments (the appropriate combination of housing, offices and the public realm), 'walkable' neighbourhoods, and 'liveable', culturally diverse urban centres.

Central to the sustainable city are issues of planning and governance. This is the domain of urban studies and planning, an interdisciplinary social-scientific field concerned with analysing urban policies, strategies and plans and how these shape, and are shaped by, institutional and organizational structures, processes and cultures. Urban studies emerged and evolved throughout the twentieth century not least as an effort to redress the ills of unchecked urban development through the professionalization of planning. At the time, this occurred under the banner of the 'garden city', 'new town' and similar concepts and movements, and these have acted as influential antecedents of the contemporary sustainable city movement (see e.g. Miller, 2002; Parsons and Schuyler, 2002; Wheeler, 2000). The field of urban studies, therefore, provides essential, critical perspectives on current discourses on sustainable urbanism. Similarly key insights are provided by fellow social science disciplines such as human geography and development studies (see e.g. Pugh, 2000; Wheeler, 2009; Dale et al., 2012) which draw attention to the fact that the sustainable city always exists in close relationship with wider regional and indeed international contexts. This prompts the need for the analysis of geographical, geopolitical, economic, cultural and other contextual factors and how these co-define and condition the sustainable city.

In particular, the tendency towards knowledge transfer between different countries and across continents raises various questions about processes of local implementation. At the most basic level, different cities have very different starting points (see Box 1.4, for example), making 'one size fits all' solutions – and even broad guidelines – at least difficult to imagine. Perhaps even more importantly, a simple binary perspective in which either solutions are 'imposed' by economically powerful actors on weaker countries, or solutions arise 'from the bottom up', fails to capture the subtleties of how globally circulating urban sustainability ideas are implemented locally. As scholars of globalization and international development have been keen to observe, policies and practices often travel at the explicit behest of actors in the localities to which they are exported, and are typically subject to significant reinterpretation and reworking as they are implemented on the ground (see Chapter 4).

This book draws on several of the disciplinary perspectives and interests mentioned above, in order to explore and discuss the sustainable city as comprehensively as possible from various, complementary viewpoints. It does so, however, by using an overarching framework designed to provide a coherent and consistent approach for inquiring into the sustainable city. This framework principally considers the sustainable city as a socio-political phenomenon in terms of interrelated policy, governance and innovation processes. The underlying assumption is that *process* is central to sustainable urbanism: this can be seen, for example, in terms of diverse innovation processes driving new techno-environmental and socio-economic approaches and solutions for sustainable urban development; it can also be seen in terms of planning and decision-making processes needed to co-ordinate action among diverse stakeholders and across scales; and it can be seen in the role of the policy process in providing strategic impetus, programmatic direction and regulatory incentives to guide various actors in their pursuit of urban sustainability. It is precisely because the sustainable city is a multi-faceted phenomenon which concurrently acts at various spatial levels; bridges environmental, economic and social issues; transcends institutional boundaries; involves diverse actors; and is future-oriented; that its process dimensions – in the form of steering, networking, co-ordination and integration – define it so centrally.

A focus on processes may seem somewhat unconventional. After all, the sustainable city is typically depicted in terms of technological systems and gadgets – wind turbines gracing the urban landscape, solar arrays, monorails, grey water recycling systems, remote sensors, and so on – coupled with futuristic design renderings of, for example, 'intelligent' green buildings, 'walkable' neighbourhoods, car-free traffic, attractive civic centres, and extensive parks and wetlands. However, the focus on process makes sense if one considers that sustainable urban development is essentially concerned with understanding the nature of, and conditions for, initiating and facilitating transitions from the present state of towns and cities towards more sustainable, future urbanism. These transitions are not a given – they do not reveal themselves without detailed, critical enquiry and much experimental and innovative work – and they do not happen without contestation, involving difficult questions about technological feasibility, political directions and social choices. Enquiring into the policy, governance and innovation processes needed to effect such transitions is, therefore, productive and central to seeking to understand the sustainable city.

Throughout this book, these processes are explored in detail and critically from conceptual perspectives, by considering the role of policy in directing urban sustainability strategy, discussing models of urban sustainability governance, and examining the role of innovation. Likewise, they are explored empirically, by analysing their practical manifestations based upon diverse examples of urban sustainability initiatives in various settings across the world. First, however, the remaining part of this chapter traces the contours of the sustainable city further by considering key principles, elements and dimensions, as identified in both the academic and policy literature.

The sustainable city in the Urban Age

As noted, the 'sustainable city' has multiple dimensions that relate to one another in complex ways. Simple, straightforward definitions are, therefore, hard to come by. Instead, a useful way of approaching the sustainable city is to consider how some of the key contributors to the field have characterized various dimensions of sustainable urban development. The sections below first compare the way that its key principles have been interpreted in recent years by three influential thinkers in the field. Following this, the discussion explores three contemporary tendencies in the interpretation of the concept in practice and policy, each differing in the way it structures the principles of sustainable development. First, however, the term 'sustainable city' itself needs some brief, basic clarification. This is done by considering what is meant, on one hand, by 'sustainability' and 'sustainable development' and, on the other, how this relates to the 'city'.

On sustainability and sustainable development

Sustainability and its sister term, sustainable development, are in themselves expansive concepts that have been developed and debated in the academic and policy literature extensively over recent decades (for an overview, see e.g. Redclift, 2005; Kates et al., 2005; Connelly, 2007). Some commentators (e.g. Dobson, 1991; Lélé, 1991) have distinguished between 'sustainability' and 'sustainable development' – for example, suggesting that the former describes a state, while the latter refers to the process of moving towards that state. However, in practice the two terms are generally now used interchangeably (Jacobs, 1999; Seghezzo, 2009). They are discussed just as much in relation to economics, international development, business management, environmental policy and community practice, as they are applied more specifically to the city.

While the origins of the concept of sustainable development can be traced back to the eighteenth century, it was during the 1980s and 1990s that it came to prominence in international policy and spawned a new field of academic research and public policy (see Box 1.1). By the early 1990s, dozens of attempts to define the concept had already been published (Pezzey, 1992: 1), but at its most basic, sustainable development valorizes economic and social activity that does not negatively impact overall on the natural environment and that can be sustained long term from human generation to generation (WCED, 1987). The concept responds to the recognition that socio-economic activity that depletes natural resources or 'capital' (water, forests, fish stocks, etc.) at a faster rate than they can be replaced is unsustainable in the long term, as it threatens the bio-habitat (the natural environment) and thereby also the livelihood of future generations.

Box 1.1   Sustainable development

The origins of the concept of sustainable development have been located in eighteenth-century German forest management (Grober, 2012). However, current uses of the term, and its widespread adoption in policy making, are more directly associated with the World Commission on Environment and Development's 1987 *Our Common Future* (also known as the Brundtland Report, WCED, 1987), and the declarations from the ensuing 'Earth Summit' conference held in Rio de Janeiro in 1992 (UNDESA, 1992a) – see Chapter 3 for further discussion of these, and the relationship between sustainable development and the city. Its standard definition, taken from the Brundtland Report, is that of 'development that meets the needs of the present without compromising the ability of future generations to meet their own needs' (WCED, 1987: 27).

Sustainable development has come to be conceptualized around three 'pillars' (or as the 'triple bottom line') of the environment, economy, and society. Rather than promoting a primarily ecological agenda, it therefore advocates a model of economic growth which encompasses human development and environmental protection. The concept has been contested in various ways (some of which are outlined below in the present chapter), and no consensus has yet emerged over what it might mean in practice or how it might be achieved.

Sustainable development, therefore, is development that does not overall exceed the Earth's biophysical capacity. 'Ecological footprint' analysis, originally developed by environmental scientists William E. Rees and Mathis Wackernagel (Rees, 1992; Rees and Wackernagel, 1996), has become one of the main methodologies for estimating and illustrating the natural resources requirements of socio-economic activity. It allows the calculation of the amount of natural resources and 'environmental services' – such as water, energy, crops for food, etc. – consumed by given socio-economic activities and the corresponding amount of land and sea area required to supply and replenish these resources, as well as to absorb the wastes produced. Taking into account the biologically productive land and sea area – the Earth's 'carrying capacity' – and the size of the global human population, calculations can be made of the average ecological footprint for each person that is sustainable: in 2007, this was calculated to be approx. 1.8 global hectares, based on a global population of ca. 6.7 billion (Ewing et al., 2010: 18). In other words, 1.8 hectares is the area of land and sea available for sustainable resource consumption to each individual person on the planet. The Global Footprint Network calculated that the actual average ecological footprint per person for the entire global population exceeds this measure by approximately 50 per cent (ibid.). This, then, is a global indicator for the current level of unsustainable human activity in these ecological terms. Similar calculations can be made – although not without some methodological difficulties – individually for countries, industrial sectors and cities (see further below). The 'carbon footprint' is used more specifically to calculate the emission of carbon dioxide (CO_2) and other greenhouse gases (GHG) of a particular entity (human being, building, business, city, nation, and so on) (e.g. Wiedmann and Minx, 2008; Ewing et al., 2010). Again, actual carbon footprint calculations can be compared with the global carbon footprint total considered to be sustainable in the context of recent debates about global warming and climate change.

When considering sustainable development, therefore, environmental, economic and social aspects have to be taken into account concurrently; they function in a direct and mutually dependent interrelationship. Contemplating the impact of human activity on the environment necessarily prompts relevant questions about the nature of economic activity – that is, whether economic development and growth can be sustained in a way which does not put undue, irreversible stresses on the natural environment. Likewise, questions about environmental degradation often have deep social and cultural implications within and across generations as, for example, poor communities – and especially communities in the Global South – may be disproportionally exposed to environmental harm; and as overconsumption of natural resources by current generations may risk the livelihood of future generations.

The close intertwining of environmental, economic and social considerations is commonly referred to as the 'three pillars, or 'triple bottom line', of sustainability (see Box 1.1). Exactly how this three-fold relationship – the relative emphasis of its elements and their articulation – is to be understood, however, is far from a settled question. Much research has gone into exploring this complex interaction conceptually, as well as empirically through case studies looking at specific contexts.

While sustainable development has over the last 20 to 30 years become a widely recognized paradigm and core element of many areas of public policy, more critical voices have raised several kinds of concerns. One such criticism addresses the fact that the translation of the concept of sustainability into policy and practice too often ends up treating each of the three pillars separately, without managing to establish interconnections in any great depth. This may lead to 'silo' practice, whereby environmental issues are addressed by certain actors in one set of policy, whereas social development is considered by other actors through a different set of policy. Another criticism is levelled against what is labelled 'weak' sustainability, which treats environmental resources or 'natural capital' – forests, water, etc. – on a par with human capital (Stern, 1997; Smith et al., 2001; Ekins et al., 2003; Rydin, 2010). According to this perspective, environmental resources (also referred to as 'eco-system services') can be traded and substituted for human capital, with the effect that increasing human capital may lead to decreasing natural capital. This idea is developed in the 'environmental economics' promoted by authors such as David Pearce (Pearce and Turner, 1990; Pearce, 2002), who see current economic models as flawed in their failure to account for ecological concerns, and therefore propose that the environment should be 'monetized' (Pearce and Barbier, 2000). In response, critics argue that ecological systems have unique characteristics that may well require the prioritizing of environmental protection over economic and social development: the extinction of a species or the depletion of a natural resource for economic gains may lead to irreparable environmental damage with unforeseen, lasting repercussions. Consequently, these critics argue that 'strong' sustainability is needed instead, to encourage socio-economic activity which protects the integrity of ecological systems. Such sustainable development, it is argued, requires alternative approaches to the 'business-as-usual' model of economic and social activity.

The conceptual fuzziness of sustainable development has had the beneficial effect of allowing an inclusive 'global dialogue' (Kates et al., 2005: 20) to take place. Equally, however, it has arguably allowed for questions of equity between the Global North and South to be downplayed in its interpretation (Jacobs, 1999; Meadowcroft, 2000). Since, as a foundational document, the Brundtland Report avoids advocating any particular economic model, it has been suggested that in mainstream discourse sustainable development has been dominated by a 'liberal consensus' which is insufficiently critical of the current form of economic globalization (Redclift, 2005: 220).

The complexities and challenges of interrelating, both conceptually and in policy and practice, the three pillars of sustainability have led to governance being proposed as a further, essential pillar of sustainable development (see e.g. Adger and Jordan, 2009; Griffin, 2010). Broadly, governance refers to the processes of co-ordinating, facilitating and steering policy- and decision-making processes. It emphasizes the need for networking across organizational boundaries and across institutional levels, and it emphasizes the opportunity for various actors to work collaboratively in partnership. The potential benefits of governance are seen in the improved capacity to co-ordinate action between organizations, to mobilize and integrate different sources of expertise – from specialist knowledge of professional organizations to lay knowledge of local communities – and to widen participation in policy deliberation and decision-making. This capacity is considered essential for achieving, for example, more sustainable transport: this requires the alignment and co-ordination of various transport systems – rail, bus, tram, etc. – to be able to offer more integrated, easy-to-use and affordable public transport services. A formal public–private partnership (PPP) may be the appropriate vehicle for financing, planning and operating such integrated transit. Elsewhere, setting up local food networks may require co-operation between various producers (farmers, allotment gardens, food companies), retailers (grocery stores, farmers' markets, restaurants and consumers (schools, hospitals, residents). Here, more informal distribution networks and community action programmes may be to the fore. In short, any discussion of sustainability and sustainable development usually prompts important questions about governance, and much innovation in sustainable development centres upon figuring out appropriate forms and processes for governing.

The city as 'battleground' for sustainability in the Urban Age

A powerful narrative has emerged which places the city at the centre of sustainability efforts. Some of the importance, urgency and opportunities attached to the sustainable city by leading international organizations and at least one mayor of a world city (London) are captured in Box 1.2.

According to this narrative, in the twenty-first century – the 'urban age' – the city becomes the centre stage for innovation and action, through which unprecedented urban development and growth is to be achieved in tandem with meeting global environmental and societal challenges. In this view, urban sustainable management and development are not just critical for cities themselves, but 'one of the critical items for the 21st century' (UN-Habitat, 2003a) altogether. In particular, cities are assigned a central role in combating global climate change: they are 'at the front line', where 'the battle for sustainable development' will either be won or lost. While the metaphor of the battleground evokes struggle and potential loss, it also promises the potential for victory. To use another analogy, cities are places where an 'exciting revolution' can take hold, sparking innovation and change in response to the 'new low energy age'. This opportunity is recognized as particularly significant – a once-in-a-lifetime opportunity – because globally economic development is closely coupled with ongoing urbanization, especially in developing countries of the Global South. In short, get urban development 'right', and ecological protection can be reconciled with economic growth. Hence, it is asserted, the key to sustainability lies in 'green cities' or 'eco-cities'.

These policy pronouncements serve an obvious purpose – that is, to raise political and public awareness and marshal support for concerted action on urban development. As such, they speak a bold, unequivocal language, portraying little uncertainty about the urgency and course of action required. A more nuanced, analytical narrative would point, for example, to the ongoing challenge of establishing more specific data and better intelligence about the extent to which individual urban sectors (transport, housing, water, food, etc.) and cities overall contribute to GHG emissions; it would

14

Box 1.2   The sustainable city in the Urban Age

'Sustainable urban management and development is one of the most critical issues for the 21st century' (UN Johannesburg Earth Summit, 2002).

'The battle for sustainable development, for delivering a more environmentally stable, just and healthier world, is going to be largely won or lost in our cities' (Klaus Toepfer, Director, United Nations Environment Programme) (BBC, 2005).

'Cities are now on the front line of the management of change and are playing a leading role in the global development agenda' (World Bank) (Suzuki et al., 2010: xv).

'Cities are at the cusp of an exciting revolution ... Cities are brimming with natural advantages and economies of scale that allow them to adapt and thrive in a new low energy age ... Cities, as the major source of global carbon emissions, have a responsibility to lead the way' (Boris Johnson, Mayor of London) (Embassy of Switzerland in the UK, 2010: 10).

'... the effects of urbanization and climate change are converging in dangerous ways. The results of this convergence threaten to have unprecedented negative impacts on quality of life, and economic and social stability. However, alongside these threats is an equally compelling set of opportunities ... urbanization will also offer many opportunities to develop cohesive mitigation and adaptation strategies to deal with climate change. The populations, enterprises and authorities of urban centres will be fundamental players in developing these strategies' (UN-Habitat, 2011b: 1).

'This unprecedented urban expansion sets forth before us a once-in-a-lifetime opportunity to plan, develop, build and manage cities that are simultaneously more ecologically and economically sustainable' (Hiroaki Suzuki, Lead Urban Specialist, World Bank) (World Bank, 2011).

'The key to sustainability lies in the concept of "green cities" or "eco cities"' (UNEP, 2012a: vi).

'How the world's largest and fastest-growing cities develop will be critical to the future path of the global economy and climate' (Global Commission on the Economy and Climate, 2014: 8).

address critically how economic growth and ecological protection are to be achieved simultaneously through urbanization; and it would delve into what forms of sustainable urban management are appropriate for specific contexts. While these policy statements, then, do not in themselves reveal much by way of such underlying analytical information, they nevertheless encapsulate the reasons why cities have become the main strategic focus of sustainability concerns.

First, cities and wider conurbations are major centres of financial and industrial activities and, as such, contribute significantly to a country's economy. For example, the OECD calculated in 2006 that large cities such as 'Budapest, Seoul, Copenhagen, Dublin, Helsinki, Randstad-Holland and Brussels concentrate nearly half of their national GDP whilst Oslo, Auckland, Prague, London, Stockholm, Tokyo, and Paris account for around one third' (OECD, 2006: 1). According to another study, the UK's 64 largest cities occupy only 9 per cent of the country's landmass, but generate 60 per cent of its GVA (an economic measure of the value of goods and services produced) (Centre for Cities, 2013: 2). Meanwhile, a report prepared for the United States Conference of Mayors observed that the metropolitan areas of New York, Chicago, and Los Angeles each 'produce more annually than countries such as Sweden, Norway, Poland, Belgium, Argentina and Taiwan' (IHS Global Insight, 2013: 1).

Relatedly, cities and city-regions are often understood to have new-found economic and political agency on the world stage, following processes of globalization which have left nation states less autonomous and less able to play a role as an 'institutional buffer between localities and the machinations of the global economy' (Hackworth, 2007: 12). Multinational organizations (privately owned companies and international government institutions) may have gained power at the expense of national state governments, but this has also left 'space for subnational resurgence' (Jessop, 1994: 264). Thus, according to some, '[l]ocal authorities – cities, states, provinces, special districts – now have more responsibilities and, some would argue, more ability to act independently of the larger bodies of government above them' (Hackworth, 2007: 12). This has been described as a 'new regionalism', associated particularly with 'global cities', and which 'stands in opposition to the view of the world as a borderless space of flows' (Scott et al., 2001: 1; for a recent comparative analysis, see also Herrschel, 2014). Rather than becoming increasingly irrelevant to globalized flows of different types, cities are 'central to neoliberal globalisation. The increasing concentration of humanity within them is in part a product of it' (Massey, 2007: 9). In parallel, while 'regions' in the traditional sense were subservient to the nation state, newly powerful city-regions often appear to display more commonalities, and have stronger direct economic connections, with other similar regions in other countries than with less prosperous parts of their own nation (Scott et al., 2001: 1; Archer, 2012: 246).

This story of the economic (and political) rise of the city in recent decades, however, has been questioned by some commentators. Although cities – as opposed to nation states – are increasingly understood as individual players in the global economy, in unmediated competition with other cities, this does not necessarily imply their free choice in the matter (Peck and Tickell, 1994). The contention that individual cities have appeared to gain power is to some extent contradicted by the evidence that so many have chosen similar policy paths, such as reducing public services and increasing co-operation with corporate actors (Hackworth, 2007), and moving away from merely 'managing' services towards a more 'entrepreneurial' approach (Harvey, 1989; Oatley, 1998: 4). It is argued that local actors have not been empowered by the newly organized economic world, so much as 'disciplined' (Gill, 1995), or 'terrorised' (Purcell, 2008), into certain developmental directions; the outcome might alternatively be characterized as 'limited-capacity urban governance' in many cases (Miller, 2007: 235). Even if we can talk of newly 'global' cities, furthermore, we may be guilty of ignoring significant inequalities within those same cities: only certain sectors and certain social groups have become globally connected, while others have been marginalized (Massey, 2007). Such reservations paint a more nuanced picture of the rise of the city, and problematize some of the discourse around it, but it remains the case that, for better or worse, cities – or at least more economically powerful ones – are implicated fundamentally in processes of globalization and the rescaling of power which has resulted (Brenner, 2004).

A second reason why cities have become a main focus of sustainability concerns lies in the fact that, as hubs of socio-economic activity, they are resource intensive – in terms of the use of energy, water, materials and land – and, consequently, they are a major draw on natural capitals and significant contributors to environmental pollution and degradation. For example, cities are estimated to be responsible for 60–70 per cent of man-made GHG emissions (calculated on the basis of emissions generated by both the production and consumption of goods and services within cities) (UN-Habitat, 2011b: 16). Third, cities often harbour stark social inequalities, with the contrast between wealthy and poor communities particularly sharp. This is most obviously the case in the developing world: according to the UN, African cities display the most income inequality on average, followed by Latin American cities – though many major metropolitan areas in the US are on a par with Latin America in this respect (UN-Habitat, 2010: 10). Ongoing urbanization in the developing world has been accompanied by the growth of informal and unplanned settlements; according to UN estimates, 32 per cent of urban residents in the developing world live in slums (UN-Habitat, 2010: 7).

Putting these arguments and observations together, it follows that if sustainability is to be achieved by jointly addressing environmental, economic and social development then action at city level seems potentially particularly effective. The city, then, is seen by many as the appropriate scale for intervention, where governance structures and processes can be designed and implemented to produce significant action and effect sustainable development.

There is a further, important reason why sustainability has become so closely tied up with cities: this relates to the unprecedented rate of urbanization globally, and especially in developing countries in the Global South. 2008 was marked as a watershed moment in human history, when for the first time half of the world's population lived in urban areas and cities (UN-Habitat, 2009b; UN-Habitat, 2011a). It is estimated that in the period between 1950 and 2011, the urban population increased by a factor of five, and that by 2030 it will have increased to 60 per cent of the world's population (UN-Habitat, 2011a). The fastest rates of urbanization in recent decades have taken place (and are expected to continue to do so) in developing countries and emerging economies in the Global South, especially across Asia, Africa and Latin America. (In comparison, the populations of Europe, North America and Oceania have increased, too, but at significantly slower rates.) For example, in China alone, it is estimated that in the period 2000–20 some 300 million people will have become city residents as a consequence of both migration to urban centres and the ongoing urbanization of rural areas. Hence, the policy importance of urban sustainability is seen not just in terms of addressing the environmental, economic and social challenges facing existing cities but, crucially, in terms of innovating in sustainable development in preparation for cities and urban regions yet to emerge.

Principles of the sustainable city: three approaches

Urban sustainability as policy priority has brought forth numerous propositions and visions for what the sustainable city should look like. Many of these propositions and visions are future-oriented and normative, expressing what their protagonists wish the ideal-typical sustainable city to look like. As such, they may be criticized for being too removed from the reality of present sustainable urban development, and steeped too much in normative thinking. This is arguably an unfair view: for one thing, such propositions and visions typically take a cue from innovative experimental and analytical work carried out by pioneers in the field; and for another, they purposely reach for ambitious goals, in order to provoke fundamental debate, creative thinking and ambitious long-term planning.

Here, three such contributions are introduced and compared (see Table 1.1): Richard Register's (1987) seminal *Ecocity Berkeley*, which subsequently led to the publication of ten 'ecocity principles'; Jeffrey R. Kenworthy's (2006) 'The Eco-city: Ten Key Transport and Planning Dimensions for Sustainable City Development'; and Steffen Lehmann's (2010) *The Principles of Green Urbanism*. These examples are illustrative of the rapidly growing literature on sustainable urban development over the last three decades or so. They are useful in showing both the common strands of conceptual thinking running through various sustainable city propositions and the nuanced differences that exist between them. Apart from different normative accentuations, these nuances are explainable also in terms of the evolving discourse: for example, Register's work predominantly relates the city to its immediate local context and associated environmental and socio-economic challenges, whereas Lehmann's contribution some twenty years later reflects the rising interest in the sustainable city from a global perspective, in terms of global warming and climate change affecting cities in the Global North and Global South alike.

Ecocity/Urban Ecology principles (Register)

The Urban Ecology movement dates back to the 1970s and centres upon the innovative work by its co-founder Richard Register, who has been a major force behind the modern eco-city movement. *Ecocity Berkeley* (Register, 1987) outlined a vision and a set of practical propositions for the rebuilding of Berkeley (California, US) as an 'ecologically healthy' city. It soon became the catalyst for this growing international movement dedicated to promoting urban

Table 1.1 *Principles of the eco-city and sustainable urbanism*

Urban ecology (Register, 1987/1996)	Eco-city dimensions Kenworthy (2006)	Green urbanism Lehmann (2010)
1. Create compact communities near transit nodes.	1. Compact, mixed-use urban form.	1. Climate and context: city based on its climatic conditions.
2. Emphasize 'access by proximity' transport strategy.	2. Natural environment permeating urban spaces.	2. Renewable energy for zero CO2 emissions.
3. Restore damaged urban environments.	3. Road infrastructure de-emphasized in favour of rail and cycling/walking.	3. Zero-waste city, through circular, closed-loop eco-system.
4. Create affordable, mixed housing.	4. Environmental technologies for water, energy and waste management, to create 'closed loop systems'.	4. Water: closed urban water management; high-quality water.
5. Nurture social justice.		5. Landscape, gardens, biodiversity: integrating landscape, gardens and green roofs to enhance biodiversity.
6. Support local agriculture and community gardening.	5. City centres as 'human centres' attracting residential growth and employment.	6. Eco-mobility: sustainable transport and good public space network – compact and polycentric cities.
7. Promote recycling and resource conservation.	6. High-quality public realm, emphasizing community, culture, equity and good governance.	7. Local, sustainable materials, with less embodied energy.
8. Work with businesses to support ecologically sound economic activity.	7. Physical structure and public space designed to meet human needs.	8. Density and retrofitting of existing districts.
		9. Green buildings and districts.
9. Promote voluntary simplicity; discourage excessive material consumption.	8. City as economic and employment centre.	10. Mixed-use, affordable communities.
	9. Planning as visionary 'debate and decide' process.	11. Local food and short supply chains.
10. Increase public awareness of ecological sustainability issues.	10. All decision making is sustainability based, inclusive and democratic.	12. Cultural heritage, identity; sense of place.
		13. Urban governance, leadership and best practice.
		14. Education, research and knowledge.
		15. Strategies for cities in developing countries.

Notes:
1 The principles listed above are abbreviated from those appearing in the original texts.
2 The Urban Ecology principles, based on Register's earlier (1987) book, appear in the 1996 Mission Statement of the so-named organization, as cited in Roseland's (1997a) influential article.

Sources: Adapted from Roseland (1997a), Kenworthy (2006) and Lehmann (2010).

sustainability through research, contributions to policy discourse and practical pilot projects. In 1996, the Urban Ecology mission statement was published in support of creating ecological cities – or 'eco-cities' – based on ten core principles (as cited in Roseland, 1997a).

The first two principles deal with transport: they call for land use policy to be focused on creating compact urban development along transit nodes – thus emphasizing 'access by proximity' – and promoting public transport. This priority reflects the problem of urban sprawl – low-density residential development in suburban areas, resulting in inner-city deprivation and the need for urban commuting – prevalent at the time in many North American cities. Counteracting the dependency on private car use and promoting more compact urban design to enable commuting on foot, by bicycle and public transport was at the very heart of Register's eco-city and the Urban Ecology movement. Concerning other environmental dimensions, the focus is on local environmental issues, such as the restoration of natural habitats and the reduction of local pollution. CO_2 and energy issues, which become a conceptual priority in later decades, are not listed. However, the principles do emphasize the close relationship of the city with its surrounding hinterland, or 'bioregion', with educational and public campaigns advocated to increase awareness of the city's wider ecological dimensions. Notably, this relationship is not just understood in functional terms (resource management and so on), but also as an aesthetic relationship to be reflected in the design of buildings and infrastructure as well as the integration of ecological features in the urban fabric. Urban Ecology also has a strong social sustainability perspective, with particular emphasis on social justice issues, including improved opportunities for women, ethnic minority groups and people with disabilities. This, again, reflects the recognition at the time that the decline of inner-city areas disproportionally affected poorer, disadvantaged communities, as the middle-class population moved to more affluent suburbs.

What stands out from the Urban Ecology mission statement and its ten principles, as well as Register's eco-city books, is the strong emphasis on, and celebration of, local activism, public engagement and 'voluntary simplicity'. This is in contrast to more technology-focused, business-oriented and management-driven approaches to the sustainable city found in many more recent concepts and initiatives.

Eco-city dimensions (Kenworthy)

Similar to the first principles of Urban Ecology, Jeffrey Kenworthy's ten eco-city dimensions are centred upon the interrelationship between urban form and transport. The widely cited article 'The Eco-City: Ten Key Transport and Planning Dimensions for Sustainable City Development' (Kenworthy, 2006) justifies the heavy emphasis on transport as follows: 'the highly auto-dependent, resource-consuming cities in North America and Australia account for a disproportionately high amount of the energy, materials and waste production of today's urban areas, and require remedial actions on an unprecedented scale' (ibid.: 67). Consequently, the ten dimensions are designed around the core issue of urban transport systems and the challenge of reducing car dependence in contemporary 'automobile cities' (ibid.: 69). This is to be achieved primarily by addressing urban form, and in particular by supporting more compact, mixed-use development, on the basis that there is a direct correlation between urban density and private car use: the greater the urban density (measured as persons per area), the smaller the amount of private car journeys. For Kenworthy, then, urban form is key to sustainability: 'How much land a city requires to house its people and accommodate its economic activities is critical in determining its sustainability, especially its transport patterns and impacts' (ibid.: 69).

Compared with Urban Ecology, and reflecting the growing use of systems thinking underpinning urban sustainability concepts, Kenworthy's eco-city dimensions put stronger emphasis on environmental technologies for energy, water and waste management in support of creating 'closed-loop systems' to improve resource efficiency: 'the overall aims of environmental technologies are to maximise the possibility that cities can meet their needs from the natural capital of their own bio-regions in a renewable way and to move to closed-loop infrastructure systems that recycle and re-use their own wastes' (ibid.: 76). This focus on environmental technologies is balanced by an emphasis on place-making that meets human needs for interaction and community. This emphasis is further strengthened by a call for a 'debate and decide' mode of planning, which places vision making and inclusive community and stakeholder engagement at its heart: aspiring to greater sustainability, for Kenworthy, crucially requires 'engagement with communities as part of a process of envisioning the future for the city, rather than just "predicting and providing" for more traffic' (ibid.: 82).

Principles of green urbanism (Lehmann)

'Transforming the city for sustainability' is at the heart of the fifteen 'principles of green urbanism' elaborated by Steffen Lehmann and endorsed by the United Nations Educational, Scientific and Cultural Organization, UNESCO. These principles are based on what the author terms the 'triple-zero framework' consisting of: (a) zero fossil-fuel energy use; (b) zero waste; and (c) zero emissions (aiming for 'low-to-no-carbon' emissions) (Lehmann, 2010: 230). This confirms the shift in sustainable city concepts towards CO_2, energy and (material) resource efficiency over the last decade or so. Consequently, the first three of the fifteen principles deal with climate, renewable energy for CO_2 emissions, and zero waste. The emphasis here is on 'the city as a self-sufficient energy producer' based on decentralized district energy systems (ibid.: 231) and 'the zero-waste city as a circular, closed-loop eco-system' (ibid.: 232). Interestingly, while place-specificity is usually discussed from a social perspective – concerning how the unique aspects of place inform and shape the city socially and culturally – Lehmann highlights the unique conditions of a place in relation to climate. According to this principle, the particular climatic conditions (topographical orientation, solar radiation, rain, humidity, prevailing wind direction and so on) of a site or place should be at the core of how urban sustainability is approached and defined. This is not too dissimilar to the Urban Ecology approach, but here the focus is more exclusively on climate.

Other principles cover dimensions of urban sustainability found elsewhere in frameworks, too, including a focus on water, landscape and biodiversity, local food and supply chains, and 'transport-oriented development' – here, too, relating land use to transport patterns (through urban densification along transport nodes) – but much of this is defined by the overarching 'triple-zero' framework. Again, similarly to other frameworks, a balance is attempted – without, however, revealing much detail about how this is to be realized – with issues of 'local identity' and 'sense of place': the essence of a place is characterized as 'the up-swelling of grassroots strategies, the protection of its built heritage and the maintenance of a distinct cultural identity' (ibid.: 238). 'Good governance' is postulated as core requirement, based on 'citizen participation' and 'empowerment', 'public consultation', 'new policy frameworks', 'holistic designs', 'shared decision-making' – in short, 'cities are a collective responsibility' (ibid.: 239).

Principles and elements of sustainable urbanism, as illustrated by the three propositions here, underscore the multi-dimensional nature of the sustainable city: from applying environmental technologies for waste management to promoting locally sourced materials; from creating compact communities near transit nodes to establishing urban parks and green roofs; from supporting affordable housing to designing 'human-centred' public space; and from developing governance leadership to facilitating inclusive decision-making; the facets of sustainable urban development are indeed manifold. Furthermore, these dimensions are not presented atomistically; they are understood as interlaced and layered over each other: concerns about cities' environmental impacts at wider regional and global levels are typically woven into concerns about local-level environmental impacts. Similarly, structural connections are made between social and economic sustainability issues and environmental issues. A focus on intervention at the neighbourhood level meshes with a focus on city-wide and city-regional intervention. Interest in technological innovations may be framed in terms of a broader interest in social innovations. And interest in institutional governance is interlaced with interest in wider civic governance.

As noted, the challenge of defining the sustainable city is in bringing these diverse principles together in a coherent way, as well as translating them into viable practices. Despite the open-ended nature of this challenge, however, certain commonalities can be observed across many initiatives. By way of illustration, three contemporary 'theming' tendencies in the organization of sustainability principles are outlined below, each privileging a different set of perspectives and goals.

Contemporary theme 1: the low-carbon eco-city

Faced with the diverse – and at times contrasting – dimensions of the sustainable city, one could be forgiven for feeling rather puzzled about what forms its core. One perspective places environmental concern centre stage. Some would say that it is mainly and most urgently about greenhouse gas emissions and energy use (see Box 1.3). Certainly, the recent rise of the sustainable city to key policy proposition globally has coincided with international debate about global warming and climate change.

One of the reasons why cities are identified as the 'front line', or 'battleground', for action against climate change is that they are

Box 1.3   The 'low-carbon' agenda

In 2006, 'carbon' was the 'word of the year' of the *New Oxford American Dictionary* (OUP, 2006), signalling that the carbon agenda had entered mainstream policy and public discourse. Atmospheric carbon dioxide (CO_2) and other greenhouse gases have over the last half a century – and especially so over the last three decades – increased measurably. There is broad scientific consensus that this increase is largely due to human activity, resulting from significant global population growth and concurrent economic development. Carbon emissions are chiefly caused by energy production and consumption using fossil fuels (oil, coal, gas). Backed by numerous scientific analyses, the International Panel on Climate Change (IPCC) in its assessments states that if carbon emissions continue to increase unabated, there is a heightened risk of global warming and associated climate change (IPCC, 2001; 2007; 2013).

The agreed global policy position is stated in the United Nations Framework Convention on Climate Change – the so-called 'Kyoto Protocol' (UNFCCC, 1998) – which was signed in 1997 by over 190 members (the US was the most notable country not to sign the treaty), and entered into force in 2005 (UNFCCC, 2008). According to this framework, the global community overall and individual nations commit to taking measures to limit global warming to no more than 2°C by 2100, in order to avert potentially catastrophic climate change. The main focus is on reducing CO_2 emissions, partly by moving from fossil-fuel based energy generation to cleaner, renewable energy sources (solar, wind and tidal energy, biofuels, etc.), and partly by reducing energy consumption levels through energy-saving technology (e.g. LED – light-emitting diode – lighting, low-energy or 'passive house' buildings) and behavioural changes.

Apart from these *mitigation* measures, the Kyoto Protocol also calls for *adaptation* measures to respond to the impacts of already happening and still expected climate change, such as sea-level rise and more extreme weather patterns.

responsible for a large share of the GHG emissions produced. According to the 2011 global report on cities and climate change by UN-Habitat – which acts as an authoritative reference and state-of-the-art report – an estimated 40–70 per cent of overall anthro-pogenic (i.e. human-induced) GHG emissions arise from within cities (UN-Habitat, 2011a: iv). This is an estimate for so-called 'production-based' GHG emissions – that is, emissions produced by various entities (buildings, factories, transport networks, etc.) located within cities. The proportion increases to an estimated 60–70 per cent for 'consumption-based' GHG emissions, which is the figure for emissions relating to the consumption of goods and services by urban residents, irrespective of whether the goods or services were produced within or outside urban areas.

As the UN-Habitat report makes clear, these figures are estimates only. The reason for this is that 'it is impossible to make accurate statements about the scale of urban [GHG] emissions, as there is no globally accepted method for determining their magnitude' (ibid.: iv). (The methodology used by IPCC for measuring GHG emissions is designed for the national level; it does not specify measurements for city-level emissions.) In addition, the report points out that the 'vast majority of the world's urban centres have not attempted to conduct GHG emission inventories' (ibid.: iv). Furthermore, the report points to the uneven contributions of cities to GHG emissions: for example, the climate and natural conditions have a direct bearing on the level of GHG emissions: a city situated in an arid, hot desert requires more energy for cooling, water supply and food supply than a comparable city in a moderate climate with readily available local water and food supply. Economic conditions and consumer culture have a bearing on emission levels, too: a city with an affluent population and thriving, energy-intensive economy will produce disproportionate amounts of CO_2 compared with an urban area characterized by low-income and resource-limited economic activity. North American cities are frequently reported as having among the highest CO_2 emissions, while European cities tend to have a comparatively lower GHG profile due to their relative compactness, lower car usage and higher public transportation rates. Large cities in the Global South – such as in Brazil, China, India and South Africa – have rapidly rising CO_2 profiles, as emerging centres of global manufacturing. The UN-Habitat report, therefore, concludes that 'urban centres have played a key role in this [the global warming] process, although the extent of their role is not yet fully understood' (ibid.: 2–3).

Yet another way of considering the contribution of cities to climate change is to consider *per capita* emissions – that is, the average emissions produced by individuals. Here, the UN-Habitat report points out that 'a striking aspect of emissions inventories is that average *per capita* emissions for many large cities are substantially lower than for the country in which they are located' (ibid.: 14). The report cites figures indicating that the average Londoner, for example, produces just over half the GHG emissions of the average UK citizen. More strikingly still, the GHG profile of a resident of New York is over three times lower than that of the average American citizen. In other words, at the individual person level, a city dweller may well be considered to live more sustainably, by this measure, than someone living in a rural or semi-rural area (in some countries of the Global North at least).

Taken together, the relationship of cities to climate change is clearly an important and complex one in equal measure: by their nature, as centres of large populations and hubs of economic and cultural activities, cities must be responsible for a significant proportion of human-made GHG emissions. However, exactly what that proportion is, and how this applies to different aspects of the city, turns out to be difficult to specify at present: there are no accepted, standard methods for measurement and no existing inventories; the definition of what counts as city or urban area – that is, where boundaries are drawn – is not straightforward; and there is significant variability in the types of cities in different parts of the world. As a consequence, the UN-Habitat report repeatedly injects words of caution in its discussion of the contribution of cities to climate change. This is worth highlighting, since the estimates of 40–70 per cent (production-based) and 60–70 per cent (consumption-based), respectively, for cities' contribution to total GHG emissions are frequently cited as absolutes. Instead, these estimates make clear the need for further, detailed analysis, as part of the wider process of defining the sustainable city.

The limited knowledge about the precise extent and nature of cities' contribution to global warming notwithstanding, there is broad acceptance that mitigating for climate change must involve cities. As such, cities have variously become 'laboratories' for developing and applying diverse carbon-reduction strategies. A recent survey of 100 'global' cities and 'mega-cities' around the world (Bulkeley and Castán Broto, 2013) discovered 627 urban climate change 'experiments' across a variety of sectors, the vast majority of which had been initiated in the last few years, and typically by local government actors. One focus of such strategies is on shifting from fossil-fuel to low-carbon energy production, to 'de-carbonize' energy use. Here, the strategy involves moving to renewable energy sources, with energy preferentially generated, used and recycled on-

Box 1.4   Tales of two low-carbon cities

Since the mid-2000s, many urban sustainability initiatives have included a strong focus on climate change issues, often seeking to minimize greenhouse gas emissions during their construction and operation, or reduce their overall dependence on fossil fuels. One reason for the appeal of this approach may be that, while resonating with the global consensus that climate change is one of the biggest problems facing the planet in the twenty-first century, carbon reduction also has direct local relevance for many cities – potentially reducing local air pollution as well as lessening dependence on national and international fuel supplies. Equally, carbon emissions represent a concrete and accessible interpretation of the otherwise perhaps nebulous concept of sustainable development; carbon emissions can be measured (though methods for doing so are contested), allowing for tangible progress to be demonstrated along with 'non-negotiable target setting' (While et al., 2010: 77).

Surat in Gujarat (India) is in the process of implementing a low-carbon initiative facilitated by national government. It is one of the cities included among the Indian Ministry of New and Renewable Energy's preliminary 'model solar cities'; eventually, it is envisaged that 60 'solar cities' will be selected across the country. While the long-term goal for Surat is to meet all energy needs from local renewable sources, the national programme as a whole will aim to help participating local authorities reduce conventional energy use by a minimum of 10 per cent over five years. In an indication of the internationalization of low-carbon urban sustainability practice, technical assistance will be provided by the Brookhaven National Laboratory (US Department of Energy). See Joss (2012: 17) for further details.

Copenhagen presents an example of low-carbon policy making in a very different political, economic and environmental context. Copenhagen's different starting point in terms of sustainability – it was recently given the European Commission's 'European Green Capital 2014' award – has allowed it to announce the rather more ambitious target of becoming fully carbon neutral by 2025, or as it puts it, 'the first carbon-neutral capital in the world' (Ministry of Foreign Affairs of Denmark, undated). Projects aimed at helping it meet this goal include investments in a range of alternative and renewable fuels, constructing a clean-burning 'waste to energy' power plant, improving its pedestrian and cycle infrastructure, expanding its district heating systems, and reducing energy use in commercial and residential buildings (Gerdes, 2013).

site via 'closed-loop' systems. An example would be district energy production linked to, say, a photovoltaic ('solar') array, or a waste ('combined heat and power') plant. The significance of this sort of approach lies in the concurrent shift to renewable energy sources and to local energy production, with opportunities to link to various urban systems and infrastructure. Another focus is on reducing urban energy consumption levels. This is to be achieved chiefly by improving the energy performance of, say, buildings (through better insulation) and various infrastructure systems (water distribution, waste management, transport, etc.); as well as by behavioural interventions, such as encouraging walking, cycling and public transport, and reducing food waste. Yet another focus is on creating 'carbon sinks' – that is, reservoirs that absorb more CO_2 than they emit – such as wetlands and forests. This may be accomplished by incorporating carbon sinks within the urban landscape, for example by transforming disused industrial land into urban parks or wetlands; or by supporting carbon sinks within the city's hinterland. The latter requires an integrated, bio-regional approach to low-carbon urban development.

Low-carbon innovation is a key plank in many a sustainable city, or eco-city strategy, reflecting the dominant focus prompted by global climate change policy (see Box 1.4). 'Low-carbon eco-city', 'solar city', 'near-zero energy town' and similarly named initiatives have in recent years been launched by national governments and local authorities across the world, in order to spearhead innovation and investment. Internationally, initiatives such as Climate Positive (or 'Climate+') Development (Climate Positive, 2013) and the Carbon Disclosure Project (CDP, 2013) support cities in implementing and reporting low-carbon developments.

Contemporary theme 2: the resilient city

Cities are implicated in global climate change not just as significant contributors of GHG emissions, but also as (potential) victims of the effects of global warming. Predicted sea-level rise, the risk of increased storms and flooding, and water shortages due to extreme weather patterns are all expected to put severe stresses on urban areas. The effects could not only threaten cities' physical infrastructure (buildings, transport systems, electricity grid, water supply, etc.), but equally economic activities, public health and other social services. These and other impacts are expected to be particularly severe in urban areas and cities in low-lying coastal areas. Some of the world's fastest-growing large cities – especially in Asia – are situated in coastal regions and, as such, are especially vulnerable to the effects of predicted global warming. As UN-Habitat (2011a: 1) puts it, 'the very urban areas that are growing fastest are also those that are least equipped to deal with the threat of climate change'. The agency calculates that approximately 13 per cent of the world's urban population live in these risk-exposed zones (ibid.: v); with increased urbanization in developing countries, this proportion is set to increase further.

The discussion about the relationship between cities and global climate change, therefore, increasingly focuses on how cities can adapt against the anticipated detrimental effects of climate change – especially sea-level rise, flooding and other extreme weather occurrences – in addition to their role in mitigating for climate change through the reduction of greenhouse gas emissions. This discussion is often conducted under the banner of the 'resilient city' (see, for example, Newman et al., 2009; UNISDR, 2012; Otto-Zimmermann, 2011).

Broadly, urban resilience refers to cities' preparedness and capability to deal with external threats, here in the form of climate-related extreme events. This includes preparing for possible events (e.g. storm surge), responding to the effects of such events (e.g. flooding of neighbourhoods and city centres) when they occur, and managing the recovery (e.g. clearing debris, restoring public services). Urban planning, therefore, increasingly addresses resilience by building related strategies into urban development. This may take the form of strengthening sea and flood defences within a city's perimeter, or it may involve work upstream along river catchment areas to slow the flow of water in the case of severe weather. Cities may implement measures to reduce the threat of storm water run-off – which can cause local flooding and water pollution – by putting in place storm water harvesting techniques, such as retention ponds and permeable paving which can both absorb and purify excess surface water. Again, cities may increasingly need to counter the urban heat island effect, characterized by higher temperatures (in comparison to the surrounding area) resulting from higher heat absorption and retention by building surfaces and reduced wind flows. Measures may include using less heat-absorbing building materials, increasing the amount of vegetation (e.g. through green roofs, and parks) and installing water features.

Urban resilience is, however, not only concerned with climate change adaptation. The concept is increasingly also applied to diverse socio-economic issues, such as food security, economic recovery and community health, as exemplified by the 100 Resilient Cities initiative (see Box 1.5). According to this view, resilience responds to both natural and human-made catastrophic events, from the devastation wreaked on a city by a hurricane to the negative impacts of a financial crisis or a severe food shortage on urban communities. As a result, resilience discourse, drawing on the concept's original elaboration by ecologist C. S. Holling (1973) and then developed in the physical sciences with a mainly technological focus, has increasingly broadened out to address economic and socio-political matters, too (Coaffee, 2008; Leichenko, 2011; Walker and Cooper, 2011). Consequently, the social sciences have become involved in conceptualizing and analysing – and critiquing – urban resilience, with particular focus on governance issues, such as institutional capacity and community cohesion and responsiveness. Certain common principles appear across the various spheres to which resilience thinking has come to be applied; in particular the values of adaptivity and flexibility are promoted, and seen as achievable through the development of short, local supply chains, as a means of defence against environmental and economic shocks from afar, along with reflexive processes of ongoing learning. Such principles are illustrated by the 'five core characteristics' of resilience outlined by the Rockefeller Foundation (see Box 1.5).

Similar to urban sustainability, urban resilience, therefore, encompasses environmental, economic and social dimensions. As such, the two conceptual perspectives overlap significantly, and some researchers and policy-makers treat them as largely synonymous. Sustainability and resilience, however, can also be seen as differing in some important ways: sustainable development is chiefly concerned with supporting development that can be sustained long term, across generations, within the planet's resource limits and mitigating for environmental degradation. In contrast, resilience is more concerned with readying a community against external, physical or human-made threats through various adaptation strategies, without necessarily engaging in corresponding mitigation strategies. Viewed positively, resilience arguably puts greater emphasis on preparing and enabling communities to respond actively to challenges. Conversely, it may be seen as down-playing sustainable behaviour and responsibility, by externalizing environmental and socio-economic challenges and focusing action on keeping these challenges at bay without necessarily addressing their underlying causes. In practice, however, these two perspectives are usually in play along-

Box 1.5   100 Resilient Cities initiative

The Rockefeller Foundation's 100 Resilient Cities initiative is an example of an international network seeking to engage cities in resilience building. Its interest in urban resilience reflects the Foundation's long tradition of supporting social and technological innovations in a wide variety of fields. Launched in 2013, the Foundation's centenary year, the initiative provides funding, knowledge and policy exchange to one hundred competitively selected cities from around the world. These cities will also be supported in employing a Chief Resilience Officer, with a mandate to co-ordinate activities and stakeholders and promote the resilience agenda locally, and in developing their resilience plans.

As the accompanying publication *Rebound: Building a More Resilient World* (Rockefeller Foundation, 2013) demonstrates, resilience is not just understood in terms of a response to the threat of global climate change. The concept relates more broadly to both natural and human-made catastrophic events and how cities (and societies more generally) can ready themselves to withstand, and bounce back from, associated shocks and stresses. Specific areas of focus within this initiative therefore include food security, housing, manufacturing and health. The types of resilient system which it hopes to encourage will have five 'core characteristics', which it describes as follows (ibid.: 2–3): (i) spare capacity, which ensures that there is a back-up or alternative available when a vital component of a system fails; (ii) flexibility, the ability to change, evolve and adapt in the face of disaster; (iii) limited or 'safe' failure, which prevents failures from rippling across systems; (iv) rapid rebound, the capacity to re-establish function and avoid long-term disruptions; and (v) constant learning, with robust feedback loops that sense and allow new solutions as conditions change.

side each other, with mitigation and adaptation being a twin strategy deployed by cities to tackle environmental and related socio-economic challenges.

Contemporary theme 3: the liveable city

The 'low-carbon eco-city' and 'resilient city' both primarily suggest a responsive relationship of the city to its surrounding and wider global environments: the former, by focusing on mitigating detrimental environmental effects, and especially reducing various GHG emissions; and the latter by adapting to emerging and anticipated external threats. In contrast, the 'liveable city' theme turns more on itself, by emphasizing sustainable development primarily as a means of rendering cities habitable and enjoyable places. The premise here is that 'at their best, cities and towns can be *wonderful* places in which to live', as the book cover of *Reclaiming Our Cities and Towns* (Engwicht, 1993) holds out. The attention, then, shifts more onto the living experience and related conditions in the city. As another volume on the topic – *Toward the Livable City* – asks of readers on its book jacket: 'Commuters, suburbanites, city dwellers: are you curious about making your life more livable and interested in knowing what that might mean?' (Buchwald, 2003). The liveable city theme, however, also encompasses more hard-nosed policy interests, as reflected more recently in a growing number of governmental, business and civil society initiatives that seek to address the link between urban liveability and health benefits, economic competitiveness, social capital and cultural appeal.

To some, liveability may be a welcome theme to be added to the sustainable city defined principally around enviro-technical issues; it may infuse an otherwise rather abstract and serious discussion with more of a human touch, social interests, perhaps a sense of enjoyment; and in doing so, it may be seen as rendering the sustainable city a more palatable, attractive proposition. Others see liveability as a more fundamental, central aspect of the sustainable city; not some convenient add-on, but intricately connected to environmental, economic and social issues and challenges. Certainly, from a historical perspective, liveability was a key motivation and concern for urban planning pioneers, such as Ebenezer Howard, Patrick Geddes and Lewis Mumford, working on the various progenitors of what is now called the sustainable city: for example, the garden city (of which more in Chapter 3) is centrally predicated on designing towns and cities with the well-being of their inhabitants – workers, residents, children, visitors – in mind. In similar vein, the starting point of many a proposition for eco-cities and sustainable communities proffered over the last four decades or so has been the question of how people (should) live, work, commute and interact in cities. As one of the key texts on eco-cities of the 1990s, *Eco-city Dimensions: Healthy Communities, Healthy Planet,* opens: 'This book is not just about cities. It's about where and how we live…' (Roseland, 1997b: vi). Not surprisingly, then, the focus in these discussions is often on the local and on social dimensions such as equality and public participation. Roseland, for example, emphasizes the vision of eco-cities as one '... that links ecological sustainability with social justice and the pursuit of sustainable livelihoods' (Roseland, 1997b: 12), while Barton (2000a: 6) highlights sustainable neighbourhoods with the purpose of 'marry[ing] welfare and ecological robustness'.

In some more recent conceptualizations of the sustainable city based on enviro-technical system thinking, liveability appears more as a background theme. Examples such as Masdar (see Box 4.5), PlanIT Valley (pp. 150–1) and Songdo (Box 3.3) remain relatively silent about how liveability relates to eco-city plans. Elsewhere, however, the theme continues to be at the heart of discussion about sustainable urban development. This is, for example, illustrated by *Towards a Liveable London*, a report published by the London branch of the Campaign for the Protection of Rural England (CPRE, 2014), which calls for more active intervention and improved, integrated planning at both community and municipal levels, in order to address the city's growing social pressures (see Box 1.6).

As can be gleaned from the Liveable London initiative, one key aspect of the sustainable city as liveable city is the focus on the built environment, especially at the local neighbourhood level. This echoes wider academic and policy debate which primarily emphasizes improving the design of, and planning for, neighbourhoods, in order to address concurrently environmental, economic and social issues affecting the city. The *Charter of The New Urbanism* (1993, reproduced in Buchwald, 2003: 277–82), the foundational text of the New Urbanism movement, states so clearly: 'The neighbourhood, the district, and the corridor are the essential elements of development and redevelopment in the metropolis. They form identifiable areas that encourage citizens to take responsibility for their maintenance and evolution' (ibid.: 280). Design and planning issues flagged up in the charter include promoting compact, mixed-use development, fostering community integration, and encouraging a short-distance lifestyle. The 'walkability' of urban areas has become a popular term to denote more sustainable urban living at neighbourhood level. For example, Portland, Oregon (US) newly emphasizes the '20-minute neighbourhood' in its most recent municipal plan, following a focus on more wider regional integrated transport planning in the preceding decades (Portland City Council, 2012; see also case study in Chapter 5).

Other aspects of the sustainable city as liveable city increasingly to the fore in urban policy include people's health and well-being. (For some observers, this represents a return to the original concerns driv-

Box 1.6   Liveable London

The 'Liveable London' campaign is run by the London branch of CPRE (Council for the Protection of Rural England). CPRE's broader 'Vision for London' ties together economic, environmental and social considerations: 'Our vision is of London as a prosperous world city. The challenge is for a better use of land and wiser stewardship of natural resources. London should have a vibrant economy and be surrounded by pleasant countryside. London should become a sustainable city with low carbon and less waste. We want to encourage a keen sense of place, with better urban design, good quality of life and greener, safer neighbourhoods' (CPRE London, undated).

Towards a Liveable London (CPRE London, 2014) focuses on opportunities for improving the built environment as the housing needs of London's growing population are met. 'Simply providing new homes', it argues, 'will not guarantee a liveable and sustainable city.' It goes on to outline five challenges:

1. Affordable housing (including incentives to encourage the increase and supply of affordable homes, social housing, and shared ownership properties, to make better use of brownfield land, and to improve the quality of privately rented homes).
2. Managing higher densities (including the intensification of suburban locations, particularly near high streets and transport nodes).
3. Integrated neighbourhood design (good connections to the surrounding urban fabric and public spaces, with a balance between privacy and openness).
4. Diversifying housing developments (with better provision for families, the elderly, and under-30s; more support for housing models other than private developments).
5. Place-keeping – neighbourhoods for life (good design as well as ongoing management of public spaces, with participation across stakeholder groups to ensure local people feel involved in the 'co-production of place').

ing the sustainable city movement, by interlinking public health and urban design issues; see Frumkin, 2002.) For example, the World Health Organization's Healthy Cities network brings together 90 cities worldwide and supports various national healthy city initiatives (WHO, undated). The Zagreb Declaration for Healthy Cities, which was signed by mayors and municipal leaders from across Europe with support from WHO, has as one of its key objectives 'making health, health equity, social justice and sustainable development key values in our vision for developing our cities' (WHO, 2009: 6). The close connection between issues of health, social (in)equality and economic development in city planning is also underlined in a Lancet Commission on healthy cities, a joint report by the medical journal *The Lancet* and University College London (Rydin et al., 2012a; also Rydin et al., 2012b). The authors note that while the features to achieve healthier cities are becoming increasingly understood, 'what is less well understood...is how to deliver the potential health benefits and how to ensure that they reach all citizens in urban areas across the world. This task is becoming increasingly important because most of the world's population live in cities, and, with high rates of urbanisation, many millions more will soon do so in the coming decades' (Rydin et al., 2012a: 1). Among the recommendations are that issues of health inequalities in urban areas require close integration into urban planning, and that for urban health action to be effective it should be directed particularly at the local level through the involvement of practitioners and community groups. In a separate publication, some of the same authors emphasize the importance and expected benefits of experimentation, and trial and error, as well as a commitment to ongoing evaluation, to policy and practice learning (Rydin et al., 2012b: 557).

A further aspect of the liveable city theme is community engagement and participation. Apart from the importance of urban policy, community involvement in design and planning is seen as essential to tackle some of the key concerns of the liveable city, such as social inequality, environmental pollution, poor health outcomes, and a lack of civic engagement (Roseland, 2012; Joss, 2014). However, while community involvement and public participation are widely embraced as 'good practice', its ideal often jars against the reality of limited opportunity for engagement in urban planning and decision-making: hence, the principle of 'deep' participation, centred upon empowering and giving 'voice' to the community, frequently ends up as 'thin' participation in practice, based on cursory debate and involvement (Joss, 2014). Among the many methods and techniques designed to give redress to this 'participatory deficit', by mobilizing and facilitating active community engagement in planning and decision-making processes, is the *Community Capital Tool* (Roseland, 2012: 12–19). Developed jointly by researchers at Simon Fraser

University (Canada) and Tilburg University (the Netherlands), the tool prompts participants to assess, and develop strategies for, 'community capital' in their particular local setting. 'Community capital' is defined in terms of six interrelating 'capitals' – natural, physical, economic, human, social and cultural. This divergence from the 'three-pillar' model of sustainability is deliberate, as the three standard categories of economic, social and environmental sustainability are considered insufficiently nuanced for effective community engagement. The tool is available free online in English, Spanish and Portuguese, so as to support community engagement in resource-poor cities in developing countries.

What's in a name?

The discussion about sustainable cities, as the preceding sections illustrate, is characterized by the concurrency of multiple dimensions, often encapsulated by reference to the 'triple bottom line' of sustainable environmental, economic and social development related to urban contexts. What is more, the term 'sustainable city' itself is frequently accompanied by multiple sister terms, such as 'eco-city', 'green city', 'energy city', 'future city', 'resilient city', 'compact city', 'low-carbon city', 'information city', 'liveable city', 'smart city' and 'knowledge city'. The question arises, therefore, whether these terms denote by and large the same proposition, in which case the particular choice of terminology may be less important and more a matter of any given fashion of the day or even personal preference. Conversely, one can ask whether these terms are each distinctive, embodying separate ideas and practices of urban development. In this case, what is the relationship between them, and does it make sense to use them in the same breath? The answer has obvious implications for the academic discourse, as it would help explain how the sustainable city is conceptually understood and thematically demarcated. Importantly, however, it potentially also has implications for guiding policy and practice.

A look at some recent practical initiatives suggests that these terms in fact often feature comfortably alongside each other and may indeed be interchangeable. Glasgow, the largest city in Scotland (UK) is a case in point: following a nationwide competition, the city was selected in 2013 by the UK government to spearhead its 'future cities demonstrator' initiative (Glasgow City Council, undated a). In a promotional article, the municipal authorities describe their planned 'future city' as having a host of aspirational attributes, including being 'the first green energy "super city" in Scotland', and a 'global low-carbon industrial hub' (*The Guardian*, 2014: 6). The plans include the City Science initiative, promoted as 'a bridgehead between academia and industry ... creating the infrastructure for a global R&D [Research and Development] hub ... for Scotland's International Technology and Renewable Energy Zone' (ibid.). The same article flags up Sustainable Glasgow, an initiative whose 'aim is to make Glasgow one of the most sustainable cities in Europe', with a main focus on investing in the development of 'low carbon energy systems' and 'low carbon and district heating systems'. Glasgow, however, is not just to be a 'sustainable city', but equally a 'green' one: 'we're striving to cut carbon emissions and become one of the greenest cities in Europe'. Efforts to date have been rewarded with the city being runner-up in the European Green Capital 2015 awards. What's more, the city has joined the Rockefeller Foundation's 'resilient cities' programme (see Box 1.5), and elsewhere in the article refers to its 'smart city agenda' (ibid.). Other examples abound of cities readily mixing terminology: for example, Melbourne (Australia) is often discussed as a model 'knowledge city' on account of its programmatic focus on knowledge-based urban development (Yigitcanlar et al., 2008); yet this term is used in tandem with the city's 'eco-city' initiative and related Eco-City Sustainability Campaign. Together, these two concepts feed into the 'healthy cities model' which the municipal authorities adopted as part of the *Melbourne Public Health and Wellbeing Plan 2013–2017*. Elsewhere, Guangzhou (China) as part of a bilateral initiative launched the 'Sino-Singapore Guangzhou Knowledge City' redevelopment programme; this is described on the official website as a 'sustainable city' that 'embodies smart, eco and learning'. Complementing the use of terminology, the initiative is to be implemented using an 'eco-city indicator' framework (de Jong et al., 2013).

If these policy and practice examples suggest that the various sister terms co-exist in close relationship, even to the point of being interchangeable, what about the academic literature? Does the latter draw conceptual boundaries between, say, the 'sustainable city' and 'resilient city', and between the 'liveable city' and 'smart city'? To investigate this, de Jong et al. (2015) carried out an extensive quantitative literature analysis relating to outputs in peer-reviewed journals covering the period 1996–2013. Using Scopus, one of the largest repositories of academic literature, the authors identified a total of 1,430 articles which concern themselves with 'sustainable city' and eleven related terms. The quantitative analysis looked at: (1) how often each of the terms is mentioned; (2) how frequently two or more terms are discussed in the same article and, thus, brought into conceptual relationship; and (3) what conceptual keywords are associated with each of the terms. The results reveal a field of conceptual relationships between 'sustainable city' and its sister terms (see Figure 1.1). The larger the point denoting a particular term, the greater the number of times it is mentioned in the academic literature; and the more central the position of a term in the field, the greater is its conceptual connection with sister terms. Accordingly, the 'sustainable city' is both the most frequently mentioned term and is most often associated with its sister terms. In other words, it occupies a central position in the relational field and, as such, can be seen as something of an 'umbrella' concept that broadly encompasses diverse aspects of environmental, economic and social urban development. In contrast, for example, the 'resilient city' has only more recently emerged in the academic literature – its occurrence is, therefore, significantly smaller than that of 'sustainable city' – and presently occupies a more peripheral position: it is conceptually more narrowly defined in relation to climate adaptation and disaster management. For its part, the 'smart city' has fast been ascending in recent years and begun to occupy a central position alongside 'sustainable city' and 'eco-city'. Interestingly, the data suggest that 'smart city' is presently developing into a conceptually distinctive sub-network of its own, closely linked with 'digital city', 'ubiquitous city' and 'information city'.

Overall, this research suggests that within the academic discourse there exists a clear interrelationship between the 'sustainable city' and what can rightly be called its various sister terms. At the same time, the analysis points to some conceptual distinctiveness among the diverse categories of sustainable urban development. Some categories, such as 'resilient city' and 'liveable city' at present occupy a somewhat more marginal, specialist position, whereas 'sustainable city' as an overarching concept takes central position. 'Eco-city' and 'smart city', too, occupy a central position, but are nevertheless characterized by some conceptual distinctiveness. The conclusion to be drawn from this research is that, at least when it comes to academic discourse, these terms are not all equal; while they all seek to conceptualize social, economic and environmental dimensions related to urban development, they do so from slightly different thematic angles and with various emphases. As to their apparently

Figure 1.1 *The 'sustainable city' and its relationship to eleven sister terms*

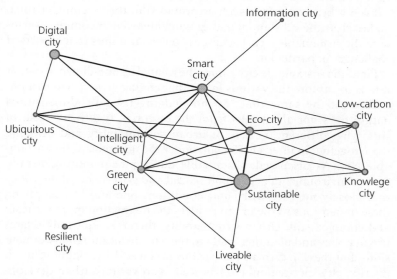

Source: Based on de Jong et al. (2015).

overlapping, even interchangeable, use in policy and practice, this need not necessarily be ascribed to conceptual fuzziness; it can be seen as policy-makers and practitioners mobilizing multiple terms to accentuate and bring into interplay concurrent aspects of urban development and regeneration and, thereby, signalling a comprehensive approach to, and high policy priority for, urban policy and planning.

Key challenges

The sustainable city is a captivating and challenging phenomenon in equal measure. It is captivating as a proposition to move towards urban development which is less resource intensive and environmentally harming, while providing opportunity for socio-economic development; and in doing so, addressing some of the major tasks confronting society – namely, dealing with environmental threats posed by cities in an age of unprecedented urbanization globally. Yet, it is also inherently challenging as a normative concept struggling for clear and cohesive definition, as an analytical field pursuing empirically grounded knowledge, and as practice striving for innovation and shared learning.

Even a brief overview, such as provided in this opening chapter, makes clear the substantial undertaking involved in coming to grips with the sustainable city. The discussion so far points to three sets of challenges in particular.

First, the sustainable city cannot be treated as one-dimensional, or it fails to capture the various facets that characterize urban sustainability. At the same time, acknowledging its multi-dimensional nature does not absolve us from the essential, if difficult, task of specifying different aspects of urban sustainability and bringing these together in interrelationship under the umbrella of the sustainable city. As discussed, sustainable development more generally entails environmental, economic, social and governance dimensions that closely interact with, and condition, one another. Applying these dimensions to the urban renders the interaction more intricate and complex still. Urban sustainability, therefore, not only relates urban policy and planning issues to the various sustainability dimensions, but these in turn also to various urban scales (neighbourhood, district, city, city-region, etc.) as well as to various urban development types (existing urban buildings and infrastructure, urban expansion and new urban developments, urban development within resource-limited, or conversely affluent, contexts, etc.), various urban sectors and systems (energy, transport, water, materials, food, waste, etc.) and, lest one forget, urban culture and community.

These multiple dimensions may risk rendering the sustainable city a convoluted conceptual, analytical and practical undertaking. However, it should be possible – and indeed be part of the process of systematizing the sustainable city – to identify certain hierarchies and priorities. Moving to low- or zero-carbon urban development may be the overriding concern informing urban sustainability strategy if one accepts that limiting global warming and climate change are of fundamental importance and that urbanization processes are centrally implicated in this. Nevertheless, even such a singular focus would immediately prompt other dimensions to come into play, raising such related issues as the appropriate mode of urban economy to support this transition or the social implications of adapting cities to climate change risks. Moreover, an overriding focus on low-/zero-carbon urban development is likely to overlay other local, environmental issues – say, combating local air pollution or protecting urban parks and waterways – as well as other socio-economic issues, such as local employment and community cohesion.

The second, related challenge consists in recognizing the importance of context. While, to an extent, it is possible and useful to abstract the sustainable city from its context to identify some generic, and thereby transferable, features and criteria – as illustrated in the preceding sections of this chapter – ultimately sustainable urbanism has to be conceptualized, analysed and practised in relation to its place-specific context. What is meant here by context is the interplay of three broad aspects: the geographical and environmental features and conditions characterizing the city; the physical structures and conditions of the city itself; and the political, social and economic conditions at work. Geographical and environmental features – the wider regional climate as well as the specific microclimate, the presence or absence of waterways, the abundance or scarcity of raw materials and food sources, etc. – define the city in important ways and, in turn, shape the present condition of and future potential for urban sustainability. For example, a city in the Northern hemisphere with ample access to water may well focus efforts on supplying energy through hydro-electric power, whereas a city in an arid region with high annual sunshine averages is likely to invest in photovoltaic energy generation.

Planning for urban sustainability, therefore, ideally takes into close account these and other geographical and environmental features. It should further take into consideration the physical features and conditions of the urban area itself. For example, a city with a pre-existing dense layout – such as seen in many European medieval towns and cities – may be particularly suitable for improving public transport. Conversely, the potential for energy efficiency in buildings may be hampered by a large proportion of historic buildings. A city with defunct industrial areas may lend itself to urban regeneration through developing derelict brownfield sites, with the opportunity to create dense, mixed-use neighbourhoods and, thereby, preventing urban sprawl on the city's fringes.

Just as decisive for planning and implementing urban sustainable development as a city's physical aspects are its socio-economic and political conditions. In the context of low-income urban communities with limited infrastructure and governance capacity, urban sustainability measures that would otherwise look modest in a well-developed, affluent city may be ambitious, signalling an important move towards more strategic, concerted planning in support of more resource-efficient urbanization. A case in point is India's solar city initiative launched in 2011 (see pp. 136–7), which has as its aim a ten per cent shift to renewable energy consumption to be achieved by the end of the first five-year period. Expecting fast expanding urban centres in developing countries to reach carbon neutrality within a few decades may not be realistic, whereas for an affluent city with well-established infrastructure and governance capacity, such as Copenhagen (see Box 1.4), this may soon become the expected norm.

Again, recognizing the importance of context is not to say that developing generic criteria and norms play no part in urban sustainability; on the contrary, in the context of finite natural resources, the threat to biodiversity and the prospect of global climate change, high-level, overarching goals and objectives may be expected to become more central. Nevertheless, local contexts and conditions co-determine urban sustainable development in decisive ways, and so require close attention by researchers, policy-makers and practitioners alike. The balance between, on one hand, overarching, global indicators and standards of urban sustainability and, on the other, local contextualization attempted by various sustainable city, or eco-city, frameworks developed in recent years is explored in greater detail in Chapter 7.

The third challenge follows on from the other two challenges and concerns the issue of complexity. As anyone working on urban sustainability can attest, complexity is an inherent, perennial feature. Attempting to analyse, say, material flows within cities (with a view to achieving greater resource efficiency), to design a public–private partnership to realize a large-scale, integrated public transit system, or to de-carbonize the urban energy grid, or to achieve many other common goals of urban sustainable development, requires sophisticated planning, management and technical systems – and all this has to be navigated through often highly complex policy processes. However, this complexity should not stand in the way of effective, active governance. The challenge, then, consists of figuring out comprehensive ways of managing multiple aspects of the sustainable city. It is precisely because of this essential requirement for managing complexity that processes of co-ordinating, integrating and networking are increasingly recognized in sustainable city planning; and it is for this reason that these processes occupy a focal point throughout this book.

There is a further, fourth challenge that needs to be taken into account: this concerns the political nature of the sustainable city. On the surface, urban sustainability may look to be all about technical information, specialist systems, expert design and advanced innovation processes. However, the sustainable city is defined just as much by socio-political issues. This becomes apparent when questions are raised about, for example, whether cities should be set targets for reducing carbon emissions, and if so who sets them and at what level; how (and again by whom) sustainability goals are prioritized in the policy process; what planning mechanisms should be used to encourage innovation and enable development; and how related decision-making is made accessible and accountable. Not surprisingly, like any other major issue of public policy, urban sustainability can provoke heated debate. Some may see urban sustainability as policy foisted upon communities by government agencies without much say by local stakeholders; others may accuse officialdom of engaging in 'greenwashing' by adopting the sustainable city as policy without, however, making any concomitant, substantive commitments; again others may express concern about sustainable urban development leading to gentrification and, thus, being the preserve of affluent urbanites to the exclusion of less advantaged communities.

Conclusions

The fact that the apparent elegance of the proposition of the sustainable city belies such a wide range of thorny conceptual and practical challenges might tempt one to conclude that it will only ever remain an unrealizable normative vision. More optimistically, however, its very tenacity in inspiring experimentation in so many varied urban settings, and the very fact that its meanings continue to be contested, point to its remarkable generative power as an idea. Its complexity does not, in other words, justify its abandonment; instead, it highlights the need for ongoing analysis, open-ended constructive debate, and critical reflection to accompany the process of its implementation in policies, plans and practices around the globe. The following chapter outlines a conceptual framework for examining and interpreting the contemporary sustainable city phenomenon and its multiple processes.

Chapter 2

Conceptualizing Urban Sustainability: The Process Perspective

CHAPTER OVERVIEW

An essential aspect of the sustainable city are the processes involved in seeking to effect a transition from the present state of urban development to goal-oriented future development guided by urban sustainability visions and targets. These processes encompass stimulating and facilitating innovation, enhancing co-operation and co-ordination among diverse actors, and providing policy and regulatory incentives. This chapter discusses how relevant schools of thought variously conceptualize the sustainable city in terms of processes, from the city as an experimental 'niche' to the city as governance network, and from the city as operating system to the city as urban metabolism. These different paradigms each add useful, complementary insights, while at the same time displaying some shortcomings, not least the relative neglect of socio-political agency. The chapter concludes by suggesting that the importance of active processes of governance – subject both to political discourses and public accountability – should be rather more obviously emphasized in accounts of the sustainable city.

Introduction: focusing on the means, not the ends

When, in 2008, the French government launched its twin ÉcoCité and ÉcoQuartier programmes as part of the national Urban Sustainability Plan (*Plan Ville Durable*), it did so as an '*initiative exemplaire*', or model eco-city initiative (see METL, 2012; 2013; *Revue Urbanisme*, 2010). At its core, the initiative is driven by three key, related aims: transforming existing cities; promoting environmental and economic innovation to achieve sustainable development and economic growth; and supporting dialogue and co-operation between central government and participating cities. Both programmes – ÉcoCité is directed at cities of 100,000 inhabitants or over, while ÉcoQuartier addresses medium-sized towns and cities of 20,000 to 100,000 inhabitants – began in the initial phase of development (2008–9) by inviting cities to come forward with proposals based on national guidelines. As a result, 13 (out of a total of 19 proposed) ÉcoCité (see Box 4.1) and 16 (out of a total of 160) ÉcoQuartier projects were selected. In the subsequent, second phase (2010–11) a further six cities were taken aboard the ÉcoCité initiative, while a further 24 projects were selected for the ÉcoQuartier award (*Palmarès national ÉcoQuartier 2011*). This second phase also saw the launch of the Club National ÉcoQuartier, a national forum aimed at encouraging dissemination of ideas and practice sharing among these and other cities; in total over 500 cities were reported to have joined the forum by 2011. In addition, on the back of the national initiative, an independent non-governmental Association ÉcoQuartier (Éco-quartiers.fr, undated) came to life aimed at bringing together civil society organizations interested in engaging in urban sustainability initiatives. The more recent development phases signal the shift from initial conceptualization to practical implementation.

A defining aspect of the initiatives is the emphasis on process. For example, in the case of ÉcoQuartier this is reflected in the overarching aims and criteria guiding the development of projects, captured in four core categories (translated): 'approach and process', 'quality of life', 'land use planning', and 'climate change adaptation and resource efficiency'. Process, thus, merits its own category and includes guiding criteria, such as: 'formalising and implementing a pilot process and governance strategy'; 'integrating costing in investment planning'; 'taking into account the practices of users and constraints of planners'; and 'putting in place an evaluation plan and continuous improvement programme' (METL, 2012). Working with these process-oriented criteria, as well as other, substantive urban sustainability categories, applicants are prompted both to carry out an analysis of their present state of urbanization and to develop a vision and strategy for realizing the ÉcoQuartier initiative in the future. The latter entails drawing up a scenario based on '24 hours in the life of the ÉcoQuartier' for the year 2030. Once the outline proposal is approved, applicants work towards obtaining pre-operational admission to the ÉcoQuartier scheme; this is seen as a particularly important step, in order to secure the necessary third-party investment. Subsequently, at the point when a project is deemed to have progressed sufficiently – defined as 50 per cent of the urban space-related work completed – and the annual audits and final evaluation result in a positive assessment, the project receives national certification (*Label ÉcoQuartier National*). Throughout, the process is designed to encourage co-operation among local, regional and national actors aimed at offering technical and planning assistance, ensuring independent auditing, and providing national recognition.

The Japanese Eco-Model City (EMC) initiative is an almost perfect echo of the French initiative; it, too, emphasizes the process character of the sustainable city (Murakami, 2011). Launched in the same year, 2008, EMCs are intended to 'trigger the transition to a low-carbon society' (ibid.: 6). They should do so, first, by presenting clear, ambitious targets demonstrating how to move beyond current urbanization to a future, low-carbon society; second, by using these targets to stimulate innovation within specific urban contexts; and third, by spreading the innovative practices gained through these pioneering EMC initiatives to other Japanese cities, and beyond to the wider East Asian region. Thirteen Japanese cities to date have been officially recognized as EMCs (see Box 4.4). In contrast to the French initiative, the Japanese EMC scheme is more narrowly defined by its focus on realizing drastic reductions in greenhouse gas emissions – namely, at least 30 per cent by 2020, rising to 50 per cent or more by 2050 (ibid.: 8) – reflecting the Japanese government's national action plan for achieving a low-carbon society. However, in terms of the types of cities, the range of proposals, and the geographic spread, the EMC scheme is similar in its breadth and variety to the French initiative. This is deliberate since, as pioneering initiatives, the EMCs are intended – beyond the transformation of the designated urban areas themselves – to act as inspirational models to be emulated by other cities. Collaboration among municipalities is an explicit expectation, understood as a necessary condition for realizing the country's action plan for a low-carbon society.

Like the French scheme, EMC proposals have not just had to specify ambitious targets for 2030 and beyond, but also to demonstrate how these targets are to be realized in the intervening period. The selection criteria, here too, include evidence of 'credible implementation plans', and a commitment to 'continuously developing new initiatives' (Gudmundsson and Fukuda, 2012: 29). Again, similarly to the French initiative, the EMC proposals have been evaluated independently, based on guidelines established by the

Japanese government; and a Promotion Council for Low-Carbon Cities (Murakami, 2011: 12) was set up to bring together national agencies, local governments and non-governmental organizations to engage in methodological development and dissemination activities.

What stands out from both the French and Japanese initiatives is their emphasis on transition, innovation and co-operation. The sustainable city is not posited as a fixed norm or ready-made entity that merely awaits implementation; rather, it is essentially conceived of as a process of innovation. This process is understood as having two underlying premises: first, that it is aimed at effecting a transition from current forms of urbanization to goal-oriented future urban sustainable development; and second, that, in order to bring about such transition, purposive active intervention is required. Hence, these initiatives are intended to spark socio-technical innovations and to enable the up-scaling of sustainable urban practice. As catalysts, they intend to do so by providing policy and regulatory guidance, by offering financial incentives and technical assistance, and by facilitating co-ordination and shared practice learning among various stakeholders involved.

Chapter 1 introduced the argument that it should be fruitful – both in terms of normative conceptualization and empirical analysis – to contemplate the sustainable city from a process perspective: that is, to study the diverse innovation and governance processes that shape urban sustainability norms and practices; to inquire into related institutional, organizational and wider socio-cultural factors which – favourably or unfavourably – condition these processes; and to consider the role of the policy process in steering and incentivizing – as well as possibly hampering – the governance of urban sustainability. This chapter follows suit by probing more deeply into the nature of these processes. In doing so, the chapter aims to outline some of the predominant ways in which the sustainable city is normatively conceptualized and analytically captured, and the centrality that is afforded to process within these schools of thought. A comparison of these approaches highlights some profound differences in what the sustainable city as process is understood to be. By placing greater emphasis on the political and social aspects of process, the chapter seeks to redress the balance in the predominant conceptualization of the sustainable city as principally concerned with system-based, enviro-technical processes. Some of the key characteristics of the three conceptual outlooks considered are summarized in Table 2.1.

Table 2.1 *Urban sustainability as process: summary of conceptual outlooks*

	Multi-level perspective	Urban metabolism	Complex adaptive systems	Governance networks
Key metaphors	Niche, regime, and landscape 'levels' Innovation processes Transition, transformation	City as living organism/living machine Material flows Symbiosis, closed loops	Feedback dynamics Closed signalling loops Self-organizing behaviour	Joined-up thinking Vertical and horizontal relationships Integration and collaboration, partnership
Intellectual roots	Energy policy/innovation studies	Ecology and biology	Electronic and computer engineering	Political science
Agency	Intermediary actors, facilitated by government	Self-organizing	Self-organizing	Steering by government, intermediary actors
Typical applications	Innovation clusters	Urban flow-based infrastructure	Urban data-based management	Public–private partnerships

Transitions towards sustainable cities

'Transition' has become a key word in recent years in the discussion about sustainable development, and especially in the context of low-carbon innovation (see, for example: Geels, 2002; Geels and Schot, 2007; Heinberg and Lerch, 2010; Lachman, 2013; Pisano et al., 2014). The term is used in policy to signal the need for a systemic shift from current fossil-fuel dependent socio-economic activity to future resource-efficient development based on drastically reduced carbon footprints. Such transition is characterized by three basic elements: first, a temporal dimension which takes in a medium- to long-term period, often with 2030 or 2050 set as the time horizon by which to achieve significant transition; second, a main thematic element focused on GHG emissions and corresponding energy and material resource efficiency; and third, a conceptual dimension informed by system theory and relating to various infrastructure systems, including energy, transport, water, waste, agriculture and communications.

Not unexpectedly, cities have been drawn into this transition-for-sustainability policy discourse. For example, according to the United Nations Environment Programme, cities are 'critical geographical units in the formulation and implementation of policies that will shape our future across sectors' and should, therefore, act as 'transformative tools' for achieving a 'transition to a green economy' (UNEP, 2009: 2). The discussion about what place and function cities – and specifically, urban systems – occupy in these transition processes is, however, still at an emerging stage. Hence, it is useful to consider how transition is understood theoretically and how, in turn, this relates to urbanization processes.

In doing so, one should bear in mind that urbanization itself is not a uniform phenomenon. Rather, urbanization occurs at various scales and rates of intensity and speed, resulting in diverse patterns of urban development and rural–urban relationships. For example, according to one study, a distinction may be made between six 'city archetypes', each defined by particular urbanization dynamics and, taken together, suggesting different development trajectories (Centre for Liveable Cities, 2014):

1. 'Underdeveloped urban centres', such as Marrakesh (Morocco), which are mainly based in developing countries and are characterized by relatively low populations and low urban density.

2. 'Underdeveloped crowded cities' (e.g. Manila, Philippines), to be found predominantly in Asia and Africa and characterized by high population (density).
3. 'Developing mega-hubs' (e.g. Chongqing, China), with rapidly growing populations, based in developing countries.
4. 'Sprawling metropolises' (e.g. Los Angeles, US), found in developed countries and defined by large-scale, low density urban form.
5. 'Urban powerhouses', or world cities (e.g. Hong Kong, China), characterized by high population (density) and an international service sector economy.
6. 'Prosperous communities' (e.g. Copenhagen, Denmark), encompassing established small- to medium-sized cities in developed countries.

Each of these city types has a different profile in terms of urbanization rates and related socio-economic development stages, as well as corresponding sustainability challenges, including energy consumption levels and material resource demands. (And within each city type, there are further differentiations, owing to the particular features and contexts of individual cities.) Other studies point to differentiated urban–rural relationships, including the emergence of extended metropolitan regions (EMRs) through polycentric, region-wide – as opposed to city-based – urbanization (see, for example, Swilling et al., 2013: section 3.2). As a consequence, among other factors, such uneven urbanization through differences in city types and urban–rural relationships can be expected to condition and co-determine the transition pathways towards urban sustainability: while the goal of the transition to low-carbon urbanism may be a common one, the routes towards it may be many.

Multi-level perspective

At the core of sustainability transitions is a dynamic relationship between emerging innovative practices – also referred to as 'sustainability-oriented innovations' (see, for example, Swilling et al., 2013: section 6.1) – and existing systems. Sustainability-oriented innovations may struggle to form and take hold within a context of well-established, dominant systems: for example, initiating and then scaling up a local, organic food network may typically be up against existing international agri-business and large food distribution and retail systems; or developing and financing a district energy scheme may be hampered by regulations and technical specifications geared towards mainstream energy systems. The *problematique* of sustainability transitions, therefore, lies as much in tackling these enduring, established systems, as it lies in focusing on the alternative, innovative practices themselves. Among the various ways of conceptualizing transitions for sustainability (see, for example, Lachman, 2013), the so-called multi-level perspective (MLP) provides a useful approach for conceptualizing the dynamic relationship between established systems, or regimes, and emerging innovative practices. MLP was originally developed by a group of Dutch researchers in the late 1990s and early 2000s in relation to a study on Dutch energy policy; it has since been developed as a distinct theory of environmental governance (Rip and Kemp, 1998; Geels, 2002; Berkhout et al., 2003; Geels and Schot, 2007; Geels, 2010; Smith et al., 2010; STRN, 2010; Geels, 2011), and more recently has been applied to cities and urbanization processes (see e.g. Hodson and Marvin, 2010a; Guy et al., 2011; Swilling et al., 2013; Bulkeley et al., 2013).

As the term suggests, MLP distinguishes between different analytical levels: at the micro-level, the 'niche', or 'socio-technical niche' refers to small-scale, relatively protected spaces. A research laboratory, demonstration project, or social network or movement may constitute such spaces. It is within these spaces that various actors (designers, technologists, environmental campaigners, funders, etc.) join forces – in different constellations – to develop and trial new socio-technical concepts, methods and practices, such as local food networks or district energy schemes. These innovative practices are generally referred to as 'socio-technical' in that they combine technological developments and applications with social functions and interests. The niche, while relatively self-contained by the innovation process at work, nevertheless interacts with the wider, meso-level 'regime', within which it is embedded. The regime comprises established systems – relating to transport, energy, water, waste, food, etc. – and associated rules, institutional arrangements and professional practices that define and support these systems. In comparison with the niche, the regime is stabilized and governed by various 'lock-in' mechanisms, from statutory regulations to established professional practices, and from binding contractual arrangements to vested interests (STRN, 2010:6). As a consequence, regimes tend to be enduring, set in their norms, rules and structures; and it is for this reason that new socio-technical developments emerging from within niches may struggle to break through and establish themselves more widely. Finding ways of unlocking, or destabilizing, the regime, therefore, becomes an important consideration in sustainability transitions. For example, the establishment of 'feed-in-tariffs' (FIT), which allows small-scale renewable energy producers to connect to national energy grids, is a mechanism for unlocking the energy system and, thus, setting the condition for district energy schemes to become viable. Likewise, providing favourable business rates or tax exemptions for small food suppliers and distributors may be an important mechanism to open up the food system and allow local food networks to establish themselves successfully.

The third element of MLP is what is referred to as 'landscape' – not to be confused with geographical landscape – operating at the macro level. This is the most static element of the three and refers to the wider context within which regimes and niches are situated. It encompasses macro-economic patterns, political (institutional) culture and environmental characteristics. Change at landscape level tends to be slow, for example in the form of long-term demographic shifts, cultural trends, and evolving land use practices. Landscape factors influence niche-level processes indirectly. For example, public and policy discourse on global warming, as an environmental as well as cultural landscape factor, provides the wider context, within which, say, the energy system may become unlocked and sustainability-oriented innovation can occur at niche level. Together, the three aspects of MLP – 'niche', 'regime', and 'landscape' – and their interaction should be understood in conceptual terms, rather than as real-life phenomena, as a means of examining and interpreting the dynamics at work in innovation processes.

How cities, and especially sustainable city initiatives, relate to the multi-level perspective is not immediately obvious. This is because MLP, in its abstract conceptualization of innovation systems and corresponding action levels, does not engage per se with the spatial dynamics of cities (Swilling et al., 2013: 56). More recently, however, the two interests have been brought together within the context of urban sustainability. As UNEP (2009: 2) puts it, cities are 'critical geographical units' and 'transformative tools' through which to achieve the transition to a green economy. In relation to MLP, they are dynamically implicated in this transition process at both regime and niche levels. From the regime perspective, cities are 'geographical units' embodying socio-technical systems: here, several regimes – energy, water, waste, food, transport, communications – come together through, and in relation to, the city as a particular spatial configuration. Any one regime may intertwine more or less with a city's spatial arrangements: for example, a transport system (say, metropolitan transit) may be closely bounded by urban space, whereas a water or energy supply and distribution network may be configured mainly in relation to wider regional and national dimensions. More or less directly, therefore, cities as spatial units embodying socio-technical regimes become implicated in the process of effecting transition, with focus on how entrenched systems can be purposefully unlocked or destabilized, giving way to new innovative practices. In this role, cities can be understood partly as recipients, and partly as generators, of sustainability-oriented transitions (Swilling et al., 2013: 56). As recipients, cities may take on the role of implementing national transitions – serving as the sites through which wider, purposive transition is enacted – whereas as generators they mediate the latter by shaping and infusing transition at higher regional or national levels. In both cases, the possibility opens up for cities to develop their own transition processes embedded within the particular spatial arrangements in place.

Cities, then, are 'geographical units' which not only embody socio-technical systems, but also harbour niches. According to Geels (2011: 12), sustainable city initiatives can be conceived of as niches through which radical innovation is envisaged and developed. As such, they stand in contrast to, and challenge, mainstream urban planning and governance – that is, the established regime(s) in place. They do so by variously combining new technology (renewable energy, waste management systems, public transit, urban agriculture, etc.) with new urban planning practices (integrated governance, social networks, etc.) and socio-cultural activity (community engagement, sustainable lifestyles, etc.). Individual sustainable city initiatives, as niches, are each defined by particular 'design communities' and specific, sequentially developed projects (Geels, 2011: 15). Moreover, they compete within particular socio-economic contexts (again, the wider regime in play). As a result, sustainable city initiatives follow along multiple possible paths, rather than a single, uniform trajectory; this accounts for the diversity of urban sustainability initiatives observed.

Such an understanding of the sustainable city underscores the relevance of process both internally within the niche, and in the relationship between the niche and the regime. At niche level, internal processes – also called 'strategic niche management' (SNM) – are central to determining how sustainable city initiatives are envisaged, designed and implemented (Geels, 2011: 20): visions have to be articulated, to guide the process of innovation and attract funding and interest; social networks have to be formed, in order to achieve a viable constituency of actors to be involved and to mobilize various (financial, technical, community) resources; and experimentation and learning have to be facilitated, to address and interconnect the multiple dimensions – from technical aspects to market considerations, and from infrastructure issues to cultural practices – involved in urban sustainability innovation. As spaces of innovation, then, urban sustainability niches are chiefly defined in terms of ongoing, evolving processes, with both the direction and outcomes subject to, on one hand, niche-internal dynamics and, on the other, external conditioning from the wider regime. This, therefore, renders these niches initially inherently unstable and fragile; and, consequently, it may take considerable time for the innovation processes to build sufficient momentum to produce transition at the wider regime level.

Beyond the focus on the niche-internal processes involved, sustainable city development should also be understood as a sequence of multiple initiatives (Geels, 2011: 22). According to this view, while individual sustainable city initiatives evolve in relation to the particular spatial contexts within which they are embedded, they collectively form a trajectory that over time may successfully challenge the dominant regime and, thus, bring about urban sustainability transition beyond specific spatial sites at larger societal level.

Both the French ÉcoCité and ÉcoQuartier initiative and the Japanese Eco-Model City programme offer interesting insight, from a practical perspective, into the dynamics involved in sustainable city innovation processes. They suggest that the value of thinking in terms of a unidirectional relationship and trajectory – say, the sustainable city, as a fragile niche, struggling to establish itself within a context of a locked-in regime – is limited; instead, a more complex picture emerges. The regime itself – the national innovation system, and urban development regime – appears to become unlocked and to begin to move along a 'purposive urban socio-technical transition' (Swilling et al., 2013: 58) pathway, in the form of the programmes spearheaded by the respective national agencies. By providing overarching frameworks, including national guidelines, technical assistance and financial support, these programmes create incentives and more enabling conditions than would otherwise be the case, with the purpose of stimulating innovation at the niche level. The frameworks, however, are not intended to be defined rigidly, to pre-determine the process and outcome of innovation; instead, they are defined deliberately openly to facilitate the flourishing of multiple niches. Hence, actors on the ground are prompted to take a lead in defining the contents and processes of sustainable city initiatives.

Consequently, the frameworks acknowledge that the resulting initiatives are expected to be diverse, following various pathways. Moreover, while some initial funding and assistance is offered centrally, both programmes emphasize that individual initiatives themselves need to generate viable networks of actors and secure investment. What is more, by forming knowledge exchange networks between participating and non-participating cities (Club National ÉcoQuartier in the case of the French programme; Promotion Council for Low-Carbon Cities in the case of Japan), an attempt is made to interconnect individual niches, so as to effect broader, more sustained urban sustainability transition. Needless to say, it remains to be seen whether these ambitions can eventually be realized in the course of the two programmes' further implementation in the years to come.

Urban sustainability as adaptive system process

The transition perspective conceptualizes the sustainable city as part of a wider socio-technical system, emphasizing the dynamic interaction between innovation at niche level and developments at wider regime level. The depiction of urban sustainability as process has in recent years also been significantly influenced by two other, interrelated theoretical perspectives which view the city as socio-ecological metabolism and complex adaptive system, respectively. These perspectives, too, conceptualize the city dynamically as part of wider system relationships, although here the understanding of system is defined more explicitly in terms of self-organizing, co-evolutionary processes. From this viewpoint, the city can be seen as a quasi-living organism – not unlike a biological organism – which forms part of a wider ecological system; or, with a more technological, cybernetic slant, as a complex, machine-like adaptive system. Common to all three perspectives is the emphasis – albeit to varying degrees – on urban processes as non-linear, co-evolutionary and self-organizing activity. In turn, the steering and co-ordination of these processes, in the form of governance networks and mechanisms, becomes a central concern. Here, the important question arises as to whether such governance should be understood as largely self-directive, or instead requiring active, purposive intervention. In the case of intervention, the further question arises as to whether this should be cast mainly in technocratic terms – based on technical criteria and led by experts – or be rendered more explicitly a wider socio-political process. This, then, also prompts a discussion about the role of intentional political agency in the quest for urban sustainability.

The sustainable city as circular metabolism

The likening of the city to a living machine, or living organism, is not new; such metaphors have been a characteristic feature of many debates about town and urban planning across the decades, often shaping the discussion of how to redress the problems arising from unchecked, detrimental urbanization (see Chapter 3). As such, there is a close intellectual connection between the city conceptualized as an organism or metabolism and the emerging discourse on urban sustainability. What is, however, relatively new is that the proposition has gone beyond serving as a mere metaphor: urban metabolism is increasingly understood in literal manner as a real, measurable and quantifiable phenomenon based on environmental scientific understanding.

In the 1930s, Lewis Mumford, building on the earlier work by Patrick Geddes and others, originally proposed that urban development should be based on an 'organic order' (see Chapter 3; Mumford, 1938, reproduced in Wheeler and Beatley, 2009: 18–22; Mumford, 1961). Informed by new insights from biology as well as sociology, Mumford discussed the city in terms of a 'living machine' which exists in intimate relationship with its surrounding natural environment and is governed by self-regenerative, adaptive processes. This contrasts with the city as a product of industrialization and defined by what he termed 'machine ideology' – that is, urban development dominated by polluting and dehumanizing industrial technology. If the notion of the city as a 'living machine' was originally used more as a qualitative metaphor as part of a far-ranging philosophical critique of the techno-industrial age, it was later, in the second half of the twentieth century, developed further into a more explicit scientific concept and methodology. Environmental scientists in particular have been instrumental in highlighting the ecological basis of cities; in doing so they have applied system thinking in an effort to analyse – including measuring and quantifying – the dynamic relationship between urban and ecological systems.

Based on the seminal work by Wolman (1965) and subsequently Girardet (1996; 1999), Barles (2009; 2010) and Swilling et al. (2013), among others, 'urban metabolism' has become a key element in the discussion of the sustainable city. This perspective views the city in relation to its surrounding hinterland, or bioregion; the latter serves the city by providing both the sources of materials and resources – energy, water, building materials, agricultural produce, etc. – required to sustain urban infrastructure and activity, as well as the sinks for absorbing urban wastes, including solid waste, waste water and greenhouse gas emissions. In the context of unsustainable development, the metabolic relationship between the city and its hinterland is linear in the sense that the resources are extracted from outside the urban boundaries, transmitted inside the city's boundaries in support of urban activities, and the resulting wastes deposited back into the external environment (Girardet, 1999: 32–46; Swilling et al., 2013: 51). Urban activity becomes unsustainable as a result of this linear relationship, when the demand – in terms of both resource inputs and waste outputs – exceeds the carrying capacity of the city's hinterland (see Chapter 1). This state of affairs is to be rectified by arranging the relationship in more circular fashion – that is, by creating 'closed-loop' urban metabolism. The significance of urban metabolism, and its method-ological application through material flow analysis (MFA), is that 'it facilitates the re-embedding of urban systems within the wider nexus of local-regional ecosystem services ... and natural resource extrac-tion' (Swilling et al., 2013: 33).

Designing, and redesigning, cities for such sustainable, socio-ecological metabolisms calls for concerted action along three fronts (Swilling et al., 2013: 47–52): first, improving resource efficiency and productivity, by achieving more material output with less (non-renewable) material input, an example of which would be more energy-efficient buildings that reduce energy consumption while maintaining living standards; second, switching to – ideally locally based – renewable resources, such as electricity generation using photovoltaic power plants, and thus further reducing demand for non-renewable materials; and third, re-cycling and re-using waste materials, such as through waste-to-energy incineration.

The sustainable city conceptualized in terms of a circular, closed-loop metabolism has been advanced by environmental scientists, in order to develop analytical techniques and practical tools aimed at achieving more sophisticated, integrated 'whole-system' approaches to sustainable urban planning and development. While still at a rela-tively early stage and as yet not applied to entire cities, nevertheless a number of experimental initiatives have sought to implement circular urban metabolism at smaller scale and mainly in relation to infrastructure (energy, water, materials, etc.), such as in the form of eco-industrial parks (e.g. Kalundburg, Denmark) and some eco-town projects (e.g. Kitakyushu eco-town and other Japanese eco-town initiatives) (see, for example, GEC, 2005; van Berkel et al., 2009). At wider national policy level, circular urban metabolism has been embraced by several countries – arguably most enthusiastically by China, whose various eco-city development programmes draw heavily on the concept of the 'circular economy' (Joss and Molella, 2013). This concept was enshrined in national law in 2009, and aims to 'integrate economy with resources and environmental factors ... based on the material metabolism mode of "resource-product-regenerated resource", which incorporates a mechanism of efficient resource use and waste stream feedback, while its metabolism is compatible with the whole ecosystem' (Li et al., 2010: 4274). The World Bank's Eco2 Cities scheme repeatedly invokes the idea of metabolism in its conceptualization of the city, and in its examples of urban sustainability best practice gathered from around the world (Suzuki et al., 2010), emphasizing the importance of understanding urban 'flows' alongside questions of urban form, and heralding the 'opportunities for integration by learning to view the city and the urban environment as a complete system' (World Bank, 2010a: 7).

Beyond this focus on infrastructure and related material flows, the notion of the city as metabolism – drawing on biology and ecology – has also been applied more widely to the city as social entity, or network. This is illustrated, for example, by research carried out by Bettencourt et al. (2007). This work set out to establish whether there is more to the notion – beyond serving as a qualitative metaphor – of the city as 'metabolism', 'organism' and 'living system'. The research – based on a comparative, quantified assessment of urban data from across China, Europe and the US – suggests a positive correlation between growth in urban size and the rate in urban activity and innovation: as cities grow and urbanization expands, so the pace of economic and cultural activity increases. This correlation applies across different types of urban form implying, the authors argue, a universality of 'urban life': 'It is remarkable that it is principally in terms of these rhythms that cities are self-similar organizations, indicating a universality of human social dynamics, despite enormous variability in urban form. These findings provide quantitative underpinnings for social theories of "urbanism as a way of life"' (Bettencourt et al., 2007: 7305). Cities are likened to other social organizations, such as businesses and corporations; and they are compared in evolutionary terms with biological organisms. This leads the authors to argue that with increased urbanization the rate of innovation quickens, involving ever shorter time scales; this stands in contrast to much longer innovation cycles (as seen by natural selection processes) in the biological realm. From this, the authors conclude: 'our analysis suggests uniquely human social dynamics that transcend biology and redefine metaphors of urban "metabolism"' (Bettencourt et al., 2007: 7306).

Notions of the city as metabolism, living organism, or living machine – understood either metaphorically or literally as quantifiable characteristic – may be useful in the discussion of urban sustainability, as a means of articulating, on one hand, the intricate, dynamic relationship between the city and its wider natural environment and, on the other, the complex nature of the city as social organization. The World Bank's Eco2 Cities programme distinguishes its approach to urban sustainability from earlier ones by proposing 'a new generation of eco cities that move beyond individual, stand-alone green measures to a systems perspective ... It requires that a city be understood as a whole and that design solutions incorporate some of the complex, multipurpose features of natural ecologies' (Suzuki et al., 2010: xx). And yet, these notions are not without their problems, including most strikingly in many cases a lack of proper articulation of the city, and urban sustainability, as an active socio-political process; Eco2 Cities may be untypical in its parallel concern with governance processes. Elsewhere, the city, as urban metabolism, may be reduced essentially to infrastructure and related material flows, often with little in-depth discussion of the implications for how urban activity is and should be governed in this respect. Where the notion of metabolism is further extended to social dimensions, the underlying biological and evolutionary analogies lead to the depiction of the city as a spontaneous self-organizing entity. From this perspective, urban organizations and actors are governed by self-similar, evolutionary processes – 'a treadmill of dynamical cycles of innovation' (Bettencourt et al., 2007: 7306) – as part of wider system dynamics. This reinforces the conceptualization of governance as a process acting upon, or happening to, organizations, communities and individuals, especially so when understood within a context of a 'universality of human dynamics', as opposed to an active process of socio-political deliberation and decision-making.

What is more, the analogies with biological organisms and systems often become stretched and arguably tenuous as seen, for example, in reference – even when presumably meant metaphorically – to the potential of cities acting as closed-loop ecosystems 'like a forest or savannah' (Benyus, 2010, as reproduced in Swilling et al., 2013: 47), or in actual measurement of urban metabolism through quantitative comparison between the ratio of walking speed to city size with the biological ratio of heart rate to body mass in mammals (Bettencourt et al., 2007: 7304/Fig.2). Such analogy risks being reductionist and thereby obscuring or negating the socially constructed and contested nature of urban activity and, in turn, failing to articulate and clarify the sustainable city as a concern for human action.

The sustainable city as complex adaptive system

The conceptualization of cities as living machines and as self-similar, self-organizing social organizations is reinforced by a further, influential theoretical perspective – namely, that of complexity theory (see, for example, Allen, 1997; Portugali et al., 2012; Batty, 2013). Here, the emphasis is not as exclusively on the analogy with biological systems as in the case of urban metabolism/organism, but rather on the analogy with complex systems and their dynamics. Within complexity science, a system can be mechanical, physical, biological or social: from stock markets to ecosystems, and from the internet to international organizations. In these terms, the city can be considered a system, too. Broadly, what defines a complex system is, on one hand, the internal organization and relationship of its constituent parts and, on the other, the dynamic interrelationship with its surrounding environment. Complexity, then, arises from the dynamic networks of interaction within the system and between the system and its environment. This interaction is governed by 'closed signalling loops' and related 'feedback dynamics' (the vocabulary here reveals the close kinship with electronic system science). A system is adaptive if its internal aggregation organizes itself and evolves in response to changes in the surrounding environment. These adaptive, co-evolutionary processes rely on the capacity of the system and its constituent parts – also referred to as 'agents' – to learn, engage in behavioural change and arrange itself. Agency, then, is a largely endogenous process, emanating from within, in the form of self-organizing behaviour.

Analysing the attributes of an individual agent – its discrete behaviours, activity, reactions, etc. – on its own will not fully reveal the dynamics of the system as a whole, because the wider system process is ultimately the result of the collective properties emerging from the interaction of the various parts (Bretagnolle et al., 2006). This, then, prompts the need for whole-system analysis. This requires empirical modelling and simulation, which is a key feature of system science: by reproducing and testing various components/agents and their networked relationship, models of complex systems can be developed and adaptive behaviour simulated, in order to develop an understanding of the co-evolutionary dynamics at work and the resulting effects in terms of system behaviour and change. Such modelling can be applied to the city as complex adaptive system; here again, similarly to recent developments in urban metabolism research, the attempt made is to move beyond the metaphorical use – the fashionable reference to the city as complex system – and try empirically to reproduce and predict a city's systemic, collective properties through simulation models (see, for example, Bretagnolle et al., 2006: 15).

In practice, sophisticated modelling of urban systems has proved to be challenging; this is partly because of the difficulty of defining and delineating the city as a bounded system, given the concurrency of diverse, overlapping urban networks (infrastructure, trade, cultural, social, etc.) as well as the relative openness of its boundaries; and it is partly also because of the methodological limitations and constraints involved in modelling and simulating what are inherently highly complex relations and interactions. In spite of these challenges, research on urban complex system suggests 'some collective common behaviour ... which is not initiated or controlled by a unique institution but self-organized. These collective behaviours contribute to ensure a social regulation of the system' (Bretagnolle et al., 2006: 20). Similar to research on urban metabolism this, too, foregrounds the 'universality' of urban system dynamics and related self-organizing governance processes; in doing so, it again obviates the question, when applied to urban sustainability, of how active governance through public and political discourse might play a role in shaping these processes.

The proposition of the city as a complex adaptive system, like that of the city as urban metabolism, has been deployed to date mainly for conceptual and analytical purposes, to advance a more sophisticated understanding of cities and of urban sustainability. Nevertheless, this scientific discourse has begun to wield significant influence on urban (sustainability) policy and practice. This can be seen most explicitly in recent developments in the area of 'smart cities' (see Chapter 3). For example, according to the British Standards Institution (BSI), in a policy report commissioned by the UK government, '"smart cities" is a term denoting the effective integration of physical, digital and human systems in the built environment to deliver a sustainable, prosperous and inclusive future for its citizens' (BSI, 2014a: 9). The smart city can thus be understood as a sustainable city defined by an explicit system approach. The BSI report duly echoes the conceptualization of cities in system terms: 'In common with many natural and man-made systems, cities are complex. Our understanding of complex systems is achieved by reducing the complexity to a manageable number of well understood fundamental parameters ... of cities' behaviour' (BSI, 2014a: 7). In a sister document, which discusses the use of smart city frameworks, the challenge is highlighted – again echoing the methodological discussion among researchers – of applying such a system approach in practice: 'However, the complexity and pace of change, combined with the need for integrated and systemic solutions, are presenting a major challenge to local authorities who, traditionally, have developed responses in a "siloed" fashion' (BSI, 2014b: 7). According to this perspective, traditional decision-making based on discrete organizational structures and compartmentalized processes – captured by conventional notions of 'government' – may struggle to engage effectively with the systemic, networked nature of urban sustainability issues as they typically transcend singular institutional boundaries, policy spheres and geographical scales. This, in turn, points to the need to consider the role of governance processes and, specifically, what might be relevant and appropriate mechanisms for governing sustainable urban development within a context of complexity.

Governing for urban sustainability

Governance, as a domain of political theory and policy analysis, mirrors innovation studies and system sciences in significant ways: it, too, has over the last few decades gained an increasingly salient position in both academic and wider policy discourses; it focuses on adaptive, interdependent networking processes across various scales; and it presents itself as a potential solution for dealing with complex, systemic issues and what are sometimes referred to as 'wicked problems' (Rittel and Webber, 1973) – of which sustainable development is a prime example – facing contemporary decision-making (see, for example, Bueren et al., 2003; Boyd and Folke, 2011; Schneider, 2012; Termeer et al., 2013). This is not coincidental, as governance has some common intellectual roots with both innovation studies and system theory. Its distinguishing feature is the explicit emphasis on decision-making processes; the institutions, organizations, structures and techniques used to manage these processes; as well as the relationships and dynamics between the diverse governmental and non-governmental, public and private actors involved. Again, it is no coincidence that governance has become implicated in urban sustainability, given the recognition of the centrality and complexity of the processes at work.

While governance, then, offers the potential to clarify and perhaps even facilitate complex, multi-level processes, it sometimes risks – especially when the emphasis is one-sidedly on governance as dissipative, self-organizing process – down-playing or obfuscating important questions about political agency, public accountability and power. In this respect, too, the resemblance with innovation and system sciences occasionally shines through. As a consequence, if governance is to be a useful perspective for analysing and explaining the sustainable city, it requires a critical engagement with the political nature of governing processes involved in sustainable urban development. This calls for a clarification of the key characteristics of, as well as the rationale for, governance in relation to sustainable development in general, and urban sustainability in particular.

'From government to governance' is a phrase used to denote a relative shift in decision-making culture, which is said to have occurred over the last half a century or so, resulting in the transformation of policy and decision processes. In its course, according to this view, the traditional 'command-and-control' function of the state (= government) has increasingly given way to a more facilitating function (= governance): rather than necessarily remaining centrally involved in, and solely responsible for, decision-making, the state assumes the role of facilitating agent by letting non-governmental actors – private companies, associations, technology firms, etc. – into the process and itself exercising a more removed, co-ordinating and steering role. On their part, non-governmental actors assume a more central and active role through collaborative policy networks and joint decision processes. Such networks and collaborative processes are sometimes referred to as 'heterarchical' (see Jessop, 2002), to denote the move away from hierarchical structures (with the state at the top of the hierarchy) towards more horizontal, decentralized and shared decision-making relationships. Another conceptual term used is that of a 'differentiated polity' (Rhodes, 1997), which similarly signals the co-existence of several separate, partially overlapping decision-making spheres, rather than an all-encompassing polity with central government at the helm.

The original predictions of a full-scale, paradigmatic shift from government to governance have since been relativized: more recent research points to a more complex picture according to which government retains an important influence, either by keeping itself directly involved in decision-making processes, albeit alongside other non-governmental actors, or by orchestrating collaborative governance – also referred to as 'imperative co-ordination' (Jessop, 2004) – and thereby continuing to exercise control more indirectly, or 'at a distance' (as it is sometimes described). Not surprisingly, this research flags up important questions – with direct implications for the discussion about urban sustainability – about the dynamics of collaborative governance, the possibility of asymmetries arising between actors involved in networking, related problems of power imbalances and control, and the place for public discourse and accountability.

The sustainable city as urban governance network

This *problematique* of governance is reflected in the discourse on sustainable development, as well as urban sustainability more particularly. The intertwined, self-reinforcing relationship between governance and (urban) sustainable development is by now widely recognized (see, for example, Adger and Jordan, 2009; Griffin, 2010; Joss, 2010; Bulkeley and Marvin, 2014; Tomozeiu and Joss, 2014). The fact that sustainable development deals with, and cuts across, the economic, social and environmental pillars of policy-making (see Chapter 1), and does so at multiple levels – from the local to the global – involving a mixture of state and non-state actors through collaborative, networked processes renders it a political concept 'replete with governance questions' (Farrell et al., 2005: 143). Here, too, calls are made for more synergistic approaches to developing policies and implementing decisions, with added relevance arising from the need for concerted, integrated decision-making across sectors and national borders as well as beyond short-term political and economic cycles (Tomozeiu and Joss, 2014).

However, it should not be read as given that a governance approach to sustainability necessarily delivers more effective or legitimate policy solutions compared with more traditional government mechanisms (see, for example, Griffin, 2010). Research into a range of sustainable development issues has shown that new forms of governance for sustainability can harbour problems, tensions and contradictions of their own. For example, the blurring of responsibility in public–private partnerships, or the hybridity of state-initiated yet privately run bodies, can lead to blockages in decision-making and cause public accountability problems (see, for example, Book et al., 2010; Joss, 2010). Elsewhere, research has indicated that governance mechanisms designed to reconcile economic and environmental sustainability goals may in fact exacerbate tensions between them (Cochrane, 2010; Joss, 2010). Much of this has been shown to be closely dependent on the particular thematic, policy and geographical contexts within which governance for sustainability occurs. Other commentators, however, cast the overall tendency towards partnership arrangements as a problematic symptom of the 'neoliberalization' of urban governance. While partnership governance models appear to be a practical solution to reduced municipal budgets, and promise both public accountability and private sector efficiency, critics have suggested that the private sector may profit while risks are transferred onto the public sector, that profitability may be prioritized over other goals including sustainability, and that governance processes may become less transparent (see, for example, Harvey, 2006; Bexell and Mörth, 2010; Book et al., 2010; Joss, 2010). The important question of accountability in these newer governance arrangements is taken up in Chapter 8.

These governance characteristics and challenges are also frequently found in relation to urban sustainability issues, where they are often particularly pronounced due to the complex intermeshing of hierarchies, networks and market mechanisms within specific local settings (see, for example, Greenwood and Newman, 2010; Rydin, 2010; Joss, 2011a; Tomozeiu and Joss, 2014). Here, it is not uncommon to observe especially intricate governance dynamics at work arising from the multiple interplay between vertical central–local relationships (international organizations, national agencies, municipal government, etc.), horizontal public–private relationships (public authorities, utilities, non-governmental organizations) and cross-sectoral relationships (economic, social, environmental policy), all played out within, and in relation to, specific urban contexts. This can lead to significant tensions, as illustrated, for example, in a study of the Thames Gateway, the UK's (and Europe's) largest urban regeneration project (Greenwood and Newman, 2010): the aim of new governance – namely, to 'join up' strategic planning and development through increased horizontal, collaborative governing – was here found to be undermined by the still considerable influence wielded by traditional government structures. The relationship between traditional planning and new forms of governance was not yet fixed; in particular, the relationship between central government and local tiers of decision-making was found to be undergoing continual change (Greenwood and Newman 2010: 108–9). In turn, this was shown to have had detrimental effects on the extent to which sustainable development policy implementation could be achieved. Similarly, an analysis of the English eco-town initiative – a government-led, but locally implemented programme aimed at developing new sustainable towns in response to a serious housing shortage – points to the influence exercised by the governance arrangements on the thematic framing of the policy, as well as the arrangements' negative impact on the initiative's overall progress (Tomozeiu and Joss, 2014). Here, too, the governance dynamics in play produced significant tensions due to the particular mix of central steering (government agencies) and local implementation (local authorities, developers); and here again, this was exacerbated by continual changes made to the national eco-town policy and the local planning processes as the initiative unfolded.

Urban sustainability governance, by definition, maps onto and relates to specific urban contexts: municipal institutions, infrastructure, services, the urban environment, and communities. A particular challenge, considering the role of cities in transition processes, is how to achieve alignment of urban governance networks with urban infrastructure, so as to enable and effect purposive urban transitions: 'The issue here is the degree to which policy agendas are separated or aligned with the power to manage urban infrastructure regimes. To use the language of the MLP [multi-level perspective], it is the extent to which the priorities of an urban governance network – and the social interests that produce them – are able to actively manage socio-technical regime change' (Swilling et al., 2013: 57). The challenge, then, for urban governance networks is three-fold: first, they have to mediate between, on one hand, existing political and bureaucratic structures and processes and, on the other, the management of infrastructure regimes; second, they have to facilitate the integration of separate socio-technical regimes (energy, water, transport, etc.); and third, they have to co-ordinate with wider regional, national and even international infrastructure networks. It cannot be assumed that existing municipal government structures can automatically deliver these networking functions, since they tend to be organized along established political boundaries and their policy remit and expertise may be limited. In London, for example, municipal waste management is the responsibility of individual boroughs and councils (of which there are over 30) with no overarching strategy or organizational capacity, as a consequence of which there is no effective alignment of waste management policy across the city as a whole. Hence, there is a recognized need for new types of governance networks to bring together actors from across organizations, policy domains and areas of expertise with a view to facilitating, co-ordinating and integrating urban sustainability policy, planning and development.

(Urban) governance networks exhibit particular characteristics relating to the space occupied, the actors involved, and the type of knowledge generated. Concerning the networking space, this can be defined as 'in-between' or 'outside' space in the sense that it typically does not reside within, and is not owned by, any particular organizational structure. This applies especially to informal, ad hoc networks – say, a local food network – but it can also be seen in more formal governance arrangements, such as public–private partnerships where the organizational structure is shared among the governmental and non-governmental parties involved, with no one single party fully owning the partnership. The 'in-between' space arises from the fact that by definition the issues considered within the governance networks reach across and are negotiated between institutional boundaries; but it is often also expressly articulated and arranged in this manner, in order to signal that the networking space not be owned by any particular interest, thereby creating a more neutral space where knowledge can be generated and solutions identified relatively unencumbered by direct vested interests.

The second characteristic of (urban) governance networks is the need for so-called 'intermediary organizations', whose function is to mediate, on one hand, between different aspects of urban sustainability issues – say, between economic development goals and environmental protection needs – and relatedly, on the other, between the various interests and priorities of the actors involved in the governance process (Swilling et al., 2013 57–9). Intermediary organizations are typically professional organizations that specialize as facilitators, and may include research organizations, consultancies, international development organizations and professional or public associations, among others. Within the 'in-between' spaces of governance networks and innovation niches, intermediary organizations occupy a unique position and often wield considerable influence over networks by virtue of co-ordinating, even setting, the agenda and orchestrating the governance process. In a global survey, Bulkeley and Castán Broto (2013) found that experimental urban climate change initiatives are typically initiated by local authorities but, in around half the cases they examined, were conducted in partnership with other actors, usually from the private sector. While not all these partners will necessarily have had a co-ordinating role, the finding nevertheless allows the authors to interpret such experiments as creating 'new political spaces' (ibid.: 371), and being linked to the 'shifting and blurring of public/private authority and the restructuring of the (local) state' (ibid.: 373). Purcell (2008: 27) is more openly critical of this tendency more generally in urban governance, contending that '[o]ligarchic institutions like public-private partnerships, appointed councils, and quasi-public agencies are increasingly making decisions that were formerly made by officials directly elected by the public ... Enterprise zones and mega-projects, for example, are creating special appointed bodies that govern only that particular project.' The involvement of third parties, then, particularly those empowered to make decisions outside traditional democratic processes, at least raises questions about democratic legitimacy and accountability.

Governance networks are further characterized, third, by the type and form of knowledge to be produced. Here, the normative emphasis is on generating new, integrated knowledge and capacity that are otherwise not readily available within individual organizations. In particular, the aim is to: promote shared understanding through the exchange of knowledge, information and expertise; encourage experimentation and learning with a view to stimulating new knowledge and innovative practices; and facilitate co-ordination among diverse actors aimed at mobilizing capacity and collective action. The intention at least is therefore that such networked governance 'creates a context for the discussion of competing priorities, helps to access fresh external knowledge ... and either provides capacity that is lacking or helps mobilise untapped internal capacity' (Swilling et al. 2013: 58). If a governance network is successful in doing so it may enable innovation niches to gain traction and establish themselves more widely; in turn, this may over time result in changes to the existing socio-technical regime as well as to established urban governance arrangements.

As noted, research into practical applications of governance processes for (urban) sustainability has indicated several challenges, highlighting what can be a considerable discrepancy between the normative ideals of governance and actual practice. This suggests the need for critical engagement with governance design and the conditions for effective governance processes. The nature of the 'in-between'/'outside' space of governance networks – including the role of the intermediaries involved and the status of the collaborative knowledge and action generated – in particular requires careful consideration in terms of public accountability and political legitimacy: creating innovation niches and governance spaces outside formal structures, specifically in order to mediate between areas of interests and facilitate co-operation among diverse actors, can have the unintended effect of complicating or even removing political accountability functionality (for a discussion of the *problematique* of accountability in sustainability governance see, for example, Joss, 2010). Where and how decisions are made, who owns these and, consequently, who can be held accountable for actions taken may become obscured as a result of networking in informal, dissipative spaces.

If the accountability of policy- and decision-making within formal government arrangements is widely taken to be an important norm and necessity then this arguably applies even more so to decentralized, collaborative forms of governance: more informal, shared decision-making suggests a need for special efforts to ensure the transparency and legitimacy of both decision processes and outcomes. This is particularly the case in contexts characterized – as urban sustainability transitions typically are – by relatively limited and uncertain knowledge, unchartered development paths and, therefore, the likelihood of political controversy and social resistance. After all, sustainability-oriented transitions imply radical and perhaps even disruptive change away from current patterns of socio-economic development. Related decision-making can, therefore, be expected to be subject to heightened political and public contestation; and it will require explicit political legitimacy to secure public support and lasting implementation.

This, then, suggests an approach to the governance of the sustainable city which pays explicit attention – more so than tends to be the case in mainstream discourse – to questions concerning governance dynamics, political accountability and power, and the role and place of public discourse. Such an active outlook avoids two assumptions that are sometimes tacit in the discussion of urban sustainability: first, that governance is a relatively non-problematic process that by virtue of its deployment produces more synergistic, integrated discourse and decision-making and, consequently, delivers the answer to the challenges posed by complex decision issues, as typified by the sustainable city; and second, that urban sustainability governance is a largely self-organizing, adaptive process – as part of the urban 'ecosystem' or 'metabolism' – which emerges and evolves bottom up in relation to wider systemic developments and following some universal natural or social principles. Instead, a more active approach seeks to analyse and define the conditions under which governance – as an inherently socio-political process, reliant on and driven by intentional agency – can facilitate urban sustainability transitions; it does so in particular by articulating urban sustainability governance networks beyond the technocratic aspects of the innovation processes involved, in relation to wider political and public discourse. This entails considering, for example, how 'in-between'/'outside' networking spaces connect with existing political structures and policy processes; how various social interests – including those of groups and communities with marginal voices – are represented within governance networks; how the influence of intermediary organizations is controlled; and how the knowledge generated within governance networks is related to public discourse. The purpose of such an active approach to governance, then, is to ensure due political oversight and public resonance and engagement; but just as important, its purpose is also to create the conditions which allow sustainable city initiatives to establish themselves beyond their initial, fragile innovation niches.

Conclusions

Contemplating the sustainable city from a process perspective brings two main advantages: first, it helps to reveal and clarify the processes that fundamentally characterize and drive urban sustainability innovation, and in particular the dynamic relationship between sustainable city initiatives and wider, systemic transition processes; and second, it draws attention to the need for an active approach to articulating and shaping governance processes as an essential part of defining, and engaging with, the sustainable city.

That the sustainable city is chiefly characterized in process terms becomes clear when one considers it as part of a wider, long-term effort to effect a fundamental, large-scale transition from current socio-economic development to future global activity which is to be radically less dependent on fossil fuel and consequently significantly more resource efficient. Within this wider process, sustainable city initiatives can be understood as constituting innovation niches and corresponding governance networks, in which diverse actors come together to engage collaboratively in articulating visions for urban sustainability, generating new knowledge, carrying out experiments and launching alternative products and practices. These niches and networks each exhibit distinct innovation dynamics and pathways owing to the particular assemblages of actors and their interests involved, as well as to the specific interactions with the urban contexts from which they emerge. Collectively, these diverse sustainable city initiatives may add up to form a wider, long-term innovation trajectory which, in turn, may over time gradually contribute to systemic urban sustainability transitions.

The four conceptual outlooks considered here – multi-level perspective, urban metabolism, complex adaptive systems and governance networks – all reveal important insights into, and provide critical analyses of, the sustainable city as process. While they each have their own take on the processes involved in urban sustainability, they share several important observations: first, they highlight the temporal dimension in play, whereby urban sustainability is essentially defined as an unfolding activity – often long term; it is not uncommon to see the sustainable city defined as 20–30 year development – rather than as a fixed goal or state; second, they emphasize the dynamic relationship of urban sustainability with wider systems, including environmental, urban and various socio-technical systems; and third, relatedly, they point to the inherent complexity arising from the systemic nature of the sustainable city; this complexity can be observed both internally within sustainable city initiatives – the niches and governance networks – as well as in their wider interactions with institutions, policy issues and processes, and various urban scales. Finally, the four conceptual outlooks highlight the diversity of urban sustainability processes resulting from the manifold systemic interactions and various contexts in play.

Consequently, the processes involved in the sustainable city need to be analysed at three levels and, importantly, these three levels need to be brought into relationship with one another. At one level, processes need to be analysed internally within sustainable city initiatives, with focus on the purposive, catalytic activity undertaken within niches and emergent governance networks; at the second level, processes need to be considered at the wider systemic urban level – the city as a whole and its various infrastructure and socio-technical systems – noting that changes at this level may be just as important and necessary to enable innovation niches to flourish and establish themselves; and at a further level, attention should be paid to the cumulative processes by which diverse sustainable city initiatives contribute, beyond specific urban contexts (particular niches and regimes), to the collective conceptualization of the sustainable city in wider policy and socio-cultural discourse (the landscape level), as input into long-term social transitions.

While the four conceptual outlooks discussed all emphasize process aspects of the sustainable city, with clear overlaps between them, they nevertheless also show up some significant differences; these differences point to some of the difficulties involved in conceptualizing the sustainable city as processes. Both the urban metabolism and complex adaptive system perspectives tend to conceive of the governing processes – albeit from different angles – as largely endogenous, self-organizing processes. Here, urban governance processes and related dynamics are understood as resulting from some collective common behaviour as part of complex systemic interactions, rather than being directed by deliberate, active intervention. Keil and Boudreau (2006: 43), for example, suggest that analyses of urban metabolism have tended to pay little attention to political changes in their study areas, to avoid asking critical questions about underlying economic structures, to underplay social and cultural factors, and to imagine the natural world as overly static and passive. An alternative perspective is advocated in the same volume, with the argument that '[p]rocesses of metabolic change are never socially or ecologically neutral' (Heynen et al., 2006), and that urban 'metabolism' and 'circulation' should not be thought of as technological or engineering issues, but rather highlight the city's character as a 'giant socio-environmental process', a 'socio-physical' hybrid with political meanings and effects, and the potential to change society for better or worse (Swyngedouw, 2006: 37). As typically mobilized at present, then, these perspectives – perhaps not unsurprisingly, given their roots in environmental and systems sciences – approach urban sustainability processes with a more technocratic understanding, with a focus on system-related adaptive self-organization. As such, to some extent at least, they arguably 'de-politicize' the sustainable city as process.

In contrast, the transition multi-level perspective (MLP) and the governance perspective place greater emphasis on urban sustainability governance as a purposive process based on intentional agency. They more explicitly engage – again, not entirely surprisingly, given their disciplinary roots – with questions of collective action, networking and co-ordination. However, these perspectives, too, arguably tend to pay insufficient attention to the socio-political conditions and criteria of the sustainable city. This is partly because they view governance as a relatively unproblematic process, with assumed positive effects of networking in terms of the ability to generate shared visions, mobilize interests and achieve co-ordinated action; and it is partly because they retreat from an active position of government – as purposive, intentional agency – to a more passive form of governance. As a consequence here, too, the sustainable city process to an extent becomes de-politicized insofar as the focus is on self-organizing networked spaces outside formal political structures and processes, occupied by new types of intermediary organizations and guided by internal specialist – and as such also technocratic – discourse.

In response to these dominant conceptualizations of the sustainable city as process, a powerful argument can be made that urban sustainability governance be rendered a more active, socio-political process. This is not to deny the importance of understanding urban sustainability in terms of dynamic, interactive processes as part of wider, complex environmental and technological system relations. However, this argument shifts the focus onto governance as purposive, collective action which is subject to political discourse and public accountability. There are two strong reasons for this shift of focus, one empirical, the other normative: first, as noted, research on sustainability governance has shown that attempts to design governance as technocratic process are often fraught with problems, as in practice governance processes frequently turn out to be 'messy', characterized by complicated government–governance relationships and raising intractable issues concerning political legitimacy and public accountability. Second, normatively, if one understands sustainable city initiatives as part of radical innovation processes aimed at effecting a large-scale, systemic transition towards significantly different socio-economic development then this arguably merits the involvement of active politics and public discourse. While sustainable city initiatives may need the relative protection of special niches and governance spaces to flourish as emerging innovative processes, this does not mean that they should be reduced to technocratic processes and shielded from political and public discourse. Otherwise, they may risk failing to engage effectively with the political and social issues that inevitably become intermeshed with urban sustainability initiatives; and they may risk failing to gain traction and establish themselves in wider urban policy and development.

To explore the case that active governance should be a powerful shaping force in these processes, it is useful first to explore the idea of urban sustainability specifically as a policy discourse, or as a convergence of policy discourses. The following chapter identifies the main characteristics of the contemporary sustainable city from this perspective, and considers how these have changed over time.

Chapter 3

Past and Present Policy Discourses

CHAPTER OVERVIEW

Recent decades have seen the sustainable city occupy an increasingly central position in international and national policy. As a consequence, concepts and practices of urban sustainability are profoundly shaped by policy discourses. Among these, sustainable development and ecological modernization are particularly forceful at a global level, applying environmental, economic and social dimensions to processes of urbanization and urban regeneration. This chapter charts the evolution of major policy discourses across time, highlighting in particular the related current tendencies for urban sustainability to be theorized in terms of interconnected systems, and understood to be a scientific-technical exercise; it discusses key actors involved in promoting and implementing policies; and it considers the implications for the practices which emerge.

Introduction: sustainabilities new and old

'The key to sustainability lies in the concept of "green cities" or "eco-cities"' (UNEP, 2012a: vi). This is one of the core recommendations of the United Nations Environment Programme, as published by the agency in its report *21 Issues for the 21st Century*, ahead of the United Nations' 'Rio20+' conference held in Rio de Janeiro in 2012. The report differentiates sustainable cities from their conventional counterparts in terms of superior environmental quality and liveability, to be achieved through the application of principles including compact mixed-used development, low-energy transportation, renewable energy generation and a reduced overall ecological footprint. Similarly, UN-Habitat, the United Nations body in charge of urban settlements, draws attention to cities as both source of, and solution to, global environmental challenges in its own annual report *Cities and Climate Change: Policy Directions* (UN-Habitat, 2011). The report predicts that the 'lives and livelihoods of hundreds of millions of people will be affected by what is done (or not done) in urban centres with regard to adapting to climate change over the next decade' (ibid. 35), positioning the 'populations, enterprises and authorities of urban centres' as 'fundamental players' (ibid. 1) in developing strategies to this end.

The UN is by no means the only international organization concerned with promoting urban sustainability policies. For example, the World Bank, which supports developing countries through loans for capital programmes, launched its Eco2 Cities policy initiative in 2009 with reference to urbanization as a 'defining feature of the 21st century' (Suzuki et al., 2010: xv). The '2' in Eco2 Cities stands for 'ecological cities as economic cities', thus highlighting the interdependence between environmental protection and economic growth. (In addition, the World Bank refers to Eco2 Cities as the 'second-generation' eco-cities, following the first generation of the 1970s.) According to the World Bank, the unprecedented urban growth, in particular in the Global South, provides a 'once-in-a-lifetime opportunity to plan, develop, build and manage cities that are simultaneously more ecologically and economically sustainable' (ibid.). In similar vein, the Organisation for Economic Co-Operation and Development (OECD), the international economic organization representing 34 European and non-European countries with high-income economies, turned its attention to cities through its Green Cities programme, again emphasizing the link between ecological and economic development: 'as key engines of economic growth, job creation and innovation, but also as major contributors to global warming and environmental problems, cities are at the heart of the transition to a green global economy' (Hammer et al., 2011: 8).

Concerns about the sustainability of cities are not new; they date back over a century and a half, when the detrimental environmental, health and social impacts of industrialized urban centres in Victorian England and elsewhere became only too apparent, and the 'garden city' was proposed as antidote (Wheeler and Beatley, 2009; Kargon and Molella, 2008). Current policy discourses on urban sustainability echo these earlier concerns, although they have taken on new dimensions. Most notably, particular local environmental issues are now overlaid with global climate change as the predominant policy challenge, and attention has increasingly turned to developing countries in the Global South, where urbanization processes are most pronounced, as well as to new actors – international technology firms,

Figure 3.1   *Overview of key policy narratives*

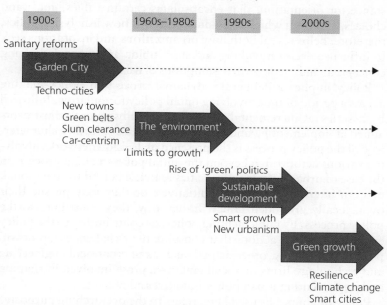

engineering groups, consultancies – that have come to play a growing role in sustainable city initiatives. Furthermore, much of current policy has become increasingly influenced by the dominant concept of 'ecological modernization', or 'green growth', according to which environmental protection and economic growth are mutually compatible, to be achieved through a transition to low-carbon economies.

In trying to understand current concepts and practices of urban sustainability, it is useful, therefore, to analyse related policy concepts and discourses, and to consider the ways in which these have evolved across decades. This is what this chapter sets out to do: first, by reviewing key policy developments across time; and second, by discussing mainstream contemporary urban sustainability discourses. The chapter concludes by raising some critical questions about recent trends in urban sustainability policy.

On policy discourse

First, though, the meanings of the terms 'policy' and 'policy discourse', as used in this context, merit a brief explanation. Policy generally refers to a course of action, or a group of decisions, rather than a specific decision or action (Hill, 1997). As such, it indicates a stance, or orientation, that encapsulates certain values, goals and choices, and from which individual decisions flow. Analysing policy, therefore, helps reveal both how organizations and institutions seek to influence decision-making and steer action and what underlying conceptual and ideological assumptions drive that process.

Policy implies a deliberate, dynamic process of policy-making across a period of time involving initial policy formulation, followed by a series of incremental decisions and subsequent adjustments aimed at implementing and evolving the policy. A further characteristic of the policy process is the presence of decision networks involving various actors often beyond the initial policy-making process. In the case of urban sustainability, cities may take a lead from national, or even international, policy initiatives; or they may pursue their own, locally grounded policy. Either way, they contribute to the policy process, by implementing policy, or contributing to the policy evolution through actions that consolidate or challenge 'top-down' policy. Increasingly, other actors, such as international engineering and technology firms or social enterprises, are involved in shaping and implementing urban policy initiatives.

Policy discourse, as used here, refers to the overarching purposive stance of policy – that is, the concepts, ideas and narratives at the heart of policy. This suggests that the policy process is political; it embodies certain values and pursues specific goals. (In several languages, such as German and Spanish, the same term is used for 'policy' and 'politics'.) Policy discourse, furthermore, refers to the communicative process of policy formulation, implementation and dissemination. Analysing urban sustainability policy discourses should, therefore, help to reveal underlying normative and conceptual perspectives, how these are communicated and by whom and, in turn, how they inform and condition urban sustainability forms and functions. Looking at, say, a national policy programme should provide useful insight into how a government conceives of the 'sustainable city', how it seeks to frame the agenda and steer and regulate practice. There may, of course, be a gap between what a certain policy espouses and actual development on the ground, be it as a result of practical problems of implementation or resistance on the part of those expected to implement the policy. Attention, therefore, also needs to be paid to alternative policy discourses and how these co-determine urban sustainability practice.

Policy also needs to be understood in terms of specific tools. These tools vary depending on the goal of policy, be it to redistribute (through taxation), to distribute (social services, benefits), to regulate (public and private activities) or to constitute (institutions) (Hill, 1997). Relatedly, their specific focus may also vary considerably; different policies may serve, for example, to set out regulatory frameworks (e.g. specifying the proportion of onsite renewable energy generation), to provide investment mechanisms and fiscal instruments (e.g. carbon credits, feed-in tariffs), to encourage action on public awareness and consumer behaviour (e.g. public transport campaigns), or to promote indicators and standards (e.g. green building codes). Some of these tools are discussed in more detail in Chapter 5, which looks at specific urban sustainability governance mechanisms, as well as Chapter 6, which discusses the use of various national and international frameworks for urban sustainability.

First, however, this chapter explores urban sustainability policy in terms of overarching discourses across the last 150 years or so and their influence on contemporary developments. Importantly, the following discussion should not be read as a necessarily linear evolution of urban sustainability concepts and policies, with each *époque* and each new proposition or initiative neatly building on the previous one. Rather, over time various discourses have emerged, influenced and preoccupied by context- and time-specific developments, concerns and traditions (see also Hall, 2002; Zhou and Williams, 2013). These narratives sometimes merge into one another; at other times they develop along diverging lines, so that contemporary sustainable city concepts and policies often reveal a rich and varied underlay of older discourses. Indeed, the diversity of contemporary sustainable city concepts and policies can at least partly be understood in terms of these multiple historical roots.

The sustainable city in response to the Industrial Age

The rise of urban sustainability as mainstream international policy and public discourse can be dated back to the 1990s: in 1992, the influential Rio Declaration on Environment and Development, and related Agenda 21 action plan (referring to an agenda for the twenty-first century), resulting from the UN 'Earth Summit' attended in Rio de Janeiro by leaders of 178 countries. Chapter 7 of *Agenda 21* addresses issues concerning 'sustainable human settlement development'. As elsewhere in the document, the emphasis is on the link between environmental and socio-economic development: 'the environmental implications of urban development should be recognised and addressed in an integrated fashion by all countries, with high priority being given to the needs of the urban and rural poor, the unemployed and the growing number of people without any source of income' (UNDESA, 1992b: 7.3). Chapter 28 also calls for local governments in each country to develop a Local Agenda 21 plan in consultation with local communities. The call for concerted, global efforts to address the various challenges identified in connection with rapidly increasing urbanization was made again on the occasion of the city summit hosted by UN-Habitat in Istanbul in 1996. Significantly, the resulting Habitat Agenda positions cities as sources of creative solutions to, rather than simply victims of, structural global problems: 'We have considered, with a sense of urgency, the continuing deterioration of conditions of shelter and human settlements. At the same time, we recognise cities and towns as centres of civilisation, generating economic development and social, cultural, spiritual and scientific advancement' (UN-Habitat, 1996: 2).

These two UN conferences and their resulting declarations laid much of the groundwork for urban sustainability policy developments in the ensuing years. The 'triple bottom line' of sustainable development – marrying environmental, economic and social sustainability – in particular has become a firm part of contemporary discourse on urban sustainability policy. This formulation is more clearly present in the 2003 re-affirmation of the *Habitat Agenda,* which asserts that 'sustainable human settlements development ensures economic development, employment opportunities and social progress, in harmony with the environment' (UN-Habitat, 2003b: 2.9).

It is important, however, following on from Chapter 1, to recall that the *problematique* of the (un)sustainable city was first identified by social commentators and writers as early as the nineteenth century. Indeed, while current policy debates about urban sustainability reflect concerns specific to the twenty-first century – global climate change and rapid urbanization in the Global South, among others – they also have clear echoes of earlier debates originating in the nineteenth and twentieth centuries.

The 'garden city' forms a particularly enduring arch between the present and past. This can be seen, for example, in the case of the Japanese government's recent eco-city programme, which builds on the legacy of the introduction of the garden city concept in Japanese urban planning in the early twentieth century (Low, 2013; see also

Chapter 4). It can also be seen in China's 'Eco-Garden City' programme run nationally for the last couple of decades by the Ministry of Housing and Urban-Rural Development (Zhou et al., 2012). Indeed, it seems likely that the 'principles of the garden city' will be applied to new towns in Britain itself, the birthplace of the garden city concept, according to proposals by the UK government (Donnelly, 2012) following the publication in 2011 of the report *Reimagining Garden Cities for the 21st Century* by the Town and Country Planning Association (TCPA, 2011).

Garden Cities of To-morrow, by Ebenezer Howard (1850–1928), published in 1902 (Howard, 1965), was a powerful response to the increasingly widely felt excesses of the modern industrial city. It soon became a classic reference work and profoundly inspired twentieth-century urban planning policy in England, Europe, the US and beyond. At its core was a conceptual and practical proposal for how to deal with the detrimental effects of unprecedented urbanization resulting from the industrial age. Manchester and other industrial cities across Victorian England had become a byword for rising social inequality, cramped urban environments lacking basic infra-structure, and coal-fired mills and iron works causing serious air and water pollution – Friedrich Engels' *The Condition of the Working Class in England* (Engels, 1987) was inspired by his experience of Manchester in the early 1840s. London had grown into the first city of the modern age with a population of one million, on the back of unparalleled urban expansion and social change, as so astutely observed in *Hard Times, Bleak House* and other novels by Charles Dickens. Technology – from the steam engine to electric lighting – began to transform urban life profoundly. In short, the modern industrial city, it was increasingly felt, had become unhinged, divorced from nature – in both an environmental and social sense.

As the term implies, the core idea of the garden city is to marry the best of rural countryside with the best of town life. This 'town-coun-try' – or garden city – would provide employment opportunities, improved living standards and cultural education, while at the same time enabling the direct experience of nature and ensuring a healthy environment: 'town and country *must be married*, and out of this joyous union will spring a new hope, a new life, new civilisation' (Howard, 1965: 48, italics in original). Howard's intention was to be both conceptual and practical, leading him to propose a concrete model of the garden city (see Figure 3.2), outlining not just its urban infrastructure and design, but also its financing, planning and management. Central to his concept were the separation of urban

Figure 3.2   *Howard's 'diagrams' for a Garden City*

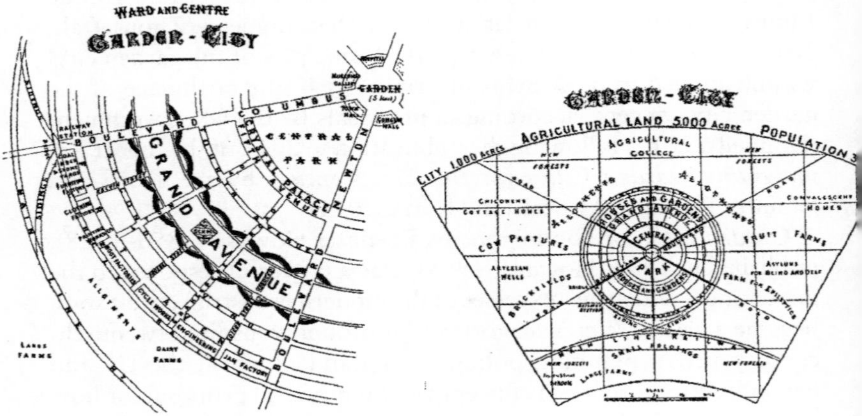

Source: Howard, 1965.

functions – disentangling places of living, work, civic participation, agriculture and nature – and decentralization. His model consisted of a core central city (designed for a population of 58,000) with large boulevards radiating out to surrounding 'slumless, smokeless' cities, each of approximately 32,000 residents. These satellite towns would be interconnected by a municipal railway, and be interspersed with industrial sites, agricultural land, forests and waterways.

The garden city concept was not only radical for its approach to integrating industrial urbanization with rural settlement types, but also for its proposed social innovation: it centred upon self-governing community organizations that would collectively own and administer the land; ground rents and profits would be available to the community to invest in the development and upkeep of the garden city. In this respect, the garden city departs from earlier company town concepts which were premised on paternalistic support from factory owners to provide well-built affordable housing to the factory workers. In contrast, the garden city subscribed to a social vision of the urban community co-owning the new developments and, thus, having a direct stake, and being closely involved, in building urban centres intended to be socially, economically and environmentally superior to their mainstream counterparts. As such, the garden city concept entails a strong social equity component that is as much concerned with socio-economic conditions of the new urban working class as with the physical conditions of city life.

The number of garden cities actually built in the first half of the twentieth century remained limited to a few dozen or so. Among the most prominent of these are Letchworth Garden City and Welwyn Garden City, the two original garden cities built in England; Greenbelt (Maryland), Greenhills (Ohio) and Greendale (Wisconsin) in the US; and Hellerau (Dresden) in Germany. None of these examples followed through Howard's vision in full, as practical implementation challenges acted as constraints on their scale and conceptual aspirations. Still, the impact of the concept as such was profound and far-reaching, influencing both urban planning theory and policy internationally for decades to come (Hall and Ward, 1998; Miller, 2002). In Britain, the Town and Country Planning Association (TCPA) arose directly from the garden city movement and, as the UK's oldest environmental charity, significantly contributed to the development of planning practice. The garden city concept informed the New Towns Act (1946) and the Town and Country Planning Act (1947), passed by the UK parliament to aid post-war urban reconstruction and development (UK Parliament, undated). In Japan, the model was adopted in town planning in the early twentieth century in an attempt to mitigate the effects of industrialization there. In Europe and particularly the US, too, the garden city was a key inspiration for urban reformist movements – such as the Regional Planning Association of America – and the post-Second World War 'new town' movement. 1950s and 1960s 'satellite towns' surrounded by 'greenbelt' and orbiting a metropolitan centre come close to Howard's original garden city proposal (Hall and Ward, 1998; Birch, 2002). Elsewhere, garden city principles were applied to various twentieth-century 'techno-cities', new towns built in conjunction with major technological projects (Kargon and Molella, 2008). These not only sought to overcome the rural–urban divide, but also to reconcile modern technology with community-based, healthy living.

Other seminal contributions to the emerging modern town planning movement, which engaged variously with themes identified by the garden city concept and can be seen as early inspirations for contemporary environmental and urban sustainability policy discourses, came from Patrick Geddes (1854–1932) and later Lewis Mumford (1895–1990), among others. Geddes's contribution included the application of sociological thought to urban planning, especially by emphasizing the interrelationship between 'place', 'work' and 'folk' (community), as a consequence of which he advocated urban planning based on the joint consideration of physical geographical, market economic and anthropological dimensions. This formulation has been interpreted as an important forerunner of later approaches to sustainable development conceptualized around the 'triple bottom line' of the environment, economy, and society (Porritt, 2004). His approach to human–environmental relations led him to develop a regional focus, highlighting the link of human settlements to wider physical geographies. Apart from introducing the concept of regional planning, he also championed the use of quantifiable survey and mapping data as the basis for urban planning, which has since become the staple tool of urban sustainability planning (see Chapter 7). Inspired by Geddes, Mumford – more a theorist than practitioner – in his work sought to counter the social as well as physical ills that the 'machine ideology' of the industrial age had brought to urban development (Mumford, 1938; reproduced in Wheeler and Beatley, 2009: 18–22). He was optimistic that new advances in biology and sociology could redefine urban planning and, consequently, that polluting and dehumanizing industrial technology would be replaced by cleaner and socially more harmonious ('neotechnic') modern technology that would achieve better integration between buildings and urban spaces. According to this approach, an 'organic order' ought to be at the heart of how cities are built and operated, and how they relate to the wider environment. Cities are conceived of as akin to 'living machines' that have self-regenerative and adaptive capacity. It is a view which would later gain further traction with the rise of environmental sciences from the 1960s onwards (see below), and which has a central place in contemporary sustainable city discourses.

While the contributions by Howard, Geddes, Mumford and others had a profound and enduring influence on twentieth-century urban planning, some aspects of modern planning practice inadvertently created problems of their own. In particular, the separation of residential and commercial land use functions – through the use of zoning codes and new town policies – enabled by the rapid rise of private car use led to a new phenomenon of unsustainable development: urban sprawl (see, for example, Gillham, 2002; Hall, 2002; Dieleman and Wegener, 2004). Hence, the ideal of the garden city morphed into the reality of rapidly expanding low-density garden suburbs. As a consequence, mass transit and the economic and social decline of inner-city areas became a new, defining characteristic of twentieth-century cities, especially in the Global North.

The original edition (1898) of Howard's book was entitled *Tomorrow: A Peaceful Path to Real Reform* (before being renamed

Garden Cities of To-morrow for the second, 1902 edition). This reflects the essentially social reform agenda at the heart of the garden city and new urban planning movement – namely, a predominant concern for improving the living conditions, socio-economic opportunities and community experience of the working class population in industrialized urban centres. Environmental effects – inner-city air and water pollution – were understood as localized problems; they mattered in as far as they negatively impacted on urban residents. It was only in the 1960s that wider environmental concerns began to be recognized; since then, these have increasingly moved to the forefront of the urban sustainability conceptual and policy agenda.

The emergence of 'the environment'

In 1956, in the Japanese port city of Minamata, a new disease was discovered which would eventually claim over 2,000 lives (Ministry of the Environment Government of Japan, undated). The 'Minamata disease', as it became known, was presented as a neurological syndrome which in extreme cases would lead to paralysis, coma and even death. Its cause turned out to be mercury poisoning, brought about by the consumption of contaminated seafood. The source of contamination was found to be industrial wastewater discarded into Minamata Bay by a local chemical factory run by Chisso Corporation. Despite early action on the part of fishing co-operatives and the formation of a patient organization to seek recognition of, and compensation for, the outbreak of the disease, it was not until the end of the 1960s that the case was fully acknowledged by officialdom and started to resonate broadly in the Japanese public. This change was prompted by a second outbreak of Minamata disease in 1965 elsewhere in Japan, in Niigata Prefecture, as well as the discovery of two new diseases caused by industrial pollution ('Yokkaichi asthma' caused by air pollution; and 'Itai-itai disease' caused by water pollution). Together, these illnesses became known as 'the four big pollution diseases', resulting in growing environmental awareness and the formation of citizens' movements supporting victims and calling for public recognition and compensation.

The significance of the Minamata case is twofold: in Japan, it was instrumental in raising broad public awareness of the detrimental impacts of some industrial production processes on the environment and public health, and of the related plight of many heavily industrialized cities. It also acted as an early catalyst for the formation of citizens' action groups and the emerging environmental movement, which in turn prompted more open, critical scrutiny of public policy- and decision-making. As such, Minamata and the other 'big pollution disease' cases significantly influenced subsequent urban sustainability initiatives promoted by the Japanese government and individual cities. Industrial ecology and industrial symbiosis – which seek to address issues of industrial waste reduction and recycling as well as to increase resource efficiency by way of co-locating businesses in such a way as to encourage the sharing of resources – have become key characteristics of Japan's 'eco-city' initiatives (for a comprehensive overview of Japan's eco-city initiatives, see Low, 2013). Kawasaki and Kitakyushu became Japan's first officially designated 'eco-towns' in 1997, aimed at addressing environmental pollution problems and assisting with regional development. As part of the eco-town initiative, city-based industries were given financial incentives to convert to zero-emission production and to reduce waste through recycling and industrial symbiosis. More recently, in 2009, the Japanese government selected 13 from a total of 82 applications for its national eco-city programme (see Chapter 4). Among them is Minamata, which has managed, since the 1990s, to overcome its infamous status as Japan's most polluted city through a concerted programme of combating industrial pollution and improving resource efficiency. It now boasts one of the country's most advanced industrial and household waste separation and recycling systems.

Beyond Japan, the case of Minamata is significant in that it signposts the start of a rapidly growing environmental movement worldwide. While Minamata brought Japan's problems of urban and industrial pollution, caused by rapid economic growth in the postwar period, to the attention of a global audience, elsewhere the environment increasingly became a matter of policy and public concern, too. *Silent Spring*, by US environmental scientist Rachel Carson (1962), was a key publication that popularized the risks to the environment from unfettered modern agriculture, industrial activity and consumer culture. Throughout the 1960s and 1970s, environmental awareness grew on the back of increasing research by environmental scientists as well as advocacy by campaigners, leading to new national and international environmental policy programmes. In 1973, Denmark became the first country to introduce an environmental protection law and to set up a 'Ministry for Combating

Pollution' (*Ministeriet for Forureningsbekæmpelse*; later renamed Ministry of the Environment).

At international level, the United Nations 'Conference on the Human Environment', held in 1972 in Stockholm (Sweden), is generally seen as a landmark intergovernmental event responsible for raising global public awareness, and setting the policy agenda, for environmental issues (Bernstein, 2001). The report (UN, 1972) is framed in terms of the tensions between environmental protection and economic development – the former appearing as a concern predominantly of the Global North, the latter of the Global South – and, as such, reflects the 'limits to growth' discourse dominant in environmental thinking at the time (Dryzek, 2005). This discourse centres upon the relationship between economic and population growth, on one hand, and limited natural resources, on the other; and the risks to environmental systems from unchecked anthro-pogenic activity. It gained influence through the seminal book *Limits to Growth* by a group of environmental scientists (Meadows et al., 1972) commissioned by the Club of Rome, an influential global think tank.

The 1972 UN report – along with other environmental policy reports at the time – recognizes the central role of cities in addressing environmental problems. Its very first recommendation relates to the 'planning, improvement and management of rural and urban settlements' (UN, 1972: 6). Urban problems, such as 'housing, transportation, water, sewerage and public health, the mobilisation of human and financial resources, the improvement of transitional urban settlements and the provision and maintenance of essential community services' are linked to 'the social well-being of the receiving country as a whole' (ibid.). Other recommendations highlight 'international implications', such as the 'export' of pollution from urban and industrial areas to international hinterlands (ibid.: 7). The report thus reflects the emerging recognition and perception at the time of cities as the major cause of wider and increasingly global environmental pollution.

1976 saw the first major UN Conference on Human Settlements, culminating in the *Vancouver Declaration* (UN, 1976) and leading to the establishment of the UN's Human Settlements Programme, or UN-Habitat for short, in 1978. The *Vancouver Declaration* built on the Stockholm Convention by linking problems facing human settlements to wider questions of social and economic relations nationally and internationally. At the same time, it arguably introduced a conceptual shift in that the city was no longer merely the site or source of environmental problems; rather, 'human settlements must be seen as an instrument and object of development' (UN, 1976: 4).

The establishment of UN-Habitat itself reflected the broader shift in international policy whereby attention was increasingly being turned towards urban centres in their own right. When the UN was first created after the Second World War, two-thirds of the world's population was rural, as a consequence of which urban issues did not feature prominently on the international policy agenda. By the time UN-Habitat was established, the global population was well on the way to becoming predominantly urbanized (2008 being a watershed moment, when for the first time in human history the majority of people lived in urban areas – see Chapter 1). Reflecting this shift, the term 'human settlements', while including rural settlements such as villages, has become increasingly synonymous with urban settlements.

Away from international policy forums, the ecological basis of cities was increasingly being discussed by environmental scientists. The concern here was partly about introducing a systems approach aimed at correlating urban and natural (ecological) systems; and partly about moving towards more quantitative methods of capturing and measuring urban parameters and relationships (Zhou and Williams, 2013: 9). In an echo of Mumford's 'living machines' and 'organic order' several decades earlier, the concept of 'urban metabolism' begun to be developed scientifically as a means of defining and quantifying urban resource and energy flows. The seminal study by Wolman (1965) in particular helped establish this field of research, which sought to measure input and output flows of materials and resources, such as water, energy, waste and pollution. A more aesthetic conceptual approach – albeit as much underpinned by quantitative measurement – was pursued in *Design with Nature* (McHarg, 1969), which called for ecological principles to be integrated into city planning by paying special attention to, and building on, a city's site-specific geographical and environmental advantages.

Arcosanti, Paolo Soleri's self-described 'experimental town' developed in the desert of Arizona (US), represents a practical attempt at developing 'arcology', as coined by Soleri, by combining and reconciling architecture with ecology (Arcosanti, undated). Arcosanti's innovations include a town layout which follows the features of the surrounding landscape, and a terraced greenhouse complex. A work in progress since 1970, the site has served mainly as an education centre offering accommodation and workshops for architecture students and visitors. Beyond its status as innovative pilot initiative,

Arcosanti is significant in that it highlights the presence of alternative ecology and urban sustainability discourses which – while not mainstream policy – have nevertheless had an important influence in shaping, often experimentally, sustainable city concepts and practices and, in turn, contributing to policy discourse. 'Radical', 'deep' and 'social' ecology represent distinct, yet related discourses that seek to define (urban) ecology in less technocratic and instrumentalist – and conversely, more normative and political – ways than mainstream policy discourses, by emphasizing goals such as environmental justice, gender and race equity and community empowerment (Dryzek, 2005).

The (re)definition of the city in wider environmental terms was at the heart of the 'eco-city' movement that emerged during the 1970s and 1980s, initially in the US. Richard Register and his Urban Ecology group based in Berkeley, California, were instrumental in developing an alternative narrative and practice of urban development centred upon explicit ecological principles. As the landmark publication *Ecocity Berkeley: Building Cities for a Healthy Future* states in its opening sentence: 'an ecocity is an ecologically healthy city' (Register, 1987: 3). While the eco-city thus has clear echoes of the earlier garden city concept, it now more centrally addresses the ecological relationship between the city and its wider 'bioregion' as well as the environmental aspects of the city itself. It tackles, among other aspects, the problems of the 'sprawled flat city' and related transportation by advocating greater urban density and 'walkability'; and it discusses the 'greening' of the city by proposing practical innovations such as rooftop gardens and urban agriculture (see Table 1.1). At the same time, reflecting the urban ecology discourse of the period, the eco-city is also designed as an 'instrument for human purpose' (ibid.: 13) around principles of social equity (creating fairness and opportunity for citizens) and aesthetics (relating urban design to the surrounding physical environment).

Elsewhere during this period, the prospect of creating an eco-city as 'a human settlement of the future in which social and ecological processes are harmonized in the best possible way' was proposed theoretically by Yanitsky (1982: 470) in connection with UNESCO's Man and the Biosphere (MAB) programme, an international research and education programme originally launched in 1971 with a focus on ecological conservation and biodiversity. It was, however, not until 2006 that UNESCO/MAB formally adopted its 'biosphere eco-city' as policy initiative (see Chapter 6).

Global sustainability agenda

For over two decades now, the discussion of urban development has been framed by a dominant, broad policy narrative – namely, that of 'sustainability' (see Box 1.1). It was the 1987 landmark report *Our Common Future* (WCED, 1987) that widely introduced the concept of sustainable development in public discourse and established it as an overarching global policy narrative guiding a broad range of policy fields, from energy to transport, and from agriculture to urban development. The *Brundtland Report*, as it also became known, was the product of the UN's World Commission on Environment and Development (WCED) chaired by former Norwegian Prime Minister Gro Harlem Brundtland.

What makes it a landmark report is the explicit linkage of socio-economic development with environmental concerns, and especially global poverty issues with the emerging global environmental agenda. At the heart of the report is a call for closer policy attention to be paid to existing patterns of economic activity and in particular how these, on one hand, fail to meet the needs of the global population – resulting in poverty especially affecting the Global South – and, on the other, produce significant environmental degradation. The report thus argues that issues of poverty and environmental damage are interconnected through economic development. At the same time, it argues that existing economic activities are unsustainable insofar as they exceed limited resource and environmental capacities. The concern for intergenerational justice is expressed in the overarching principle of 'meet[ing] the needs of the present without compromising the ability of future generations to meet their own needs' (WCED, 1987: 8).

At its core, then, is a call for a new economic model, which promotes economic growth that concurrently addresses, and takes care of, human development and environmental issues. This formulation, which has since become widely known as the 'triple bottom line' (or 'three pillars') of sustainable development – economic, environmental and social – has increasingly permeated different spheres of policy-making, and entered media and public debate, over the last couple of decades. Accordingly, it has profoundly informed the way in which both the concepts and practices of the sustainable city have been advanced since the 1980s.

The 1992 UN 'Earth Summit' held in Rio de Janeiro (Brazil) was an important step in establishing sustainable development as global policy goal. The *Brundtland Report* provided the conceptual framework for the Rio summit, from which several influential policy documents emerged, including the *Rio Declaration on Environment and Development*, the *UN Convention on Biological Diversity*, the *UN Framework Convention on Climate Change*, and *Local Agenda 21*. The latter was the Summit's local sustainable development action plan which was subsequently adopted by numerous countries and implemented by local authorities – chief among them towns and cities – around the world. ICLEI – Local Governments for Sustainability (originally called International Council for Local Environmental Initiatives; hence, ICLEI), an international association of local governments founded in 1990 and presently including over 1,200 members across 70 countries, has been a key global network of towns and cities through which information about Local Agenda 21 has been disseminated and urban sustainability initiatives championed on the ground.

The second and third UN 'Earth Summits' were held, respectively, on the tenth and twentieth anniversaries of the original conference. The 2002 summit took place in Johannesburg (South Africa), while the 2012 summit was again hosted in Rio de Janeiro. The former produced the *Johannesburg Declaration* (UN, 2002), which addressed sustainable development in particular relation to human development in developing countries (focusing on issues such as poverty and hygiene). The 2012 conference did not produce a binding declaration per se, but instead reaffirmed the earlier sustainable development agreements (including *Agenda 21*), while calling for a new set of 'sustainable development goals'.

The evident appeal and success of the concept of sustainable development in establishing itself as a key policy discourse must at least in part relate to its ability to interconnect closely environmental, social and economic concerns; and in doing so, to postulate that economic growth can be reconciled with present and future social equity and environmental protection if its negative impacts are addressed. However, for the same reason, sustainable development is seen by its critics as a problematic concept (Hopwood et al., 2005). Too often, it is argued, sustainable development is used to perpetuate existing, 'business-as-usual' economic development models, with the environment treated as one of several 'capitals' (alongside financial, physical, human, etc.) that can be substituted for each other (Goodland and Daly, 1996; Giddings et al., 2002). Within such a 'weak' conceptualization of sustainability, environmental degradation resulting from economic activity may be acceptable, as negative capital cost, if it is outweighed by gains in, say, financial or physical capital. Critics argue that such an approach renders the environment subservient to economic interests and fails to account properly for the inherently unique aspects of ecological systems, which may be difficult to rehabilitate, once damaged, or impossible to replace, once depleted (Wackernagel and Rees, 1997).

Critics also argue that sustainable development, as it is understood in mainstream policy, too often glosses over more deep-rooted problems of inequity and inequality at the heart of social developments (Haughton, 1999). According to this view, by adopting and pursuing a 'weak' sustainable development narrative, the status quo of dominant large-scale economic relations is maintained – with only marginal adjustments made – and, consequently, social problems are insufficiently addressed or indeed exacerbated (Meadowcroft, 2000). In response, this view advocates giving a greater voice to small and marginalized communities, particularly in developing countries, and finding alternative economic development approaches to stimulate local economic growth that is compatible with environmental protection and mindful of cultural factors and traditions.

What these debates lay bare, then, is the risk of trade-offs between environmental, economic and social sustainability dimensions (particularly if environmental and social goals are deprioritized in practice relative to economic ones). Finding effective synergies instead, both conceptually and through practice, between the three pillars of sustainable development remains a key challenge for researchers, policy-makers and practitioners alike.

The *Brundtland Report* displays continuity with the UN's earlier (1972) *Stockholm Report* in distinguishing between the 'third world' and the 'first world' in terms of problems faced and possible solutions. At the same time, it heralds an increasing focus on cities specifically within policy debates; it acknowledges that 'the world's economic system is increasingly an urban one' (WCED, 1987: 235), and includes a chapter of its own on urbanization.

Nevertheless, its discussions of urban sustainability focus mainly on third-world cities. These are presented as facing a dual challenge: as well as being confronted with severe local environmental problems – such as overcrowding, poor sanitation, polluted air and water, poor transport, and crumbling infrastructure – they also lack the resources and governance structures to address these problems. The solution, according to the report, consists of implementing concrete improvements – for example, more low-cost housing, and better use of resources – as well carrying out essential reforms to governance structures. Concerning the latter, the report pays unprecedented attention to the differing roles of agencies at different scales. Among these, central governments are singled out for having a responsibility to mitigate the 'pull' factor of emerging 'megacities' through investment in smaller cities and towns. At the same time, the need to rethink local government models is advocated to allow urban development to be adapted to local contexts and needs, and for local authorities to assume a greater role as stewards of urban sustainability. Finally, the report calls for international co-operation through bilateral mechanisms between developing countries, as well as support from developed countries and international organizations for local governments and civil society organizations.

First-world cities, meanwhile, are singled out for using more than their fair share of the world's resources, and for exporting environmental pollution. As the report puts it, they 'have a global reach and draw their resources and energy from distant lands, with enormous aggregate impacts on the ecosystems of those lands' (ibid.: 9.15). Elsewhere, the report acknowledges that cities in the developed world may face environmental challenges of their own. However, these are not seen as particularly severe, since developed countries have ready access to financial resources and advanced technology to redress urban problems. Thus, comparatively little attention is paid to problems of urban sustainability affecting cities in the developed world. Rather, it is assumed that a move to urban sustainability is broadly inevitable in the West. In contrast, 'developing countries are not in the same situation. They have a major urban crisis on their hands' (ibid.: 9.23).

While focusing mainly on third-world cities, the *Brundtland Report* at the same time introduces a new dimension in its emphasis on the international interconnection of cities, reflecting the growing recognition of the global dimension of sustainability. The report engages with global climate change as an emerging policy challenge for the international community. This was subsequently echoed in the 1992 Rio Summit, which emphasized both global climate change and biodiversity as key concerns. As a consequence, urban sustainability became defined as concurrently consisting of local and global issues and challenges. Apart from global environmental issues, the international dimension attributed to cities arguably also reflects the fact that *Our Common Future*, and the subsequent Rio Summit, were spearheaded as international initiatives by the UN.

The centrality of cities in global policy discourse was consolidated in 1996 through the UN-Habitat II conference hosted in Istanbul

(UN-Habitat, 1996). Some argue that it was at this point that cities fully moved centre stage in global environmental and development policy (Myllylä and Kuvaja, 2005). This 'city summit' resulted in the *Habitat Agenda*, which was subsequently adopted by 171 countries, and whose key recommendations shaped the UN's *Millennium Declaration on Cities and Other Human Settlements* (UN, 2001). The significance of cities to human progress is here justified by the fact that 'half of the world's 6 billion people will be living in cities' (ibid.: 2). This has subsequently become the dominant narrative in international policy, with cities seen to be holding the key to future sustainable development. As a subsequent UN document proclaimed, concerning progress on implementing the UN's sustainable development targets: 'the battle for the Millennium Development Goals (MDGs) will be won or lost in cities' (UN-Habitat, 2007: 1). The narrative was reinforced in 2008, when the actual watershed moment was reported to have occurred; it is now commonplace in policy documents and media debates to assert that mankind has become a predominantly urban species.

'Coming to terms with the Urban Age' was the theme of the World Urban Forum (WUF) hosted by UN-Habitat in Vancouver in 2006 – reflecting the entrenchment of the policy stance that the future is an essentially urban one and, hence, that cities are key loci of innovation and action in the quest for sustainable development. It also reflects the growing participation in this discourse by cities themselves. As UN-Habitat (2006b) reported, the first World Urban Forum held in Nairobi in 2002 attracted 1,200 'Habitat Agenda Partners'; at the second WUF held in Barcelona in 2004, the number had risen to 4,400; at the third WUF gathering in Vancouver, as many as 10,000 were present.

By this stage, the North–South urban sustainability divide exhibited by previous UN documents had been replaced by 'converging approaches to sustainable urban development policies between developed and developing nations' (UN-Habitat, 2006a: 6). Furthermore, the 2006 WUF report highlights the 'recognition that each region face[s] particular challenges that [are] best addressed by a more systematic exchange of best practices and good urban policies among all stakeholders at the local, national and international levels' (ibid.: 7). This suggests a multi-level governance approach as key to planning for and realizing urban sustainability, with knowledge exchange and practice learning among various stakeholders to the fore and perhaps a more limited role for 'top-down' intervention by international bodies such as the UN.

Such an assessment reflects the reality of cities, national governments as well as a range of civil society organizations having been at the forefront of developing and implementing urban sustainability policy. The sustainable development discourse spearheaded by successive UN conferences and declarations since the 1970s has clearly been instrumental in framing policy contents and affording cities global policy status, but it is through numerous initiatives on the ground that urban sustainability policy has taken concrete shape. Some of these initiatives – especially Local Agenda 21 – have been a direct consequence of, and have closely built on, the UN's (urban) sustainability policy programmes. Others have taken on more home-grown dimensions, based on national and local policy programmes and reflecting particular, context-specific priorities. Often, these international and national policy narratives have coalesced and combined to shape urban sustainability practices at the local level.

One enabling contextual factor in the growing focus on urban environments within sustainability policies and practices at this time may have been the more general shift in perceptions of urban living through the 1990s – in post-industrial Western cities at least. The late 1980s and 1990s were marked by a wide variety of regeneration schemes led by national government policies in older industrial districts (Loftman and Nevin, 1994), often to attract young professional residents and workers, and encourage tourism (Macleod, 2011): a return of residential populations to the inner city, and a reworking of city centres as places of consumption and leisure, rather than of production – a process more critically described in terms of gentrification (Featherstone, 1994; Zukin, 2010). In the US, calls were increasingly made to halt suburban sprawl (Freilich and Peshoff, 1997; Bruegmann, 2006), and new residential developments following the intertwined pro-urban principles of 'smart growth' and 'new urbanism' began appearing (see, for example, Katz et al., 1994; Talen, 1999; Duany et al., 2010); new urbanism has been described as strongly influenced by the ideas of the garden city movement (Stephenson, 2002). These principles, embraced by the American Planning Association, emphasize greater density, more efficient use of infrastructure, pedestrian access to services and provision of open space, and aim to build social capital in neighbourhoods through the strengthening of 'community'. 'Smart growth' and 'new urbanism' were at least strongly aligned with the principles of sustainable development increasingly being adopted within urban policy-making internationally.

Europe too demonstrates well the coalescing of different policy narratives over this period. While it would be wrong to suggest that a uniform experience is applicable to all European countries and cities, overall Europe has warmly embraced urban sustainability as key policy (see, for example, Jörby, 2002; Smardon, 2008). In particular, many European cities signed up to Local Agenda 21 agreements. In some cases – prominent examples of which include Freiburg (Germany), Graz (Austria), and Oslo (Norway) – this was done unilaterally, on a voluntary basis. In others – such as France, Sweden and Switzerland – this followed the national adoption of *Agenda 21* policy and the subsequent requirement for local authorities to put in place related action plans. At pan-European level, Local Agenda 21 received its biggest boost through the Aalborg Charter signed in 1994 by a coalition of 80 towns and cities from across Europe (see Box 3.1).

Europe's embrace of the sustainable development agenda in the wake of Rio Earth Summit 1992 built on the European Commission's own *Green Paper on the Urban Environment* (CEC, 1990). This policy input document – aimed at stimulating 'debate', 'reflection' and identifying 'possible lists of action' – itself emphasized the three pillars of sustainable development: 'finding lasting solutions to the environmental problems facing our cities requires ... addressing not just the proximate causes of environmental degradation, but examining the social and economic choices which are the real root of the problems' (ibid.: 1). As a consequence, the Green Paper argues that the problems of cities require a fundamental reconsideration of models of economic organization and urban development. It identifies individual cities as the primary focus of action, but at the same time argues that co-operative partnership at both national and European levels will be required – with each level having specific roles and responsibilities – to effect a transition to more sustainable urban development.

The Green Paper informed *Towards Sustainability* (CEC, 1992), the European Commission's fifth environmental action programme. The programme, the Commission's main policy framework for the environment, identified a gap between 'top-down' policy formulation, on one hand, and 'bottom-up' implementation, which risked inhibiting the achievement of sustainable development. In response, it called for closer alignment and integration of various decision-making levels – local, regional, national and international – and emphasized the importance of public engagement. Furthermore, it reiterated the need to reconcile environmental concerns with economic and social development issues.

The Green Paper also led to the establishment of the European Expert Group on The Urban Environment in 1991. The group, together with the European Commission, launched the European Sustainable Cities programme, which ran from 1993 to 1996. The programme was centrally 'concerned with identifying the principles of sustainable development and the mechanisms needed to pursue it' and 'disseminat[ing] good practice at local level' (CEC, 1996: Abstract). Together, these early European initiatives, then, are reflective of the wider international development of policy discourses at the time: (i) they had environmental problems – mainly defined in relation to local issues, such as pollution, waste and green spaces – as their starting point; (ii) environmental issues were, however, closely linked to economic and social issues, within the emerging framework of sustainability/sustainable development; (iii) cities and urban areas became seen as pivotal to applying and achieving sustainable development; and (iv) pluralistic, multi-level governance was recognized as an essential approach to effect policy and implement action.

Graz and Växjö are examples of European cities which, in adopting Local Agenda 21 programmes, established a reputation well beyond their countries' borders as innovators in urban sustainability. Based on its Local Agenda 21 initiative, Graz declared itself an *Ökostadt* ('eco-city') in 1995 and set targets for 2000 for combating air, noise and water pollution; reducing waste; increasing public transport; lowering energy consumption; and preserving green spaces. The city's initiative was recognized in 1996 with a European Sustainable City Award by the European Commission. Växjö's approach built on earlier efforts set against the background of the oil crisis in the 1970s, which prompted city planners to seek alternative energy sources – namely, the use of locally sourced wood. The efforts were broadened out in its Local Agenda 21 action programme, to encompass waste treatment, organic waste-to-energy production, and public transport improvements.

Many other cities in Europe and elsewhere mobilized interest around the emerging sustainability debate in the 1990s, and particularly Local Agenda 21, to initiate their own urban improvement programmes. Here, too, there were several notable commonalities at work, including an initial focus on local environmental challenges, the catalytic function of the emerging sustainability policy discourse, and action at local level being initiated and implemented with encouragement from wider national and international – in these two cases, European and UN – policy frameworks.

Box 3.1 The Aalborg Charter and European Sustainable Cities Platform

The *Charter of The European Cities and Towns Towards Sustainability* signed in the Danish city of Aalborg in 1994 – hence, the 'Aalborg Charter' – is a pan-European declaration inspired by the Rio Earth Summit's Local Agenda 21 initiative. It was initiated by the European Union in conjunction with its Environmental Action Programme Towards Sustainability, and signed by the participants of the first European Conference on Sustainable Cities and Towns. The original signatories have now been joined by over 2,700 towns and cities in more than 40 countries. The charter sets out a commitment to sustainable development at local level, with particular focus on urban settlements:

> We, cities and towns, understand that the idea of sustainable development helps us to base our standard of living on the carrying capacity of nature. We seek to achieve social justice, sustainable economies, and environmental sustainability. Social justice will necessarily have to be based on economic sustainability and equity, which require environmental sustainability.
>
> (European Commission, 1994)

The charter comprises three parts: (1) a consensus declaration of 'European cities and towns towards sustainability'; (2) the creation of the European Sustainable Cities and Towns Campaign; and (3) an action plan for local government engagement in Local Agenda 21 initiatives.

Beyond its impact at local level, the charter led to several pan-European follow-up initiatives, including:

- the Aalborg Commitments, agreed in Naples in 2004 on the charter's tenth anniversary and since signed by over 700 organizations;
- the Green Capital Award, of which Stockholm was the first recipient in 2010;
- the Covenant of the Mayors, a voluntary agreement to improve energy efficiency and to achieve CO_2 emission reduction of 20 per cent or more by 2020; and
- the EU Reference Framework for European Sustainable Cities, a practical toolkit for urban sustainability planning launched in 2008 (see Chapter 6).

These diverse activities are brought together by the European Sustainable Cities Platform (www.sustainablecities.eu).

The experience of the two cities, however, exemplifies a further important characteristic of urban sustainability policy over the last couple of decades or so: its evolving nature. Växjö, for example, more recently introduced an 'eco-budgeting' process in its central operation, on the premise that integrating sustainability in the budgeting process is an effective way of influencing decision-making across policy fields. Meanwhile, Graz has moved to position itself as a leading European centre of renewable energy and environmental technology. It is the hub of the so-called 'Green Tech Valley' in which over 150 green-technology companies participate. These developments are indicative of a wider shift in urban sustainability policy, from a primary focus on combating pollution and other environmental degradation, to a concurrent focus on economic opportunities from green-technology investment. This arguably reflects a more general trend towards emphasizing the 'green growth' agenda of cities in the twenty-first century.

Ecological cities as economic cities

If sustainable development was the dominant, overarching discourse influencing urban policy and planning in the 1990s, the 2000s arguably saw a shift to a new policy stance centred upon 'green growth' and 'ecological modernization'. This shift should not be understood as the abandonment of the sustainability agenda. Rather, the focus of attention has shifted towards re-casting local and global environmental challenges in terms of economic opportunities, with cities at the centre of a managed transition to a low-carbon, 'green' economy and society. Within this shifting narrative, the triple bottom line of sustainability has become largely normalized and embedded within policy (while critical conceptual engagement with the *problematique* of sustainable development continues). Most cities nowadays routinely use sustainability plans and targets to guide decision-making, and sustainability is a key component in most urban development projects.

Zürich, Switzerland's largest city, illustrates this point (Joss, 2011b): one of the original signatories of the Aalborg Charter, the city regularly scores highly in international sustainability and quality of life rankings and urban sustainability has gained a central place in the city's policy agenda. For example, it launched the 2,000-Watt Society, which was supported by three-quarters of the electorate in a municipal referendum in 2008 and which has as its goal the reduction of per capita energy consumption by a factor of three (from 6,000 watts per capita per year) and CO_2 emissions by a factor of five. However, the city does not appear to feel the need to promote itself as an eco- or sustainable city as such. One of the reasons may well be that sustainability is a key commitment in Switzerland's constitution: the Swiss population voted in a referendum in 1999 in favour of amending article 2 of its federal constitution to state that all public policy- and decision-making must be guided by the principle of sustainability. Consequently, Zürich – alongside all other Swiss towns and cities – is mandated to pursue urban sustainability measures, and the introduction of these requires neither explicit policy justification nor publicity. Neverthless, while Zürich exemplifies the long-term normalization of urban sustainability in many specific cases, the broader picture is still characterized by a shift towards a more explicit emphasis on global economic growth, based on technological innovation, as key to environmental and social transformation.

The World Bank's Eco2 Cities initiative and the OECD's Green Cities programme are illustrative of this discourse taking hold in international policy. Eco2 Cities was launched in 2009 as part of the World Bank's Urban and Local Government Strategy, and is aimed at cities in the developing world. Under the banner 'ecological cities as economic cities', the initiative's rationale emphasizes the need for urban innovation through synergy between economic and ecological sustainability: 'innovative cities ... can economically enhance their resource efficiency (realizing the same value from a much smaller and renewable resource base), while simultaneously decreasing harmful pollution and unnecessary waste' (Moffatt et al., 2012: 7). In turn, it is argued that this helps cities enhance economic competitiveness and resilience, and strengthen their fiscal capacity. Eco2 Cities, then, 'are more likely to survive shocks, attract businesses, manage costs, and prosper' (ibid.: 7). The conceptual approach emphasizes the need for an integrated systems approach and related change management in urban planning and policy. This, it is claimed, distinguishes Eco2 Cities, as 'second-generation' eco-cities, from previous eco-cities: the latter focused on innovation in relation to separate urban sectors and centred upon environmental performance (e.g., transport, water, green space), whereas Eco2 Cities pursue a 'one-system' approach by bringing together various sectors and co-ordinating the actions of key stakeholders within the 'whole urban system'. This is underpinned by an investment framework that incorporates sustainability and resilience planning.

To date, the World Bank has used its Eco2 Cities framework mainly in South East Asia. In Indonesia, five cities – Jakarta, Surabaya, Makassar, Palembang, Balikpapan – have embarked on 'catalyst' initiatives, with the Philippines and Vietnam following suit. Chapter 4 discusses the integrated governance approach of Eco2 Cities in more detail.

The OECD's Green Cities programme was launched in 2011 (OECD, 2011a). It builds on OECD's *Declaration on Green Growth* (OECD, 2009), and complements the organization's *Green Growth Strategy*, also launched in 2011 (OECD, 2011b). As such, it gives useful insight into the policy direction of its 34 member countries. 'Green growth' is defined by the OECD as 'fostering economic growth and development, while ensuring that natural assets continue to provide the resources and environmental services on which our well-being relies ... it must catalyze investment and innovation which will underpin sustained growth and give rise to new economic opportunities' (OECD, 2011b: 9). Furthermore, the OECD makes clear that 'green growth also recognizes that environmental policies that do not also support economic growth and wealth generation are not sustainable in the long term' (OECD, 2011a: 2).

The aim of the OECD Green Cities programme itself is to establish 'how urban green growth and sustainability policies can contribute to improve the economic performance and environmental quality of metropolitan areas and thus enhance the contribution of urban areas to national growth, quality of life and competitiveness' (ibid.: 1). In particular, the programme seeks to assess the impact of urban green growth and sustainability policies on employment, competitiveness and green investment opportunities. In doing so, it responds to a call for guidance on green growth policies, issued by mayors and ministers from 21 cities and 34 countries at the 2010 OECD Urban Roundtable of Mayors and Ministers on Cities and Green Growth.

Cities as key sites of change

The idea that mankind has entered the 'urban age', as discussed in Chapter 1, has particular resonance with the 'green growth' policy discourse, in which cities are privileged as key sites globally where change leading to sustainable development can be achieved. According to the World Bank, '[c]ities are now on the front line of the management of change and are playing a leading role in the global development agenda' (Suzuki et al., 2010: xv). This leading role derives partly from an understanding that cities form the 'engines of economies' (ibid.: 3). In addition, it derives from their political significance as centres of interaction between different networks and scales of actors: '[o]nly at the city level is it possible to integrate the many layers of site-specific information and to work closely and rapidly with the many stakeholders whose input may influence the effectiveness of a sustainability pathway and who have a stake in its successful implementation' (ibid.: 3). The leadership role of cities as drivers of change is further enhanced by ongoing globalization processes whereby certain powers of the nation state are devolved to the city through fiscal and administrative decentralization. At the same time, this optimistic view of cities is counterpoised with an acknowledgement that they are 'responsible for a majority of the resource and energy consumption and the harmful emissions' (ibid.: 3). This notion of responsibility, however, only serves to strengthen the argument that cities are the key sites where changes need to occur.

In similar vein, the OECD refers to the 'logic of city scale action', identifying cities as 'critical drivers of national and aggregate growth' (Hammer et al., 2011: 18). Given its remit to promote co-operation at state level, the OECD does not seek to argue that national governments have lost significance. It outlines the various important roles which national governments can play in enhancing cities' 'capacity to act on green growth' (ibid.: 93). Yet the approach which it advocates for the governance of urban green growth is explicitly not a 'top-down' one. Rather, it acknowledges the emergence of various forms of horizontal governance which increasingly give '"voice" or influence in the policy dialogue process to research and non-governmental organizations', with actors working 'across organizational boundaries to influence outcomes', and relevant horizontal 'linkages increasingly being forged between cities, regions and national governments' (ibid.: 93). Within this framework, cities have agency in their 'potential for delivering social and technical innovation that is not possible at a broader scale' (ibid.).

The OECD also acknowledges the 'negative externalities' of cities – that is, detrimental impacts on the regional and global 'hinterland' resulting from urban activities – including water and air pollution, the loss of ecosystems, higher health costs (due to pollution impact on human health) and loss of productivity (due to congestion and long commuting times), among other factors (Hammer et al., 2011: 19–20). It points to cities as major sources of energy demand and

CO_2 emissions; and it highlights their increased vulnerability – including the risk of flooding, water scarcity and urban heat island effects – due to the effects of climate change (ibid.: 24–5).

Like the World Bank, the OECD sees the responsibility of cities for these negative externalities as a further argument for focusing attention on the city as key site of change:

> cities ... are well positioned to develop innovative policy solutions that can be scaled up into regional or national programmes, and to provide a laboratory for national pilot programmes on the urban level ... they are promising testing grounds for green technology development ... [they] are magnets for highly skilled people and advanced firms, and they are responsible for developing infrastructure and the built environment, as well as providing waste, water and transport services. (OECD, 2011a: 2)

The *Green Cities* concept document continues by arguing that urban sustainability policies not only directly benefit cities themselves, but also contribute to national environmental and economic performance. As the report asserts, 'synergy between environmental and economic policies is stronger at the urban level'; at the same time, it acknowledges that '[d]eveloping green growth strategies at the city scale is not an easy task' (ibid.). Hence, it repeats its call for governing efforts based on systematic and long-term integration and co-ordination between local and national levels, and between public- and private-sector organizations (a theme discussed in greater detail in Chapter 5).

Ecological modernization

The 'green growth' discourse, and cities' global role within it, incorporates conceptual notions of 'ecological modernization' and the 'circular economy'. Originally an economic theory developed in the 1980s, ecological modernization has since gained momentum in policy-making, especially within the context of rapid urbanization in the Global South and the rise of global climate change as policy concern. (For an overview, see Mol et al., 2009; Young, 2000; for a critical perspective, see Fisher and Freudenberg, 2001.) Ecological modernization shows parallels with the concept of sustainable development in that it, too, interrelates environmental and economic issues. However, it does so with a stronger focus on how environmental productivity – that is, the productive use of natural resources and ecosystems – can stimulate economic growth and capital productivity. Ecological modernization, then, is understood as the re-adaptation of economic and industrial development by integrating environmental productivity. Environmental management, innovation in 'clean' technologies, sustainable supply chain management, and ecologically efficient industrial metabolism, are all elements of the environmental re-adaptation of the economy. Ecological modernization significantly relies on technological innovation and self-regulatory business innovation as its drivers. In short, without denying the importance of wider social sustainability dimensions, it does not, as such, engage with them.

The ecological modernization paradigm is central to the strategies adopted within both the Eco2 Cities and Green Cities initiatives. In the case of the former, '[t]he objective of the Eco2 Cities initiative is to help cities in developing countries achieve a greater degree of ecological and economic sustainability' (Suzuki et al., 2010: xvii). The Eco2 Planning Process prompts policy-makers and planners to define urban sustainability in terms of 'capital assets' (manufactured, natural, human and social) and the services they provide; these assets should be appropriately valued or priced, and monitored through indicators (ibid.: 30, 37–8). In OECD's case, green growth is postulated as 'a means to create jobs and economic growth while reducing costs and environmental impacts over the long run' (Hammer et al., 2011: 8). This objective, however, is not merely a balancing act: 'Complementarities and synergies between environmental and economic objectives are at the heart of the ongoing green growth debate, and they are particularly strong in cities' (ibid.: 25).

In applying their initiatives more specifically to the urban context – rather than the more abstract industrial-economic focus of ecological modernization theory – both initiatives, however, also concurrently engage with social dimensions. As such, they relate more firmly back to the 'triple bottom line' perspective of sustainable development. Hence, the *Green Cities* concept document takes up issues of social sustainability: 'the traditional efficiency paradigm is giving way to a richer definition of societal progress, where efficiency, equity and environmental sustainability are closely interrelated' (ibid.: 13). It identifies the need 'to ensure that green growth policies do not generate or exacerbate social inequalities', but rather lead to 'a more equitable distribution of environmental and economic benefits' (OECD, 2011a: 2). For its part, Eco2 Cities has

Box 3.2   China's ecological modernization agenda

Ecological modernization is a key plank in China's current national economic development policy. Both the eleventh (2006–10) and twelfth (2011–15) Five-Year Plans include commitments to improving environmental protection as part of the country's economic growth and urban development agenda. These high-level policy commitments come on the back of unprecedented urbanization rates in recent years: by 2007, some 45 per cent of the population lived in cities; by 2025 this is projected to rise to over 60 per cent, with additional urbanized land areas of 65,000 km^2 required to accommodate this rise (World Bank, 2009: 1). The ecological modernization policy is closely linked to the objective of creating a 'circular economy', which refers to the circular flows of materials and energy: industrial and urban developments are to form a 'compound system' by interlinking industrial processes and urban systems to promote circular material and resource flows and, in doing so, to improve environmental protection and restoration. According to governmental sources: 'China is trying to explore a rapid path for industrialisation that features efficient use of natural resources, protection of ecological environment, and co-ordination between socioeconomic development and the environment and natural resources' (PRC-UN, 2012: 4).

The ecological modernization agenda is the key force behind China's enthusiastic embrace of eco-city initiatives of various kinds in recent years (see Chapter 4). As the official declaration resulting from the first government-sponsored China Binhai Tianjin International Eco-City Forum stated: 'we shall follow the developmental path that accords with natural laws and combines cities into the balance of matter and energy circulation in the entire eco-system' (*China (Binhai Tianjin) International Eco-City Forum Journal* 2010: 15). As a consequence, individual eco-city initiatives are routinely promoted using the ecological modernization and circular economy discourses. Among many examples, Suzhou Industrial Park in the city of Suzhou (Jiangsu Province) became the first 'national eco industry demonstration zone' officially recognized by the government. In some cases, however, actual implementation practice has been found to fall short of the rhetoric (see e.g. Joss and Molella, 2013).

as one of its guiding principles the use of 'collaborative design and decision-making' to involve 'key stakeholders' in the process of planning, implementing and monitoring urban sustainability initiatives; and it emphasizes the 'importance of incorporating within any development program the unique aspects of place' (World Bank, 2010b: 4).

China is arguably the country that has most enthusiastically embraced ecological modernization as a principle of economic development and urban planning, driving much of the country's current, ambitious low-carbon eco-city programme (see Box 3.2, and Chapter 4). Ecological modernization is here seen as instrumental in realizing current, and future predicted, high rates of urbanization in a way which is environmentally sustainable and helps meet China's stated target of reducing CO_2 emissions by 40–45% by 2020 from 2005 levels (measured as 'intensity target' – CO_2 emissions per GDP – rather than absolute emissions target) (CCICED, 2009). Social sustainability is not overlooked in Chinese eco-city initiatives; it is typically understood in terms of specific environmental and economic benefits to residents (e.g. access to clean water, health provision, urban safety). However, the focus on ecological modernization means that social concerns have a less prominent and articulated place, especially in the case of new-build cities. The resulting understanding of the city mainly in terms of an urban metabolism, as part of a wider circular economy, risks producing overly technological and technocratic conceptualizations and practices of the eco-city, devoid of a strong articulation of the city as a social, political and cultural place (Joss and Molella, 2013).

Smart city

The current policy focus on the city as part of a green growth strategy is, then, typically accompanied by a focus on technological innovation (Joss et al., 2013). This works in complementary ways: on one hand, the 'green city' is seen as the site from which innovative high-tech green technologies will emerge and, thus, where economic growth and urban renewal will occur. It serves to attract international financial and technological investment through 'science parks' and acts as an 'incubator' for start-up renewable technology firms and various 'green' businesses. For example, the mayor of London in 2010 announced the launch of a Green Enterprise District in East London, as part of the wider Thames Gateway eco-region initiative and anchored by Siemens' Urban Sustainability Centre

(Mayor of London, 2010). The European Commission launched a Smart Cities and Communities initiative in 2011, with a budget of €365 million to fund projects in the energy, transport and ICT sectors. Elsewhere (and seemingly without any intended hint of post-modern irony), Vancouver's Greenest City initiative declares the city's ambition to become 'the Mecca of green enterprise' (City of Vancouver, 2012: 14), while the Middle Eastern city of Masdar boasts of becoming a 'cleantech cluster', and the 'silicon valley of green technology' (Masdar City, undated).

On the other hand, technological innovation is the main means through which the sustainable city is to be realized. The use of various 'green' technologies – from renewable energy technology to waste management tools, and from sustainable building methods to integrated transport systems – has long featured prominently in urban sustainability policies. Contemporary policy discourses, however, appear to conceive of the sustainable city more generally as high-tech city: it is not just various 'green' technologies that chiefly define this city, but also the integral use of 'smart' or 'ubiquitous' technology. This refers to the central use of information and communication technologies for digitally linking up and co-ordinating various urban systems in an overarching information system. In its *Green Growth* strategy document, the OECD (2011b) expects that IT solutions will be important in shaping the 'new paradigm' of development in the future.

South Korea has, since the mid-2000s, pursued a national strategy to apply 'ubiquitous technology' to urban planning (see Box 3.3). Elsewhere, in Japan, the city of Fujisawa together with technology firm Panasonic are in the process of converting Panasonic's former factory site into Fujisawa Sustainable Smart Town, designed as a high-tech city with advanced solar power generation, heat-pump and hot-water systems. All new homes are to be connected to a 'smart grid', providing real-time information on electricity use so that supply can be exactly matched to demand.

This heightened technological focus brings with it a shift towards greater involvement of technology firms in shaping and applying sustainable city policies. Cisco, General Electric, Hitachi, IBM, Panasonic, Siemens and Toshiba are among leading international companies that now readily assist municipal policy-makers in developing and implementing urban sustainability strategies. Some of these have developed tailor-made 'smart-city' concepts and applications of their own, which are marketed to local and national governments as urban sustainability tools and solutions.

Box 3.3   South Korea's u-city strategy

In 2009, South Korea launched its green growth strategy, aimed at developing synergy between economic growth and environmental protection. Within the strategy, cities form a key platform for implementing green growth policies and fostering related innovation (Shwayri, 2013). Both national agencies and local authorities launched various initiatives, such as the 'greening cities' initiative, the 'eco-rich city' competition, the 'climate change adaptation model city' and the 'eco-city' project. Songdo, to the west of Seoul, was one of the early flagship eco-city projects, with the ambition of setting a new international standard for 'green' design for large-scale urban developments. At the same time, it was to be a flagship 'ubiquitous' eco-city – or 'u-ecocity', based on the central integration of 'smart' (wired and wireless) information technology in urban systems to deliver public and private services.

South Korea's national u-city policy (spearheaded by the Ministry of Information and Communication, and the Ministry of Construction and Transport) envisages the development of some 15 smart-city projects, of which Songdo, whose completion is expected in 2015, is the largest. Local government authorities are expected to lead on the funding of and planning for ubiquitous IT infrastructure, while business is expected to develop and operate the ubiquitous (communication) services. This multi-level governance arrangement has been blamed for ineffective co-ordination and lack of co-operation among actors involved (Kim et al., 2009; Dong-Hee, 2009; Shwayri, 2013).

Carbon agenda

The recent push for sustainable cities as part of a wider green growth policy discourse, coupled with a strong focus on 'smart green' technological innovation, has to be understood in close connection with calls, at both international and national levels, for a transition to a low-carbon economy and society. The OECD's Green Growth strategy sees reducing greenhouse gas (GHG) emissions as one of four 'key environmental challenges' facing the world alongside premature deaths from air pollution, people living under severe water stress, and world threats to biodiversity (OECD, 2011b: 19). This is echoed in its Green Cities programmes: 'cities are central to the green growth debate, as they are both the locus of economic activity and the drivers of energy consumption and greenhouse gas emissions' (Hammer et al., 2011: 11).

The World Economic Forum's SlimCity initiative, which ran between 2008 and 2010, is another instance of a policy approach to sustainability defined mainly as an international knowledge transfer project focused on 'the sustainable development of all aspects of a city to achieve reduced carbon emissions and increased resource efficiency across all sectors, involving the following industries: chemicals, engineering and construction, energy, information technologies, mobility, and real estate' (WEF, 2009: 2).

The growth in eco-city initiatives of various kinds since the early 2000s, then, has been linked with the mainstreaming of the 'low-carbon' policy discourse (Joss et al., 2013). The centrality of carbon discourse helps explain the dominant focus on energy systems and related renewable energy technologies in the construction of new, and the retro-fitting of existing, urban areas. District energy systems, onsite renewable energy technologies and low-carbon building technology are part and parcel of the modern eco-city. Some initiatives have an almost exclusive focus on energy systems and related goals of achieving 'low carbon' or even 'carbon neutrality': for example, the Indian Ministry of New and Renewable Energy (MNRE), under the government's 11th Five-Year Plan (2007–12), launched a Development of Solar Cities initiative aimed at reducing conventional energy demand by at least 10 per cent through the implementation of solar and other renewable energy sources, energy conservation and solar passive architecture (Joss, 2012: 17; see also Chapter 4).

When the concept of the 'eco-city' began to emerge in the 1980s and 1990s, the initial focus was mainly on redressing particular adverse local urban conditions (urban sprawl, inner-city deprivation, environmental degradation, etc.). An understanding of cities' impact on wider climate change issues only gradually began to be reflected in policy, and initially this was subsumed within a decidedly local narrative. Freiburg (Germany) was an early pioneer when its city council adopted the Climate Protection Protocol in 1996, committing itself to reducing CO_2 emissions by 25 per cent below 1992 levels by 2010. It is telling that key texts of the period (see e.g. Register, 1987; Roseland, 1997b) barely mention climate change or CO_2 emission reduction – or only do so indirectly. It was only following the adoption of the UN's Kyoto Protocol in 1997 that the focus of attention began to shift towards cities' international role and responsibility concerning global CO_2 emissions and climate

change (see While et al., 2010). Overall, cities are currently estimated to account for 60–70 per cent of (consumption-based) global
GHG emissions (UN-Habitat, 2011b: 16). In addition to existing
cities, particular concerns are expressed about the rapidly emerging
urban centres across much of Africa and Asia, which significantly
add to global greenhouse gas emissions and are, therefore, seen as
critical to developing strategies and implementing solutions to tackle
climate change.

Since the late 1990s, then, cities have come to be recognized in
international policy discourse as a key source of, and potential solution to, global climate change. As a consequence, they have also
become leading international policy actors. This was illustrated, for
example, by the Copenhagen Climate Summit for Mayors, held in
2009 on the occasion of the UN Climate Change Conference
Copenhagen; the resulting *Copenhagen Climate Communiqué*
(CCSM, 2009) signed by 79 mayors asserts that 'cities act!' and
urges national governments to 'acknowledge the pivotal role of cities
fighting climate change'. One further illustration among many is the
Cities Climate Leadership Group, or C40, which brings together
world cities in a collaborative network with the mission to reduce
carbon emissions and adapt to climate change. Among the C40's
recent initiatives is the Carbon Disclosure Project, for which 140
large cities around the world were invited to provide information on
their water usage, greenhouse gas emissions, and strategies with
regard to climate change (C40, 2011).

Against this evolving international policy context, the concept of
the eco-city – in terms of its substantive focus, local context and
international role – has undergone significant changes, framed by an
increasingly strong 'carbon discourse'. According to the 2011 global
census of eco-cities (Joss et al., 2013), more than 70 per cent of
initiatives surveyed directly engage with climate change in their
policy statements, master plans and/or action plans. Approximately
60 per cent of initiatives include specific reference to 'CO_2', 'carbon'
and/or 'greenhouse gas' emissions. These examples are evenly
spread across global regions, and evenly distributed between new-
build, in-fill and retro-fit eco-city types – further indicating the
pervasiveness of carbon discourse. Climate change issues are in fact
mentioned in some of the initiatives launched in the pre-2000
period, but such mentions are rather less frequent and less prominent compared with the 2000+ period.

Accordingly, a whole new vocabulary has, seemingly effortlessly,
entered policy and public discourse couched in the language of

'carbon'. The term 'carbon neutral' was even the *New Oxford American Dictionary*'s 'word of the year' for 2006. Hence, urban sustainability concepts and initiatives are now labelled using terms such as: 'low-carbon city'; 'low-carbon zones/districts; 'carbon-neutral city'; 'zero-carbon city'; 'zero-energy city'; 'zero net energy cities'; 'near-zero-energy satellite town'; 'solar city'; and 'climate-positive development'. In China, the terms 'eco-city' and 'low-carbon city' appear to be used interchangeably, and sometimes combined into 'low-carbon eco-city'.

The focus on (low) carbon does not mean that other dimensions of the sustainable city have become marginalized. A broad range of issues relating to economic, social and environmental sustainability continue to be captured under the 'eco-city' banner, with particular local features distinguishing individual initiatives from others. Nevertheless, the carbon discourse has created a markedly more international focus, with cities adopting a common global language and engaging as international policy actors in relation to climate change. And this is also reflected in socio-technical approaches to the modern eco-city.

The policy landscape: so what's new?

The historical perspective and the focus on policy discourses together reveal a rich and complex picture of what the sustainable city is understood to be. Rather than a neat, coherent concept, and rather than a policy discourse that has progressed consistently across time, what the analysis in this chapter exposes is a cumulative, multifaceted, and at times contradictory, phenomenon: the sustainable city has been understood differently depending on historical periods, ideological stances, national and cultural experiences, specific socio-political processes, technological innovations and, of course, various forms and processes of urbanization themselves. What makes the policy perspective useful, then, is not so much that it offers any conclusive insight into, or ready-made definition of, the sustainable city. Instead, it offers useful analytical insights into the different ways that urban sustainability is conceptually and programmatically framed, who the actors involved in these processes are, and what context- and place-specific factors and contingencies are in play.

If the policy perspective on the sustainable city does not facilitate an easy and coherent characterization, it arguably still allows for the observation of some broad, key trends. These trends point to long-term shifts in urban sustainability policy.

First, earlier exclusive concerns about the liveability of cities have been complemented with concerns about the external impact of cities on their surrounding local and global environment. The original proposition of the garden city was mainly a response to the directly detrimental social effects of industrialized urban centres on city dwellers themselves. By introducing design and planning principles, such as the separation of work and life, the introduction of green spaces and community amenities, and the use co-operative governance mechanisms, the garden city was to combine the best elements of 'the country' with those of 'the town' in new form for the benefit of individuals and the community.

Growing awareness of indirect, external impacts of urban economic and industrial development on the environment added a new aspect to the sustainable city: how it should be designed and planned to minimize environmental degradation. This introduced a new dimension to urban planning concerned with the functional relationship between the city and its surrounding hinterland. Initially predominantly understood within a local context, this new concern soon extended to the global level, as the wider reach of the city's environmental impacts – beyond regions and across continents – became evident and as the combined environmental impact of cities globally was being considered. As a consequence, nowadays, urban sustainability policies and practices typically concurrently engage with how cities can be improved to redress local environmental problems (e.g. air pollution, water shortage), lessen their global environmental impact (energy demand, greenhouse gas emissions) and enhance their liveability for residents.

Arising from this wider environmental dimension of the city, the second trend relates to the increasing conceptualization of the city in general, and urban sustainability in particular, in terms of wider, interconnected systems and networks. Hence, policy discourses now routinely – sometimes explicitly, other times implicitly – discuss the city as a form of 'urban metabolism', linked to wider circular economic systems and natural ecosystems; and urban sustainability is conceptualized in terms of resource and material flows (water, energy, air, industrial processes) and how these can be rendered more efficient by improving urban infrastructure and applying new technology. In other words, since the 1960s, environmental and engineering sciences have increasingly been applied to the study of the city and have informed policy discourses on urban sustainability. In addition, economic theories have contributed to the discussion of urban sustainability in terms of adapting urban economic development to environmental goals as part of ecological modernization processes.

As a consequence, many policy discourses on urban sustainability have taken on a markedly more scientific-technical tone. This is only to be expected, given the recognition of cities' wider environmental and economic relations and functions. Still, it brings with it a distinctive abstraction of urban sustainability, in the sense of distancing it both from place-specific features of the city and from the social dimension of sustainability. Finding synergy between the technical, environment-focused dimension and the place-specific social dimension of urban sustainability, therefore, remains a key challenge in the quest for the sustainable city.

A further, third, trend concerns the increasing diversity of actors involved in, and the range of governance mechanisms used to implement, urban sustainability initiatives. Growing attention in policy is, therefore, paid to the fundamental importance of governance in defining and facilitating urban sustainability strategies and plans. Substantial parts of policy documents, such as the World Bank's *Eco2 Cities* (Suzuki et al., 2010) and UN-Habitat's *Planning Sustainable Cities* (2009b) reports, address the requirements for, and forms of, governance. Planning issues have always been at the heart of the sustainable city – the history of urban planning as a discipline is closely linked to the emergence of the garden city and related schools of thought in the twentieth century – but arguably these have taken on added relevance due to the increased complexity and the related need for co-ordination across urban systems and between a growing number of actors. It is not uncommon these days for urban sustainability initiatives to entail the simultaneous involvement of local authorities, national agencies, international organizations, private-sector developers, civil society organizations and the community; and such involvement is increasingly managed through elaborate public–private partnerships and other complex governance arrangements. This requires contemporary urban sustainability policy to address critical questions about the efficiency of new governing processes, about their legitimacy in relation to traditional forms of policy- and decision-making, and about their role in (re)shaping the city.

Finally, a marked policy shift can be seen in the internationalization of urban sustainability. Prior to the 1970s, the (un)sustainability of cities was a concern mainly of industrial nations in the Global

North. Since the 1970s, interest in the sustainable city has become globally ubiquitous, applying to the Global North and South alike. Cities in the Global North are interested in urban sustainability as part of socio-economic and cultural regeneration processes against the background of the transition from industrial to post-industrial society; cities in the Global South pursue urban sustainability initiatives to facilitate, and mitigate negative effects of, rapidly expanding urbanization and industrialization processes. Across the world, cities engage in sustainable development policies in order to address the global climate change challenge, as well as to position themselves as attractive places of investment and business within the global economy. This globalization of urban sustainability has been reflected in growing international policy activity – centred upon sustainability, green growth and environmental policy discourses – involving international governmental organizations (UN-Habitat, World Bank, OECD, etc.), non-governmental organizations (BioRegional, Clinton Climate Initiative, LEED, etc.) and businesses (Hitachi, IBM, Siemens, etc.).

Conclusions

The sustainable city has over the last century undoubtedly become a firm fixture in policy-making. More recently, in the last half a century, urban sustainability has become a distinctly global policy discourse, framed by a few overlapping dominant narratives, including sustainable development, ecological modernization and global climate change. These narratives suggest some general trends: increasing recognition of cities' global environmental impacts; a systems approach to conceptualizing urban sustainability; the salience of governance; and the internationalization of urban sustainability policy. However, their circulation has not resulted in the production of a unified understanding of what constitutes the sustainable city. Optimistically, one might say that these policy narratives have contributed to the identification and clarification of various aspects of urban sustainability. More pessimistically, one might say that they have highlighted unresolved tensions and contradictions between varying normative and analytical dimensions of the sustainable city. The *problematique* of urban sustainability policy is further compounded by the manifold diversity of practical initiatives and experiences on the ground, which inevitably can only be properly understood as part of specific (local, cultural, etc.) contingencies. Capturing and analysing that practical diversity – a task attempted in the next chapter – is an essential part of developing a critical understanding of the contemporary sustainable city.

Chapter 4

The Global Picture

CHAPTER OVERVIEW

Across regions and continents, a multitude of eco-city initiatives have begun to be implemented. These display considerable diversity of form, reflecting different approaches to sustainability and place-specific characteristics. Making sense of this variety may require us to survey the phenomenon as a whole, to gain a comprehensive picture of how urban sustainability is currently envisaged, conceptualized and practised in various organizational, national and cultural contexts. However, this task poses some methodological challenges: How should the 'sustainable city' be captured? How should the information be collated and analysed? This chapter provides an overview of contemporary 'eco-city' initiatives identified through a comprehensive global census. The analysis is complemented with specific examples from across the world, illustrating the manifestation of urban sustainability initiatives in different regional contexts and as championed by various organizations. While the overall picture is varied, it reflects in its totality the discursive shift, already identified in Chapter 3, towards a more systems-based and technological understanding of the sustainable city.

Introduction: the evidence on the ground

Driving from Beijing through Hebei Province past the city of Tanghai towards the Bohai Sea, about 270 km to the south-east of China's capital, the visitor eventually reaches a vast new urban development project: the Tangshan Caofeidian International Eco-City (Joss and Molella, 2013). An initiative by the provincial government, planned with input from Swedish engineering group Sweco and financed through a mixture of public and private investment (estimated to total approximately US$9 billion), this brand new eco-city is designed to accommodate the 1.5 million residents expected to settle in the rapidly growing Caofeidian Industrial Area by 2025. Upon completion, the city is to cover an area of over 74 km², dominated by a 12 km² high-rise city centre and flanked by an 18km² mixed-use district to the north and a 44 km² mainly residential district to the east. To the south and west, the city will be surrounded by a 45 km² wetland park, which also acts as a natural barrier separating the fresh water habitat from the sea shore to the south of the city. The city's plan includes an extensive public transport system – including monorail and rapid bus transit – designed to put 90 per cent of residences and offices within 500 metres of transport services. 95 per cent of energy use is to be met from renewable sources, with wind, solar and geothermal energy generated onsite. The purpose-built 'city service quarter' will accommodate a multifunctional resource management centre where the city's water, waste and materials will be recycled and the district energy will be based. The planning process, which makes use of an overall master plan complemented by individual zone and site plans, is guided by an elaborate, specially developed 'eco-city indicator' system comprising 141 individual indicators.

Visiting the site in 2010, one could not help but be struck by the sheer scale and speed of this development: an entirely new eco-city built from scratch, and at relentless pace, across a vast area of reclaimed land. Following the decision by the provincial government in 2007 to build a new eco-city, a competitive process to identify an appropriate site took place in 2007–8, as a result of which Caofeidian was selected on the basis that it would be an area of reclaimed land and, therefore, not encroach on valuable agricultural land. Construction proper commenced in early 2009, underpinned by a tightly orchestrated schedule of sequential development phases. The target is to progress completion such that by 2020 the first 800,000 residents will have moved into the city. By autumn 2010, only 18 months after the start of construction, a vast area of land had already been reclaimed from the sea, with infrastructure and building work well under way (see Illustration 4.1). In fact, horizontal development (land reclamation and preparation) and vertical development (building construction) have been progressing in parallel: large dredging ships continue to reclaim land to add to the growing area, water is drained from the land, dams are erected, roads are constructed, buildings go up, even landscape work is under way – all at the same time. Turning left, one can see heavy construction vehicles engaged in laying the foundations of building complexes; turning right, one sees a long line of trucks carrying soil used for further land reclamation; looking ahead, and amidst the mud and infrastructure work, half a dozen gardeners are seen engaged in planting trees and grass in the

Illustration 4.1

Caofeidian International Eco-City

Source: Photograph taken by the author, 2012.

emerging green space. In the middle of it all, the new visitor centre displays numerous models and shows a film (in 3D) of what the future eco-city will look like. In front of the centre – tellingly located on '1 Future Boulevard' – the sign says: 'Welcome to the City of the Future'.

Halfway around the world from Tangshan Caofeidian International Eco-City, work has been under way for the last decade or so to 'green' the streets of Portland, Oregon (US). The Green Streets initiative was prompted by the problem of storm water running off into the city's Willamette River – a serious local environmental challenge given the considerable annual rainfall there. The initiative seeks to capture stormwater run-off through designed and landscaped areas integrated into the road system. By absorbing a large proportion of rainwater falling onto the roads, these planted areas not only reduce run-off, but also act as purification system through which the groundwater is replenished. The initial approach focused on traditional engineering solutions, such as run-off pipes connected to the sewer system. Over time, this was complemented by incorporating natural functions (through the planted areas) into the physical infrastructure system. At the same time, the green streets features are used to enhance the streetscape more generally, by introducing additional green spaces into urban neighbourhoods (see Illustration 4.2). A further element of the initiative – and characteristic of the city's wider approach to urban sustainability – is the

Illustration 4.2

'Green street' design, Portland: junction of SW 5th Avenue and
SW Montgomery Street

Source: Photograph taken by the author, 2010.

active involvement of residents and business in both the design and maintenance of the green street projects. Local residents are invited to get involved in discussing design details – such as the choice of trees and shrubs, and the incorporation of artistic work – with city planners, as well as to take responsibility for maintaining the system in order to ensure its ongoing effectiveness.

The Green Streets programme is just one of several urban sustainability initiatives for which Portland has gained an international reputation. Going back several decades, the city initially focused its effort on achieving an integrated public transport system and the pedestrianization of the city centre. Sustainability was incorporated into the remit of the city's planning office, resulting in action programmes on energy efficiency, waste management and green building design, among others. The city and surrounding regional authorities joined forces to co-ordinate metropolitan land-use planning, including the establishment of substantial green zones in and around the city to control urban expansion.

More recently, in 2009, the mayor set up the Portland Sustainability Institute with the remit of spearheading innovative urban sustainability programmes. Among these, the EcoDistricts initiative is an ongoing partnership between the city and five neighbourhoods, aimed at promoting sustainable neighbourhood development across different parts of the city. Each of these partnerships is characterized by place-specific elements: for example, the South of Market (SoMa) EcoDistrict project involves Portland State University (PSU) together with over a dozen other major property owners in the area; the aim is to improve the district through green streets and public transit and, thus, attract businesses and visitors to the area. PSU itself contributes to this through its substantial sustainability research base. Another example is the Foster Green EcoDistrict, encompassing a cluster of suburban neighbourhoods in the north-eastern part of the city. Here, the focus is on enhancing the quality of life and addressing community needs and priorities, by improving economic vitality, public safety, public transportation and access to open space. Overall, the EcoDistricts initiative is of interest because it points to the question of the appropriate scale for intervention and innovation in urban sustainability (see Chapter 5). The Portland Sustainability Institute argues that 'we've learned how to green buildings. The next stage is to green whole neighborhoods. It starts with the vision of the people who live and work there' (PSU ISS, undated). At the same time, the case of Portland suggests that higher-level intervention at the city and wider regional level – as exemplified in its approach to sustainability over the last few decades (in terms of regional transport and zoning strategies, etc.) – may often in fact be a precondition for effective action at neighbourhood level.

Tangshan Caofeidian International Eco-City and Portland's Green Streets and EcoDistricts initiatives are typical, if hugely contrasting, examples of the growing number of eco-city projects around the world. They point to the broad spectrum of initiatives presently found: at one end, entirely new, large cities built from scratch; at the other end, ongoing innovation carried out within existing cities through various 'retrofit' programmes. At one end, developments driven by rapid urbanization in the Global South; at the other, developments motivated by urban regeneration and socio-economic revitalization in cities of the Global North. And at one end, a focus on technological innovation, while at the other an emphasis on co-operation among planners, business and community groups.

Understanding the nature, and grasping the extent, of contemporary urban sustainable development, therefore, requires not only theoretical considerations (see Chapters 1 and 2) and comparative policy analysis (Chapter 3), but also a closer empirical look at practical initiatives in various settings. The aim of this chapter, then, is to provide an overview of the kinds of eco-city initiatives that have emerged in recent years and decades in various parts of the world. In doing so, the chapter seeks to explore: what types of development can be discerned; what some of their key characteristics are; how far they have progressed to date; what regional variation there is; and which international, national, municipal and non-governmental actors are spearheading these initiatives. Providing such a broad, global overview is useful, in order to understand and demarcate contemporary urban sustainability concepts and practices. At the same time, this is also a methodologically inherently difficult task: how should one capture, and make sense of, the diversity of initiatives? How can Tangshan Caofeidian International Eco-City and Portland's EcoDistricts initiative – and similar initiatives – be compared, given the striking differences involved? And how can global trends and general features be identified from among the many place- and context-specific features shaping the sustainable city? The next section addresses these methodological questions, before the global state of the art is explored.

Methodological considerations

There are several methodological challenges involved in developing a global picture of contemporary sustainable city initiatives. One such challenge concerns the fact that there is no commonly agreed, standard definition of what an eco-city is. While the literature discerns various 'dimensions' of the eco-city, these are not consistently applied, and applicable, across initiatives (see Chapter 1). This is both because important normative-conceptual differences exist concerning how the eco-city is defined by various protagonists, and because place-specific characteristics fundamentally co-determine the design, development and implementation of eco-city initiatives. Consequently, when trying to survey the field, one is inevitably confronted with wide-ranging diversity: some eco-city initiatives may emphasize social and environmental equity issues, while others conceptualize the city more technologically as an urban metabolism. Again, some initiatives may incorporate comparatively modest goals and targets due to relatively low base levels of urban sustainability (say, in a developing world context characterized by rapid, large-scale urbanization processes and limited existing sustainability efforts), while other initiatives pursue more ambitious targets within a context of already advanced achievements. This poses the question of how comparable these diverse initiatives are.

Another methodological challenge relates to the potentially huge numbers of initiatives and how these can best be captured. This reflects the fact that recent years and decades have seen an impressive mushrooming of urban sustainability initiatives of various kinds. The challenge, then, lies in ensuring that the number and range of initiatives to be surveyed are large enough to provide a sufficiently reliable global picture, while at the same time not rendering the analysis unwieldy with too large a data set to process. Relatedly, there may be a difficulty in managing to capture relevant initiatives, where information is hard to come by, for example because no information is available internationally in English. It is important, therefore, to be aware of potential biases and limits built into global surveys of the sustainable city.

A further challenge is posed by the rapidly evolving nature of urban sustainability initiatives. Any time-restricted survey can by definition only ever provide a 'snapshot' of sustainable city development at any given time. Longitudinal surveys that track initiatives across time would offer the opportunity to analyse the progression of urban sustainability efforts; this, in turn, would provide useful information about the scale and significance of individual initiatives and the extent of development across cohorts of initiatives. However, longitudinal analysis can be time-consuming and resource-intensive.

Finally, the question of how best to identify common patterns and trends, against a background of place- and context-specific diversity within the dataset, is far from straightforward. For example, is there a trend towards new eco-city developments of the kind represented by Tangshan Caofeidian International Eco-City, and if so, in which regions might this be most apparent? Or is there perhaps a tendency towards defining the sustainable city in technological terms, in response to climate change concerns and the related focus on renewable energy? The challenge, then, consists of finding useful analytical categories that help identify such common features within a context of diverse developments across various parts of the world.

Defining parameters

These challenges, however, do not constitute insurmountable barriers to the development of a comprehensive global picture of contemporary eco-city initiatives – especially if the main goals are to establish their global spread and scale, and to capture the diversity contained within this. Doing so requires the adoption of an approach where the criteria for inclusion are broad – but also clearly specified and justified (since, without this specification, it will be unclear what the sample represents). To this end, in the survey described in this chapter, the following three core principles were applied:

1. *Size of development.* The focus of analysis is on initiatives relating to neighbourhoods, districts, towns, cities and metropolitan areas. Hence, a broad range of initiatives is captured, from the types represented by Tangshan Caofeidian International Eco-City to the types represented by Portland's EcoDistricts. However, sustainability initiatives at the individual building (block) level, or relating to rural settlements, are excluded from the survey. This corresponds with the analytical interest here in *urban* sustainability – that is, sustainable development concepts and actions relating to various urban scales and systems.

2. *Cross-sectoral reach.* Initiatives are captured that deal with issues involving two or more policy areas (e.g. transport, housing, energy) relating to urban infrastructure and services. The rationale for this is that urban sustainability typically acts as integrated intervention in infrastructure and services across individual policy boundaries. For example, renewable energy measures may be implemented in relation to housing, transport and waste management.

3. *Policy resonance.* This relates to the importance of policy engagement and political leadership as key drivers of eco-city initiatives. Clearly, where municipal authorities, regional or national governments, or international organizations adopt sustainable city policies, this attests to the significance attributed to related initiatives. In turn, this increases the likelihood of eco-city initiatives gaining policy traction and being implemented in practice. In contrast, an eco-city proposal without any policy support may remain just that: a concept on paper – however ambitious and innovative – without any prospect of practical realization.

Together, these criteria should ensure that all those initiatives can be captured where there is evidence of significant and substantive engagement in urban sustainability, and where projects and programmes are promoted explicitly as policy initiatives by relevant municipal authorities, national governments, private developers and international organizations. The approach is also sufficiently broad to take into account the diverse range of initiatives developed under the banner of 'eco-city' and related sister terms, such as 'low-carbon city', 'solar city' and 'sustainable city'. At the same time, this approach is not prescriptive in terms of evaluating substantive achievements (e.g. specified environmental performance or socio-economic features) as criterion for inclusion/exclusion. As noted, this would otherwise mean imposing a particular eco-city definition or threshold and, thus, privilege some initiatives over others based on normative preferences.

Data capture

If the definitional challenge is addressed through the above approach, then another challenge is how to deal with the potentially large amount of data available for analysis. This required the comprehensive scanning and detailed analysis of relevant sources, including policy documents, project reports, master/sustainability plans, academic literature, website materials and media reports. Following a gathering process of this type, verification of data is essential, so as to ensure their robustness. This was accomplished through a triangulation process in which information was cross-referenced between different sources.

A mixture of qualitative and quantitative data was captured. Qualitative information allowed for the eco-city initiatives to be characterized in narrative form and to provide explanatory contextual information. This helped to 'tell the story' and situate initiatives within their place-related contexts. Measurable information was also captured so as to allow for consistent comparative analysis using quantitative variables. These related to factors including the size and type of an urban development, the prevalence of certain sustainability features (e.g. CO_2 emission targets, renewable energy technologies), and the types of actors involved.

Needless to say, even a thoroughly rigorous methodological approach cannot prevent missing out certain developments and initiatives. This is particularly likely to be the case, as noted, where information about initiatives is not readily available in the international literature. Inevitably, then, the global picture of sustainable cities may be skewed to an extent by the international over-reporting of some initiatives and the under-reporting of others, respectively.

Data analysis

Analysis of the data yielded by a survey of this type would ideally be geared towards providing both an overarching picture of eco-city developments, and a complementary more in-depth discussion of relevant specific features. In this case, a descriptive analysis of the dataset as a whole was facilitated by the capture of a series of specific salient variables at the data gathering stage. First, the analysis looked at how the overall number of captured initiatives is distributed across global regions, thus indicating where activity is more or less pronounced. In addition, the key types of development, and patterns among these, were identified. Here, the distinction between 'new development', 'urban expansion' and 'retrofit development' proved useful: the first relates to entirely new cities built from scratch; the second includes in-fill projects, such as new urban districts built on brownfield sites; and the third applies to existing urban infrastructure, buildings and services. The analysis also took into account the development phase of eco-city initiatives, by distinguishing between developments 'at planning stage', currently 'under construction', and 'implemented'. This gave an indication of how far eco-city initiatives have advanced in practice beyond conceptual stage. A further key variable informing the analysis described the main implementation mode, distinguishing between 'technological innovation', 'integrated sustainability plan' and 'civic engagement'. This points to whether eco-city initiatives are mainly defined through technological solutions, focusing on the integration of economic, social and environmental dimensions of sustainability, or placing community engagement at the centre of activity (noting, of course, that in many cases there will be a mixture of the three).

A typological approach of this kind, it was hoped, would allow for the identification of broad, global trends and patterns and, as such, provide useful insight into the current conceptualization and practice of the sustainable city. At the same time, it was intended that the general trends should be juxtaposed with the place- and context-specific features of urban sustainability initiatives, since the sustainable city is also essentially defined by local contexts.

The following sections discuss key global developments in respect of practical eco-city initiatives – individual projects, national programmes, international networks – that have taken place since the 1990s and that have been characterized by a remarkable acceleration and global proliferation since the early 2000s. The materials are drawn from a comprehensive global survey following the methodology outlined above – see Joss (2011) and Joss et al. (2011; 2013).

Figure 4.1   *Number of eco-city initiatives launched, globally and by region*

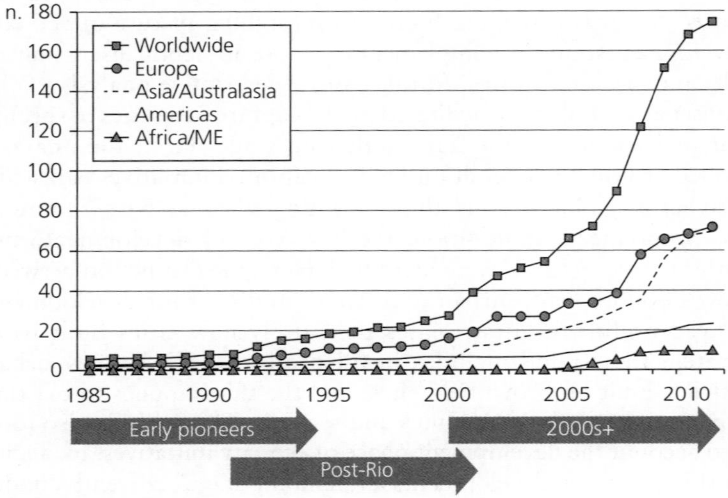

Source: Joss et al., 2013.

Global trends

However difficult it may be, for the aforementioned methodological reasons, to determine the exact number and extent of eco-city initiatives of various kinds, the last decade or so has certainly seen a significant increase and regional proliferation of such initiatives. As Figure 4.1 indicates, the increase and proliferation have been particularly pronounced since the mid-2000s. The figure shows the launch of eco-city initiatives for each year, both region by region, and overall globally. The resulting longitudinal perspective suggests three consecutive, partially overlapping phases (Joss, 2011b), which mirror the evolution of key policy discourses across the period (see Chapter 3).

Longitudinal shifts

1. *Phase I: early pioneers (1980s–early 1990s).* Throughout the 1980s and early 1990s, the 'eco-city' was mainly a normatively prescriptive concept, 'a collection of ... ideas about urban planning, transportation, health, housing, economic development,

natural habitats, public participation and social justice' (Roseland, 1997a: 197). Practical examples were relatively few and far between. This is echoed by Barton (2000b: chapter 5), who also noted that there was initially a considerable gulf between aspiration and actual achievement. Barton's explanation for this was that various economic, political and behavioural constraints inhibited the realization of eco-city developments. Through his empirical survey of developments in that period, he showed that there were but a few city-wide urban sustainability initiatives, with practical activity initially focused more on individual buildings and at the neighbourhood level. In other words, sustainable urbanism, while attracting growing conceptual interest, had not yet fully established itself as a broad policy priority. Nevertheless, there were a few cities that pioneered urban sustainability through policy and practice. Among these were Curitiba (Brazil), Freiburg (Germany) and Växjö (Sweden), all of whose activities can be traced back to the 1970s: Curitiba, under its then mayor Jaime Lerner, began by developing an integrated, affordable bus system aimed at easing traffic congestion and increasing public transport across the rapidly expanding city; Freiburg, dubbed Germany's 'eological capital', was one of the first municipalities to adopt a city-wide sustainability master plan (in 1986), with a focus on sustainable energy; for its part, Växjö became active in the field as a result of the 1970s energy crisis, focusing its efforts on substituting fossil fuel with locally sourced alternative energy. All three cities became international showcases of urban sustainability innovation in the 1980s and 1990s. Significantly, all three cities continue to be leaders in the field, having adapted their strategies with the evolving sustainability policy discourses.

2. *Phase II: post-Rio local and national experimentation (1992– early 2000s)*. The 1992 'Earth Summit' and resulting Local Agenda 21 (see Chapter 3) formed the background against which eco-city concepts were increasingly translated into practice. As discussed in the previous chapter, the Local Agenda 21 was particularly embraced by European countries and cities, inspiring the Aalborg Charter (*Charter of The European Cities and Towns Towards Sustainability,* European Commission, 1994) and the European Commission's European Green Capital Award. Schwabach, a small German city, was selected by the federal government for a pilot study to design a model for urban sustainability development to be emulated elsewhere in Germany, while,

in Sweden, all local authorities were required to implement
Agenda 21 plans to encourage environmental sustainability
(Mega, 2000). In New Zealand, Waitakere sought to integrate
Western and Maori concepts of sustainable resource manage-
ment in its eco-city master plan (Laituri, 1996).

3. *Phase III: global expansion/policy mainstreaming (2000s–
present)*. The most recent phase is characterized by the concurrent globalization – in terms of geographic spread and
international profile – and mainstreaming – in terms of policy
uptake and practical implementation – of the eco-city phenomenon. This period coincides with the adoption of climate change
policies at international and national levels following the Kyoto
Protocol (the UN's climate change framework convention),
which was adopted by the UN in 1997 and came into force in
2005. The period also coincides with the landmark moment in
2008, when it was estimated that for the first time in human
history the majority of the world's population now lived in urban
areas. While the third phase overall has been characterized by a
significant global growth in eco-city initiatives from the early
2000s, this has been particularly marked since the second half of
the decade. Thus, eco-city initiatives are now dotted in growing
numbers around the globe, and several high-profile initiatives at
national and international levels have begun to promote eco-city
innovation systematically. These include: the Indian pilot eco-city
initiative to retrofit six pilgrim cities (2002–7); the French
government's ÉcoCité and ÉcoQuartier initiatives (launched
2008); Japan's national eco-city programme (launched 2008); the
World Bank's Eco2 Cities programme (launched 2009, initially in
Indonesia but with wider focus on South East Asia); and the international city network C40 Cities Climate Leadership Group
(which in 2011 merged with the Clinton Climate Initiative's
Climate Positive Development Program, and now includes over
60 cities worldwide).

Apart from the evident difference in the rate of increase in practical eco-city initiatives, the three phases, then, also differ in terms of
the degree of policy engagement (as explored in greater detail in
Chapter 3): the first phase was characterized by a pioneering
approach underpinned by conceptual explorations informed by
normative ideas and local challenges as yet not fully embedded in
policy. The second phase signalled a shift to a more regulatory
approach. The concept of eco-city became increasingly standardized

by the policy framework of sustainability in the wake of 'Rio 1992' and within the context of Local Agenda 21. In turn, eco-city initiatives took on a standardizing role in that – through practical implementation – they collectively contributed to the conceptualization of sustainable development policy. Schwabach was an example of this regulating process whereby standards are defined through initial piloting and subsequent use, becoming models to incentivize and guide eco-city development more widely. Finally, as discussed more fully in Chapter 3, the most recent phase signals a further shift towards a policy agenda focused on innovation, particularly economic ('green growth') and technological ('smart city') innovation. Under this recent policy perspective, the eco-city is associated with the opportunity to stimulate socio-technological innovation, business development and cultural branding. The focus on 'decarbonizing' urban infrastructure and systems suggests a further standardization, reflected in the centrality of the 'carbon discourse' in mainstream eco-city policy (Joss et al., 2013).

As noted, calculating the exact number of eco-city initiatives at various points of this longitudinal trajectory is difficult to accomplish. For China, for example, the World Bank (2009: p.ii) estimated that there were some 100 eco-city initiatives under way in 2009 (see also reference to 100 'low-carbon city' initiatives in Wang, 2010: 52). More recently, the Chinese Society for Urban Studies (CSUS, 2011a: 27) reported that 259 cities above prefecture level (constituting about 90 per cent of the country's cities) had declared the intention of becoming an 'eco-city' or 'low-carbon city'. As neither of these reports includes full lists of eco-city projects referred to, and as this is clearly an evolving situation, it is difficult to ascertain the exact state of play. Figure 4.1 (Asia/Australasia) includes 25 Chinese eco-cities, on the basis – in line with the requirements of the survey methodology – that there was internationally reported evidence of their ongoing development in 2011. It seems fair to conclude that different types of activities related to urban sustainability, and often labelled as 'eco-city' initiatives, are rather more widespread in China than this figure would suggest; the lack of readily available documentation, however, precludes a reliable assessment of their specific characteristics.

Europe poses a similar challenge: since its launch in 1994, the Aalborg Charter has been signed by over 2,700 cities, towns and municipalities (including local authorities below the size of towns) that are now part of the European Sustainable Cities Platform (www.sustainablecities.eu). Viewed positively, this suggests that

urban sustainability has become normalized and is now well embedded in municipal policy and action across swathes of European cities
and towns. More critically, one can argue that signing up to an
urban sustainability charter – however significant in itself – does not
automatically make a sustainable city. Figure 4.1 (Europe) 'only'
includes 73 initiatives, based on clear evidence of concerted urban
sustainability policy and action under the banner of 'eco-city',
'sustainable city' or similar labels. What is arguably more important
than trying to establish absolute figures, then, is to track longitudinal developments and to consider regional trends.

Regional contexts

It would be difficult to argue that there are distinct regional eco-city
models or types – say, the 'European' or 'Asian' eco-city. Instead, it
is more convincing to make a case that increasing internationalization is at work, within which distinct types of eco-city development
– such as 'new build' versus 'retrofit' – can be discerned across
regions, as explored further below. Nevertheless, adopting a
regional perspective is beneficial in that it provides further understanding of the specific contexts in which particular developments
have taken place over the last decade or two.

Europe

The widespread adoption of sustainable development policies across
Europe – both at the European-wide level (through the institutions
of the European Union) and at individual national levels – in the
1990s has meant that historically Europe was at the international
forefront of practical sustainable city initiatives. This is confirmed
by Figure 4.1. During this period, cities such as Almere (the
Netherlands), Linz (Austria) and Helsinki (Finland), with its newly-
built *Eko-Viikki* community, joined earlier pioneers Freiburg and
Växjö in spearheading urban sustainability initiatives; and these
cities continue to play an important role today. Significantly,
however, they have been joined since the early 2000s by a larger
group of existing cities and new developments from where a new
generation of eco-city initiatives has been emerging.

Many of these new developments take the form of urban expan-
sions; some based on greenfield, others on brownfield, sites.
Examples of greenfield development include Ecociudad Logroño
(Ecocity Logroño), a new CO_2-neutral neighbourhood (3,000
homes) planned for Logroño, the capital of the Spanish region of La

Rioja; and PlanIT Valley, a new 'high-tech' 4,000-acre development (for 225,000 inhabitants) currently in the process of being built in the Portuguese town of Paredes (near Porto). Other cities have adopted sustainability strategies as part of the socio-economic regeneration of brownfield sites, or 'in-fill' projects. For example, Brøset is planned as a carbon-neutral district (approximately 2,000 new homes) situated on an 86-acre former hospital site on the outskirts of Trondheim (Norway). The initiative, which is being developed as an interdisciplinary research-into-action programme involving Trondheim University, has gained support from the Norwegian government through its Future Cities programme. Hamburg-Harburg Eco-City (Germany) is another example of a regeneration project. Styling itself as 'Germany's first entirely sustainable creative-industrial corporate development' (Ecocity, 2009), the project is based on the transformation of the former port facilities into a new office and residential area. Energy consumption is to be cut by 30 per cent (compared with 2010 levels) and GHG emissions are to be reduced by 80 per cent by 2050. In 2011, Hamburg-Harburg was the first European large urban development to receive LEED Platinum certification (see Chapter 6 for further information on sustainable city certification schemes, including LEED).

Hammarby Sjöstad, another internationally acclaimed brownfield regeneration project, was one of the reasons why the city of Stockholm received the first European Green Capital award in 2010. The project was originally part of the city's 2004 Olympic Games bid. While the bid itself failed, the Hammarby Sjöstad project, which encompasses twelve neighbourhoods, has continued to be developed, with completion expected in 2018. It has been made possible through a co-operative partnership between investors, architects, developers and land owners. The project includes an integrated transport system aimed at achieving 80 per cent public transport by 2010, including free ferry transport. Solar panels on most buildings, and water and waste recycling systems, are other features of the new district. By 2011, 8,700 out of an eventual total of 11,500 flats were completed. Elsewhere in Sweden's capital, work on the regeneration of the 236-hectare Stockholm Royal Seaport began in 2010, with completion expected in 2025. The new district will provide 10,000 homes and 30,000 office jobs, and aims to be fossil-fuel free by 2030. While there are plans to introduce solar energy and a biomass plant, the main focus is on improving energy efficiency, including a smart grid system. Sustainable transport initiatives include the introduction of biogas buses, charging points for electric vehicles, and new lanes for pedestrians and cyclists. To reduce emissions into the harbour, docked boats will be able to plug into the electricity grid instead of using diesel. The largest current building on site, a gas works, will become a new cultural centre including an opera stage. The initiative is part of the Clinton Climate Initiative's Climate Positive Development Program.

In the UK, the Thames Gateway (to the east of London) is significant in that it is currently Europe's largest urban regeneration project. It stretches along the river Thames, incorporating parts of London and the counties of Essex and Kent. The 'eco-region', as it is promoted, comprises urban, brownfield and green space, and is to be developed according to economic, social and environmental sustainability criteria. The area will include several distinct urban (industrial) sustainability projects. These include: (a) the London Sustainable Industries Park, styled as 'clean-tech' hub for low-carbon technologies, launched in 2009 with funding support from both the Greater London Authority and the UK government; (b) the Green Enterprise District, which was launched by the mayor of London in 2010 and covers six East London boroughs; (c) the Royal Albert Basin, situated within the Green Enterprise District, a mixed-used development with focus on retrofitting existing buildings, providing waste infrastructure and decentralized energy schemes, as well as remediating brownfield sites; (d) the Thames Gateway Institute for Sustainability, launched in 2010 as a cross-institutional research and innovation centre to support the development in the region; and (e) the Crystal, Siemens' new global urban sustainability headquarters (opened in 2012).

As examples of the new generation of European sustainable city initiatives, these projects have in common a strong focus on urban regeneration through the redevelopment of brownfield sites, and on urban expansion through the development of greenfield sites. As part of these major urban projects, sustainability is seen as a key driver for stimulating economic growth, especially by transforming former industrial sites into new hubs for low-carbon 'clean-tech' industries and attracting international business, and for revitalizing cities by creating desirable, environmentally friendly residential and cultural quarters.

Similar developments can be observed in France. Significantly, here the impetus for concerted eco-city development has come from central government, which in 2008 launched the ÉcoCité and ÉcoQuartier initiatives (see Chapter 2 for details). Mirroring other recent European eco-city projects, both initiatives are characterized

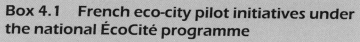

Box 4.1 French eco-city pilot initiatives under the national ÉcoCité programme

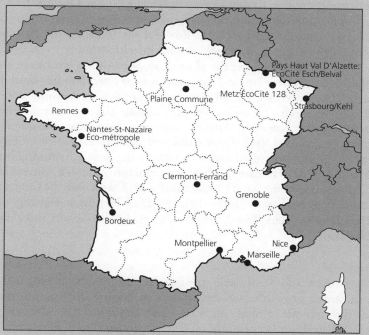

Locations of French ÉcoCités – not including the *ÉcoCité insulaire et tropicale* project on La Réunion island (Territoire de la Côte Ouest).

The 13 original pilot locations selected by the French national government display great variety both socio-economically and in terms of their geography/natural setting; the plans for each were developed to reflect these very different local contexts. Common to all 13, however, is the aim to accommodate significantly growing residential populations, and an emphasis on economic development – reflecting the key goals of the ÉcoCité programme. More specific themes, which appear variously across the initiatives, without being common to all, include: regeneration of ex-industrial or inner city areas; densification; improvements to public transport; creating environment-technology jobs; and protecting the natural environment. (For further details of each, see Joss et al., 2011 and *Revue Urbanisme*, 2010.)

by their focus on: (a) transforming existing cities, (b) promoting environmental and economic innovation to achieve sustainable development and economic growth – funding comes from the €1bn national economic stimulus programme (*Le Grand Emprunt*) – and (c) supporting dialogue and co-operation between central government and participating cities. Box 4.1 summarizes the thirteen ÉcoCité projects originally selected for development.

Specific policy frameworks at the European Union level have also guided eco-city development. International co-operation has since the early 2000s been supported by two European Commission-funded action research programmes: the first, the Ecocity: Urban Development towards Appropriate Structures for Sustainable Transport project (2002–5), included seven European cities working as part of a network: Bad Ischl (Austria), Barcelona Trinitat Nova (Spain), Györ (Hungary), Tampere (Finland), Trnava (Slovakia), Tübingen (Germany), and Umbertide (Italy). The second, the Concerto Eco-City Programme (2005–10), included Helsingør/Helsingborg (Denmark/Sweden), Trondheim (Norway), Tudela (Spain) and Zilina (Slovakia).

Asia
Across Asia and Australasia, the last decade or so has seen particularly strong growth in eco-city initiatives, contributing significantly to the overall global increase (see Figure 4.1). Altogether, Asia/Australasia is currently on a par with Europe in terms of the number of eco-city initiatives.

Back in the 1990s, only a few pioneer initiatives emerged from the region, such as: Auroville, a small-scale non-governmental, self-styled ecological urban development in India, originating from the 1960s; Kawasaki, named the first 'eco-town' by the Japanese government in 1997; and Waitakere, New Zealand's fifth-largest city, whose eco-city strategy blended Agenda 21 principles with traditional Maori values. Since the early 2000s, the launch of several national programmes has given eco-cities an increasingly high policy and media profile across the region, against the background of accelerated urbanization and economic development processes. These national programmes generally act by facilitating national (and international) expertise and knowledge sharing, and providing technological and planning guidance as well as financial support. Within these overarching frameworks, local actors (municipal authorities, developers, etc.) are responsible for developing and implementing specific initiatives on the ground.

India is a case in point. It demonstrates the increasing governmental interest in, and backing for, eco-city initiatives, and also highlights the partial shift of policy interest, from a more exclusive focus on the environment and development, to a broader focus encompassing commercial and techno-industrial interests. In 2001, as part of its tenth Five-Year Plan (2002–7), the Indian Ministry of Environment and Forest chose Kottayam as the first of six pilot eco-city initiatives, which aimed to make various retrofit adaptations to existing cities. Puri, Thanjavur, Tirupati, Ujjain, and Vrindavan were subsequently selected (see Box 4.2). All six projects focused on the same key objectives: (a) improving sanitation in public spaces; (b) making public transport more efficient and environmentally sustainable; (c) improving urban management; and (d) improving facilities and conditions for tourists. Individual projects were administered by the Indian Central Pollution Control Board (CPCB), and the programme overall received funding support from the German international development agency (*Gesellschaft für Internationale Zusammenarbeit*). From the limited literature available, it would appear that progress on the implementation of the eco-city programme has been slow, with many recommendations in each city not getting beyond the planning stage (Joss et al., 2013).

More recently, the Indian government has sponsored two further eco-city initiatives which differ significantly from that of the Ministry of Environment and Forest. The first comes from the newly established Ministry of New and Renewable Energy (MNRE), which in 2008 announced plans to develop 60 'solar cities' to be implemented during the eleventh Five-Year Plan (2007–12) (MNRE, undated). The cities of Surat and Gandhinagar (both in Gujarat) are included among the preliminary 'model solar cities' (see map in Box 4.2). The programme's rationale is that ongoing economic growth and urbanization are expected to lead to demand for energy outstripping supply. Hence, the programme provides support for municipal corporations in promoting the use of renewable energy, energy efficiency measures, water conservation measures, and the use of solar passive architecture. The target is to reduce conventional energy use by a minimum of ten per cent over five years in each city. Ultimately, the goal is for solar cities to meet all energy needs from local renewable sources. Apart from providing the overarching planning framework for the solar city initiative, the ministry also facilitates international input, including technical assistance from Brookhaven National Laboratory at the US

Box 4.2   India: three national programmes

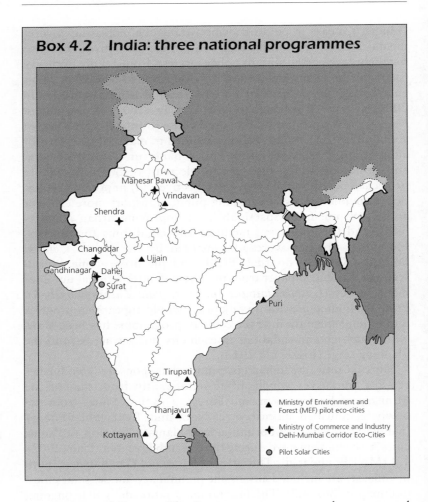

Department of Energy. The Japanese government also expressed interest in collaborating in the programme. Such international input is seen as particularly important, in order to overcome local capacity problems. By 2011, MNRE had given the go-ahead for 36 solar city programmes.

The other recent national initiative comes from the Ministry of Commerce and Industry, which in 2010 launched its plans for four new-build 'eco-friendly cities' within the designated Delhi-Mumbai Corridor, or DMC (see Box 4.2). Besides the eco-cities – Changodar, Dahej, Manesar Bawal, and Shendra – the DMC will have 11 investment regions and 13 industrial areas. The four eco-cities are expected to cost US$90 billion, with costs shared between India and Japan. The eco-town design is based on the Kitakyushu eco-town model in Japan. The initiative follows a system of urban planning new to the area and will represent the biggest urban development programme since Chandigarh was built in 1953. Key features are compact, vertical developments, an efficient public transportation system, the use of digital technology to create smart grids for better management of civic infrastructure, recycling of sewage water for industrial use, re-use of industrial waste, green spaces, cycle tracks and easy accessibility to goods, services and activities, designed to foster a sense of community.

Elsewhere in India, the Ministry of Urban Development collaborated with the US Department of Energy and its Brookhaven National Laboratory to create eight 'near-zero energy satellite towns'. Rajarhat, a fast growing new township near Kolkata, was selected in 2010 to be the first of these initiatives.

China is at present arguably the most ambitious country in Asia – if not the world – concerning the development of eco-city and low-carbon city initiatives. As noted earlier, in this fast evolving context, it is difficult to establish exact figures, but safe to say that there are dozens of such initiatives currently under way in various parts of China (see Yu, 2014: 7678). One of the most high-profile initiatives is Tianjin Binhai Eco-City, which was officially endorsed in 2007 by Premier Wen Jiabao and is a showcase of China's international engagement and ambitions: it is being developed through bilateral co-operation with Singapore, and has been host to the annual 'China International Eco-City Forum' since 2010 (see Box 4.3; and also discussion in Chapter 6).

China's recent enthusiastic embrace of eco-cities is a clear attempt to redress the negative environmental consequences of rampant urbanization (Joss and Molella, 2013). According to the World Bank (2009: 1), some 45 per cent of the country's population lived in cities by 2007, which is projected to rise to over 60 per cent by 2025, covering an additional urbanized land area of 65,000 km^2. The paradigms of 'ecological modernization', 'eco-civilization' and 'circular economy' – all enshrined in the country's policy framework (see Box 3.3) – are intended to effect a transition to a low-carbon economy and more sustainable urban development. Eco-cities play a central part in this national agenda, and as such are supported through national governmental programmes. These include: the National Standards for Eco-Garden City by the Ministry of Housing and Urban-Rural Development (MOHURD), first developed in 1992 as

Box 4.3   Tianjin Binhai Eco-City

Tianjin Eco-City is a new district of the historic city of Tianjin. It forms part of the Tianjin Binhai New Area, and is adjacent to the Tianjin Economic Development Area (TEDA). It is being built with technology and expertise from Singapore, drawing on the two countries' previous experience of developing the Suzhou Industrial Park. While initially the district will derive energy from a waste incinerator plant, several other options for energy generation are under consideration, including clean fuel, renewable (solar) and geothermal energy. All buildings will conform to stringent energy efficiency standards. The district is planned to allow for up to 90 per cent public transport, cycling and walking. Advanced water saving and waste management systems will be implemented. The existing wetlands around the city will be protected to enhance biodiversity. Work began in 2008 and is scheduled to take between ten and fifteen years to completion. By 2010, several building complexes were completed, and work on a light rail transit system is under way. The city layout is based on integrated mixed land-use 400m × 400m 'eco-cells', every four to five of which combine to form differently landscaped 'eco-neighbourhoods' of 20,000 residents. Green 'eco-valley' corridors, serving as the main public open spaces, will run through the city. By May 2010, 125 companies had registered in the eco-city, and in July 2010 it received a US$6m grant from the World Bank's Global Environment Fund to support the development of policy, monitoring and regulatory mechanisms. The first public housing project was opened in 2011. Overall completion is expected by 2020.

In a recent detailed analysis of Tianjin Eco-City, Caprotti (2015) acknowledges its ambitious and experimental character, but raises the possibility of it becoming an exclusive 'eco-enclave' within the increasingly environmentally degraded Bohai Rim Metropolis region. He suggests that the initiative may teach us relatively little about social sustainability – observing, for example, that Tianjin's residents were not involved in the planning process and that its public housing policy effectively excludes certain social groups.

National Garden City Standards and re-issued in 2004 as the Eco-Garden City programme; and the Indices for Eco-County, Eco-City and Eco-Province by the Ministry of Environmental Protection (MEP), first developed in 2003, and re-issued in 2007. Together, these programmes were estimated (by the Chinese Society for Urban Studies, as cited in Weskamp, 2013: 43) to have been responsible for an average of 29 eco-city projects year-on-year since 2003. More recently, in 2010, the National Development and Reform Committee (NDRC) launched its own Low-Carbon Demonstration Cities and Provinces initiative, adding a further 133 initiatives to the total (ibid.).

These national incentive schemes and regulatory frameworks are one key characteristic of current Chinese eco-city development. Complementing this, however, the situation is also characterized by initiatives taken by cities and provinces themselves, which has led to a proliferation of eco-city projects of various kinds, ranging from new builds to retrofit developments, and from towns to large cities and city-regions. Many of the new eco-cities are strategically located in new urban agglomerations, city clusters, metropolitan areas and coastal regions – including Tangshan Caofeidian International Eco-City, which is situated in the nationally designated Circum-Bohai-Sea growth region. As such, they serve to absorb urban migration, respond to environmental challenges and, as iconic developments, are designed to help enhance regional economic aspirations both in the national and wider global contexts.

However, while the Chinese eco-city development programmes seek to address some of the negative externalities of recent urbanization processes, they are arguably to an extent also caught up in them (Joss and Molella, 2013). This is apparent, for example, in the partially overlapping and fragmented policy initiatives by MEP, MOHURD and NDRC, each of which pursues its own demonstration projects and approval processes (World Bank 2009: 3–4). It is also apparent in the unilateral efforts made by local governments and real-estate companies to launch their own eco-city initiatives, resulting in a lack of effective policy co-ordination and regional co-operation. In Hebei Province alone, in addition to Tangshan Caofeidian International Eco-City, there are at least seven other, seemingly unconnected, eco-city initiatives currently under way: Baoding, Huanghua, Shijiazhuang, Tangshan Nanhu, Wanzhuang, Zhangjiakou, and Zhuozhou. There is, then, a risk of uncontrolled development stoked by strong inter-city competition, fragmented policy-making, and a lack of unified regulation. In response, the Chinese authorities have begun to address the need for better co-ordination and agreed standards, by seeking to develop an overarching 'eco-city development index system' (CSUS, 2011a).

In Japan, too, eco-city development has been facilitated by strong national governmental programmes. The first such programme was launched in 1997 by the Ministry of Economy, Trade and Industry, jointly with the Ministry of Health, Labour and Welfare (now the Ministry of Environment). This programme was primarily aimed at reducing industrial waste and emissions. Under the scheme, Kawasaki was named the first national eco-town. More recently, in 2009, the Ministry of Environment jointly with the Ministry of Economy, Trade and Industry selected Kitakyushu, Minamata, Obihiro, Shimokawa, Toyama and Yokohama from a total of 82 applications for eco-city development. The choice was made both on the basis of the six cities' track records as sustainability champions and their plans for future innovation. A further seven eco-cities were recognized later in 2009: Chiyoda, Iida, Miyakojima, Kyoto, Sakai, Toyota and Yusuhara (see Box 4.4). The initiative aims to encourage other cities to follow the example set by these 13. This current eco-city initiative is rather broader in scope than the earlier 'eco-town' programme.

In one important respect, however, Japan differs from other Asian countries: current eco-city innovation is steeped in historical values and traditions, while at the same time incorporating specific contemporary features. Low (2013) points to three distinct historical developments as having directly contributed to the current eco-city movement in Japan (see also Chapter 3): first, nineteenth-century industrialization, whose effects led to the adoption and adaptation of the Garden City concept in the early twentieth century; second, the environmental crisis of the 1950s and 1960s resulting in local environmental activism; and third, more recently in the 1990s, the internationalization of sustainable development policy. The national experience of environmental crises in the last half century in particular explains the focus of Japanese eco-city initiatives on waste recycling and reduction, retrofitting of existing urban (infra)structure and active citizen participation. According to Low, the historical perspectives, reinterpreted within a contemporary context, result in certain tensions in the conceptualization of the eco-city between tradition and modernity.

Elsewhere in the Asian/Australasian region, in South Korea five eco-city projects – Gwanggyo Ekonhill, Incheon Eco-City, Magok/Seoul, Sejong and Songdo International Business District – have been developed under the umbrella of a national urban policy programme (see Box 3.3; Shwayri, 2013; Joss et al., 2011). With support from the World Bank's Eco2 Cities Initiative, significant urban sustainability initiatives are under way in Indonesia (Balikpapan, Jakarta, Makassar, Palembang,

Box 4.4   Japan's national eco-city programme (2009 to date)

Although the 13 initiatives in this programme were selected by the Japanese national government, there is little sense of a prescriptive framework of sustainability being imposed 'from above'. While all have in common a technological focus, and take the form of 'retro-fits', their concrete goals vary considerably to reflect local contextual factors and priorities. Chiyoda's strategy for reducing CO_2 emissions concerns workplace-related energy consumption, for example, since it is home to many of the country's major political and economic institutions. In some cases, emphasis is given to improving the natural environment (Obihiro's activity, for example, includes a reforestation programme, reflecting its location in a biodiverse area), or making better use of specific local resources (Iida's plans, for example, are centred on solar energy, given the region's abundant sunshine). In others, historical continuity appears to be a key factor: Toyota is aiming to lead the way in changing car use; and Miyakojima, already a popular visitor destination, aims to encourage eco-tourism, to include the development of a 'South East Asian eco-house' model for local developers to follow (for more details of each, see Joss et al., 2011).

Surabaya), the Philippines and Vietnam. Notable Australian projects include Barangaroo in Sydney and Victoria Harbour in Melbourne.

The Americas
Compared with Asia and Europe, the increase in eco-city developments in the Americas has been less pronounced and mainly focused on the US and Canada. Still, from a regional perspective, there has been a marked change. As one urban sustainability specialist noted:

> Before this watershed decade [the 2000s]...urban sustainability [features] were found in only a handful of North American cities. Today, these hallmarks of green cities are popping up *everywhere*. Big cities like New York, Los Angeles, Vancouver, Toronto, and Chicago are actively trying to 'out-green' each other, while suburbs like Boulder, Colorado and Alexandria, Virginia, are rolling out their own localized sustainability solutions. (Karlenzig, 2010: 303)

It is indicative, then, that of the 17 US initiatives captured in Figure 4.1 (Americas), twelve were launched in the 2000+ period (and earlier urban sustainability initiatives have in some cases been followed by more recent developments, as exemplified by the case of Portland's EcoDistricts earlier in this chapter). At the same time, there is also good reason to suppose that a growing number of other local initiatives are taking place, in spite of a relative lack of engagement at national policy level.

While urban sustainability policies in two of Canada's three eco-city initiatives (Toronto and Vancouver) can be traced back to the 1990s, the more concerted and explicit eco-city initiatives are recent: the Live Green Toronto initiative was launched in 2008; Vancouver's EcoDensity Charter was unveiled in 2008 and its Greenest City initiative launched in 2010.

Across Latin America, two of the five eco-city initiatives were launched in the mid-2000s: Panama Pacifico, a new district of Panama City (Panama), styles itself as 'Latin America's first green city'; while Pedra Branca is a new compact district of Palhoça (Brazil) being built by private developers. Both initiatives are members of the Climate Positive Development Program of the Clinton Climate Initiative (see further below). The other three initiatives date back to the 1970s–1990s: Curitiba (Brazil) is one of the earliest, internationally recognized eco-cities; Bahia de Caráquez and Loja (both Ecuador) embarked on 'eco-transformation' in the 1990s.

Africa and the Middle East
Africa and the Middle East have seen comparatively modest development, starting in the mid-2000s: of the ten initiatives captured in Figure 4.1 (Africa/ME), Masdar (UAE) has generated by far the most media interest globally (see Box 4.5). Notable African initiatives have emerged in Kenya (Hacienda Ecocities/Mombasa), Nigeria (Eko Atlantic City/Lagos), South Africa (Ivory Park Eco-City/Johannesburg; Menlyn Maine/Pretoria; Zonk'izizwe Town Centre/Johannesburg), and Uganda (Kampala; Sseesamirembe). Despite the slow progress to date, ongoing environmental pressures associated with the unprecedented rate of urbanization across Africa and the Middle East make it possible that the region will see a surge of eco-city developments in years to come.

From new city to retrofit innovation

Confronted with this myriad of eco-city initiatives of various kinds across regions, it can be useful, for comparative purposes, to categorize them according to three types (Joss, 2011b):

1. *new build* – that is, entirely new cities built from scratch;
2. *urban extension/in-fill* – consisting of new neighbourhoods or districts, built on either greenfield or brownfield sites; and
3. *retrofit* – represented by sustainability innovation applied to existing urban structures and services.

This categorization is instructive in that it points to arguably fundamentally different types of urban sustainability intervention: in terms of scale, resource requirements, governance processes and socio-technical systems, significant differences can be expected between, say, an entirely new city built from scratch in a desert or on reclaimed land and the retrofitting of an existing district or town. Again, urban in-fill projects offer unique opportunities – namely, bringing about substantial urban regeneration and development with sustainability at the core of planning and operation – while also presenting particular constraints, such as rendering new development compatible with the existing, wider urban environment. (These

Box 4.5 Masdar

Launched in 2006, Masdar proclaimed itself the world's first fully 'zero-carbon' and 'zero-waste' city in the making. Built from scratch in the desert near Abu Dhabi with governmental support, the project is an attempt to transform the Emirate into a global leader in sustainable energy technologies. The city's masterplan mixes principles of traditional Arab architecture (providing natural ventilation and minimizing heat impact) with modern high-technology innovation. The new city aims to become an international hub for renewable energy research and development, led by the Masdar Institute of Science and Technology (in co-operation with MIT, Cambridge, US). Work started in 2008 but, due to the global recession, the overall completion date has been put back from 2016 to 2021–5, with the final costs expected to be in the region of US$20 billion.

Since the project was launched, some of the envisaged environmental sustainability features have been scaled back. For example, its planned 'personal rapid transit system' has not been expanded beyond a pilot scheme; plans for a hydrogen power plant and a solar manufacturing plant have stalled; and the goal of having 100 per cent renewable energy generated on site has been abandoned. Masdar is now expected to become a 'carbon-neutral' rather than, as originally envisioned, a 'zero-carbon' city. Construction continues apace, however. In 2010, the first building phase was completed, including six main buildings, over 100 apartments and the Masdar Institute of Technology. Its 10MW photovoltaic plant ▶

different governance and innovation features and requirements are explored in greater detail in Chapters 5 and 6.)

Judging by media reports, one could be forgiven for assuming that the typical twenty-first-century eco-city falls into the first category: new cities built pursuing a clean-slate approach. Certainly, projects such as Masdar, Tianjin Binhai and Sejong have enjoyed high media profiles due to their novelty as iconic symbols and the flagship status accorded to them by their sponsors. The promotion of Masdar as the world's first 'zero-carbon' and 'zero-waste' city, and Tangshan Caofeidian International Eco-City as 'city of the future', speaks of the ambition and determination of their promoters to claim a central stake in the international competition to re-invent the city fit for the twenty-first century and, in doing so, set a universal standard for

▶ is now connected to the Abu Dhabi national grid. By 2015, some 7,000 people are expected to live in, and 12,000 people to commute to, the city.

The considerable, and generally positive, international media coverage of Masdar has more recently been tempered by some more critical questions from the academic community. Cugurullo (2013), for example, identifies a gap between Masdar's promotional images and what is actually being developed. He suggests that its social sustainability features have been crowded out by the predominant emphasis on the city acting as a 'living lab', or 'permanent showroom', aimed at incubating and displaying various new 'smart' environmental technologies. This, he argues, raises the spectre of Masdar developing into a 'non-place', bereft of an organic society and built on an unattainable vision of a global 'zero-carbon, zero-waste' eco-city. Caprotti (2015: 82) similarly interprets Masdar as 'largely driven by economic and technological concerns', and questions the nature of the social environment which will result. Crot (2013: 2820) suggests that Masdar's 'imported' model of sustainability may afford it 'legitimacy in the eyes of the international community' but does not guarantee 'internal legitimacy': declining state support can be partly explained by the unacceptability of some of the project's features to the local population. The case of Masdar, Crot argues, points to the importance of considering local and national political contexts when studying urban sustainability initiatives, and suggests that technological fixes in themselves may not be enough to secure a sustainable future.

eco-city innovation. However, not only is there often a discrepancy to be found between these promotional claims and actual achievements – which requires critical engagement (see e.g. Cugurullo, 2013; Joss and Molella, 2013; Shwayri, 2013) – but eco-city innovation is just as likely to take place within existing cities through either retrofit or in-fill developments.

In fact, out of the total of 178 initiatives captured in Figure 4.1, the number of new builds is relatively small (24), when compared with the roughly equal numbers of retrofit (78) and in-fill (76) developments (see Figure 4.2). This is not to deny the significance of the contribution of new-build projects to the current eco-city phenomenon: of the 24 captured here, 21 have been developed in the most recent, 2000+ period; and of these 15 are located in Asia.

Figure 4.2   *Types of eco-city initiative by global region*

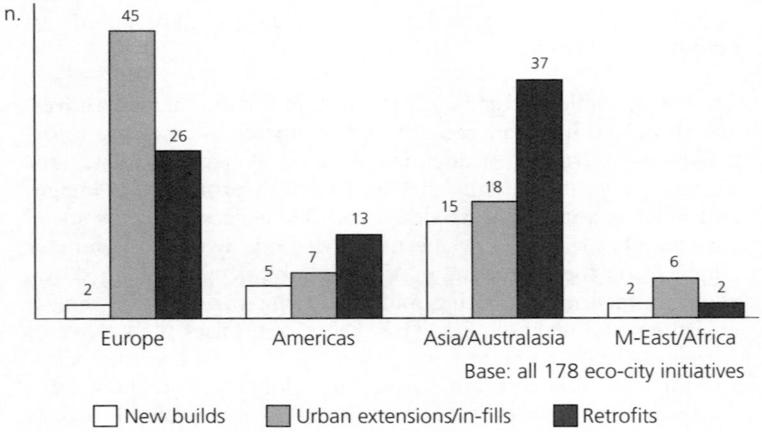

Base: all 178 eco-city initiatives

☐ New builds   ▨ Urban extensions/in-fills   ■ Retrofits

Source: Joss et al., 2013.

New-build eco-cities, however, are not the norm: current eco-city innovation is more typically centred upon existing urban areas through either urban extension/in-fill or retrofit developments. This, then, also suggests that the process of learning about, and scaling up, urban sustainability is not – as is sometimes assumed – one that necessarily starts within new-build developments and is subsequently applied to existing urban areas. A powerful (counter) argument can be made that innovation in urban sustainability should spring just as much from within existing urban systems and communities. As Figure 4.2 shows, there are interesting significant regional variations concerning the three categories of eco-initiatives. In Europe, there is a prevalence of in-fill developments, including the regeneration of brownfield sites, suggesting a close linkage of urban sustainability initiatives with socio-economic urban regeneration programmes, as illustrated by Hamburg-Harburg, Stockholm Royal Seaport and the French ÉcoCités. Meanwhile, in Asia, despite the significance of new builds, developments most often consist of retro-fits, indicating a particular need to render existing infrastructure and systems more environmentally sustainable. One way of interpreting these figures is to argue, in the case of Europe, that the concept or label of 'eco-city' (or similar sister terms) has come to be predominantly used to denote, and nationally and internationally publicize, a new sustainable approach to urban expansion and regeneration. In comparison, the smaller proportion of retrofit initiatives could be explained by the 'normalization' of urban sustainability across much of Europe (as discussed in Chapter 3), whereby it has gained an accepted place in policy and is routinely practised in everyday planning and, hence, does not require special policy measures or promotion.

In the case of Asia, the large proportion of retrofit initiatives may suggest a particular need to address pressing environmental issues within existing, rapidly expanding cities that have exhibited a comparatively low level of sustainability performance to date. In this context, explicit 'eco-city' policy commitments and mentions may be necessary to effect change and secure support from relevant domestic and international audiences. At the same time, from a methodological perspective, one should note that particularly within a context of rapid urbanization – as is the case across much of Asia – the distinction between retrofit and urban expansion may sometimes be more difficult to make: a municipal authority may pursue overarching urban sustainability policy applicable across the city area, within which individual in-fill projects contribute to ongoing urban expansion.

A further, useful way of gauging the international state of play is to analyse the rate of development of the initiatives included in Figure 4.1. To this end, it is useful to distinguish between three stages of development:

1. 'planned' projects, whereby policy commitment is secured but implementation has not yet begun;
2. projects 'under construction'; and
3. 'implemented' initiatives (in the sense that their original plans have been achieved, whether or not further changes have since taken place or are anticipated).

Looking at the eco-city phenomenon from this perspective might at first suggest that relatively little concrete progress has been made internationally, in spite of the overall finding that the number of initiatives has recently surged. Only 44 of the 178 initiatives can be considered as implemented (see Figure 4.3). Significantly, however, the highest proportion of implementation is found in retrofit initiatives – namely, 28 out of the 78 cases; urban expansion and new-build types are rather more likely to be either at planning stage or under construction. This difference is explained if launch dates are

Figure 4.3   *Development phases in relation to eco-city types*

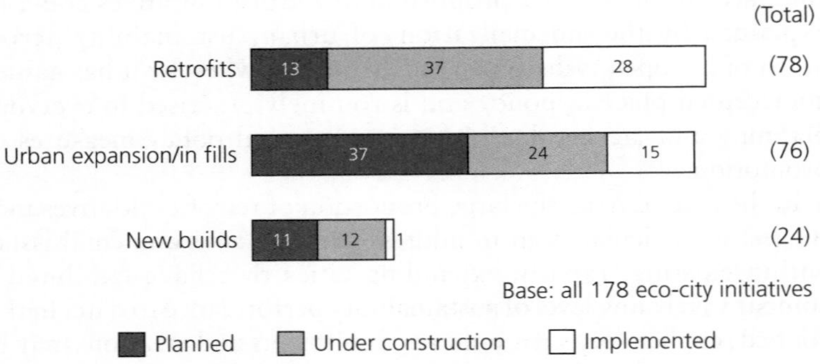

Base: all 178 eco-city initiatives

■ Planned   ▨ Under construction   ☐ Implemented

Source: Joss et al., 2013.

also taken into account, given that the time to implementation for in-fills and new builds is in many cases stated as requiring 15–20 years: 66 of the total of 76 in-fills, and 21 out of the total of 24 new builds, were only launched in the 2000+ period. In the case of these more recent initiatives, then, it is still too soon to assess the rate and nature of progression from planning stage to implementation, or to evaluate their substantive impact on the ground.

Technological versus social

While the distinction between 'retrofit', 'urban expansion' and 'new build' is certainly a useful way of identifying major types of eco-city innovation, each with particular characteristics and involving specific governing processes, there are two additional key features that further help differentiate recent developments: the level of technology use, and the extent of involvement by international organizations. The first concerns the relative focus on technology – that is, the degree to which technological aspects are embedded within the conceptualization, design and practice of eco-city initiatives. It should come as no surprise that technological solutions feature prominently in numerous eco-city projects, given the recent widespread emphasis on renewable energy generation and CO_2 reduction targets. Nevertheless, there are significant differences in approach, with some eco-city projects pursuing an almost exclusive technological strategy, while others strive to realize more nuanced concepts that seek to integrate technological, social and cultural dimensions.

Tangshan Caofeidian International Eco-City exemplifies the type of project where technological solutions are centre stage, with the visitor centre and promotional materials describing it as 'a scientifically developed model city' and a 'city based on science and technology' (Joss and Molella, 2013). This explicit focus works at four distinct levels: the first is the most overt, concerning the visible use and display of various 'green' technologies as key features and functions of eco-city, from geothermal energy pumps to a monorail system, from an underground pneumatic solid waste system to an integrated water sourcing and treatment system, and from solar power to tidal energy systems. Together, these technological features are to deliver the city's environmental benefits, including: 60 per cent solid waste recycling; 80 per cent biodegradable waste used for methane gas production; 90 per cent rainwater collection; 90 per cent public transport access (within a 500 m radius from offices/residences); 95 per cent onsite renewable energy generation; and 100 per cent waste water treatment. At the second level, technology is less immediately visible, but arguably just as pervasive, in the form of 'smart' systems: the use of digital (wired and wireless) technology to steer and monitor centrally – from the city's 'multifunctional resource management center' – various municipal services and functions, such as district energy heating, water distribution and collection, and traffic control. Hence, Tangshan Caofeidian is also promoted as China's first 'information city'.

At the third level, science and technology are privileged in the eco-city's envisaged role as an innovation hub: its prominent planned features include an 'innovation science and technology park' and a 'science and education city center'. Finally, the fourth level concerns the underlying scientific rationality guiding the concept of, and planning for, the eco-city. As the promotional literature proclaims: 'after scientific estimates, a city begins its perfect and calm transformation. With its natural advantage, Caofeidian will go down into history of the scientific attempt to build an innovative eco-city' (Administrative Committee of Tangshan Caofeidian International Eco-City, 2009: Preface). The city is, thus, conceived of as rationally planned based on scientific methods and guided by technology. Its designers are clear about the city's mission as pioneer in 'concept innovation': 'this is a more vigorous eco-city mode, which will become a model and sample [sic] for China and even the whole world' (Tangshan Bay Eco-City Management Committee, 2011: 14). Or, as another one of the city's planners put it: 'there is a fever of eco-city in China, and what we urban planners and researchers should do urgently is to identify, clarify, and put in practice the eco-city principles scientifically and rationally' (Qiang, 2009: 519).

This fourth – conceptual – scientific-technological aspect of the eco-city is arguably the most striking as well as baffling: it goes to the very heart of how the eco-city is defined and rationalized. The explanation for it may partly lie in the current rapid development of eco-city initiatives across China within a context of partially fragmented policy-making, strong inter-city competition and a relative lack of unified regulation (Joss and Molella, 2013). As a consequence, reference to scientific rationality and reliance on technological solutions may provide planners and developers with the necessary assurance and guidance in this rapidly developing environment. The conceptualization of Tangshan Caofeidian International Eco-City as a 'scientific' city, then, resonates with efforts elsewhere across China to develop eco-city initiatives according to scientific principles. This was demonstrated by the declaration issued at the first 'China International Eco-City Forum', which in its opening section proclaimed that 'we shall identify a correct concept for urban development ... and scientific assessment of eco-city development' (Joss and Molella, 2013: 126).

The prominence of technology in contemporary eco-city concepts and designs is, however, not just confined to China. It is widely found elsewhere in eco-city initiatives, from Fujisawa Sustainable Smart Town (Japan), to Neapolis Smart EcoCity (Cyprus), and from Portugal's PlanIT Valley to South Korea's Songdo (Joss et al., 2011). PlanIT Valley, a new urban development for 225,000 residents near Porto (Portugal), is noteworthy for the claim by its planners that it is 'the benchmark for future urban communities' and 'city of the future' (Living PlanIT, undated) on the basis of the advanced use of technology. The design of the PlanIT Valley project, which has received endorsement by the Portuguese government and been given Project of National Importance status, includes the use of hi-tech innovation at urban scale for power generation, water distribution and waste treatment. It will use sensor technology to achieve efficiencies in energy and resource use, both during construction and in service provision to residents and workers. Homes are designed to use at least 50 per cent less energy and 80 per cent less water than those inhabited by regular city dwellers.

The new city is the concept of Living PlanIT, a private company specializing in the development and application of digital and communication technologies to provide sustainable solutions. With completion expected in 2015, Living PlanIT envisage its 'city of the future' to 'serve simultaneously as a living laboratory for partner companies, test bed for their smart technologies, innovation center, incubator for technology start-ups, and demonstration of how Living PlanIT will collaborate with its partners and property developers to replicate its approach in other locations' (Living PlanIT, undated). While the developer emphasizes that PlanIT Valley will provide 'its citizens with a higher level of information about their built environment than has been possible previously' (ibid.), it is clear from the promotional materials that the main beneficiaries will be municipal managers who will have access to enhanced monitoring of infrastructure and services: 'managers will be able to optimize normal daily operations of the city and provide greater certainty in reacting to extraordinary events' (ibid.). The ultimate beneficiaries, however, may well be Living PlanIT and other technology firms supplying various technological hard- and software. It is the developers' intention that 'PlanIT Valley will exercise all the capabilities of the PlanIT OS™' (ibid.).

While the likes of Tangshan Caofeidian International Eco-City and PlanIT Valley, with their almost exclusive interest in high technology, may be at the far end of the scientific-technological spectrum, they are indicative of a more general trend in which technology is taking a more central place in contemporary eco-city concepts, designs and practice. This trend can only partly be explained by the focus on environmental issues. To be sure, the emphasis on climate change, CO_2 and other GHG emissions produces a strong articulation of the eco-city in terms of sustainable technological solutions. Of the 178 initiatives captured in Figure 4.1, 129 explicitly engage in climate change issues (Joss et al., 2013): of these, 105 specifically mention 'CO_2', 'carbon', and 'greenhouse gas' in their plans, while 106 mention 'energy' (energy consumption, energy efficiency, etc.) and 87 flag up 'renewable energy' production. However, the trend is in no small part also due to the prominence of various 'smart' technological paradigms and agendas at the heart of many contemporary eco-city initiatives. The conceptualization of urban sustainability (policy) predominantly in terms of green growth and ecological modernization (see Chapter 3) evidently produces strong incentives and opportunities for the combination of ecological strategies with technological innovation, with technology firms at the ready to step in and act (often concurrently) as designers, planners and deliverers of advanced technology for sustainable urban infrastructure and services. This is reinforced by the conceptualization of the eco-city – based on environmental and engineering sciences – in terms of 'systems' and 'metabolisms': statements, such as 'cities are both organic and controlled' and 'cities are complex systems and just like human beings they each have their own unique metabolism' – here made, respectively, by Peter Roberts, board member of the UK's Homes and Communities Agency (HCA), and by Stefen Behling, the head of research and development on new sustainable designs at international architect group Foster and Partners (Embassy of Switzerland in the UK, 2010: 28; 34) – are now quite commonly heard, albeit often with little critical engagement. This reflects the influence of a science-based approach to contemporary urban sustainability and explains the preponderance of technological concepts and solutions applied to the eco-city.

There are, of course, many examples of eco-city initiatives found towards the other end of the spectrum, with a stronger articulation of social and cultural dimensions of urban sustainability and a more subjugated role for technology. Sydney (Australia) and Tajimi (Japan) are illustrative of this category (Joss et al., 2011): the former has since the early 1990s pursued a concerted sustainability programme that seeks to address environmental, socio-economic and cultural issues in equal measure. To this effect, the city authorities formed a partnership with civil society groups and launched a public campaign on conservation and sustainability. In 2009, the city endorsed the Sustainable City 2030 plan, which covers social and cultural sustainability as well as the physical environment. In similar vein, Tajimi, which won the country's Top Eco-City award for the first time in 2003, has followed an urban sustainability approach that combines community involvement with transparent information on environmental performance. New developments and the retrofitting of existing buildings are carried out by prior public consultation. Characteristically, urban sustainability as a planning issue is integrated across all of the city's administrative departments. In these two, and similar, initiatives, technology is by no means sidelined – both have explicit CO_2 and GHG-related targets and corresponding technological measures – but, conceptually and practically, technology does not define these eco-cities as centrally and stridently as it does in the cases of, for example, Tangshan Caofeidian International Eco-City and PlanIT Valley.

Consideration of the technology dimension, then, seems to reveal a positive correlation between new-build and urban extension initiatives and the central application of hi-tech solutions. This arises partly from the 'clean-slate' approach associated with new-build and urban expansion initiatives – whereby new developments can be built from scratch on either greenfield or brownfield sites (or reclaimed land, as in the case of Tangshan Caofeidian International Eco-City) – which provides the opportunity to apply a systems approach and integrate technology centrally in the eco-city design; and it also arises from the corresponding core involvement of developers – engineering and technology firms in particular – in the planning and implementation processes. In contrast, in the case of pre-existing urban structures – that is, retrofit initiatives – the need to work within existing social, cultural and political boundaries, combined with the application of urban sustainability measures to existing infrastructure (often century-old) and services, necessarily brings socio-political and cultural dimensions to the fore and requires more 'blended' and moderated technological adaptation. This contrasting approach can be expected to be particularly strong in cases with an existing participatory culture – where urban policy is routinely subject to political discussion and public discourse – and a legacy (dating back to the 1990s) of embedding sustainability in urban planning.

International partnerships

The other additional key feature characterizing the types of eco-city initiatives is the extent of involvement of internationally active organizations. This refers to the international export – and related local import – of eco-city design, master planning and development, with international governmental organizations, private businesses and social enterprises variously engaged with local actors. Such international policy and knowledge transfer has been highlighted more generally as a key feature of planning in the 'global era' (e.g. Rydin and Thornley, 2002; Hodson and Marvin, 2010); and it has been identified specifically also in relation to several recent eco-city initiatives (Chang and Sheppard, 2013; Cugurullo, 2013; de Jong et al., 2013; Hult, 2013; Joss and Molella; 2013; Shwayri; 2013). International knowledge transfer can be defined as the central involvement – ranging from master planning to development, and from co-financing to providing accreditation – of foreign actors in the design and implementation of eco-city initiatives, and the resulting transfer and exchange of conceptual and empirical knowledge, expertise and practice.

Of the 178 initiatives captured in Figure 4.1, 89 were found to include international knowledge transfer of some kind (Joss et al.,

2013). Of these, 83 initiatives were launched in the 2000+ period – that is, more than half of all the initiatives launched within this period. Business organizations – consultancy, architecture, engineering and IT firms, among others – are particularly strongly represented in this recent process, with the flow of knowledge transfer to date mainly occurring from Europe, and to a lesser extent from the US, to Asia (especially China, India and South Korea). At the same time, there is growing evidence of knowledge transfer between Asian countries, as exemplified by the bilateral co-operation between India and Japan in connection with the four Delhi-Mumbai Corridor eco-cities, and between China and Singapore in connection with the development of Tianjin Binhai Ecocity.

Six major types of organizations can be seen to be involved in international co-operation, with the nature of policy and knowledge transfer varying according to type. (They are listed below in order of frequency, with consultancy firms most often involved in international knowledge transfer.) Significantly, the vast majority of these organizations have become active on the scene within a relatively short period of time, since the mid-2000s:

- *Consultancy firms*: This involves architecture, planning, engineering and information technology consultancies that operate internationally and have become a dominant feature of the recent wave of eco-city initiatives. Such firms are involved in carrying out feasibility studies, designing master plans, providing financial investment, and acting as developers. Swedish consultancy and engineering group Sweco, for example, was commissioned – following an international competitive tendering process – by the municipal government of Tangshan to prepare the master plan and corresponding indicator system for Tangshan Caofeidian International Eco-City. Such involvement is mostly in relation to new-build and urban expansion initiatives, and most often in Asia, although international private firms are also involved in several recent initiatives in other global regions. It is not uncommon to see consultancy firms – such as British engineering group Arup and Dutch architecture firm MVRDV, among many others – involved in several eco-city initiatives in different regions simultaneously.
- *International governmental bodies*: Organizations such as the World Bank and the UN are not only involved in championing global policy on urban sustainability (see Chapter 3), but they also take a more hands-on approach by initiating and facilitating prac-

tical eco-city initiatives. The Eco2 Cities programme is currently being applied with the collaborative involvement of the World Bank and local partners in a number of Asian cities, including in Indonesia, the Philippines and Vietnam. UNESCO's Biosphere Eco-Cities initiative (launched in 2006) and the older UN Sustainable Cities Programme (a joint initiative of UN-Habitat and UNEP, dating back to the 1990s) have similarly partnered up with municipal authorities across different global regions. The European Union, for its part, has launched a variety of initiatives under its Sustainable Cities Platform (see Box 3.1), including the Reference Framework for European Sustainable Cities, which provides a set of guidelines for the design and implementation of urban sustainability action plans. Together, these and other organizations play a facilitating role, by providing practical frameworks and developing collaborative relationships with partners on the ground.

- *City networks*: Cities themselves have formed collaborative partnerships aimed at facilitating knowledge exchange and developing standardized approaches to urban sustainability. The C40 Cities Climate Leadership Group has become a particularly prominent player, with currently 63 participating world cities. The network was initiated in 2005 by the former mayor of London to develop concerted action among the world's largest cities to tackle global climate change. In 2011, the C40 group merged with the Climate Positive Development Program of the Clinton Climate Initiative (which includes district-level pilot projects in 17 cities, with focus on climate-neutral development). Across the US, some 50 cities teamed up in 2008 to form STAR Communities (STAR = Sustainability Tools for Assessing and Rating Communities) designed as a common framework for urban and community sustainability initiatives. The framework was launched in 2012, in association with ICLEI. These municipal networks point to the role assumed by cities themselves as international players, as part of which they engage in joint policy development and contribute to the standardization of urban sustainability concepts and practice.
- *Non-governmental organizations*: This group consists of a mixture of internationally active social enterprises, such as British-based BioRegional, and professional bodies, such the US Building Council (LEED / LEED ND) and BRE Global (BREEAM Communities). Through its 'One Planet Communities' initiative, BioRegional is involved in projects as diverse as Ivory Park EcoCity (Johannesburg/South Africa), Masdar (UAE), Mata de Sesimbra (Portugal) and Sonoma Mountain Village (US) (BioRegional,

2013). For its part, the US Building Council is involved in applying its LEED Neighborhood Development programme to a similarly diverse range of projects, from Hamburg-Harburg to Songdo, and from Panama Pacifico to Vancouver. Both organizations provide developers with frameworks for designing and implementing urban sustainability programmes, and offer multi-stage accreditation schemes. Elsewhere, the International Ecocity Framework and Standards (IEFS) was launched in 2012 by Ecocity Builders (US), the social enterprise arising from Richard Register's pioneering work on eco-cities dating back to the 1980s. (The role of standardization, and associated accreditation processes, is explored in detail in Chapter 6.)

- *Research organizations*: International research co-operation can play an important role in conceptualizing the eco-city and supporting technological innovation. For example, Masdar (UAE), which was launched in 2006 and completed the first phase of development in 2010, has teamed up with the Massachusetts Institute of Technology (MIT) to establish the Masdar Institute of Science and Technology, aiming to become an international hub for renewable energy research and development. The feasibility study for Mentougou Eco Valley, a proposed new district near Beijing, was carried out by VTT Technical Research Centre of Finland, with Finnish consultancy Eero Paloheimo EcoCity Ltd. and Eriksson Architects in charge of the masterplan. European-wide research co-operation has been fostered through the aforementioned European Commission-funded Ecocity and Concerto Eco-City programmes involving 11 cities and associated research organizations.

- *National governmental agencies*: Another growing route of co-operation is through bilateral governmental initiatives. Apart from fostering knowledge exchange, these initiatives are seen as an opportunity to develop trade relations. For example, the Chinese cities of Chengdu, Chongqing and Shenyang are in the process of being retro-fitted in line with the French ÉcoQuartier concept, following an agreement in 2010 between the French and Chinese governments. The agreement seeks to facilitate the exchange of information and technical expertise on environmental policy and innovation. Within each pilot city, an *éco-quartier* is to be developed with input from French companies. As noted, elsewhere bilateral agreements have been put in place between: India and Japan (relating to the four 'eco-friendly' cities in the Delhi-Mumbai Corridor); between India and the USA (relating to

the solar-city and Near-zero Energy Satellite Town initiatives);
between China and Singapore (Tianjin Binhai Ecocity); and
between China and Switzerland (relating to the Low Carbon City
China Programme – see Joss, 2012).

As these types and examples show, the internationalization of eco-city
development has increased significantly over the last decade or so,
contributing to growing bilateral and multilateral inter-city partnerships and concurrent attempted standardization processes. As such,
this has contributed to the increasingly 'ubiquitous' character of eco-
cities (Joss et al., 2013). The attraction of international engagement is
clear to see: for cities – including regional and coastal cities jostling for
advantageous market positions – it provides an opportunity to advertise themselves as attractive centres for international business and
investment. For international firms, it opens up new markets, especially in areas of rapid urbanization and accompanying economic
development. For governments, it is a useful means of fostering bilateral development and trade relations. Finally, for international organizations, it provides an opportunity to develop urban sustainability
standards and to influence policy and practice on the ground.

Viewed more critically, the influence of internationalization can be
seen as contributing to the globalization and marketization of eco-city
innovation in a way which risks subordinating local concerns and
features, or in extreme cases even emptying eco-city concepts and
designs of local content altogether. A disregard for local context,
furthermore, raises the possibility that some schemes function as
premium 'ecological enclaves' (Hodson and Marvin, 2010b, 2010c),
which 'by-pass existing infrastructure and build internalized ecological resource flows' (Hodson and Marvin, 2010b: 299) in order to
protect the interests of their socially elite residents, while doing little to
promote social equity or environmental sustainability in their broader
surroundings. Looking at the design renderings and promotional literature of Tangshan Caofeidian International Eco-City, for example,
one can be forgiven for thinking that this could be a city potentially
anywhere – a 'ubiquitous' eco-city in the true sense of the word, and
an impression which cannot have been entirely unintended by its
developers (Joss and Molella, 2013).

Such impressions may be misleading, of course. In the case of the
eco-city (as in other fields of policy-making), it may be too simplistic
to interpret what Peck and Theodore (2001) label the tendency
towards global 'fast policy transfer' as a process whereby the practices of the 'Global North' are crudely imposed on the 'Global

South'. Just as local economic outcomes are determined by the inter-action between place-specific factors and global forces (Shatkin, 2008), 'imported' policies are typically translated and reinterpreted by local actors in specific contexts (see e.g. Peck and Theodore, 2001: 428; Nasr and Volait, 2003; Watson, 2009: 7; McCann, 2010: 123), and often reshaped by specific interactions between actors during their 'journey' from one country to another (McCann, 2010). Chang and Sheppard (2013) come to similar conclusions in their study of the Chongming Eco-Island and Dongtan Eco-City projects (both located near Shanghai); while both clearly 'belong to a global diffusion of urban sustainability initiatives', they are equally 'embedded in and layered onto pre-existing socioeconomic institu-tions and cultural contexts' (ibid.: 61). Similarly, Rapoport (2014) has observed that, although master planning of large new-build eco-cities is usually conducted by a relatively small group of North American and European firms, this is very much at the invitation of local actors. The generic (and Western) appearance of what is envis-aged may belie the fact that master plans are understood by local clients as constituting an initial stage of the development only, more like a 'bundle or menu of options' (ibid.: 5) from which to choose. It would seem likely, furthermore, that the geographies of this knowl-edge transfer may change in future as Middle Eastern and Asian firms are developing an 'increasingly global reach' (ibid.: 4). If the business of the eco-city reflects other trade patterns evident within globalization, then what has become known as 'south-south global-ization' (Murshed et al., 2011) may come to be increasingly impor-tant – with China's growing economic involvement in infrastructural projects in Africa (Power et al., 2012) being one relevant example.

While, then, the 'globalization' of urban sustainability is a far from straightforward process, it nevertheless points towards a mindset in which policies and technologies are fundamentally transferable, even if they are likely to be modified to some extent when implemented in different locations. In contrast, the example of Portland points to an alternative approach in contemporary eco-city development; one that is more deeply anchored within established, local urban policy and culture and, therefore, more directly defined by place-specific features and processes. Tellingly, however, even with its longstanding tradition of local engagement in urban sustainability and home-grown eco-city initiatives, Portland recently felt the need to collaborate more interna-tionally when it signed up, in 2012, to the Climate+ Development Program of the Clinton Climate Initiative. However, the converse argument can be made, too: in the case of Songdo, the original intention by its developers to render the city essentially as an international ubiquitous eco-city evolved – due to a lack of international investment and local political processes – into a development much more closely characterized by local features and dynamics, in what Shwayri (2013) dubbed a process of 'Koreanization'. Either way, internationalization has clearly become a key feature of contemporary eco-city development – even if this trend is only one of many factors shaping plans and practices on the ground.

Learning from the big picture

Any attempt to develop a global picture of the sustainable city aimed at revealing both the breadth and depth of development will inevitably encounter some conceptual difficulties and reach methodological limits. For one thing, there is the challenge of how to deal with the diversity of approaches and initiatives in a meaningful way – that is, in a way which recognizes and makes sense of diversity, while at the same time managing to identify overarching trends, patterns and themes. Focus the lens too narrowly – say, exclusively on new-build eco-cities – and the gain in sharpness of focus may be outweighed by the loss of sight of the wider picture, which includes the significant eco-city innovation taking place within existing cities and through urban expansion. Focus the lens too widely – say, on any initiatives carried out loosely in the name of urban sustainability – and the gain in wide focus may result in a blurred picture overall. For another, there is the methodological challenge of how to capture the multitude of eco-city initiatives given their global reach and, relatedly, how to process and make sense of the associated abundance of information in a way which is analytically robust and practically manageable.

There is a further inherent difficulty involved in developing a global picture of contemporary eco-cities: what the picture manages to capture inevitably always remains limited and partial. After all, the sustainability of a city is closely defined in terms of its particular place: the specific geographical, socio-economic, political and cultural features, dynamics and contexts. Only close-up and in-depth analysis will properly reveal what makes the sustainable city. Moreover, as a majority of eco-city initiatives are still under development, what the picture reveals are glimpses of what the future eco-city might look like – based on master plans, policy declarations and promotional literature – as projected by those promoting these very initiatives. The full picture may only come into view in due course if and when eco-city initiatives are implemented; and then, again, it will need to be viewed and interpreted in relation to specific places and contexts. What is more, a city is, or at least should be, so much more – more multifaceted, complex and rich – than can be captured through a singular focus on the 'eco-city' – or, for that matter, 'energy city', 'solar city', 'low-carbon city', 'smart city', 'resilient city' etc. The focus on the eco-city may reveal one picture – albeit arguably an important one – when there are several other pictures equally characterizing and representing the life of the city.

In spite of these limitations and reservations, trying to develop a global picture of contemporary eco-city developments is both useful and necessary, in order to track developments across time, identify trends and characterize patterns. What such a picture reveals are several telling developments in urban sustainability over the last few decades. First, there have been significant longitudinal shifts: the 1970s and 1980s were something of an experimental phase, during which ideas and concepts of the eco-city were developed against the background of raising environmental awareness and with practical initiatives few and far between. The 1990s saw a significant main-streaming of urban sustainability in terms both of the concept of the sustainable city taking hold in policy-making and of increasing prac-tical applications on the ground. As discussed in Chapter 3, this period coincided with the establishment of sustainable development as a broad, global policy goal following the 1992 Earth Summit in Rio. More recently, since the early 2000s, eco-city initiatives have become more ubiquitous still: they are found in growing numbers across global regions – the eco-city has become as much a phenome-non of the Global South, as it used to be one mainly of the Global North; they involve more diverse actors – individual cities; city networks; national governments; international governmental organ-izations; global architecture, engineering and technology firms; social enterprises – and they are developed through increasing inter-national co-operation.

The second broad trend concerns the shift towards urban in-fill and new-build developments. Throughout the 1980s and 1990s, eco-city innovation was mainly conceptualized and implemented in relation to existing cities. Since the 2000s, a new breed of eco-city initiatives has emerged, defined by the large-scale, commercial rede-velopment of urban brownfield sites – such as the transformation of defunct port areas into sustainable creative-commercial hubs (e.g. Hamburg-Harburg, Stockholm Royal Seaport, Thames Gateway) –

and even larger-scale new-build initiatives aspiring to become regional and international commercial and cultural centres (e.g. Masdar, Songdo, Tianjin Binhai). Back in the 1990s, the call to take up the cause of urban sustainability was chiefly directed, under the global policy framework of Local Agenda 21, at municipal governments and other public local authorities. Consequently, urban sustainability – encompassing the 'three pillars' of environmental, economic and social development – was discussed as part of municipal policy-making and translated into initiatives applied to existing urban infrastructure and services. This discussion continues unabated, but it has since been complemented with a turn towards urban in-fill and new-build developments. This turn has brought new, private actors – land developers, architecture practices, engineering consultancies, technology firms, financial institutions etc. – onto the stage, who drive forward various eco-city initiatives on a mainly commercial basis. Under the currently dominant conceptual perspective of 'green growth' and 'ecological modernization', the eco-city has indeed become squared: the ecological city is (propositioned as) an economic city. In this context, the analytical distinction between 'retrofit', 'urban expansion' and 'new-build' developments is particularly useful as a way of identifying global trends and pinpointing key differences in conceptual and practical approaches found in contemporary eco-city initiatives.

A third trend concerns the more overt and explicit use of technological concepts, systems and solutions in the way eco-city initiatives are envisioned, designed and implemented. This is partly explained by the concerted global policy focus on climate change, and particularly CO_2 and other GHG emissions, in the post-Kyoto era, prompting in some cases an almost single-minded perspective on energy-related technological schemes and solutions. It is, however, also partly explained by the realization of related commercial opportunities: as cities and national governments look to private developers, engineering groups and technology firms to finance, design and implement urban sustainability strategies as part of urban expansion and new development projects, it is not surprising to see a shift towards a more technologically formulated concept of the eco-city. The eco-city conceptualized as an 'urban metabolism' and 'urban operating system' reflects a current predilection for technocratic discourses, which naturally call technological approaches and solutions onto the plan.

Noting these broad features of the contemporary eco-city, it once again needs emphasizing that the current diversity of initiatives includes many an example where these trends are moderated by local contexts and conditions, as a consequence of which the picture of urban sustainability on the ground is often particularly intricate and complex, defying easy categorization. Furthermore, there are also notable counter-examples predicated on alternative visions of, and approaches to, urban sustainability. These need equal attention in the effort to develop an in-depth understanding of the sustainable city.

Conclusions

The last three decades or so have seen a remarkable evolution in the practice of sustainable city development, from the original, few pioneer projects in the 1980s, via the proliferation of local urban sustainability initiatives in the post-1992 period, through to the current breed of international 'energy', 'low-carbon' and 'smart' eco-city initiatives spread increasingly across the Global North and Global South. A core direction of development has long been along the route of sustainable development, emphasizing the three pillars of environmental, social and economic development and embedding this within existing municipal policy and contexts. Complementing this, a more recent tendency has emerged for high-profile, iconic urban in-fill and new-build developments to be promoted as major innovation hubs and investment opportunity to an international audience. In the pursuit of 'green growth' and 'ecological modernization', this more recent development has brought onto the scene a new set of global players and has foregrounded a more technocratic discourse centred upon the notion of the sustainable city as 'metabolism' and 'operating system' to be guided by hi-tech solutions. In turn, this has prompted new ways of thinking about how best to plan, co-ordinate, implement and monitor urban sustainability. In other words, governance has moved centre stage in the discussion of how to bring about the eco-city.

Chapter 5

New Governance Challenges

CHAPTER OVERVIEW

There is widespread recognition of the need for a new paradigm of governance for urban planning and development. This is centred upon the demand for greater integration across urban scales and systems, and stronger engagement of diverse stakeholders in policy- and decision-making processes. The need is particularly pronounced in the debate about urban sustainability; some even see governance as the core constituting element of what makes the sustainable city. Based on two case studies of contemporary urban sustainability initiatives – Treasure Island (San Francisco) and Portland (Oregon), both in the US – this chapter provides insight into what this new-mode governance looks like, how it is conditioned by particular contexts, and how it reflects and shapes the contemporary discourse on the sustainable city. In doing so, the chapter highlights the strong normative influences at work which re-cast the city and sustainability in significant – and potentially problematic – ways.

Introduction: questioning the governance consensus

A consensus appears to be emerging, according to which the sustainable city is to be realized through new governance, based on collaborative partnership and integrated planning and development. What is more, governance is not just understood as a necessary means by which to achieve urban sustainability; rather, it is considered a core essence of what defines the contemporary and future sustainable city.

The centrality of governance is typically explained with reference to three distinct, yet related arguments, as outlined in Chapter 2. First, sustainable development in general, and urban sustainability in particular, bring together environmental, economic and social considerations in complex interplay; in turn, this directs attention to how the resulting multiple relationships are governed and what types of intervention might be appropriate to help facilitate sustainable development. In the urban context, particular questions are raised about how sustainability initiatives are related to different urban infrastructure, systems and scales and, especially, how urban sustainability intervention at one level – say, the neighbourhood or district – is interconnected with policy and planning at other levels – the wider city or urban region, for example – and vice versa, so as to effect integrated development. Attention to governance, then, is seen as essential to be able, on one hand, to analyse and understand and, consequently, on the other, to facilitate and steer the processes of co-ordination and integration required for sustainable urban development.

Second, governance has moved centre stage owing to the recognition of the need to mobilize diverse actors in urban sustainability processes. There is by now an established assumption and acknowledgement that municipal authorities – or for that matter, national governments – cannot go it alone and that they, therefore, need to develop and implement sustainable city initiatives in partnership with other public and private organizations. In particular, commercial developers, technology and consultancy firms, and financial investors are widely seen as instrumental to realizing large-scale initiatives which require substantial financial, technical and organizational input. Relatedly, the third argument for the focus on governance is the demand for collaborative, public engagement. The expectation here is that by involving relevant stakeholders – residents, neighbourhood associations, interest groups, civil society organizations, etc. – the openness and accountability of planning and decision-making processes can be assured and enhanced. What is more, since sustainable urban development is increasingly recognized as being decisively conditioned by, and thus dependent on, individual and social behaviour and action – and so no longer exclusively a matter of government- and expert-led policy and planning – a focus on engagement becomes a key concern for governance processes.

This three-fold argument has created a powerful, normative governance paradigm for urban sustainability; this favours collaborative forms of urban planning and innovation which focus on building co-ordinative capacity – that is, the ability to facilitate and achieve integration across urban sustainability policies, systems, action levels and actor networks. In doing so, it creates and privileges a particular discourse on the sustainable city, which is cast essentially in terms of governance. This discourse is often presented as something new and innovative, a departure from previous ways of conceptualizing urban sustainability and related planning and decision-making.

Two recent examples illustrate the emergence of this new paradigm, not least in policy circles. The first relates to the World Bank's Eco2 Cities initiative (for an overview, see Chapter 3). The choice of terminology – Eco2 Cities – not only refers to the close interrelationship between environmental and economic urban sustainability – 'ecological cities as economic cities' – but also signals the arrival of what the World Bank calls a second generation of eco-cities following in the footsteps of the first wave of pilot eco-cities emerging from the 1970s and 1980s: 'Eco2 city is a useful term for recognizing a new generation of eco cities that move beyond individual, stand-alone green measures to a systems perspective ... It requires that a city be understood as a whole' (Suzuki et al., 2010: xx). Consequently – echoing the discussion in Chapter 2 of the city conceptualized as urban metabolism and adaptive system – a 'one-system approach' is advocated, with a corresponding focus on integration:

> The one-system approach aims to take full advantage of all opportunities for integration by promoting a view of the city and the urban environment as a complete system. Once we see the city and the urban environment as a system, it is easier for us to design the elements to work well together. This may mean enhancing the efficiency of resource flows in an urban area through integrated infrastructure system design and management ... By applying the one-system approach, cities and their surrounding natural and rural areas can strive to coalesce into a functional system that works well as a new whole. (Suzuki et al., 2010: 4–5)

On the basis of this 'one-system approach', one of the core principles of the Eco2 Cities initiative is collaborative governance, which is defined as '... an expanded platform for collaborative design and decision-making that accomplishes sustained synergy by co-ordinating and aligning the actions of key stakeholders' (Suzuki et al., 2010: 3). The benefit of collaboration is seen in the joining up of interests, skills and expertise to enable the realization of urban sustainability projects:

> All stakeholders and project partners bring a unique combination of policy tools based on their mandates, skills and resources. Part

of the challenge in cities implementing new projects is ensuring that all stakeholders have aligned their existing policies and programs and are using their particular strengths to support the project goals and strategies. By collaborating with senior levels of government, local utilities, private sector corporations, and nongovernmental organizations, one creates the potential for a broad and diverse suite of policy tools. A collaborative process may be able to identify potential actions for the public at large and for individuals with special talents or interests. (Suzuki et al., 2010: 81)

The second example demonstrating the new urban sustainability governance paradigm at work comes from the French think tank La Fabrique de la Cité ('the urban factory'), which was founded in 2010 with the mission to 'promote discussion and leadership on urban innovation' centred upon three thematic strands: adaptation of existing cities, sustainable mobility and urban economy (La Fabrique de la Cité, 2013: 2). Based on an international gathering of several dozen urban experts in 2013 in Stockholm – where the city's Hammarby Sjöstad and Royal Seaport urban sustainability initiatives (see Chapter 4) served as inspiration and case studies – the think tank published an overview report on the 'city of tomorrow' which, in response to the challenges of urban sustainability and regeneration, places new governance at the heart of urban innovation processes:

Making the city more innovative is about rethinking the urban model to give it the opportunity of inventing new ways of working. First of all, this means a change of governance, which must now be a collective and inclusive process involving public decision-makers, the private sector, non-profit organizations, the academic world and citizens themselves. (La Fabrique de la Cité, 2013: 6)

Cities that have succeeded in rethinking their governance models have embraced dynamic transformation. Decision-makers and investors understand that bringing all stakeholders together massively increases the chances of successful delivery of urban projects, regardless of whether those projects focus on housing, shops, transport, inter-community links or public spaces. The era of top-down thinking has had its day, to be replaced by collaborative and co-operative working. (La Fabrique de la Cité, 2013: 7)

Governance is not only given prominence here, but also apparently celebrated as a departure from previous schools of urban policy and planning. The strong normative stance towards searching for and applying innovative forms of collaborative decision-making and development, evident in both examples above and elsewhere, prompts important questions about the nature, validity and significance of this purportedly new paradigm. This chapter seeks to make a critical contribution to this discussion by addressing the following three interrelated questions: (1) what form such collaborative governance takes, and what related governance dynamics arise; (2) what kind of urban sustainability is produced as a result; and, (3) how this shapes and recasts the discourse on, and politics of, the sustainable city. These questions are discussed based on two empirical cases of the new urban governance at work: Treasure Island, a sustainable urban in-fill development in the city of San Francisco (California); and the EcoDistricts retrofitting initiative originating in Portland (Oregon). The two cases are introduced here because they each exhibit some telling characteristics of new governance; indeed, the initiatives have been explicitly defined by their promoters in terms of the centrality of new modes of collaborative planning and development. At the same time, both initiatives have emerged from, and are necessarily set within, existing wider regulatory and decision-making structures; this provides nuanced insights into the dynamics – and some tensions – between 'old' and 'new' governance processes in play.

While the examples of Treasure Island and EcoDistricts contribute useful perspectives on the emergence of new urban sustainability governance processes in practice, they should at the same time not be read as epitomizing new-mode urban sustainability governance per se. After all, there are diverse other examples – approaches, tools and practices – of integration, co-ordination and collaboration to be found in relation to sustainable city initiatives; and the particular experiences of the two cases here have to be understood closely in relation to their specific contexts. (And there may even be places and instances, where governance plays only a limited role compared with traditional government.) The governance features and dynamics observed can, therefore, be expected to look somewhat different in other initiatives and contexts. Nevertheless, as exemplars, Treasure Island and EcoDistricts both point to tendencies that, beyond their particular context specificity, are arguably more widely symptomatic of recent discourses on urban sustainability governance. These common tendencies are considered in detail following the discussion of each case in turn.

Treasure Island

'A signature project' is how Treasure Island, a 450-acre (1.8 km²) new urban development planned for San Francisco, is heralded by the city's planning department in its sustainable development programme (San Francisco Planning Department, undated). With similar enthusiasm, the city's statutory body charged with overseeing the development of Treasure Island promotes it as a 'demonstration project' of how urban sustainability can be realized, and promises that the life of the built environment in this new city district 'will be measured over generations, not decades' (TIDA, undated). Such a long-term view will be needed, considering how long the project has already been in the making to date and how long it is yet expected to take until completion: for the last ten years or so, Treasure Island has been planned as an exemplary sustainable urban initiative involving lengthy negotiations with various private developers and public bodies and following extensive public consultation. Development agreement was eventually reached in 2011. By early 2014, land preparation was ongoing, as this former US naval base first requires extensive decontamination before construction of the 8,000 new homes, plus additional commercial buildings and retail space, can begin. Meanwhile, the private developers involved have had to renew their search for investors, following the sudden withdrawal in 2013 of the China Development Bank and the Chinese Railway Construction Corporation from a financing deal which the city's mayor had been involved in brokering (Matier and Ross, 2013). Consequently, the date of completion may well eventually have to be revised from the original target of approximately 2020–5.

As an exemplary sustainable city initiative, Treasure Island exhibits many of the characteristics typical of 'new' urban sustainability governance (Joss, 2011a): it consists of a complex web of governance structures and processes, with a multitude of actors – municipal government, regulatory authorities, federal agencies, global architecture and consultancy firms, housing developers, non-governmental organizations, community groups, international financiers, professional associations, etc. – involved in various capacities, at numerous levels and in multiple relationships; it includes extensive development periods marked by elaborate planning, negotiation and implementation processes; and it entails a complex governance discourse mixing technical data, policy information and public debate. Treasure Island is concurrently defined in terms of economic growth, social opportunity and environmental benefits; and it is constituted not only as a neighbourhood development, but also as a city initiative, a landmark regional destination, a national project, and an international collaborative enterprise, with diverse networks and processes to match. Inevitably, then, when attempting to capture and make sense of this initiative – as is similarly the case with many sustainable city initiatives – one is confronted with a wealth of complex information and elaborate arrangements and relationships. Not surprisingly, therefore, when the different players involved are asked to discuss the initiative, they invariably draw attention to the central issue of governance.

Key features

Treasure Island's promoters do not hold back with ambition: the initiative is to become an 'exemplary model of sustainable living' (TICD, 2006: 4), a 'new regional destination', even 'the most sustainable large development project in the United States' (San Francisco Office of Economic and Workforce Development, 2010). Treasure Island is planned as a mixed-use, high-density city district consisting of some 8,000 residential units designed to accommodate around 18,600 people, and about 240,000 square feet of new commercial and retail space (the following targets and indicators are taken from the official sustainability plan: TIDA, 2011). A large proportion of the island – some 300 acres – will be converted into open space, including a 22-acre organic farm, recreational parkland, and about 15 acres of wetlands. The latter are designed to treat storm water, as well as to provide natural habitat for native species. The transport strategy favours integrated public transit infrastructure consisting of ferry and bus services to the city centre, while on the island itself public transport is to be provided by electric shuttle buses. The street layout integrates bicycle lanes and pedestrian walkways. A congestion charging scheme is planned for private car use. The overall aim is for 90 per cent of the population to live and work within 15 minutes of public transit and the town centre; the shift to public transport based on these measures is expected to avoid an additional 12,000 person trips across the existing Bay Bridge – the bridge connecting the island with San Francisco city centre – and to reduce transport-related CO_2 emissions by 2,800 tonnes annually.

The waste reduction and recycling strategy includes: provision for 25 per cent waste water recycling (for grey water use) and biogas capture from waste water; the recycling of 75 per cent of non-

Table 5.1 *Treasure Island's urban sustainability features*

Key features/data
- 450-acre in-fill development (of which two-thirds will be open space/parks)
- Up to 8,000 residential units (estimated population 18,640)
- Average density of 95–100 dwelling units per acre in residential zones
- Lower-density, clustered development on neighbouring Yerba Buena Island
- 24,000 sq. feet of commercial space
- New ferry (and improved bus service) will connect to downtown San Francisco
- Positioned to achieve LEED Neighbourhood Development Gold certification

Environmental	*Social*	*Economic*
On-site renewable energy	New parks/open space including Urban Agricultural Park	A quarter or more homes 'affordable'
Reduced GHG emissions, in-home smart meters, and ambition of carbon neutrality	New pedestrian/hiking and cycle trails	Retail, hotel and office space
Limited parking spaces, electric vehicle charging stations, and congestion charging for cars	Short walk for most residents to transit hub and retail services	Active encouragement for green businesses
On-site waste water treatment	Preservation and adaptive reuse of historic properties	Positive net revenue for City's General Fund
Wetland habitat creation	Financial help to rehouse existing residents	Job creation (during construction and permanent)
Landscaping with 'native or regionally appropriate' species	Wide range of community facilities/spaces	Sustainable funding mechanism being sought for transport, open space maintenance, adaptive management, and affordable housing development
Land allocated for urban farm	Fibre-optic broadband for all households	
All organic waste used to produce energy or compost	Natural ventilation and daylight	
Bins for recyclables and compostables in public areas	Street grid maximises solar exposure on open spaces, provides shelter from wind, and views of regional landmarks and downtown	
Construction and demolition waste recycled or salvaged		
Possible central utility plant and automated waste system		
Able to manage 'more than 55" of sea level rise'		

Source: Treasure Island Sustainability Plan (TIDA, 2011).

hazardous solid waste; onsite organic waste composting and biogas facilities, to treat and recycle 100 per cent of organic waste produced on the island; and the use of recycled materials (ten per cent of total construction materials) in buildings. Concerning energy production and consumption, all grid-source power is to be from renewable hydro-electric power, with on-site photovoltaics providing 5 per cent of peak energy demand. Building and infrastructure energy efficiency is estimated at 15 per cent compared with the 'lowest cost alternative' (ibid.: 9). Carbon neutrality in operations – thus, excluding carbon emissions during construction – is envisaged 'over the long-term if economically and technically feasible' (ibid.: 11).

The project also includes various social and economic sustainability components including: 25–30 per cent affordable residential housing; 435 units for formerly homeless people managed by the Treasure Island Homeless Development Initiative (TIHDI); local employment through the creation of 2,000 jobs during construction, followed by 2,500 permanent jobs in the commercial centre. Table 5.1 summarizes the initiative's key features and sustainability measures. While the Treasure Island sustainability plan is tailor-made, with unique design and performance specifications, it also incorporates city-wide policy frameworks, such as the City of San Francisco Sustainability Plan and the Healthy Development Measurement Tool, as well as complying with various statutory requirements. Furthermore, it integrates several international frameworks and standards, including LEED ND (a sustainability standard for neighbourhood development – see Chapter 6), the Climate Positive Development Program (Chapter 6) and the UN Urban Environmental Accords.

Extensive preparations

Given the expectations set up by images in design renderings, sustainability documents and master plans, envisioning Treasure Island as a future urban sustainability landmark, a visitor to the site in 2010, and again a couple of years later, could easily have been underwhelmed. Despite the initiative's decade in the making, very little visible progress can be detected; on the surface at least, there is barely any evidence of the profound transformation in store for this brownfield site (see Illustration 5.1). Two factors account for this: first, while Treasure Island constitutes a 'clean-slate' approach – a new sustainable neighbourhood development built from scratch – it nevertheless requires substantial preparatory horizontal development even before vertical construction can commence, owing to the fact that the site is a decommissioned naval base situated on an artificial island. Following the closure of the US Navy base and the official hand-over of the site to the State of California in the late 1990s, by the early 2010s laborious soil decontamination work – including the removal of industrial sludge and radioactive waste – was still ongoing, overseen by the Navy (Smith and Miezskowsk, 2014). Once decontaminated, further horizontal development will be required to get the site ready for the significant vertical development planned, and especially to prepare this low-lying island in San Francisco Bay for sea level rises (estimated to be in the region of 30 inches) anticipated over the course of the next century. The second reason for the lack of visible transformation to date lies in the lengthy and complex process of putting in place a comprehensive governance arrangement for the Treasure Island initiative, in the form of an elaborate public-private partnership (PPP). This process was initiated in 2003 and reached an intermediate conclusion in 2011 when the development agreement was signed by all parties involved (TIDA, 2011).

Public–private partnership as governance instrument

If and when Treasure Island is eventually built, residents and visitors will likely judge its accomplishment in terms of the quality of the built environment and the performance of the various sustainability measures currently promised. Probably less noticeable, but arguably just as important for its success or otherwise, is the underlying public–private partnership (PPP). Certainly, according to a representative of the Treasure Island Development Authority, this tailor-made governance arrangement is a unique feature of Treasure Island and 'the single key aspect that will allow the project to be implemented' (Joss, 2011a: 334).

Public–private partnerships come in multiple forms and sizes, but invariably – as the term implies – they consist of a partnership between one or more public organizations and one or more private organizations; this partnership is formalized through a binding agreement that sets out the individual and joint responsibilities of the partners involved, and defines the various elements and phases of the project to be implemented (for an overview, see e.g. Rosenau, 2000; Akintoye et al., 2003; Hodge and Greve, 2007). Following the call for 'partnerships for sustainable development' made at the UN 'Earth Summit' in Johannesburg in 2002, PPPs of one form or

Illustration 5.1

Treasure Island: (i) future prospect (ca. 2020–25);
(ii) interim situation (2010)

Sources: (i) http://sftreasureisland.org; (ii) author's photograph.

another have become increasingly popular as a governance mechanism for sustainable development (see e.g. Pattberg et al., 2012).

In the case of Treasure Island, the centrepiece of the PPP is a statu-
tory Disposition and Development Agreement (henceforth, DDA)
(TIDA and TICD, 2011), a legal contract between a redevelopment
agency (the public partner) and developers (the private partner). The
Treasure Island Development Agency (henceforth, TIDA) is constituted as the redevelopment agency, a legal entity of the State of
California but in practice run through the office of the mayor of San
Francisco. The private side is represented by the Treasure Island
Community Development (henceforth, TICD), which is a consortium of two main private actors each with a 50 per cent share:
Lennar, the third-largest US home builder, backed by several silent
investors; and Wilson Meany Sullivan, a major building company
with expertise in retail and commercial building, joined by capital
investment firms Stockbridge Capital and Kenwood Investments.
Also involved in the PPP – although without formal incorporation –
are the Treasure Island Citizens Advisory Board, a consultative body
of TIDA, and the Treasure Island Homeless Development Initiative,
a non-governmental organization representing the interests of
homeless and low-income residents. Numerous other regulatory
agencies and public and non-governmental organizations have been
indirectly involved in the PPP by, for example, providing environmental impact assessments and making various interest representations during public consultation and the formal decision-making
process leading up to the signing of the DDA.

The disposition aspect of the Treasure Island PPP defines the way
in which the land is conveyed from the Navy to TIDA and subse-

quently to TICD and the related financial transactions involved. TICD pays the Navy for the purchase of the land on behalf of TIDA. In addition, TICD pays on behalf of the city for the various sustainability and public benefit elements built into the DDA. This is done through the sequencing of the project into consecutive development phases: the first of four phases runs from 2011 to 2015 and is mainly defined in terms of horizontal development; the subsequent three phases will entail vertical construction – residential, business and retail buildings, parks, the community farm, etc. For each phase, TICD is required to raise performance bonds on the financial market as security for the completion of the work. TICD will be able to recoup the investment during the later phases by developing the designated private land and subsequently selling residential and business properties, and/or selling land off to third-party private developers. (All public buildings and space will remain in public ownership, to be administered by TIDA.) From TIDA's perspective, this arrangement means that the agency will not have to access general public funding to finance the project – Treasure Island does not feature on the city's budget – and it will not pay upfront for the significant horizontal costs. Instead, it will repay these costs over a period of three decades once the new district is completed through tax and service charge income generated from residents and businesses based on the island.

The PPP and sustainability

Significantly, closely knitted into the DDA are extensive, binding sustainability goals – including detailed specification concerning the creation of biodiverse wetlands and green parks, and the generation of onsite renewable energy – as well as various social and economic benefits, such as affordable housing, sheltered accommodation and local business development. The close integration of substantive sustainability components into the governance mechanism is arguably a unique, innovative feature of this PPP; this centrally defines the approach to urban sustainability (Joss, 2011a). The process by which sustainability became so firmly integrated into the PPP reveals an interesting and perhaps unexpected relationship at work: initially, in the late 1990s when TIDA was set up as a public corporation and subsequently in the early 2000s began planning on the redevelopment of Treasure Island, the agency proposed a low-density suburban development alongside an adult entertainment centre. Sustainability only played a marginal role in this original vision. This met with increasing public opposition, with residents and community organizations vociferously calling for the significant scaling up of the project's sustainability aspects. This coincided with a push at the time by the then mayor of San Francisco for a decidedly more green development agenda for the city, culminating, among other initiatives, in the UN World Environment Day 2005 hosted by the city, which produced the international Urban Environmental Accords signed by 60 mayors from across the world.

The actual change to an explicitly more sustainability-oriented development for Treasure Island itself only fully occurred in 2003, once TICD entered into an exclusive negotiating agreement with TIDA. TICD was, therefore, an important catalyst for the initiative's redirection and the emerging new urban sustainability vision. As representatives of TICD partners explained, it was at around that time, in the early 2000s, that developers began to consider sustainability as a serious commercial proposition (Joss, 2011a: 338). Adopting the sustainability agenda began to make business sense, with major opportunities to develop urban markets and work on urban (in-fill) projects. As one partner explained, it was the TICD partners who first had to reach a decision to embrace sustainability – even if it was more risky in terms of cost control and acceptability than conventional development – since in the PPP arrangement being negotiated all capital risks would come to rest with the private developers. It was at this point, as a consequence of TICD's engagement with the sustainability agenda, that TIDA itself began to show more active interest and leadership in the sustainability vision for Treasure Island. Since then, the agency has been instrumental in defining the various urban sustainability components and related targets and performance measures, as reflected in the DDA documents.

A consequence of the rigorous attempts to integrate the urban sustainability features in the PPP is the detailed and rather technical specification of various sustainability elements. The way sustainability is articulated is ultimately the product of lengthy, contractual negotiations between TIDA and TICD: the former tried to build as many sustainability elements and related targets as possible into the agreement; the latter – while committed overall – was commercially wary of the associated costs to be incurred and the level of investment return achievable. The sequential phasing of the development, while helpful in terms of managing the project across a long time trajectory, according TICD representatives, nevertheless required 'walking a fine line' between TIDA and TICD, and created something of an 'understandable tension' between managing the financial risks and limiting guarantees (TICD's concerns) and ensuring public benefits at each phasing stage (TIDA's concerns) (Joss, 2011a: 342).

The focus on mutually agreeable targets in this closely negotiated relationship may have meant that urban sustainability in this case is less ambitiously defined than for some comparable initiatives in terms of, for example, green building requirements, sustainable transport modes and carbon emission performance (Joss, 2011a). This may be compounded by the fact that neither side of the partnership – as public agency overseeing the development and as private developers focusing on commercial opportunities – is necessarily known as sustainability innovators per se, and neither will be directly involved in developing and implementing the various sustainability solutions. For example, the sustainability plan – a central plank in the DDA – was developed on commission by an international engineering consultancy external to the PPP; and the various planned sustainability features will need to be designed, tested and put in place by as yet unspecified sustainability specialists. For example, the sustainable development plan envisages district energy which, however, will depend on 'partner[ing] with a third party to deploy and deliver district energy and/or waste to energy services should they be technically and financially viable' (TIDA, 2011: 34).

A further challenge in developing an urban sustainability strategy through a PPP, such as in the case of Treasure Island, is to achieve a productive balance between specifying urban sustainability targets and measures upfront in a binding way and retaining sufficient flexibility to be able to adapt planning at later stages, for example in response to emerging new technologies or changing environmental or socio-economic parameters. As noted, the sustainability plan assumes a continuous scaling up towards 'progressively higher standards', but this is expressed in the form of ambitions rather than binding mandates, given the nature of the PPP.

The PPP and public accountability

As a formal, contractual relationship, Treasure Island's PPP might run the risk of impeding open, collaborative planning and decision-making – as often called for under 'new' governance for sustainability – beyond the partnership itself. Certainly, elsewhere there have been examples of PPPs where public accountability, transparency and legitimacy were severely tested due to the complexity and technicality of the arrangements involved as well as the use of commercial confidentiality arguments (Joss, 2010; Pattberg et al., 2012). In comparison, the Treasure Island initiative appears relatively open, as judged by the ready access to materials – all DDA-related documents are in the public domain, listed on TIDA's website (TIDA, undated) – the level of public deliberation, and the degree of media scrutiny. Those involved in the initiative put this down to San Francisco's freedom of information legislation, locally known as 'sunshine ordinance': this requires an 'open book' approach, according to which all meetings hosted by TIDA are open to the public, and all PPP parties involved are required to work from one set of publicly available plans (Joss, 2011a: 339). TIDA has led extensive consultation processes, through the Treasure Island Citizens Advisory Board, dozens of public hearings and community meetings involving local residents. From TICD's perspective, this open, transparent process means that the PPP relationship amounts to 'negotiating in a fish bowl' (ibid.: 341). Evidence of this can be seen in media reporting, including several probing, in-depth reports by investigative journalists (see, for example, the special issue on Treasure Island by *San Francisco Public Press*, 2010; or reports by *The Bay Citizen* such as Bay City News Service, 2011; Mieszkowski and Smith, 2012).

In spite of this relative openness, there are factors in play that impact on the collaborative potential of the governance arrangement. This includes the fact that, as a PPP, Treasure Island's financing is wholly dependent on TICD, whose partners are, in turn, dependent on 'silent investors' and other third-party backers. This removes an element of financial transparency and related possibility for public scrutiny that would be expected in comparable initiatives realized through public funding. Furthermore, the nature of the PPP is such that the partners have effectively formed a joint project team, working closely together on a daily basis. (And it may be a surprise for a researcher, when arranging to interview TIDA representatives about the initiative, to be invited to a meeting in the city hall's offices at which TICD partners are present (Joss, 2011a).) Such a project-based, close working relationship is clearly a necessity if the partnership is to be strong and effective; nevertheless, the unintended consequence could be that the relationship between the partners becomes blurred or even indistinguishable, at least in the public's eye.

Additional factors impacting on the open, collaborative potential of the initiative are both the sheer volume and the technical nature of information produced. While documents can be accessed with relative ease, this does not automatically mean that information is readily accessible to non-experts. For example, the DDA (TIDA and TICD, 2011) is a lengthy document of 961 pages: it comprehensively sets out the Treasure Island project and the contents of the PPP and it includes an array of supporting documents – so-called 'exhibits' – including the sustainability plan. As such, all relevant materials are presented in their entirety, open for scrutiny. Yet it requires a level of expertise to be able to engage with technical and legal information pertaining, for example, to the minimum slopes between grade breaks in the 'saw tooth grading scheme' for streets (TIDA and TICD, 2011: 736), to 'reversionary quitclaim deeds' (ibid.: 39), or to a 'transitioning household that is not a post-transition household' (ibid.: 268). Even investigative journalists, accustomed to scrutinizing complex issues of public interest, refer to the 'immensely complicated' nature of this PPP (Joss, 2011a: 341). TICD partners themselves concede that the PPP has created a large amount of documentation which may not be easily accessible to the wider public due to the technical complexity and jargon involved (ibid.).

A paradox?

It is too early yet to say how Treasure Island will eventually come to look and whether the initiative will manage to fulfil its promise of being an 'exemplary model of sustainable living', and even 'the most sustainable large development project in the United States'. What is certain is that, assuming the project proceeds as planned, it will take another decade or so until completion, following more than a decade already spent intensively planning and developing this signature initiative. What is, moreover, evident is the centrality of governance processes in driving forward, and as a consequence profoundly shaping, Treasure Island.

One could be forgiven for gaining the impression that the PPP at work in this case produces a mode of new urban sustainability governance that is somewhat paradoxical: on one hand, the form of, and mechanism for, urban sustainability are made very clear and explicit through the formal partnership arrangement; on the other, they are inherently technically and legally complex and sophisticated; at one level, the arrangement is open, with transparent information about the nature of the PPP; at another level, it remains opaque, with a wider hinterland of private interests and connections difficult to scrutinize; again, on one hand, the arrangement places the city authorities centre stage – Treasure Island is to be a showcase of San Francisco's claim to being a premier sustainable destination – while, on the other, it creates a fundamental dependency on private, even international, investment beyond the control even of the city's mayor; and, relatedly, at one level, the PPP mechanism embeds Treasure Island in the city's urban planning and sustainability strategy whereas, at another level, it removes it from this framework by treating the initiative as a separate project, even based on a separate parcel of land away from existing communities.

Of course, this seemingly paradoxical nature of the Treasure Island PPP might need to be appreciated as the complex reality of contemporary urban sustainability governance at work. Still, it invites some preliminary reflections on how this 'new' governance for urban sustainability is to be understood, given the frequently unequivocal, optimistic claims made (see Introduction to this chapter). First, in this case at least, the continuous importance of government involvement is clear to see. While a collaborative partnership approach is to the fore – epitomized by the formal PPP in place – the city authorities nevertheless retain a pivotal role in spearheading and facilitating the initiative. This echoes recent findings from governance research (see Chapter 2) which counterbalances earlier claims and expectations of a radical shift away from government to new networked governance. Instead, a more complex picture emerges, which suggests the need for close consideration of the continuous, if changing, role of government and related aspects of political and public accountability. Second, the more complex reality of collaborative governance indicates that a 'whole-system' approach to urban sustainability cannot be taken for granted. If anything, at least in this case, the particular nature of networked governance suggests a more pronounced compartmentalization – Treasure Island treated as a separate project, explicitly delineated as a consequence of the contractual nature of the PPP – rather than a more integrated approach to the sustainable city as posited by those invoking 'new' governance. Furthermore, third, the assumption that a more co-operative governance-based approach automatically creates the conditions for civil society organizations, citizens and residents to be able to collaborate in urban sustainability initiatives must be carefully considered, not least given the new forms of complexity generated by governing processes which suggest the possibility of less accessible engagement in the sustainable city.

Portland's EcoDistricts

> The Portland region is several steps ahead: we 'get' sustainability.
> (PoSI, 2010a)

Over the years and decades, the city and people of Portland and surrounding communities have invested a great deal of effort into nurturing a profile and reputation as a sustainable city-region. Straddling the Willamette River, the Rose City – as Portland is also known – and its neighbouring districts and counties can indeed boast considerable achievements: unlike many other American cities, Portland has benefited from concerted regional policy-making and planning first introduced in the 1970s and since co-ordinated through Metro, the elected government agency for the Portland metropolitan area; development has been guided by a set of overarching policies, including land use planning aimed at maintaining the urban growth boundary and preventing urban sprawl as well as related regional transport planning; and there is a thriving research and development base – from universities to small start-up companies, and from professional practices to international firms – specializing in green building, renewable energy and public transit products and services. Just as important as all the sustainable 'hardware' – the 'green street' infrastructure, waste collection facilities, extensive cycle networks, integrated public transport system, etc. – many Portlandians like to define their city's vaunted 'eco-friendliness' in terms of active community and neighbourhood engagement, a pioneering spirit and a strong cultural identity. Some call it 'the Portland way' (e.g. Adams, 1997).

One of the latest chapters in the city's foray into sustainable urban innovation is the EcoDistricts initiative, which was launched in 2009 as '… a comprehensive strategy to accelerate sustainable neighbourhood development in the Portland region' (PoSI, 2010a). Similarly to Treasure Island, the initiative is centrally defined in terms of governance processes, accompanied by a pronounced narrative calling for more integrated approaches to – and, therefore, moving beyond conventional ways of – planning for urban sustainability. And, similarly to Treasure Island, while EcoDistricts was conceived of as offering a new model for facilitating and co-ordinating partnerships involving public, private and voluntary organizations, the experience to date points to several challenges of their own kind; these relate to both the initiative's particular take on neighbourhood-level intervention as well as the resulting interaction with the city's wider policy-making and planning system and tradition.

A legacy of regional sustainability planning

As an initiative launched with the active support of the mayor of Portland and intended to accelerate sustainable neighbourhood development across the metropolitan region, EcoDistricts has to be considered against the background of the city-region's legacy of urban sustainability policy and planning. This legacy can be traced back to at least the 1970s and is built upon the principle of regional cross-jurisdictional co-ordination in the areas of land use and public transport planning (see e.g. Poracsky and Houck, 1994; Abbott, 1997; Lang and Hornburg, 1997; Suutari, 2006). This approach is not specific to Portland, but as a state policy – arising from Senate Bills 100 (1972) and 101 (1973), respectively – has been mandated for all metropolitan areas across Oregon; its primary purpose has been to define and periodically review urban growth boundaries and, in turn, to protect agricultural land and greenbelt areas around towns and cities, while concurrently promoting land development and urban growth in designated zones. In the case of the Portland metropolitan area, some 25 towns and cities across three counties came together in the late 1970s to form a joint regional government entity – now known as Metro – to develop and implement framework policies and to coordinate planning in support of designating and maintaining the urban growth boundary. Uniquely, Metro is the only directly elected regional government body in the US; it serves an area of 364 km^2 and a population of over 2.3 million, including some 600,000 residents living in Portland itself. The Metro Charter, approved by ballot in the early 1990s, sets out the principles and areas of responsibility for the agency; this includes regional framework planning concerning: land use; public transport; waste management; and park land and wildlife habitat conservation. In addition to its responsibility for co-ordinating regional policy and issuing planning guidance, Metro is in charge of providing related services, such as waste management and regional transit, delivering an economy of scale with collective costs shared across the individual cities involved.

Greater Portland's regional planning approach is, however, only partly characterized by Metro; it is concurrently defined by policy- and decision-making at individual city level and, further below, planning at neighbourhood level. According to a representative of the Portland Development Commission (PDC) – the city's economic development agency – co-ordination between these tiers of government is both critical, and in actual practice 'exceptionally strong' (interview with PDC, 25 October 2010). This echoes Abbott's (1997) description of the Portland region as one 'where city and suburbs talk to each other – and often agree'. The Portland city-region's approach to urban sustainability planning, therefore, has been defined for a considerable time now by integration and co-ordination, both across government levels (regional, municipal, neighbourhood) and across policy issues (land use, transport, waste, etc.). This comprehensive regional planning strategy provides a robust regulatory framework to guide day-to-day development; in addition, it encourages long-term planning – what Metro calls the region's 'stubborn belief in the importance of thinking ahead' (Metro, undated) – such as that illustrated by the 2040 Growth Concept, adopted in the 1990s as a long-range plan to set the parameters for development for a 50-year period, until 2040. It is not least for these combined reasons that the region has gained a reputation as something of a pioneer in sustainable urban development.

Within this wider regional governance context and across a timeline of several decades, the city of Portland itself has pursued an active urban sustainability policy agenda. The initial emphasis in the 1970s was on revitalizing the city centre, with the 1972 Downtown Plan forming an important step towards tackling the twin urban ills of environmental pollution and socio-economic decline. This was followed in 1980 with the city-wide Portland Comprehensive Plan, whose focus was on the pedestrianization of inner-city areas, the development of public transport mainly through an integrated light rail and bus system, and mixed-use (retail and residential) development and affordable housing. The opening of the McCall Waterfront Park – named after state governor Tom McCall, the driving force behind Oregon's urban growth boundary policy – and the creation of Pioneer Courthouse Square (dubbed by locals the city's 'living room'), both in the early 1980s, were significant further milestones in the city's regeneration process. Sustainable development gained formal structural status within the political system with the launch of the Office of Sustainable Development in 2000; the office was amalgamated with the city's planning department in 2008 to form the Portland Bureau of Planning and Sustainability, thus placing urban sustainability even more centre stage. The city's mayor was quoted as saying that this move would 'ensure that sustainability principles are at the core of everything the city plans and builds' and that it would help the long-term plan 'to position Portland as the global epicentre of sustainable practices and commerce' (Mitchell, 2008).

More recently, the city adopted a Carbon Action Plan, which commits it to cut CO_2 emissions – in comparison to 1990s levels – by 40 per cent by 2030, increasing to 80 per cent by 2050 (City of Portland, 2009). And in 2012, following an extensive public consultation process to develop a new comprehensive Portland Plan to replace the original 1980 plan, the new 25-five year framework strategy came into force (Portland City Council, 2012). Describing itself overall as a 'framework for equity', the plan lays out three 'integrated strategies', relating to education, economic prosperity, and becoming a 'healthy connected city' (with most of its specific environmental goals falling into the third category), and interrelates these to provide 'a coordinated approach to providing services that meet multiple goals with limited funding' (ibid.: 6).

Alongside these strategic policy and planning frameworks, the city has over recent decades supported several ongoing, practical initiatives including: the promotion of green building innovation and practice through, among other measures, a tailor-made Portland LEED certification scheme and a district energy initiative; the development of an extensive network of bicycle lanes, resulting in the city being named 'America's top bike-friendly city' in a 2012 survey by *Bicycling* magazine (Dille, 2012); the extension of the light rail system and addition of a streetcar (tram) system; and the launch of the Green Streets initiative, which combines natural storm water management – using plants and soil to treat storm water at its source – with improved pedestrian footpath and bicycle lane design.

An overview of Portland's sustainable urban development legacy would not be complete without a mention of the important role played by neighbourhood associations (Suutari, 2006; City of Portland, Oregon, undated). Historically, these have been instrumental to various land use and urban policy decisions, by facilitating public participation and on occasions successfully raising opposition to controversial large-scale projects, such as proposed new motorways. In parallel to governance innovation at regional level, during the 1970s neighbourhood associations gained more formal status in the planning process, with the Portland Office of Neighbourhood Involvement (ONI) set up to implement various community and neighbourhood involvement programmes (City of Portland, undated). The number of associations has since grown to over 90; these are organized into seven autonomous district coalitions which are publicly funded but independent of the city's administration. ONI, as a municipal organization, acts as the link between the city's government and the neighbourhood associations.

EcoDistricts: innovation at neighbourhood level

Given the Portland region's well established, comprehensive policy framework supporting sustainable urban development, as well as the numerous initiatives and activities put into effect at various levels and in relation to a broad range of policy issues, the launch in 2009 of the Portland Sustainability Institute (henceforth, PoSI) and its flagship EcoDistricts initiative may have come as a surprise to some observers. After all, Metro has a well-honed regulatory framework; the city has put sustainability at the heart of government in the form of the amalgamated Portland Bureau of Planning and Sustainability; the original, and new, Portland Plans place central emphasis on environmental, economic and social aspects of urban sustainability; and there appear to be thriving activities and engagement at neighbourhood level. Yet, those backing the new venture – which was spearheaded and financially supported with a seed fund by the city's mayor – clearly felt that there was a need for 'accelerating urban innovations', according to the strapline used for PoSI (2010a). As the launch literature explains, 'the Portland Sustainability Institute was founded in 2009 to systematically bring together business, higher education, non-profit and municipal leaders to drive a set of next-generation initiatives for urban sustainability in the Portland metro region' (ibid.). Underlying this rationale are two interrelated arguments – namely, that efforts to date, one, lacked the necessary integration across various actor groups and consequently, two, were slowing down the innovation cycle:

> But [the Portland region's] own efforts, despite some excellent policies and investments, have been largely isolated from one another. We have significant existing goals unmet and newer, more ambitious goals in jeopardy, like 2030 carbon reduction targets. As the pace of challenges quickens, our region must create integrated strategies to tackle climate change, community health and sustainable economic development. Our public policies, business innovations, financing strategies and home-grown initiatives should work together. (Ibid.)

A fresh approach to governing sustainable urban development, therefore, appears to have informed the launch of the new initiative, with the *raison d'être* of PoSI centred upon integrating strategies and fostering innovation through new partnerships and networks. This is reflected in the institute's four-pronged approach, emphasizing 'whole systems integration', 'faster investment cycles', 'policy breakthroughs' and 'monitoring, documentation and engagement', the latter aimed at creating 'robust learning networks' (ibid.).

EcoDistricts was undoubtedly PoSI's signature initiative. The other launch projects included the Oregon Sustainability Center, billed as a major new sustainability education, research and innovation hub to be based in the world's most sustainable high-rise building; as well as the Portland Metro Climate Prosperity Project, aimed at driving 'a rapid and wholesale transformation to a green economy by aligning the numerous economic development and climate-related initiatives in the region under a single framework' (ibid.). For its part, the EcoDistricts initiative – again, reflecting the institute's overarching emphasis on integrative governance processes – is defined ambitiously as:

> a comprehensive strategy to accelerate sustainable neighbourhood development, at the intersection of buildings, infrastructure and people. It focuses on creating robust public-private partnerships with municipalities, utilities and district stakeholders to remove barriers and create an enabling strategy for EcoDistrict implementation. (Ibid.)

Five pilot projects were selected for implementing the EcoDistricts initiative in an initial three-year period starting in 2010. The aim was to form partnerships between PoSI and district stakeholders who would work with their local communities. The institute itself would provide technical assistance and financial resources for the work on the ground. The pilot process has been structured into five overlapping phases: (i) district organization – setting up local governance structures; (ii) district assessment – carrying out status-quo assessment and preparing future visions, based on targets and corresponding metrics; (iii) project feasibility – identifying potential projects and carrying out feasibility studies; (iv) project development – using phasing and implementation plans to realize priority projects; and, (v) district monitoring – conducting ongoing monitoring across all stages. The five pilot areas selected include three inner-city districts – Lloyd District, SoMa ('south of market', the area around Portland State University), and South Waterfront – and two outer-city neighbourhoods – Foster Green and Gateway, situated to the south-east and east, respectively, of the downtown area. Table 5.2 summarizes the key features of the five pilots.

Table 5.2 *Portland's five EcoDistrict pilot initiatives*

	Key characteristics
Foster Green	• Defined as a 'collaboration of neighbours' along the Foster Road corridor (several miles to the south-east of downtown), with focus on 'improvement projects within the community', including local park regeneration • Vision adopted in 2011, with focus on building on existing assets and active community involvement • District assessment across nine performance areas completed in 2012
Growing Gateway	• District centred upon existing Gateway urban renewal area (several miles to the east of downtown), plus surrounding area within 20-minute walking distance • District assessment completed in 2011 • Public meeting held in 2011 endorsing the 'Growing Gateway: Gateway EcoDistrict' plan • 'Re-Energize Gateway' project launched in 2012 aimed at energy retrofitting (building retrofits, especially for low-income households) and renewable energy generation (solar production) • Activities on hold as of 2013, but associated 'Gateway Green' project going forward, using crowdsourced funding to redevelop local unused land as public park and regional off-road cycling centre
Lloyd District	• Business district across the Willamette River from Portland's central business district (currently less than 10% of land use is residential) • Coordinated by specialist staff, with salaries funded by landowners • 'Roadmap' published in 2012, with plans including retrofitting of older buildings, new dense commercial and residential LEED Gold building programme, onsite renewable energy, district water utility, new greenery/parkland, and better connectivity including new pedestrian/cycle bridges over adjoining freeways

SoMA	• Spearheaded by Portland State University (located to immediate south of main downtown area), with focus on engaging surrounding private, residential and community groups
	• Developed in conjunction with University District Framework Plan and Climate Action Plan
	• SoMA 'roadmap' published in 2012, with key focal areas on improving: mixed-use development; bicycling and pedestrian network; green infrastructure, including green street initiative; expanding district energy system; and building retrofits
	• Emphasis on fostering sustainability research and education
South Waterfront	• Connected by tram to southern end of downtown area, and by cable car to Oregon Health & Science University campus (which is planning new building inside the EcoDistrict)
	• Around a third of the land was built out before EcoDistrict formed, with mostly residential high-rise buildings (mostly upmarket, though with some 'affordable housing')
	• One among several sustainability initiatives defined as 'model of LEED-certified building practices and stewardship of green spaces' (SWCR, undated)
	• District assessment report published in 2011
	• Early projects have focused on district energy and rooftop photovoltaics, river habitat improvement, and a district-wide bicycle sharing scheme

Guiding the five pilots is the EcoDistricts framework developed by PoSI; to date, this has been mainly used in the five pilots for progressing phases 2 (assessment) and 3 (project feasibility). At the centre of the framework are eight 'performance areas' that define and structure the urban sustainability contents: (i) equitable development; (ii) health and well-being; (iii) community identity; (iv) access and mobility; (v) energy; (vi) water; (vii) habitat and ecosystem function; and (viii) materials management. For each of these performance areas, an overarching goal is defined – for example, 'net-zero energy usage annually' for the energy category, and 'zero waste and optimized materials management' for the materials management category – and matched with a series of specific objectives. The assessment process, undertaken by experts commissioned on behalf of the local EcoDistrict steering group, entails a 'baseline' performance assessment to determine existing district conditions, following which performance targets are set to guide the identification of strategic development opportunities centred on a number of prioritized projects. For each identified project, a feasibility study is to be conducted to inform the subsequent implementation process. Throughout, monitoring is to be performed using established metrics.

It should come as no surprise that – even based on a co-ordinated approach facilitated by PoSI and involving a common assessment and planning framework – the five pilots have evolved somewhat differently. Lloyd, SoMa and, to a lesser extent, South Waterfront appear to be at a more advanced development stage, which may well be due to three reasons: first, in these district areas there are established institutions – business organizations, a university, a large hospital – with available professional expertise and organizational and financial capacity to be able to engage readily in sustainability planning; in the case of Lloyd, the EcoDistrict organization closely builds on an earlier district sustainability initiative (with a focus on integrated transport planning and urban redevelopment) dating back at least a decade; in the case of SoMa, the initiative has been tied in with PSU's District Framework Plan and a Climate Action Plan to which the university was already committed. Second, the EcoDistrict projects here are defined in relation to existing infrastructure needs and capacity of the organizations involved, such as those concerning transport and district energy. And third, as business and professional organizations, the actors spearheading these initiatives would already be familiar with planning and related technical assessment processes, thus being able to engage readily in this new initiative as equal partners with the city. In contrast, in the case of the Foster Green and Gateway initiatives, organizational capacity – which mainly relies on community volunteering – may be more limited at the preliminary stages at least; likewise, it cannot be assumed that technical capacity – enabling participants to relate to and engage with expert discourse, as illustrated by the use of performance metrics – is automatically available without additional training and support. What is more, reflecting the fabric of these outer-city districts, the focus of proposed action is perhaps more on 'soft' sustainability measures – such as community well-being and engagement – which may be more difficult to capture and specify.

EcoDistricts as governance narrative

As is the case for Treasure Island, it is too soon to try to assess fully the five EcoDistricts pilots; their fruition beyond initial assessment stage is still outstanding. But the overall development of the initiative invites some critical reflections. What is of particular interest is the strong steer on the part of PoSI and its backers towards urban sustainability intervention at neighbourhood/district level, especially in the context of the Portland region's existing multi-tiered approach to encouraging sustainable urban development. There appears to be a dominant rationale at work that privileges the neighbourhood level as the optimal scale at which urban sustainability integration can be effected, thereby accelerating innovation. Based on discussions with various actors on the ground, three distinct narratives are deployed to explain and justify the district-level focus. According to one narrative – most strongly represented by PoSI itself – neighbourhoods are the next logical step up from intervention at building level, which allows significant scaling up and, therefore, encourages integration among individual projects and improved 'economy of scale'. At the same time, intervention at this level is not too expansive to hinder effective innovation:

> [EcoDistricts] are an important scale to accelerate sustainability — small enough to innovate quickly and big enough to have a meaningful impact. District-scale projects, such as district energy, green streets, smart grid, demand management and resource sharing, are well known. However, the widespread deployment of these strategies has been slow to develop due to a lack of comprehensive policy or implementation frameworks at the municipal level. EcoDistricts ... [are] an initiative to help cities remove these

implementation barriers and create an enabling strategy to accelerate neighborhood-scale sustainability. (EcoDistricts, 2012: 2)

Representatives of the Portland Bureau of Planning and
Sustainability concur with the first part of this explanation: 'we
have done a lot on the building level ... so there is a perception that
we need to take the next step and look at the economies of scale
with doing this [sustainable urban development] with multiple
buildings' (interview with BPS, 27 October 2010). However, the
PoSI statement also makes the additional assertion that by lacking
'comprehensive policy' and 'implementation frameworks', municipal authorities have failed to support sustainable development at
district level, which is what the EcoDistricts framework seeks to
remedy. This view is not echoed by the Portland Bureau of Planning
and Sustainability officials, whose alternative reason for district-
level intervention is to focus on making the city more walkable:
following previous emphasis on city-level comprehensive planning
and investment – such as city-wide and regional transport routes –
the focus should now be more on the notion of the 'twenty-minute
neighbourhood', whereby amenities and services should be within
walking distance, thus reducing the pressure on urban transport
systems and related infrastructure investment. (This focus is also
reflected in the 2012 Portland Plan, which under its 'healthy
connected city' theme emphasizes the importance of complete,
walkable neighbourhoods.) These two narratives are interesting in
that one foregrounds the need for scaling up, from the building level
to the neighbourhood, whereas the other puts emphasis on scaling
down, from city-wide intervention to consolidation at neighbourhood level.

There is a further, third narrative in play, centred upon the need
for public–private partnerships – and in particular, leveraging
private investment – to realize urban sustainability initiatives.
Although this narrative appears more in the background in the official literature, it comes through as perhaps the most salient driver of
the EcoDistricts initiative in discussion with various players
involved. The case is made particularly strongly by a representative
of the PDC – the city's economic development agency – which has
co-funded the five EcoDistricts pilots: 'it is an acknowledgement
that the public sector can only do so much ... we are very clear as we
go on to do EcoDistricts that this is not something that is going to
come from the city down. This is something that has to have property owners, business owners, home owners and renters [on board]'

(interview with PDC, 25 Oct 2010). According to this view – and South Waterfront and Lloyd are highlighted as exemplars by the PDC official – major private property owners and landholders should take a lead in 'self-identifying' their priorities; these would then be considered in terms of how they can be related to wider sustainability decisions, such as district energy and water management. Once again, 'this is not a top down effort … it is a question of "okay, we provide you with these targets as EcoDistricts; you tell us what makes the best business sense for you, for this district or this neighbourhood, to go pursue it"' (ibid.).

Confirmation of this economic driver also comes from the Portland Bureau of Planning and Sustainability representatives: they contrast the previous period, where large-scale public investment was the norm, to the current economic context which requires private-sector investment: 'It tended to be fairly regulatory in its orientation and it was a different climate because there weren't the monetary constraints that we have today. You could pretty much put any transportation investment into the plan and no-one would wince, but now people are going to ask you to show how you're going to pay for it, usually. So, there's a different climate' (interview with BPS, 27 October 2010). As a result, the city authorities have to ask '"what can we do to entice further private investment?" The EcoDistricts fall within that context' (ibid.).

The privileging of private-sector interests in urban sustainability initiatives, such as EcoDistricts, is particularly significant coming, as it does, from the municipal side, especially in the context of a strong – and certainly in the case of Portland, proud – tradition of innovation in sustainable urban development achieved through concerted city-regional policy and planning. Within this new governance perspective, government itself may even be viewed – here expressed by the director of the Portland Bureau of Planning and Sustainability – as putting up potential regulatory impediments, implying that additional flexibility is required to enable new governance:

> EcoDistricts offer the promise of delivering projects on a much-accelerated timeline, and one that is driven by the businesses, residents, and property owners in a district, not by the city … EcoDistricts don't necessarily require a role for the city government, and there is a great deal the private sector can do without the city's involvement. Often, however, city regulations may complicate options, and the city needs to be ready to explore

ways to meet the outcomes that regulations are intended to accomplish in ways that may depart from the prescribed pathways. (Anderson, 2011)

A place, a tool, a product?

The discussion of what drives the EcoDistricts initiative invites the question of what precisely an EcoDistrict stands for. This point is addressed by an architect involved as consultant in the initiative, when commenting that 'EcoDistricts are not places; all it is, is a tool. It's a tool box for where [urban sustainability] should be evolving, focusing in a different way than we have before, to make great neighbourhoods' (interview with SERA Architects, 27 October 2010). PoSI itself uses the analogy of a toolkit to explain the role and contribution of its flagship initiative:

> Cities need new options to do more with less – they need an expanded toolkit to deliver sustainable solutions ... The Eco-Districts initiative looks at sustainable solutions on the scale of a district or neighbourhood. System-wide views and integrated thinking across a district help to coordinate action and amplify business opportunity – from professional service firms to manufacturers – and in the process, accomplish more significant sustainable work. (PoSI, 2010b)

As a toolkit, then, EcoDistricts offer cities a 'new option' – compared with conventional ways of government. In an echo of the Portland Plan's intention to meet 'multiple goals with limited funding' (Portland City Council, 2012: 6) through the strategic coordination of services, it proposes that system-wide integration will allow local authorities to do more with less, while simultaneously amplifying business opportunities for the private sector; in turn, this promises to accomplish more significant sustainable work than hitherto possible. Characterizations such as the ones above suggest that Portland's particular conceptualization of an 'eco-district' is primarily process-centric and systems-based; considerations of place and community retreat into the distance. What is more, the process – which, after all, is to be a district-level, neighbourhood-based process – is expected to generate products that can ultimately be exported. Consequently, EcoDistricts are less about a planning strategy than economic development and related export strategy:

One of the drivers from the mayor's perspective – if not the only driver from the mayor's perspective – is really that [EcoDistricts] is part of our economic development strategy, to be investing in green innovation and technology, and so I think he sees it as less of a planning strategy and more of an incubator of innovation and knowhow. So, it's less about the end product of the building than it is about developing a group of companies in Portland that know how to do that building. (interview with BPS, 27 October 2010)

This view is echoed by the PDC official, who characterizes the innovation process driving the EcoDistricts initiative in terms of 'how do we align innovation to meet new product opportunities and to handle new export opportunities' (interview with PDC, 25 Oct 2010). According to this perspective, EcoDistricts are expected to fit into, and be a catalyst for, a business development strategy aimed at identifying local opportunities for green product development. The head of the Portland Bureau of Planning and Sustainability concurs with this dominant framing, when summing up the *raison d'être* for EcoDistricts:

One final value proposition of EcoDistricts is in showing what is possible. The world is searching for solutions to urbanization, to resource scarcity, to poverty, to climate change, to a host of issues that are growing in urgency. We need examples of what a super high-performance district looks like, what technologies it uses, how it links natural and built environments, how it can be financed. Whoever develops these solutions will be well positioned to export their expertise and products to cities throughout the world, and that means jobs in the near term and environmental and social benefits for decades to come. (Anderson, 2011)

In the discussion of Treasure Island, it was suggested that the emerging new governance model has produced something of a paradox, in terms of an initiative emerging from within a city but evolving into something akin to a separate project and removed at some distance. A similar observation can be made for Portland's EcoDistricts initiative. Here, the paradox arguably arises most sharply from the bifurcated development of the initiative as partly a series of community-based pilot projects, and partly a governance process that – in spite of the district focus at the centre of its name – appears less oriented towards, and rooted in, specific place, and more geared towards economic innovation opportunities. This apparent tension may well have played a role when, in 2012, it was officially announced that the five pilot projects would no longer be guided by PoSI and instead be transferred to the municipal authorities, who would continue to provide developmental support to the communities concerned (City of Portland, 2012; Williams, 2012). The Oregon Sustainability Center, which had also been spearheaded by PoSI, was abandoned altogether, for lack of funding. PoSI itself, meanwhile, was renamed EcoDistricts, severing its formal link to Portland. As a free-standing organization, it now offers the EcoDistricts framework and toolkit to cities and communities across the country and beyond. EcoDistricts itself, then, appears to have become a product ready for export, in a reflection of the way its framework conceptualizes urban sustainability.

As for the five Portland eco-district pilot initiatives, the future looks somewhat uncertain. 'It's a work in progress ... We're building new relationships and figuring out how we can help them', the city's green building and development manager is quoted as saying (Williams, 2012). The same official confirmed that the EcoDistrict pilots would be matched with existing municipal resources and programmes, rather than consolidated as an initiative of its own. Interestingly, the new *Portland Plan* (Portland City Council, 2012), which addresses various dimensions of urban sustainable development in detail and with specific objectives attached, does not mention EcoDistricts once, either as concept or as existing pilot initiatives. Of the five programmes, Lloyd EcoDistrict appears the most advanced and active, most probably because it had previously developed a district sustainability initiative of its own volition, on which the current development phase seems to be building. Its leading status was confirmed by the announcement that the city authorities would fund 'the most sustainable business district in North America' with a US$1 million grant for a ten-year period (Hogue, 2014). Relatively little information is available about the other pilot initiatives, with only partial updates since the earlier assessment period stretching back to 2011.

At the heart of the original EcoDistricts initiative, launched 'as part of the Portland region's broadening commitment to sustainability' (PoSI, 2010b), was the claim that moving from the traditional way of planning for urban sustainability to this new form of governance would help to realize more 'accelerated urban innovations' through 'whole-system integration', 'policy breakthroughs' and 'faster investment cycles'. While EcoDistricts (formerly PoSI) hails the Portland pilot initiative a 'success' (EcoDistricts, 2013: 3), developments to date would suggest that the promise and potential of new-mode governance for urban sustainability – certainly when assessed against its own original, ambitious claims – remain to be fully tested, at least in this case.

Common features of new-mode governance in practice

Taken together, the Treasure Island and EcoDistricts initiatives provide useful insights into the rationale for, and nature of, new modes of governance for urban sustainability as widely advocated in policy and increasingly applied in practice. The two initiatives confirm the emergence of what some call a new paradigm for how urban sustainability is understood and promoted, and the centrality played in this by governance as dominant norm and practice. At the same time, the initiatives also point to several features of this new governance which may sit uneasily with some of the positive assumptions and claims made, such as those concerning the expected improved integration across urban systems and scales as well as more inclusive, co-operative planning and decision-making involving all stakeholders. If anything, the two exemplars point to the need for critical, context-specific analyses, in order to arrive at a sophisticated and nuanced understanding of the dynamics created by new governance processes and their impact on sustainable city initiatives.

The first, and perhaps most salient, commonality between the two case studies is the key role of financial and economic interests in shaping governance relations and policy discourse. The intertwinement of environmental ambitions with these interests – and arguably the subordination of the former to the latter – would seem to be aligned with the international spread of 'green growth' policy-making, as discussed in Chapter 3. One effect of this may be that urban sustainability is chiefly defined in terms of large-scale investment requirements, with the public sector unable or unwilling to shoulder the financial burden, and with business partners seizing potential investment opportunities. The related discourse is cast predominantly in terms of how to create economic value for cities: 'close collaboration between the public and private sectors is an effective way of changing the [governance] paradigm in ways that enable the delivery of ambitious projects that create value for cities' (La Fabrique de la Cité,

2013: 25). Within this framework, 'public decision-making bodies create the conditions under which private companies and public authorities can come together to develop the city and identify innovative funding methods ... these partnerships have made it possible to respond effectively to the expectations of the local economic fabric and transform the city by creating jobs and enhancing its appeal' (La Fabrique de la Cité, 2013: 7).

This discourse is most overtly at work in the case of Treasure Island, where the urban sustainability contents have become intimately bound up in financial interests and transactions: from the outset, TICD as a consortium of private developers was instrumental in enabling urban sustainability to be incorporated in the initiative; and the project's further realization will be contingent on TICD's ability to continue to secure investment throughout the further development phases. A similar discourse can also be found at work, if perhaps less explicitly, in Portland's EcoDistricts initiative: here again, the premise is that the city's role now consists more of acting as a convenor by facilitating new collaborative arrangements with various private and civil society organizations, accompanied by a relative retreat from government-led intervention and public investment. Beyond the five EcoDistricts pilots – whose future looks more uncertain following the re-structuring of the Portland Sustainability Institute – the emphasis on 'working smarter' through collaborative public–private partnerships is firmly reflected in the new Portland Plan, as key guiding principle for realizing the city's sustainable urban development strategy and initiatives in the coming decades.

The governance discourse in the two cases above – and repeated time and again in contemporary urban sustainability initiatives elsewhere – is not necessarily to be criticized. After all, it reflects, on one hand, the substantial scale of investment required to realize urban sustainability initiatives and, on the other, the reality of limited public spending power following successive decades of fiscal squeeze imposed on many local and municipal governments, compounded by the global financial crisis and economic downturn occurring in the late 2000s. However, it is important to recognize the way in which this discourse moulds thinking about urban sustainability – especially in terms of economic value – and how, in turn, this shapes governance relations, with the effect of privileging the interests of some actors over those of others. As a consequence, new governance processes are not as value-neutral and unproblematic as is often assumed in the urban sustainability literature.

A second feature emerging from the two initiatives – and, again, reflected more widely in urban sustainability initiatives (Joss, 2010; 2011b) – concerns the technical discourse produced by governance processes. The language of urban sustainability is already typically framed in terms of scientific knowledge and technical expertise. This is further compounded by the use of governance discourse, which comes with its own particular vocabulary and specialist language. It is not just technical terms, such as 'carbon partnership facility' and 'whole-system integration', that can render governance discourses potentially inaccessible to non-specialists; the use of broader analogies for urban sustainability initiatives, such as that of 'laboratory', 'incubator' and 'implementation toolkit' – favoured by professionals to emphasize experimentation and innovation – further underlines the expert-driven approach to sustainable urban development. This matters if the assumption is – as frequently stated, often as a matter of course – that governance should be inclusive, based on co-operation and participation among all stakeholders, including the wider community: residents, neighbourhood groups and the citizenry at large. It suggests the need for close attention to be paid to the conditions which enable (and conversely, those which hamper) various participants – and especially non-specialists – to engage effectively in governance processes.

While in both the cases of Treasure Island and Portland's EcoDistricts pilots, genuine and substantial efforts seem to have been made to mobilize and engage community groups, nevertheless much of the process has arguably remained cast in overt technical expert discourse. This was readily acknowledged as a challenge by the partners involved in Treasure Island, although at the same time accepted as perhaps an inevitable consequence of the use of an elaborate, formal public–private partnership. Even in the case of the more overtly community-centred approach of the EcoDistricts pilots, the assessment reports produced deploy a strong expert discourse. While ostensibly written on behalf of the local community, they were carried out by professional consultants and academic and policy experts on the basis of the standard framework issued by PoSI. Viewing the reports alongside each other, it is striking how similar they look in terms of presentation of data and use of language; they seem much more closely oriented towards PoSI's standard framework – the EcoDistrict as 'toolkit' – than reflective of a predominantly community-based framing – the EcoDistrict as 'place'.

Reinforcing the tendency towards technical discourses, a third feature of new governance processes is the frequent definition of urban sustainability initiatives in the form of projects (e.g. Book et al., 2010; Joss, 2011a). This approach is particularly common in the context of public-private partnership arrangements (of one kind or another) used to realize large-scale urban sustainability initiatives involving often long development trajectories. Here, urban sustainability initiatives are carried out by forming a temporary, separate project between several organizations. Within the project, participating partners come together around an agreed set of objectives and targets, and related organizational and control processes. The intended benefits are that a focused, project-based approach increases the efficiency of delivery and responsiveness to evolving circumstances, while also better harnessing various skills and mobilizing learning across organizations. However, such a project-based approach brings with it the risk that initiatives insufficiently relate to wider, long-term strategic policies and processes, and that they lack the necessary transparency and accountability (Book et al., 2010). Furthermore, such 'projectified' organization risks, once again, infusing urban sustainability with specialist discourse with which professionals can be expected to be familiar, but which may prevent non-specialists from effective engagement.

Both cases exhibit project-based organizational characteristics, closely related to the governance interactions at work; they both make use of framework documents and processes, which define various project elements and phases, and related objectives and performance targets. In Portland's EcoDistricts initiatives, the project period for each of the five pilots is segmented into distinct phases (organization, assessment, feasibility, implementation, monitoring) and overseen by a professional team drawn together from several organizations. Additional external consultants are hired to deliver specific inputs, such as the assessment reports. In the case of Treasure Island, 'terms sheets' define the contributions of, and relationship between, the partners involved in the PPP; in turn, this defines in minute detail both project contents and related delivery modes (e.g. phasing). Here, too, the partners involved have effectively formed a joint project team, working closely together on a daily basis. Interestingly, while both initiatives profess to strive for more integrative, 'whole-system' governance – to overcome the compartmentalized 'silo' approach of traditional planning and decision-making – their project-based definition imposes a delineation on the initiatives which may well inadvertently hinder effective integration.

Conclusions

A close examination of these two cases suggests that new-mode governance in urban sustainability may in practice be rather more problematic and contextually constrained than some of its champions would acknowledge. The combination of the three governance features observed in the two case studies – a predominant economic rationale centred upon mobilizing private financial leverage and economic value creation, the prevalence of technical discourses, and a project-based approach to organizing urban sustainability initiatives – produces an overall mode of governance which is defined by two interrelated, overarching features: namely, what may be referred to as, on one hand, a 'de-contextualization' and, on the other, a 'de-politicization' of urban sustainability initiatives. As noted, importantly, 'new-mode' governance does not represent a wholesale shift away from traditional government, but occurs in complex relationship to it; and so these two features should be understood here as tendencies, rather than as fully formed characteristics of all contemporary sustainable urban development. As tendencies, they are arguably observable in sustainable city initiatives beyond the two cases here – even if they always need to be considered and interpreted carefully in close relation to the specific institutional, national and cultural contexts within which such initiatives take place.

The 'de-contextualization' of the two sustainable city initiatives considered here, and potentially in many others elsewhere, directly stems from the governance-focused, process-oriented conceptualization at work. What is meant by 'de-contextualization' is a certain separation of urban sustainability initiatives from the context from which they have originally arisen. In the case of Treasure Island, this manifests itself in several ways: for example, in physical terms, the initiative relates to a separate site, which is not surrounded by and directly connected to any other part of the city; relatedly, in programmatic terms, the sustainability features are contained within themselves, unrelated to the surrounding area and wider municipal context; in financial terms, the realization of the new city district is entirely dependent on raising sufficient external funding on the market, with the project appearing nowhere in the city's budget; and in organizational terms, the project is defined through a separate legal entity and corresponding project management structure. The element of separation in the case of Portland's EcoDistricts initiative is, of course, most pronounced by the recent rededication of the Portland Sustainability Institute as EcoDistricts and the institute's relinquishing of the five community projects; but even during the initial pilot phase, the separation was apparent in the conceptual distancing of the initiative from municipal government which – perhaps surprisingly, given the record accumulated over decades – was presented as lacking in effective integration and implementation. It is significant that in both cases separate new organizational entities were set up (TIDA/TICD, and PoSI), purportedly in order to achieve more effective integration and co-ordination among diverse partners; if anything, however, this appears to have had the contrary effect of further de-contextualizing the initiatives from their municipal settings.

The second feature mentioned above, that of 'de-politicization', refers to a deliberate, quite pronounced distancing from the notion of traditional government in the narratives used to describe and justify the new types of urban sustainability initiatives. Conventional municipal government is portrayed, overall negatively, as 'top-down', preventing effective integration and slowing development; it is suggested that regulatory frameworks stand in the way of innovative practices; and, above all, there is ready acceptance that investment in urban sustainability can no longer be achieved other than by presenting it as a business opportunity to private investors. To the external observer, this moment of de-politicization is most acutely apparent in Portland's EcoDistricts initiative, where the case for a fundamentally changed approach seems to be pressed almost hardest by representatives of municipal government themselves. It is also apparent in Treasure Island, although here it seems presented more as an already settled case, normalized by similar precedents (especially the decommissioning of naval bases through redevelopment agencies using public–private partnership mechanisms) and seemingly, therefore, publicly accepted.

Such 'de-politicization' is, of course, in itself inherently political; and it can, therefore, be viewed in terms of a concurrent 're-politicization' process: the new urban sustainability politics emerging is cast in terms of a changing political and organizational culture of governance effected through various public–private partnerships. In these new partnerships, private interests and actors are seen as the enablers and drivers of innovation through essential funding and dynamic 'whole-system' integration and co-ordination, while public interests and actors appear to retreat from a leading, interventionist position to a more facilitating, convening role. As noted, this de- and re-politicization should only be understood as having occurred partially to date, rather than representing a complete shift to new-mode governance. This is illustrated by both Treasure Island and Portland's EcoDistricts, where the essential steering function of municipal government remains in evidence, including through TIDA's role as redevelopment agency in shaping and controlling Treasure Island's sustainability agenda, and the city of Portland's continuous co-ordinative and regulatory influence in the form of the Portland Plan and other comprehensive policy and planning frameworks.

In combination, the suggested 'de-contextualization' and 'de-politicization' (and related 're-politicization') tendencies – again, essentially to be understood as partial, rather than complete shifts – are realized through inherently complex, and in many ways problematic, hybrid governance relations and dynamics. The problematic nature of such arrangements calls into question the positive normative view of new urban sustainability governance – see Introduction – as axiomatically providing 'expanded platforms for collaborative decision-making', 'accomplishing sustained synergy' and 'massively increasing success'. In turn, it calls for a critical re-appraisal of the role of governmental steering and regulation, often so readily dismissed as hindering and slowing innovation and development, when in reality they seem to continue to play a pivotal function of co-ordination and integration. Detailed, probing empirical analyses of practical initiatives such as Treasure Island and Portland's EcoDistricts are essential for developing a more fine-grained picture of the processes at work in the production of urban sustainability and its discourses.

Chapter 6

The Rise of the Urban Sustainability Framework

CHAPTER OVERVIEW

There is a thriving, competitive market for urban sustainability frameworks offering replicable models for the design and implementation of sustainable city initiatives. The growing popularity of these frameworks is partly driven by the need to scale up sustainable urban development and partly by demands for more standardized approaches to defining, measuring and managing urban sustainability. It is further explained by the opportunities for non-traditional actors – including professional bodies, technology firms and social enterprises – to engage in urban sustainability as a business proposition. This chapter closely examines and compares three prominent examples: the Climate Positive Development Program, focusing on greenhouse gas neutrality for urban in-fill projects; the One Planet Living framework, underpinned by ecological footprint analysis and applicable at different scales; and the Tianjin Eco-City Key Performance Indicators, designed to offer a national framework for the numerous eco-city initiatives currently under way across China. The significant differences between these three frameworks suggest an ongoing diversification – rather than consolidation – of urban sustainability practice. They further highlight the creative tension between defining sustainable city initiatives as generic, replicable models and considering urban sustainability as context-specific, local practice.

Introduction: global standards for local practices?

International frameworks should aim to outline high-level principles and goals, rather than to achieve overly detailed and technical standards. These goals and principles should be ambitious as well as aspirational. They should engage with both the substance and processes of urban sustainability. They should aim to assist

planners, policy makers, developers and communities in designing, applying and monitoring urban sustainability indicators.
(Bellagio Statement, in Joss, 2012)

There has been a flurry of activity in recent years aimed at defining
international indicators and standards to guide sustainable city
innovation. In this process, a central question arising time and again
is which aspects of urban sustainability can and should be defined
globally, and what should essentially be a matter for local consideration. This discussion has produced a wealth of literature, not least
illustrated by the Bellagio Statement, a report published following
an international gathering of experts in the small Italian town of
Bellagio in autumn 2012. (For a wider view of the literature, see also:
Miller, 2005; Hezri and Dovers, 2006; Keirstead and Leach, 2008;
Rydin, 2010; Joss et al., 2012; Zhou and Williams, 2013.) More
significantly still, the discussion has produced a growing number of
practical responses in the form of various international frameworks,
each seeking to offer guidelines, protocols and tools for sustainable
urban development.

These frameworks respond to a growing demand for standardized
approaches aimed at scaling up and replicating the design, implementation and reporting of sustainable city initiatives based on
common methods and ready-made processes. This demand has been
fuelled by the combination of three forces: the first arises from the
high rate of urbanization currently occurring in many developing
countries, in particular across Asia and in large parts of Africa (see
Chapter 1). In the words of the World Bank, whose own Eco2 Cities
framework has focused to date mainly on East Asia: 'Global urban
expansion poses ... a once-in-a-lifetime opportunity to plan,
develop, build, and manage cities that are simultaneously more
ecologically and economically sustainable. We have a short time
horizon within which to affect the trajectory of urbanisation in a
lasting and powerful way' (Suzuki et al., 2010: xv). This unprecedented, large-scale urbanization and the related short 'window of
opportunity', so the argument goes, call for methods and processes
of urban sustainability planning that can be replicated and readily
deployed in various contexts and at different scales. Relatedly, the
second force arises from the trend towards standardizing sustainable
city concepts and practices: as urban sustainability is increasingly
viewed from a global perspective – both in terms of being defined by
global concerns (e.g. global warming and climate change, rural–
urban migration) and recognized through global policies (e.g. inter-

national conventions, urban charters, mayoral declarations) – so the expectations grow for common indicators and agreed standards to define overall urban sustainability and to guide its application across contexts (see e.g. Joss, 2012; Joss et al., 2012; Zhang et al., 2011; Sustainable Cities International, 2012; Williams et al., 2012; ISO, 2013). One such notable recent attempt is the standard – called ISO 37120 – for 'sustainable development and resilience in cities' developed for the first time by the International Organization for Standardization, a global federation of national standards organizations (ISO, 2013). In addition, the third force relates to growing opportunities for various actors – from architecture practices to technology firms, and from engineering consultancies to social enterprises – to become active internationally in marketing urban sustainability strategies and solutions (see Chapter 4). Being able to offer generic 'toolkits' and corresponding procedures is expected to lend businesses and social enterprises a competitive advantage and potentially open up lucrative markets across global regions.

Sustainable city frameworks respond to this demand for generic, standardized processes for designing, implementing and reporting urban sustainability strategies and programmes. What is meant by 'frameworks' here are sets of guidelines and techniques designed to assist policy-makers, planners, developers and community groups in conceptualizing, assessing, implementing and accrediting urban sustainability initiatives. They typically entail a series of core principles that together define the underlying approach to urban sustainability, coupled with clusters of indicators specifying various aspects and related targets of sustainable development, and accompanied by practical design and assessment tools. As such, frameworks variously systematize both the contents of urban sustainability and the processes recommended for implementing sustainable city initiatives. The degree of standardization varies between frameworks, ranging from highly prescriptive sets of indicators to more broadly defined principles and goals open to local interpretation and adaptation. Some frameworks put greater emphasis on prescribing substantive aspects of urban sustainability, leaving the precise methods of implementation to local decision-making, whereas others put greater focus on stipulating step-by-step processes aimed at articulating urban sustainability contents. Frameworks, as discussed here, are designed to be replicable – that is, they are meant to be applicable in different and potentially quite contrasting urban contexts. For example, as noted in Chapter 2, the French ÉcoQuartier and the Japanese Eco-Model City frameworks have been implemented in a variety of towns and cities – of differing characteristics – across France, and Japan, respectively; what is more, they have more recently been applied overseas (ÉcoQuartier in China, and Eco-Model City in the wider East Asian region). As such, these replicable frameworks are distinct from specific frameworks designed for exclusive use in individual cities.

While the number of sustainable city frameworks has grown rapidly within the space of only a few years since the late 2000s, each apparently vying for influence and a share of the market, practical experience to date is still somewhat limited and, hence, empirical evidence of how (well) these frameworks perform – that is, on one hand, how transferable they are across different contexts and, on the other, how effective they prove to be within specific local policy, planning and development processes – has yet to be fully gathered and analysed. What can, however, be expected to emerge as a central question is what interactions arise from the application of generic, standardized frameworks of urban sustainability within specific local (organizational, policy, socio-cultural and physical) urban contexts. There may well be a tension between, on one hand, defining global standards and generic processes and, on the other, articulating goals and designing procedures from within local settings. The discussion in Chapter 5 argued that new forms of governance used to realize sustainable city initiatives run the risk of 'de-contextualizing' and 'de-politicizing' urban sustainability. A similar risk may manifest itself in the case of replicable frameworks – which themselves constitute a new mode of governance – if they turn out not to be sufficiently closely attuned to, and embedded in, particular, local contexts of decision-making and practice. The EcoDistricts framework, analysed in detail in Chapter 5, is arguably a case in point: it was initially defined in relation to specific neighbourhoods in Portland, but ended up being de-contextualized, now serving as a generic framework (of the kind discussed in this chapter) promoted for use across different cities and even beyond the US. Other questions arising from recent developments include whether these frameworks – viewed together – point to a conversion and consolidation of how urban sustainability is considered; or on the contrary, whether they signal a diversification driven by an increasingly competitive, global market for sustainable city initiatives.

The focus of discussion in this chapter is on exploring the constituent dimensions of replicable frameworks for sustainable city initiatives; how these frameworks engage in defining the contents and processes of urban sustainability; and what related innovation and governance dynamics arise. This is done, first, by providing an overview of the range of frameworks that have recently emerged, followed by a brief conceptual discussion centred upon how these frameworks variably embody urban sustainability dimensions and related intended governance functions. These considerations are then applied to three specific frameworks which illustrate different approaches at work: the Climate Positive Development Program (CCI, 2011); the One Planet Living framework (BioRegional, undated); and the Tianjin Eco-City Key Performance Indicators framework (Singapore Government, 2013). Comparing these three exemplars is useful to tease out both commonalities across the range of frameworks as well as particular features specific to individual frameworks and their specific applications.

Conceptualizing eco-city frameworks

The term 'urban sustainability framework', or 'eco-city framework', is used here as an analytical category, to consider and compare a variety of approaches to standardizing the design, assessment and implementation of sustainable city initiatives (Joss, 2012; Joss and Tomozeiu, 2013). (It should be noted that several of the empirical examples analysed here include the term 'framework' in their official titles – such as the International Ecocity Framework and Standards (IEFS), and the Reference Framework for European Sustainable Cities (RFSC); as such, the term has practical application beyond the analytical use here.) The category is defined by three characteristics: first, the frameworks each bring together a range of sustainable urban development aspects and criteria, rather than consisting of single sustainability indicators. As such, they differ from attempts – which used to be more prevalent in earlier phases of sustainable city innovation – to define urban sustainability in the form of individual indicators focusing on, say, transport, or water. By bundling together a spectrum of urban sustainability dimensions and indicators, these frameworks seek to interconnect individual dimensions and, thus, to prompt a more cohesive approach to urban sustainability design, assessment and development. As such, they reflect the 'whole-system' conceptualization that characterizes much of contemporary policy and practice on urban sustainability (see Chapter 2).

The second, and most central, characteristic relates to the intended replicability of frameworks – that is, their design to be applicable in various settings. Frameworks, therefore, are not constituted exclusively in relation to a singular urban sustainability initiative or a particular urban context. Instead, they are purposefully defined in a sufficiently generic way to allow their potential deployment within diverse organizational, policy, cultural and geographical urban contexts. By emphasizing the systemic nature of urban sustainability, common characteristics both relating to the substance – such as resource efficiency, metabolic flows, and the interdependence between environmental, economic and social dimensions – as well as relating to the process – for example, integrated design and co-ordinated governance – of the sustainable city are placed at the centre of these frameworks, with the articulation of specific local attributes expected to follow from the individual application of a given framework within a particular, context-specific situation. A borderline case – included in the categorization here, and illustrated further below by the case of the Tianjin Eco-City Key Performance Indicators scheme – are frameworks that are initiated in relation to a specific project or urban setting, but that are nevertheless deliberately defined generically from the outset with the potential for application elsewhere. Finally, the third characteristic concerns the dissemination and promotion of frameworks at national and international levels, as opposed to use only at local or regional levels. This (inter)national focus reflects the intended transferability of urban sustainability frameworks, as generic sets of principles and guidelines, across particular local jurisdictions and cultures. Together, these three criteria exclude frameworks defined in relation to specific urban initiatives and contexts. This is, however, not to say that the latter are of no analytical interest or practical significance. Rather, these criteria are used here to achieve a clear analytical focus on internationally emerging, replicable processes for conceptualizing, assessing and managing urban sustainability initiatives. These processes, it is argued, constitute a key element of how the contemporary sustainable city is conceptualized and practised.

Based on this analytical categorization, a global survey reveals the degree to which urban sustainability frameworks intended for replicable application have rapidly gained in popularity in recent years. A total of 43 such frameworks could be identified through a comprehensive international research effort (Joss and Tomozeiu, 2013). As shown in Table 6.1 and further illustrated in Figure 6.1, only three out of these 43 frameworks date back to the 1990s; all the others have come about since the early 2000s. Indeed, no fewer than 34 frameworks (79 per cent of the total number) were launched in the period between 2008 and 2013 alone. This closely mirrors the

Table 6.1 *Replicable urban sustainability frameworks:
global overview 2013*

Name of framework	Year	Type of organization
ASEAN ESC Model Cities	2010	1
Biosphere Eco-City	2006	1
BREEAM Communities	2008; revised 2012	6
CASBEE for Urban Development/ Cities	2007; city version 2010	6
Charter of Eco Mayors (Les Eco Maires)	2010; indicators published 2011	3
City Biodiversity Index ('Singapore Index')	2008; guidelines published 2010	1
CityGrid	2009	5
Climate Positive	2009	5
Community Capital Tool	2012	5
DGNB NSQ	2009; pilot launched 2011	6
Eco-city Development Index System	2011	6
EcoDistricts	2010	3
Eco-Model Cities	2008	2
ÉcoQuartier	2008; second phase 2011	2
Eco2 Cities	2009	1
Enterprise Green Communities, USA	2011	5
Estidama Pearl Community Rating System	2009	2
European Common Indicators	2002	1
FSA	2013	5
Global City Indicators Facility	2008	5
Global Urban Indicators	1991; revised 2006	1

Table 6.1 *(continued)*

Name of framework	Year	Type of organization
Green Cities Programme	2011	1
Green City Index	2009	4
Green City Index	2009	4
Green Climate Cities	2012	3
Green Communities	1996–7	2
Green Star Communities	2012	6
IEFS	2012	5
IGBC Green Townships Rating System	2008; final version 2012	6
LEED ND	2010	6
Living Building Challenge	2006; revised 2012	5
National Eco-County, Eco-City and Eco- Province	2003; revised 2007	2
National Eco-Garden City	2004; revised 2010	2
One Planet Communities	2008	5
RFSC	2010; pilot completed 2012	1
Selo Casa Azul Caixa	2009	2
SlimCity	2009	5
Smarter Cities Challenge	2011	4
Star Community Rating System	2008; registered 2012	
Sustainable Cities Index	2012	5
Sustainable Communities	1998; revised 2010	
Tianjin Binhai Ecocity	2008; KPIs revised 2010	3
Urban Sustainability Indicators	2012	5
REAP for Local Authorities	2010	6

Notes: Organizational type: 1 = international (governmental); 2 = national agencies; 3 = local authorities (incl. networks); 4 = technology/engineering firms; 5 = social enterprises/non-governmental organizations; 6 = professional bodies.

findings of the global census of individual eco-city initiatives, as discussed in Chapter 4, which also indicates a surge of interest and activities since the 2000s and particularly since the mid-to-late 2000s. Taken together, these findings confirm not only a marked increase in individual sustainable city initiatives in recent years but, significantly, at the same time a growing, international interest in standardizing and replicating urban sustainability practice through frameworks of one kind or another.

While replicability, the combination of multiple urban sustainability dimensions, and national and international reach are their unifying features, the 43 frameworks also contain significant diversity. This is apparent alone from the range of organizations involved in their promotion. As Table 6.1 and Figure 6.1(ii) show, a distinction can be made based on six organizational types, from international (governmental) organizations to local government networks, and from social enterprises to professional bodies. Whereas the engagement of international and national governmental agencies is to be expected – they have traditionally been well placed, and have the technical capacity, to lead efforts to co-ordinate and standardize policy and related practice guidance – the growing involvement of non-governmental organizations and professional bodies is remarkable: more than half of the 43 frameworks are promoted by a variety of social enterprises and several green building councils. Some of these, such as the Sustainable Communities framework by Audubon International (undated a), or the LEED Neighborhood certification scheme of the US Green Building Council (USGBC, undated), grew out of particular national contexts, but have since been applied internationally; others were defined from the outset as international frameworks, as illustrated by the Community Capital Tool (Telos, undated), jointly developed by researchers at Simon Fraser University (Canada) and Tilburg University (the Netherlands), and the International Ecocity Framework and Standards (IEFS) (Ecocity Builders, 2011) initiated by Ecocity Builders, the social enterprise founded by Richard Register. Again, some frameworks – such as BREEAM Communities (BRE Global, 2013), DGNB NSQ (German Sustainable Building Council, undated) and CASBEE for Urban Development (Japan GreenBuild Council, undated) – emerged from green building certification schemes, but have since been further developed to offer sustainable development guidance at neighbourhood or even city level; while others have been defined a priori with a city-wide perspective, as exemplified by the Global City Indicators Facility (University of

Figure 6.1 *Eco-city frameworks:*
(i) launch years; (ii) organizational types

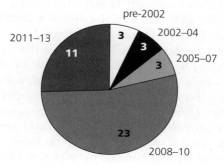

(i) Launch year

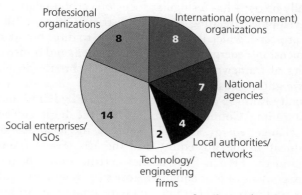

(ii) Organizational type

Base 43 eco city frameworks

Source: Joss and Tomozein, 2013.

Toronto/Government of Ontario) (GCIF, undated) and the Chinese
Eco-City Development Index System (Chinese Society for Urban
Studies) (CSUS, 2011b).

Diversity is also in evidence concerning the ways in which urban
sustainability is defined and prioritized, and the range of governance
functions assigned to individual frameworks. While the frameworks
captured here share a comprehensive, systemic approach to defining
urban sustainability, there is nevertheless considerable variation in
the relative emphases on specific dimensions. At one end of the spectrum are frameworks that prioritize a particular aspect of sustain-

able urban development, while at the same time relating this to wider aspects; at the other end, some frameworks deliberately embrace a broad range of sustainability dimensions, with each dimension equally or similarly weighted. Examples of the former include the UNEP-endorsed City Biodiversity Index (CBD, 2010) and the Climate Positive Development certification scheme by the Clinton Climate Initiative (CCI, 2011). In the case of the City Biodiversity Index, the core focus is on native biodiversity within cities (twelve out of a total of 23 indicators that make up the framework), although this is closely related to wider 'ecosystem services' dimensions (two indicators, focusing on recreational and educational services provided by parks and natural areas) as well as related governance and management criteria (nine indicators, such as local biodiversity strategy and action plans, institutional capacity, and public participation and partnerships). For its part, the Climate Positive Development Program certification scheme – to be explored more fully below – has a singular focus on carbon-neutral, or positive, development relating to urban districts (either in-fill or new district projects), which it defines in relation to three broad, overlapping dimensions: energy use, waste management and transportation. Examples of frameworks with a deliberately broad range of similarly weighted sustainability dimensions include the Star Community Rating System (jointly developed by ICLEI and the US Green Building Council), which covers the built environment, climate change, energy, natural resources, the local economy and jobs, education, health, equity and the arts (Star Communities, 2014); and the French ÉcoQuartier certification scheme, whose structure consists of four equal categories (each with five indicators) relating to land use planning, climate change adaptation and resource preservation, quality of life, and governance (METL, 2012).

Apart from the multifaceted, interrelated sustainability dimensions, what stands out from the 43 frameworks is the frequent inclusion of governance-focused sustainability criteria. A key theme of this book – and increasingly echoed elsewhere in the discussion of sustainability – is the growing recognition of the importance of governance for sustainable urban development (see in particular Chapters 1, 2, and 5); this is reflected in many of the frameworks, which feature indicators relating to institutional sustainability alongside indicators relating to more conventional (environmental, economic and social) sustainability dimensions. For example, any municipal authority adopting the City Biodiversity Index framework would not only be prompted to identify and measure native biodiversity (e.g. plants, birds, butterflies) in built-up areas, or determine the carbon storage and cooling effect of vegetation, but also address the number of city or local government agencies jointly engaged in biodiversity co-operation, or establish the range of partnerships involving various public and private organizations working in the area of biodiversity. Similarly, the ÉcoQuartier certification scheme includes specific indicators prompting planners and decision-makers to consider, for example, how (well) sustainability issues are integrated in investment planning and procurement, and what ongoing evaluation and improvement measures are in place to track progress with urban development and regeneration.

Looking beyond the sustainability dimensions themselves, governance is central to the purpose of eco-city frameworks: they are variously designed as structured processes aimed at enabling the development, implementation and assessment of urban sustainability initiatives. Yet here again, there is considerable diversity concerning the intended governance functions. One sub-set of frameworks has performance assessment as its main governance function, which has been conventionally associated with the use of indicators: these serve to define – and typically quantify – specific aspects of sustainable development; related targets can be set to measure and assess performance over time. For example, in the case of the City Biodiversity Index, the first and arguably most basic indicator relates to the proportion of natural areas in the city (calculated on the basis of the total area of natural areas divided by the total area of the city); the framework provides a scoring tool, which allows for base line measurement and performance assessments across time of this and the other indicators for individual cities, as well as for comparisons between cities. Indicators and related performance assessment methods have become a firmly established – if not uncontested – part of the processes of constructing and generating knowledge about urban development and the sustainable city (see Chapter 7); and so it is not surprising to see this functionality featuring centrally among the frameworks captured here. This is also illustrated by the frequent reference to 'index' or 'indicators' in the names of the frameworks within this particular sub-set, such as the Eco-City Development Index (CSUS, 2011b), the Green City Index (Siemens, 2012), the Sustainable Cities Index (Forum for the Future, undated), the Global City Indicator Facility (GCIF, undated), the Global Urban Indicators (UN-Habitat, 2004) as well as the City Biodiversity Index (CBD, 2010).

Characteristically, however, many of the frameworks include additional governance functions, as part of a more comprehensive process of guiding urban sustainability planning, implementation and monitoring. This often includes 'planning toolkits' of one sort or another, intended to provide practical step-by-step guidance on methodologies, tools and structured processes for taking a given urban sustainability initiative through its various stages, from baseline assessment to strategic vision, and from development to post-implementation monitoring and reporting. As part of this process, some frameworks emphasize the integral role of community engagement, which may serve to mobilize local 'lay expertise' (as opposed to expert knowledge provided by professionals) and/or to enhance the accountability of decision-making and to increase public participation. For example, the Biosphere Eco-City Framework (UNESCO) is defined as 'a framework for action and sharing', with a strong element of community engagement based on public and stakeholder participation (three of its five core objectives are headed 'involve everyone', 'link stakeholders' and 'share information') (Ottawa Biosphere Eco-City Initiative, undated). In the case of Audubon International's Sustainable Communities, the framework lists possible indicators from which a participating community is prompted to put together a set of indicators relevant to the site in question (Audubon International, undated b). Similarly, the Green Communities framework (US Environmental Protection Agency) serves as an open-access 'assistance kit' to guide community-led sustainability action plans (USEPA, 2013). This framework, too, does not prescribe any indicators, but gives possible examples. Part of the multi-stage process of using the framework consists of the participating community itself defining indicators for the site in question.

A further governance function to the fore in a growing number of eco-city frameworks is that of certification. This approach typically entails performance assessment and some form of multi-stage planning processes (the latter occasionally involving community engagement). At the same time, it is distinguished from open-access processes: certification is normally achieved through a membership-based multi-stage accreditation process, typically against some fee payment. The trend towards certification is one of the key features of the recent operationalization of urban sustainability initiatives. It is partly explained by several national green building councils extending their certification schemes for buildings to in-fill and retrofit development at neighbourhood level, of which LEED ND and BREEAM Communities are two prominent examples. It is further explained by the uptake of (not-for-profit) certification by city networks (e.g. Star Community Rating), social enterprises (e.g. EcoDistricts, Enterprise Star Communities, One Planet Communities; Sustainable Communities), and at least in one case – ÉcoQuartier – by a national agency. Certification-based frameworks tend to be favoured by developers and utility companies, as they provide a formal accreditation process, which may be essential for securing third-party investment during the development phases and, subsequently, for lending a project a sustainability 'kitemark' for marketing purposes.

It is to specific eco-city frameworks that one has to turn to gain a fuller picture of how urban sustainability is articulated both as content and process: which sustainability dimensions are emphasized and brought into relationship with others; and how these frameworks are intended to intervene in the design, planning and assessment of urban sustainability initiatives on the ground. This is done here by comparatively discussing three such frameworks as illustrative examples of the range of approaches that have emerged within the last few years: the Tianjin Eco-City Key Performance Indicators scheme, developed in conjunction with China's flagship national eco-city project and serving as a template for similar developments; the Climate Positive Development Program, a certification scheme used to guide urban district projects in eighteen cities across the world to date; and the One Planet Living framework, first developed in the UK and since applied globally in 21 urban sustainability projects.

Similar but different: three replicable frameworks in comparison

An overview analysis of the sustainability dimensions and intended governance functions for the three eco-city frameworks reveals distinctive profiles; these not only highlight the particular ways in which each framework defines sustainable urban development and its intended contribution to facilitating that process, but consequently also the considerable contrasts between them (see Figure 6.2).

The radar charts shown depict particular constellations for each framework relating to sustainability dimensions and governance functions, respectively. In the case of the sustainability radar chart,

Figure 6.2   *Sustainability dimensions and governance functions of three eco-city frameworks*

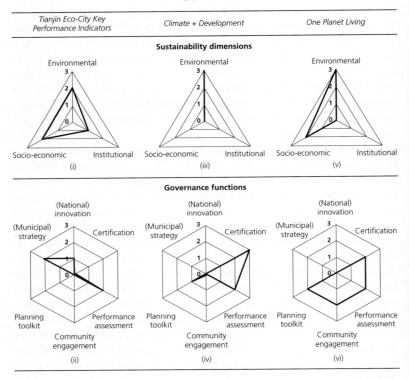

the dimensions used include 'environmental sustainability', 'socio-economic sustainability', and 'institutional sustainability'. While 'environmental sustainability' is a sufficiently clear, albeit broad, category relating to the natural and built environment (energy, water, transport, biodiversity, etc.), an exact demarcation between 'social' and 'economic' sustainability can prove difficult, as frameworks often define social and economic dimensions and related indicators in a cross-boundary manner. Hence, the two categories are represented here in a combined 'socio-economic sustainability' cluster. Given the explicit engagement in many eco-city frameworks with issues of institutional capacity – such as whether sustainability investment strategies or sustainability partnerships are in place – an additional 'institutional sustainability' category is included.

For its part, the governance radar chart is made up of six distinct process-related functions that can be found assigned to eco-city frameworks in varying degrees. In addition to the four functions – '(performance) assessment', 'planning toolkit', 'community engagement', 'certification' – introduced in the preceding section, the radar chart includes '(national) innovation' and '(municipal) strategy' functions. The former refers to the possibility of eco-city frameworks embodying, as well as contributing to, national innovation processes, as exemplified by the French ÉcoQuartier certification scheme and the Tianjin Eco-City Key Performance Indicators (see below), while the latter refers to frameworks' potential contribution to municipal strategy on urban sustainability. For both sustainability and governance radar charts, a scale of 0–3 is given, which allows the weighting of the various dimensions based on how centrally they define any given eco-city framework. For example, the Climate Positive Development Program does not directly engage with either socio-economic or institutional sustainability issues and, therefore, receives a score of 0 in both categories in the sustainability radar chart. Conversely, since its key role is that of a certification scheme based on performance assessment, it scores a maximum (3) and medium (2) for the corresponding functions in the governance radar chart.

Comparing the sustainability profiles of the three frameworks, both the Climate Positive Development Program and the One Planet Living frameworks score highest in the environmental category. This is due to the exclusive focus on measuring and assessing net-carbon urban development in the case of the Climate Positive Development Program certification process; and in the case of One Planet Living due to its use of ecological footprint analysis (see Chapter 1) as its core guiding principle. The latter does, however, also include several socio-economic sustainability principles, such as equity and well-being, as an integral part of the framework, resulting in a medium score. As for the Tianjin Eco-City Key Performance Indicators, these include a substantial element of environmental dimensions (17 out of a total of 26 indicators), but this is balanced out by seven broad socio-economic indicators and two institutional indicators; together, this results in a more balanced triangulation in the sustainability radar chart, in comparison with the other two frameworks (neither of which address institutional sustainability criteria). Overall, then, two of the frameworks define urban sustainability broadly, encompassing various environmental, socio-economic and some institutional dimensions, while one framework pursues a much more focused approach centred upon carbon-positive development.

Significant contrasts are also in evidence concerning the assigned governance functions. The primary function of the Tianjin Eco-City

Key Performance Indicators scheme – as its name suggests – is to provide a set of indicators and related targets, so as to allow the monitoring of performance during the initiative's implementation as well as subsequent performance management during the city's operational phase. As Tianjin Eco-City is a new-build city and, as such, enjoys the status of national flagship initiative, the framework also scores well – albeit in a less pronounced way – in relation to the 'national innovation' and 'municipal strategy' functions. The Climate Positive Development Program framework has a similarly strong, singular governance focus, based upon certification and related performance assessment. The One Planet Living framework, in contrast, subscribes to a broader governance approach, combining 'performance assessment' with 'planning toolkit' and, characteristically, 'community engagement'. While it can be used on an open-access basis, the framework is also offered as a multi-stage, membership-based certification process.

Tianjin Eco-City Key Performance Indicators

The quest for urban sustainability indicators and related governance frameworks has been particularly pronounced in China (CSUS, 2011b; Dong, 2013; Joss and Molella, 2013; Li et al., 2014), which is why the Tianjin Eco-City Key Performance Indicators scheme has significance beyond its original application in Tianjin Eco-City, intended as a potential model for a national urban sustainability framework. Four factors are jointly responsible for China's ongoing efforts to come up with standardization for eco-city development: first, the rapid growth in eco-city initiatives of one kind or another in recent years has created an acute demand for practical guidance on how to plan, implement and monitor sustainable urban development. As noted in earlier parts of this book (see in particular Chapter 4; also Yu, 2014: 76–8), estimates of current Chinese eco-city projects range from several dozens to a few hundreds; to this can be added further, more recent 'low-carbon' and 'smart' city initiatives. Together, this has led to calls for a more concerted, systematic approach to eco-city development. As Jianguo Wei, a senior government official, put it in the foreword to *Beautiful China: Eco-City Indicators Guidebook* (Dong, 2013), 'our thoughts on the construction of eco-cities have, in recent years, rapidly developed from theoretical explorations, to feeling an urgent need to take action, then realising the complexity of the issue, and now researching relevant system models and mechanisms' (Wei, 2013: i). Allied to this, the second factor relates to the complex, partially fragmented and, consequently, at times internally contradictory governance context within which eco-city development takes place in China – it is not unknown for different government ministries to have issued separate eco-city initiatives with little co-ordination between them – which risks impeding the establishment of an overarching governance framework and agreed guidelines (Joss and Molella, 2013). Consequently, the purpose of Tianjin's eco-city framework is not least to define a coherent set of indicators that effectively engages with the requirements of different national eco-city policies and regulations; in doing so, it promises to offer a standardized approach to eco-city development in the country.

A third factor accounting for the interest in urban sustainability indicator frameworks is the dominant discourse in much of the Chinese academic and policy literature on the scientific rationality of eco-city development (for an overview, see Joss and Molella, 2013: 125–8). According to one city planner, 'there is a fever of eco-city in China, and what we urban planners and researchers should do urgently is to identify, clarify, and put in practice the eco-city principles scientifically and rationally' (Qiang, 2009: 519). This stance is echoed in the Tianjin Eco-City declaration published on the occasion of the inaugural 'International Eco-City Forum' in 2010: 'we shall identify a correct concept for urban development, and establish an index system for the scientific assessment of eco-city development' (*China (Binhai Tianjin) International Eco-City Forum Journal*, 2010: declaration/first paragraph). In similar vein, in his foreword to *Beautiful China: Eco-City Indicators Guidebook* (Dong, 2013: Foreword II/ii–iii) – the overarching approach of which is based on indicator frameworks acting as 'integrated quality control system' to guide eco-city development – the head of urban and environmental studies at the Chinese Academy of Social Sciences declares that 'the answer [to the question of how to ensure effective eco-city development] is through scientific planning, rational eco-city standards and implementation protocols'. Finally, a fourth factor in play is China's ambition to shape eco-city development beyond China, as an international leading player. Tianjin Eco-City (see profile in Chapter 4, Box 4.3) is not just a national flagship project; it is heralded as the first inter-governmental eco-city initiative between China and a foreign country (Singapore), and its eco-city indicator framework is presented as potentially standard-setting in the wider international arena. The joint Sino-Singapore ministerial conference established to co-ordinate the Tianjin Eco-City initiative is reported to have declared that the indicator framework 'is the first descriptive guide in China, even around the world, which comprehensively discussed eco-city planning and implementation...It is an important innovation within the process of SSTEC [Sino-Singapore Tianjin Eco-City] construction and will have vital significance in leading and guiding the construction and evaluation of eco-cities' (Dong, 2013: 72).

Tianjin Eco-City is, thus, presented as a 'model for sustainable development'; and its indicator framework, which was approved at bilateral governmental level between China and Singapore through the Ministerial-level Eco-city Joint Working Committee, is described as 'replicable' and 'scalable', whereby 'the principles and models of the Eco-City could be applied to other cities in China and even elsewhere' and that they could be 'adapted for another project or development of different scale' (Singapore Government, 2012). In order to enable replicability, according to the official website the two governments co-ordinated and adjusted the formulation of the various key performance indicators: 'in formulating the KPIs, due consideration was given to the national standards in China and Singapore, and the higher of the two standards was adopted wherever feasible' (Singapore Government, 2013). As such, the framework represents an effort to integrate and amalgamate existing, partial indicator systems (Dong, 2013: 42–3).

The set of 26 indicators (Singapore Government, 2013) is subdivided into four headline categories: (i) 'good natural environment', including six indicators; (ii) 'healthy balance in the man-made environment', with three indicators mainly relating to the built environment; (iii) 'good lifestyle habits', comprising nine indicators; and (iv) 'developing a dynamic and efficient economy', with four indicators. Environmental, economic and social sustainability indicators are not segregated, but rather interwoven as a result of the framework's structuring along these thematic strands. For example, the 'good lifestyle habits' includes an indicator defining the limit of per capita domestic waste production, alongside an indicator specifying the level of affordable housing. Similarly, under 'dynamic and efficient economy', one indicator defines the proportion of renewable energy consumption, next to an indicator measuring jobs in research and development. Of the total of 26 indicators, across the four thematic strands, 17 can be considered as falling into the 'environmental', seven into the 'socio-economic', and two into the 'institutional', sustainability categories. The latter two are qualitative indicators, defined in terms of 'adopting policy to promote regional collaboration' and 'promoting the orderly development of surrounding regions', respectively. The majority of indicators are quantitative in nature, defining specific targets for 2013 – a mid-term point, when the start-up area was due for completion – and a second set of targets for 2020 (the due completion date) for the city as a whole. Some quantitative indicators provide a high degree of specification, while others are defined more broadly with limited quantification. For example, the water consumption indicator is defined as follows: 'the daily water consumption per day each person [sic] should not exceed 120 litres by 2013'; whereas the noise pollution indicator is defined thus: 'noise pollution levels must satisfy the stipulated standards for different functional zones'. The latter appears to conform to basic standards applicable to Chinese cities more broadly.

The framework's governance function overall is defined as guiding 'the planning and development of the Eco-City' (Singapore Government, 2013). As a broad, overarching planning and monitoring tool, it informs and works in tandem with the master plan and the phased development schedule. In doing so, its specific intended function in relation to the project itself is: first, to provide strategic direction in the planning process by defining specific aspects of urban sustainability and setting related targets; and second, to provide a mechanism for quantitative performance assessment across various stages of development (with 2013 and 2020 acting as key milestones), as a means of evaluating progress towards completion. In addition, third, the framework is designed to be used upon completion as a means of ensuring ongoing monitoring during the operational phase. The overall approach is summarized as follows: 'a set of integrated KPI goals that cross multiple disciplines and sectors are [sic] adopted to measure performance. This is similar to a navigation system for the city, which allows for the development of a governance-integrated quality control system' (Dong, 2013: Foreword II/ii–iii).

As noted, beyond its specific application in the Tianjin Eco-City initiative, the 'model' framework is also intended to contribute to the national – and potentially even international – standardization of eco-city development. It does so with a clear emphasis on performance assessment, while remaining relatively silent about other governance functions: little information and guidance are given concerning how the framework is supposed to be integrated in planning and decision-making processes. Furthermore, there are no elements of, for example, community engagement and practical

planning tools, such as are characteristic of other eco-city frameworks; this is at least partly explained by the slant towards the technocratic conceptualization of the eco-city and related indicator
frameworks in terms of systems and engineering sciences.

In reviewing the experience of the Tianjin Eco-City Key
Performance Indicators framework and similar 'pioneering indicator
systems' in China to date, Dong (2013) highlights in particular the
need for achieving more integrated planning, 'to overcome the current
mode of planning in which executive departments only operate in
their own functional areas and lack a holistic picture of the eco-city's
needs' and, relatedly, to provide training to planners since 'experience
has proven that many high level plans, though approved by governments and planning committees, are difficult to be understood and
therefore unhelpful to executive departments' (ibid.: 49). This recommendation flows from Dong's conclusion that, while it is one thing to
establish the basic elements of an eco-city indicator framework, it is
another thing – currently lacking sufficient experience in China – to
determine 'how to implement an indicator system within an existing
urban management and planning system', how to equip planners and
developers with the necessary skills to use indicator systems effectively
and, once applied, 'how to make use of the results of data analysis
outputs' in subsequent planning and management (ibid.: 50).

Climate Positive Development Program

In contrast to the Tianjin Eco-City framework's comprehensive,
'whole-system' and city-wide approach to sustainable development
and urban planning, the Climate Positive Development Program is
more delimited – deliberately so – in its scope and intended function:
its one guiding principle is 'carbon-positive' urban development; its
focus is on neighbourhood- or district-level projects; and its main
mechanism consists of a certification process. The framework
belongs to a growing number of market-based tools for sustainable
urban development and, as such, is mainly geared towards commercial developers or public–private partnerships involved in large-scale
urban in-fill and new urban development projects. However, in
purposefully delimiting sustainable urban development in this way,
the framework necessarily also comes into relationship with wider
aspects of urban sustainability and related governance processes so
that its significance should be considered beyond its immediate
sphere of application.

The Climate Positive Development Program styles itself a 'framework for climate positive communities' which 'aims to create large-scale models for urban development that reduce greenhouse gas emissions below zero in an economically viable manner' (CCI, 2011: 2). The resulting 'Climate Positive Developments' 'will reduce the emissions they create and offset the remainder by removing emissions from their adjacent communities. The creation of the new development will thus reduce overall carbon emissions. We refer to this as a Climate Positive Outcome' (ibid.). The framework's singular focus on carbon-neutral urban development arises from the core mission of the Clinton Climate Initiative (CCI) to help cities reduce their carbon emissions. CCI, together with the US Green Building Council, launched the Climate Positive Development Program in 2009 and has since enlisted 17 projects on six continents – all of which are ongoing, with none having achieved full certification to date – from Menlyn Maine in Pretoria (South Africa), to Nordhavn in Copenhagen (Denmark), and from Dockside Green in Melbourne (Australia) to Parque de Citade in Sao Paolo (Brazil). Both Treasure Island (San Francisco) and Portland's EcoDistricts in the US, which are discussed in detail in Chapter 5, are also enlisted projects (the full participant list can be accessed at CCI, undated). In 2011, CCI merged with the C40 Cities Climate Leadership Group (see Chapter 4), thus reinforcing the focus on climate-oriented urban development centred mainly upon efforts to reduce greenhouse gas emissions.

With its focus on 'climate positive outcomes', the framework primarily addresses carbon emissions at the operational stage of an urban development post completion, thereby excluding construction-related emissions. This seems a considerable omission, given that emissions produced during often lengthy development phases can be substantial. The reason for this omission is not explicitly stated in the framework (CCI, 2011: 5), but (in personal communication with the author) a CCI representative explained it in terms of addressing 'legacy' issues: a developer undertaking a large-scale regeneration project (especially on brownfield sites) may have to carry out substantial, carbon-intensive remediation and development work to realize a large-scale urban project; this could put the developer at a disadvantage relative to another developer working on a project with comparably fewer legacy issues. While construction-based emissions, then, are not formally included in the assessment method and certification process, the framework nevertheless requires developers 'to identify strategies to reduce emissions associated with their largest construction phase emissions sources' so that 'addressing construction emissions represents a meaningful opportunity for Development Partners to demonstrate early leadership in green design and construction' (ibid.).

Again, with its focus on carbon-positive outcomes, the framework does not prescribe particular indicators concerning the means by which this outcome is to be achieved. Rather, it provides a broad categorization in terms of emissions relating to: (i) on-site thermal energy and electrical use, relating to energy consumed in buildings, project infrastructure and water usage; (ii) solid waste and waste water; and (iii) transportation, including a percentage of the total emissions associated with vehicular trips that start or end within the community. According to the framework document, 'these parameters are not meant to be prescriptive; they are too broad to serve such a purpose. Instead, they are intended to guide Development Partners to understand the emission impacts their development will have and to ensure that solutions are identified and implemented in order to reduce emissions' (ibid.: 4). The framework nevertheless sets some broad targets, such as relating to transport emissions:

> Based on the advice of transportation experts, it is suggested that Development Partners include 40% of transportation emissions from trips that start or end on-site. 40% was selected as a proxy for the percentage of emissions associated with the development; Development Partners may submit another figure for consideration, so long as such a figure is substantiated by local circumstances. (Ibid.: 4)

Apart from the transport-related emission calculation, the interrelationship between the project site and its wider surrounding urban area also comes into play in respect of the use of 'carbon credits'. Where a site produces clean energy – for example, through waste-to-heat incineration – any excess energy not used on-site can be exported to the surrounding area, thus earning 'carbon credits'. These credits can be used to offset any remaining on-site operational carbon emissions: 'abated emissions in the broader community serve to cancel out emissions generated within the development itself' (ibid.: 5). However, the framework does not only see 'carbon credits' as a carbon accounting mechanism, but also as an instrument to encourage on-site innovation with the potential for wider uptake in the surrounding community. One such 'catalyzation example' illustrated in the framework document is the application of LED (light-emitting diode) street lighting on the project site: if 'subsequently the same Development Partner meaningfully catalyzes the adoption of the same technology in neighbouring communities both for retrofit and new construction projects ... they can claim credit for all or a portion of the annual energy savings in those communities' (ibid.: 7).

While flexibility is built into the framework concerning the specific means by which a 'carbon-positive outcome' is to be achieved, all carbon emission calculations have to be quantifiable to determine a development site's overall 'emission impacts' – the total emissions, measured in metric tonnes of CO_2, resulting from energy use, waste and transportation – as basis for the 'Climate Positive Development' rating. Furthermore, the process of achieving certification itself is prescriptive and includes a carefully designed multi-stage accreditation procedure (ibid.: 9–13). The first stage entails vetting the developer's initial application outlining the project plan and explaining how a 'Climate Positive Outcome' is to be achieved. If successful, the development is invited to join the Climate Positive Development Program and the developer is admitted as a 'Climate Positive Candidate'. This triggers the second stage of the recognition process, for which the developer is required to prepare detailed documentation – including a 'climate positive roadmap', a measurement and verification plan, and a set of milestones – demonstrating the strategies and implementation tools that will result in a 'Climate Positive Outcome'. Apart from technical data relating to carbon emission profiles for various aspects and phases of the development, the documentation must provide evidence of how the Climate Positive Development Program initiative corresponds to, and is integrated into, other planning and design requirements for the development. This assumes that other, complementary urban sustainability frameworks may be used, for example to address wider environmental or socio-economic aspects (here, again, the framework is defined by its interrelationship with wider urban context). Once the detailed plans have been approved by the independent evaluation panel appointed by CCI, the developer's status progresses from 'Climate Positive Candidate' to 'Climate Positive Participant'. As the project moves along the stated development phases and if the corresponding milestones are met – there are three intermediate milestones at 25 per cent, 50 per cent and 75 per cent of construction – the development receives the 'Climate Positive Progress Site' mark. The fourth and final step, upon project completion, consists of the verification of a carbon-positive outcome at operational stage, with successful evaluation leading to certification as 'Climate Positive Development'. Subsequently, annual data reporting is required to retain the site's designation.

The framework identifies the benefits of this 'membership-based "recognition platform"' (ibid.: 3) at three levels. First, at the most immediate level, the framework provides a structured planning process with built-in verification mechanism for large-scale urban development initiatives. As the official literature explains:

> Why a framework? New developments of this size can take decades to complete. A framework encourages Development Partners to: (a) set realistic plans for achieving the emissions target by project completion, (b) demonstrate that their implementation conforms with those plans at important milestones; and (c) adjust implementation as circumstances and technologies change over the course of development. (Ibid.: 3)

At a second level, by creating a partnership between the local developer and the CCI, the aim is to mobilize relevant expertise: developers have access to the CCI's Technical Resources Panel and Advisory Council, and will benefit from the external evaluation of the Vetting Committee. Furthermore, by establishing a network of 'Climate Positive Participants' – the 17 current projects are brought together in workshops and online forums – the aim is to facilitate knowledge transfer and shared practice learning across individual sites. Finally, a third benefit is seen in terms of encouraging market-based innovation and 'best practice' learning through the structured yet flexible approach pursued by the framework:

> This flexibility is essential to achieve Climate Positive outcomes, since it affords Development Partners the opportunity to refine their strategies and seek continuous improvement. Given the embryonic state of large-scale real estate developments pursuing net-negative emissions, there is a lot to learn from experimentation and little to be gained from rigidity... it is premature to codify best practices or emission protocols into concrete evaluation criteria. Instead, the Program relies in part on the market to identify and deliver these solutions and protocols. (Ibid.: 13)

One Planet Living

Of the three frameworks, One Planet Living is arguably the broadest in conceptual scope: while the Climate Positive Development Program is geared towards urban development projects at neighbourhood/district level, and the Tianjin Eco-City Key Performance Indicators framework is designed for city-wide intervention, the One Planet Living framework is intended yet more extensively for sustainable living overall. This is in no small part due to the social enterprise behind the framework: BioRegional, which has its origins in the UK but is engaged globally in over 20 endorsed projects in partnership with businesses, communities, local authorities, municipal governments and international organizations, defines its vision as one 'of thriving economies where we meet more of our needs from local, renewable and waste resources, enabling people to enjoy a high quality of life within their fair share of the earth's resources, and leaving space for wildlife and wilderness – we call this One Planet Living' (BioRegional, 2014: 5). As such, the One Planet Living framework is concerned with enhancing sustainable living irrespective of whether this relates to a community, a business, a city or a metropolitan region. Yet, while its scope is comprehensive, the One Planet Living framework is nevertheless conceptually rooted in urban sustainability: the framework was designed drawing directly on the experience of BedZED, a mixed-use sustainable urban housing development. (BedZED stands for 'Beddington zero energy development', named after the development's location in Beddington, a neighbourhood area in the Borough of Sutton in south-west London.) And a majority of the endorsed partnerships relate to urban development projects at neighbourhood, district, and in some cases city, levels.

Based on this broad approach, and to account for the application of the framework in various contexts, BioRegional has developed a customized application: One Planet Living serves as the overarching framework enshrining ten core sustainability principles (see below); within this master framework, One Planet Communities is the framework tailored to neighbourhood- or district-level developments, while One Planet City and One Planet Region are the respective frameworks for use at city and regional levels. Finally, One Planet Company is the framework adapted for businesses. All frameworks share the same ten principles, but with some variation concerning specific performance indicators and certification mechanisms. These principles bring together environmental, economic and social sustainability dimensions, which the framework presents as interdependent. Nevertheless, the environmental dimension is accorded central position:

> A sustainable future will need to consider environmental, social and economic factors and the ten One Planet principles and their associated targets have been developed in recognition of this. However, we subscribe to the view that society and the economy cannot exist long-term outside a healthy environment. Consequently, there are three overarching environmental drivers behind the One Planet initiative: sustainable ecological footprint; sustainable carbon footprint, and clean (non-polluting) activities (BioRegional, 2011a: 1).

Hence, the framework at its core is informed by the concept and method of ecological footprint analysis (see Chapter 1), with the aim of sustainable development that ensures regenerative resource consumption within the planet's overall capacity. This central focus is also reflected in the framework's 'one planet' name tag. The corresponding One Planet Communities international target is for an ecological footprint of 1.2 gha (global hectare) per person by 2020, assuming a biocapacity of 1.6 gha per person for sustainable planetary living (ibid.: 2). Within this overall international target, One Planet Communities accommodates differentiated targets depending on country and region. Applied to the 'zero-carbon footprint' – the framework's first, core principle – this is explained with the notion of 'contraction and convergence': 'the One Planet initiative adopts the principle of Contraction and Convergence which means that countries with high *per capita* emissions will have to reduce their emissions much more rapidly than countries that currently have low *per capita* emissions. The end result being that *per capita* emissions from each country will converge at a more equitable level and the global total of emissions will contract' (ibid.: 3). Therefore, for each project, community-specific targets are agreed between BioRegional and the local partners involved, within the parameters of the overarching zero-carbon international target – namely, for all buildings and structures to achieve net-zero-carbon emissions by 2020.

The other principles – again, informed overall by the concept of the ecological footprint – include 'zero waste', with international targets of 70 per cent of domestic waste, and 95 per cent of construction and demolition waste, reclaimed or recycled reclamation;

'sustainable transport', with targets set to result in carbon emissions 'consistent with the overarching greenhouse gas emissions reduction target' (ibid.: 9), which for the UK, as an example, is calculated as one tonne of CO_2 per person per year; 'sustainable materials', calling for materials used for construction and consumer goods to be made from renewable or waste resources, have low embodied energy, and be locally sourced; 'local and sustainable food', based on the vision for 'diets high in local, seasonal and organic produce, as well as healthy diets high in vegetable protein and lower in animal protein than is the norm in many countries with a high ecological footprint' (ibid.: 11); 'sustainable water', defined in terms of safe potable water, efficient water use, water conservation and recycling, and flood risk management; and 'land use and wildlife', with a target of 'net positive contribution to local native biodiversity and natural habitats' (ibid.: 13). In comparison, the targets across these principles range from very specific quantifiable ones – such as for waste management – to more generic, qualitative ones, as in the case of sustainable food and water. This is not to say that the latter are less ambitious and demanding; rather, it suggests that international calculations and standards are less well established and, therefore, greater efforts are required on the part of BioRegional and local partners to define and calculate targets specifically for the individual locations concerned.

Finally, there are three further principles relating to social and economic sustainability aspects; by their nature, however, these are not directly informed by the concept of the ecological footprint: (viii) 'culture and heritage', with the target of developing 'a thriving sense of place and build connectedness and social capital' (ibid.: 14); (ix) 'equity and local economy', with a focus on promoting jobs in the green economy as well as social and physical equity and inclusiveness; and (x) 'health and happiness', with local targets to be set in respect of, for example, 'overcoming chronic illness and unhealthy lifestyles' and 'facilitating inter-generational skills sharing or activities' (ibid.: 16). While these principles are arguably less tangible compared with their environmental counterparts, the framework nevertheless includes some specific indicators: for example, under the 'culture and heritage' principle, a stated 'key measure' of the strength of community is defined as 'the number of neighbours known by name', which is to be surveyed annually (ibid.: 14); under 'equity and local economy', 'two priority groups within the local context will be identified and through discussion with them or their representatives, actions taken to improve their welfare' (ibid.: 15);

and for 'health and happiness', one indicator target is to 'complete two showcase initiatives to promote health and happiness in the community. Suitable projects will be identified using baseline data to benchmark the local context, identifying specific areas of need... Residents' satisfaction levels will be monitored on an annual basis' (ibid.: 16).

One Planet Living – and its specific tools for neighbourhoods, cities, regions and businesses – is offered both as an open-source framework for self-use by interested parties and – like the Climate Positive Development Program – a membership-based certification scheme based on a multi-stage assessment and accreditation process. Certification is promoted as 'a stamp of recognition and reserved for exemplary communities, businesses and regions' (BioRegional, 2011b: 7); it is 'only used for major projects and programmes where our One Planet partners have made commitments in a One Planet Action Plan. These plans include time-bound targets allowing for equitable and sustainable use of resources... Performance against targets is assessed periodically and the plans updated' (BioRegional, 2014: 5). As part of the accreditation process, monitoring is seen as 'essential to understand and evaluate progress' and – again like the Climate Positive Development Program – it is accepted that other rating mechanisms and monitoring tools may be used: 'To ensure minimal additional workloads for partners, wherever possible monitoring a One Planet Action Plan uses the partner's existing environmental performance management system.' (BioRegional, 2011b: 7). BioRegional's role in this process is two-fold: on one hand, it acts in an advisory and facilitating capacity, to assist the partner involved in engaging with the One Planet principles and developing the project's action plan; this is done through a series of workshops aimed at sharing information and practice learning. On the other, BioRegional acts as the certifier through its endorsement panel which operates at arm's length to ensure independence and transparency. On their part, partners can use independent expert reviews as third-party verification for reporting.

According to one evaluation report, 'the [One Planet Living] framework is deemed by those who have used it as "accessible", "easily adaptable", "flexible" and "comprehensive"' (UK Green Building Council, 2013: 2). At the same time, the report concludes that the process of setting targets can be 'very challenging', especially those needing 'creativity, for example setting sustainable food targets'; and consequently, 'the training and induction of employees and project teams is needed to ensure that sustainability principles are embedded across all levels of management as well as within organisational or project thinking' (ibid.: 2). Overall, the report considers it a particular strength that the framework 'uses ecological and carbon footprinting to benchmark projects against absolute sustainability, and then regularly updates these figures during occupation. This offers a challenge to the sector, as current industry practice is rooted in modeling and benchmarking of pre-occupancy technical building performance rather than lifestyle and occupancy performance models' (ibid.: 4). Arguably, however, this strength, coupled with the additional comprehensive approach to socio-economic sustainability dimensions, may also harbour the risk of 'over-stretch': broad societal issues, such as a sustainable food chain, healthier eating habits and 'happy lives' reach beyond the traditional sphere of responsibility of local governments and developers alike and may, therefore, be difficult to influence positively in a manner that is measureable and verifiable as part of a formal recognition platform as provided by One Planet Living.

From 'innovation niches' to standardization?

The recent rise in replicable, standardized urban sustainability frameworks – as illustrated by the three schemes examined in this chapter – is characterized by three significant concurrent developments. First, these frameworks point to a shift towards defining sustainable urban development in a comprehensive and concerted way, indicative of a prevalent 'whole-system' approach driving contemporary theory and practice of urban sustainability. This stands in contrast to earlier periods, which frequently saw the discussion – especially concerning the *problematique* of defining indicators for sustainable urban development – conducted in a more atomistic, fragmentary manner (relating exclusively to, say, energy, or buildings). Characteristically, the attempt through these emerging frameworks to relate various sustainable development dimensions to one another as well as to different urban scales is not just considered a theoretical exercise, but as much intended for practical innovation and application.

Relatedly, second, the frameworks are significant in that they demonstrate the increasing recognition of governance as a key ingredient of, and condition for, sustainable urbanism. It is not uncommon to see urban sustainability defined equally in terms of institutional capacity, collaborative practice and social engagement as in more conventional, technical ways of specifying environmental, economic and social data. Several of the eco-city frameworks have produced a pronounced if not exclusive focus on the 'institutional sustainability' dimension, matched by related process-oriented governance functions: for example, the World Bank's Eco2 Cities initiative (see Chapter 3) describes itself as an 'analytical and operational framework' with all 19 of its indicators defined in terms of collaborative, 'whole-system' planning and assessment processes; and even the City Biodiversity Index, ostensibly a technical performance assessment tool, includes several explicit indicators addressing governance capacity to deal with, and enhance, biodiversity issues. Governance, then, is presented as rather more than an 'add-on' set of assessment criteria; this functionality is increasingly understood as central to a framework's ability to facilitate urban sustainability planning, implementation and assessment. Hiroaki Suzuki, as Lead Urban Specialist at the World Bank, encapsulates the frameworks' governance function as follows: 'the real value of eco-city indicators is not to show quantitative output but to help the policy-makers and practitioners...in this sense, eco-city indicators and their implementation framework are core building blocks of cities' governance system' (Suzuki, 2013: i).

Finally, the third significant characteristic of the eco-city frameworks captured here is their intended replicability. By broadly applying a 'whole-system' approach and related governance criteria, sustainable urban development is rendered a generic process that can be set out in principle and then applied – potentially repeatedly, across a variety of urban settings – locally within specific contexts. In response to the perceived need for up-scaling and accelerating sustainable urban development, the availability of generic, replicable frameworks and tools must be welcomed by policy-makers, planners and practitioners alike. And yet, replicability raises important questions about the extent to which urban sustainability (governance) can be adequately defined and addressed through such generic frameworks; who are involved as intermediaries in translating these into local contexts; and what interactions arise on an individual basis in the course of their local implementation.

In Chapter 2, the innovation perspective was introduced as a useful way of considering the emergence and evolution of sustainable city initiatives, both individually and collectively. The perspective can be extended here to eco-city frameworks, which can be partly understood as 'innovation niches', and partly as processes of consolidating and ultimately standardizing innovation practices to become the new 'regimes'. Viewed as 'innovation niches', eco-city frameworks provide spaces for diverse actors to come together to generate new knowledge and apply this knowledge in practice contexts to produce new innovations. By defining overarching parameters, setting out methods and tools, and offering (technical, organizational, financial) assistance, the frameworks provide some sort of a protected space – characteristic of 'niches' – within which actors can innovate. Experimentation is encouraged and collaboration between experts, planners and practitioners is facilitated, with several frameworks actively pursuing international–local and local–local partnerships. In different ways, all three examples featured in this chapter embody this role as 'innovation niches': in the case of Tianjin Eco-City, the development of the key performance indicator framework itself constitutes an ongoing innovation process, through which the eco-city has been conceptualized and defined for the Chinese context; in the case of both the Climate Positive Development Program and One Planet Living, the frameworks set out the overall parameters – net positive carbon emissions and ecological footprint, respectively – within which local actors are encouraged to come up with custom-made solutions. In both of these cases, the parent organization (CCI and BioRegional, respectively), acting as intermediary, forms collaborative partnerships with the local actors; in addition, knowledge sharing and transfer between individual initiatives may be facilitated through networking co-ordinated by the parent organization. Viewed from this 'innovation niche' perspective, the generic, replicable nature of the frameworks need not be seen as imposing an inflexible standard approach on local contexts; rather, it can be appreciated as providing the necessary assurance (through the recognition, or certification, process) while at the same time allowing flexibility to engage in innovation.

The innovation literature points to the possibility of the collectivity of 'innovation niches' forging a path across time that ultimately manages to destabilize the established, and in its place create an alternative, 'regime' – here, new modes of sustainable urban development replacing conventional, relatively unsustainable urbanism. The discussion in Chapter 2 suggests that taken together – that is, beyond their individual, local significance – sustainable city initiatives can be seen as working towards a new urban sustainability 'regime'. Eco-city frameworks add to this process; they can even be seen as representing the next step in that process: by generically and replicably setting out principles, defining rules and providing techniques – in relation to sustainability itself as well as, importantly, in relation to corresponding governance processes – they actively aspire to define the new 'regime'. Some do so by seeking to redefine the official policy and planning processes – as in the case of the Tianjin Eco-City Key Performance Indicators framework – others by developing alternative processes, such as the market-based certification approach of the Climate Positive Development Program. In the course of doing so, several of the frameworks have begun to advertise their ambition of becoming the new standard for urban development. For example, the Tianjin Eco-City Key Performance Indicators framework is promoted beyond its application in Tianjin as the first comprehensive standard of its kind 'in China, even elsewhere' (see above). For its part, following its initial experimental development phase, the French ÉcoQuartier framework introduced a national labelling (certification) scheme, to standardize and recognize individual initiatives. At international level, the organization involved in the Global City Indicators Facility framework recently teamed up with the International Organization for Standardization to develop ISO 37120, which is promised to be the first officially recognized global standard for 'sustainable development and resilience in cities' (see Introduction).

If and when eco-city frameworks move along this innovation path, what they can be expected to gain in terms of a standardizing role and influence they may well lose in terms of their original 'innovation niche' character: the level of experimentation may gradually diminish and the degree of flexibility be replaced by more prescriptive rules and standard methodologies. In parallel, there may well follow a consolidation towards a few dominant, mainstream frameworks. Current signs, however, are of a still proliferating field marked by a plurality of frameworks – the analysis here identified as many as 43, many of which have sprung up within but a few, recent years – opening up experimental niches, promoting innovative practices and vying for a market share. The three frameworks discussed in detail in this chapter alone are testament to the diversity of approaches found. The Tianjin Eco-City Key Performance Indicators framework is representative of a more technocratic, and as such arguably more conventional, approach which emphasizes comprehensive scientific methodology and detailed technical specification. At the same time, its definition of urban sustainability and related indicators and targets are relative, reflecting current trends in urban development (policy) in China. In contrast, both the Climate Positive Development Program and One Planet Living frameworks use a more absolute baseline for urban sustainability – namely, net positive carbon emissions and ecological footprint, respectively. While these are ultimately defined by established scientific knowledge, the frameworks themselves entail less extensive technical specification and deploy a more communicative discourse aimed for use by a range of practitioners. They – and especially One Planet Living – do so with the purpose of serving essentially as collaborative planning and assessment platform, involving local partnerships and even community participation, rather than acting mainly as a technical instrument for expert use as in the case of Tianjin Eco-City.

Diversity also manifests itself in terms of the urban scales for which the frameworks are designed: the Climate Positive Development Program is exclusively directed at large-scale urban developments – mostly real estate – at neighbourhood and district level, whereas the Tianjin Eco-City Key Performance Indicator framework is designed for city-wide level. One Planet Living is unique among the range of frameworks in that it constitutes a variable scheme, with application possible at urban neighbourhood, city, and city-region, levels (in addition to commercial organizations). Furthermore, the various frameworks sit along a state–market–community spectrum: for example, the Tianjin Eco-City and the ÉcoQuartier frameworks are sponsored by governmental bodies and directed at official planning bureaus and related professionals; the likes of Climate Positive Development Program, LEED ND and BREEAM Communities are primarily directed at developers and utility companies (often in partnership with local authorities); and Community Capital Tool and Sustainable Communities are examples of frameworks designed particularly with community engagement in mind. Finally, as noted, there can be a marked variation in the sustainability focus, with some frameworks deliberately broad in scope – as illustrated by One Planet Living – and others providing more narrow thematic perspectives, such as the Climate Positive Development Program and the City Biodiversity Index. Generally, environmental aspects tend to be defined more technically and concisely – reflecting the availability of established research data and methodologies – in comparison with more narrative, qualitative descriptions for social sustainability dimensions.

Conclusions

The application of replicable urban sustainability frameworks in particular local contexts is designed as an intervention in governance processes: they serve to provide strategic and technical guidance on how sustainable city initiatives are defined, facilitate collaboration and networking among relevant stakeholders, assist with perform-ance assessment, and obtain endorsement, among other functions. The interactions arising from such intervention may inevitably cause some tension concerning what is defined generically, 'top down' as part of a replicable framework, and what is fashioned locally, 'bottom up' reflecting the particular conditions on the ground. What constitutes an appropriate balance between the standard aspects of eco-city frameworks and the local variation of particular applica-tions remains an open discussion in need of ongoing conceptual and practical exploration. One way of considering this interaction would be to postulate that replicable eco-city frameworks should enshrine global standards pertaining to substantive aspects of urban sustain-ability: this could, for example, be grounded in the principles of ecological footprint or zero-carbon emissions (as in the case of the One Planet Living and Climate Positive Development Program frameworks). Based on these absolute, outcome-oriented global standards, the process-oriented implementation could be defined flexibly by the frameworks, reserved for local determination and adaptation. This would also allow room, depending on individual circumstances, for additional locally relevant sustainability dimen-sions to be integrated into the overarching global framework. For example, the United Nations Environment Programme recommends such an approach, in what it calls a 'two-layered, nested model combining local and global assessments' (UNEP, 2012b: 5). Similarly, Williams et al. (2012: 12) suggest that 'developing a set of very few core indicators, supported by city-specific non-core indica-tors, presents a practical solution to the issue of compatibility and standardised evaluation'. The advantage of such an approach is that eco-city frameworks would be defined by absolute, global stan-dards; however, this would require international agreement on what these should be – in the case of environmental dimensions most likely relating to the world's ecological carrying capacity (footprint) and/or carbon emission reduction targets.

Another way of considering the interaction would be to forgo any attempt to standardize substantive aspects of sustainable develop-ment and instead centre the definition of frameworks upon proce-dural dimensions. This would be based on the argument that there exists too much variation concerning what constitutes sustainable urban development across vastly different cities and global regions to be able to expect to arrive at global standards that are meaningful and practical. Instead, the focus should be on facilitating 'good practice' concerning institutional, organizational and social processes to enable actors on the ground – especially in situations with limited existing governance capacity – to engage effectively with sustainable urban development. The strength of this approach is its ability to promote knowledge transfer and common practice learning across different settings; its weakness, arguably, is that it leaves untouched the essential question of what the minimum standards for global urban sustainability should be.

However exactly the balance ends up being struck between the standard aspects of eco-city frameworks and the local variation of particular applications – an important but as yet not fully exhausted discussion – the implications of using replicable frameworks within specific local contacts need careful consideration. At present, most of the frameworks are too recent and their applications in practice only at pilot stage to allow a more definitive verdict based on empirical evidence. What is clear, though, is that as practical experience accumulates, these frameworks require closer, in-depth examination to determine their potential and actual contribution to sustainable urban innovations – and the importance of critically reflecting on this development will only grow if certain frameworks come to dominate the field in the future. Far from being a peripheral concern, standardization looks set to become a major – even a decisive – factor shaping the outcomes of sustainable city initiatives, the relationships among various actors, and the process of generating and translating knowledge about urban sustainability.

Chapter 7

Sustainability Through Knowledge

CHAPTER OVERVIEW

Contemporary sustainable city initiatives are sometimes labelled 'knowledge cities'. From this perspective, economic and social activity that is knowledge-intensive – based upon education, research, innovation and creative industries – is fundamentally implicated in processes of sustainable urban development. The connection between sustainability and knowledge does not, however, only manifest itself programmatically; even the spatial designs of recent initiatives such as Sejong (Korea) and Caofeidian International Eco-City (China) are shaped by the concept of knowledge city. More generally, knowledge plays an increasingly ubiquitous role through the integration of digital information technology. Various 'smart-city' strategies are deployed to collect, process and interpret large sets of data; this not only affects urban infrastructure and utilities, such as transport and energy networks, but – potentially more profoundly – also creates new 'knowledge infrastructures' resulting from the digital interaction of people with urban environments. Meanwhile, data and information – in the form of indicators, metrics and modelling – have become central to how the sustainable city is conceptualized, assessed and warranted. Consequently, the altogether pervasive status of knowledge vis-à-vis the sustainable city opens up a critical discussion about how it should best be understood and, importantly, actively governed.

Introduction: the centrality of knowledge

Of the many possible ways to characterize the sustainable city, 'knowledge' may not be an attribute that immediately springs to mind. And yet, knowledge reveals itself as a defining aspect of the sustainable city and its contemporary discourses. Knowledge forms an important narrative in the normative construction of the sustain-

238

able city, and it plays an increasingly central role in the techniques and methodologies used in sustainable urban development and related governance processes. In turn, the sustainable city produces and privileges certain kinds of knowledge, reflecting what sustainable urbanism is understood to be and expected to achieve. As a consequence, inquiring into the *problematique* of the sustainable city – how it is conceptualized, analysed and applied in practice – prompts pertinent questions about the nature and role of knowledge.

Knowledge as a key attribute of the sustainable city can be seen reflected in a growing number of initiatives. Sejong, a new city currently under construction in South Korea, is a case in point: it is served up by the Korean government as 'Asia's green metropolis of the future' (MACCA, undated). Its name refers to a defining period in the country's history, in the fifteenth century under King Sejong, which was marked by the introduction of the Korean alphabet system as well as several significant technological innovations. This knowledge legacy forms the background and inspiration of the new city which is defined spatially and programmatically through six major functional zones situated around the city's central park. Five of these zones are variously designated knowledge centres, with the sixth zone forming the hub of local government. The Central Administrative Zone is to be home to 16 national government research institutes relocated from their original base in the capital Seoul; the Culture and International Exchange Zone is designed to host international conference facilities, libraries and various cultural institutions; the University and Research Zone and the Medical Service Zone are to become an international centre for research and education in the fields of science, medicine and the arts; and the High Technology Industry Zone is described as 'a hub of high-tech innovation ... for international IT companies to develop new products and solutions for domestic and foreign markets' (ibid.: 6). Altogether, 'Sejong will house R&D and training centres and commercialise new knowledge' (ibid.: 9); and this is all to happen in what is promised as 'one of the greenest cities in the world' (ibid.: 8) on account of its extensive green space (making up over 50 per cent of the city's area), green rooftops, renewable energy use and an integrated public transport system, among other environmental features. In addition to being the seat of new learning and innovation to be realized through the six multifunctional zones, knowledge plays another important, if deliberately less visible, role in this 'green metropolis of the future': the use of digital information through various 'smart' technological systems – such as 'intelligent traffic system' and 'integrated information networks' – is to be omnipresent throughout the city and centrally managed through the Integrated City Information Center (MACCA, 2011: 22). This ubiquitous application of digital information and data management is not only intended to help make Sejong a 'green city' but also an innovative 'u-city' (short for 'ubiquitous city') characterized by 'human-oriented technology' (ibid.: 22).

Knowledge, then, is implicated in the contemporary sustainable city in two defining ways. First, it occupies a central position within the mainstream economic rationale for urban sustainability. Here, the sustainable city acts as 'hub' and 'incubator' for a new mode of economic activity that is based on information- and knowledge-based development and production. This economic activity is not only more knowledge-intensive; it also promises to have reduced negative environmental impacts in comparison with more tradi-tional energy- and waste-intensive industries. Often centred upon science parks and business innovation clusters, the emphasis is on high-tech and creative industries, such as renewable energy technol-ogy, environmental services and media companies. The wider sustainable city forms the backdrop of such knowledge-based economic activity – it provides a convenient, healthy and 'liveable' urban environment for the skilled workers and professionals employed in the various knowledge industries – and it may also serve as testing ground for the application of new technologies and serv-ices emerging from these urban economic clusters. Conceived of as such, the sustainable city is as much – if not more essentially – a proposition for transitioning towards a sustainable 'knowledge economy' and 'knowledge society', as it is a proposition for redress-ing environmental ills and related socio-economic challenges. Figuring out what precisely constitutes, enables and consolidates this 'knowledge society', therefore, becomes as central an aspect of the sustainable city, as does delivering particular environmental benefits.

A second, important way in which knowledge has come to define the sustainable city is through the application of information and communication technologies. This refers in particular to the increas-ing deployment of tools and methods based on digital technology, such as geographical information systems and urban modelling. The use of digital information can be seen both in the development and the operationalization of sustainable city initiatives. Proponents welcome the application of such ubiquitous 'big data' as an opportunity to achieve more comprehensive, system-based urban planning, development and management; critics fear that this may lead to a new technocratic era, unless the dominance of large information technology and engineering companies can be limited and the role of communities in the co-production of sustainable urban development strengthened. Even if the level of applications of 'big data' technology is currently still somewhat limited, with the benefits for sustainable urban development yet to be fully tested in practice, at least conceptually sustainable city initiatives are increasingly defined in terms of such knowledge-based, 'smart' technology.

There is an obvious, close interconnect between the sustainable city as the product of the application of knowledge-based technology and the sustainable city as the producer of knowledge-intensive economic activity and social life. This particular conceptualization of the sustainable city, arguably dominant in contemporary policies and practices, stands in contrast to urban sustainability propositions of earlier periods which were more directly and overtly informed by environmental considerations (see Chapter 3); and it competes with alternative visions and approaches which favour more low-tech, economically less intensive and locally grounded urbanism. Beyond its conceptual manifestation, the central role of knowledge in mainstream sustainable urbanism can be expected to influence urban form and function: in the case of Sejong, the city is structured and organized according to the principle of 'multifunctional administration' in the form of a series of specialized zones, each focusing on particular knowledge functions (research, education, technological development, cultural exchange, etc.); the city is further structured and organized based on the particular design and arrangement of various 'smart' technologies.

There is a further, third manner – equally to be explored in this chapter – in which knowledge is implicated in the sustainable city. In the preceding chapter, the role of urban sustainability frameworks was discussed; these essentially engage in generating, analysing and interpreting knowledge about sustainable urban development. They do so variously by using indicators, performance assessment tools, even community engagement processes. As such, they highlight the centrality of the knowledge process in the normative conceptualization, the practical development and the assessment of sustainable city initiatives. A core concern of this book is to understand the sustainable city in terms of processes of transition and related innovation and governance. From this perspective, sustainable city initiatives individually and collectively chart a process of steering, or attempting to steer, urban development towards more sustainable performance in terms of various environmental and associated economic and social outcomes. That process fundamentally entails constructing, gathering, analysing and interpreting knowledge about the goals and corresponding targets of sustainable urban development, about the means – systems, techniques, and practices – by which these objectives are to be achieved, and about related methods of recording, measurement and assessment.

If the sustainable city constitutes an evolving process, we should not be surprised that the related knowledge produced is typically found to be fragmentary, uncertain and, consequently, often contested and occasionally conflictual. If coming by comprehensive information and intelligence about the present state of urban development is challenging enough then developing grounded knowledge about future urban sustainability can be more precarious still. What is more, the process of generating relevant knowledge is likely to introduce certain biases arising from normative assumptions, value preferences and methodological choices at work. Indicators and systems models may sometimes be posited as comprehensive and objective representations of urban sustainability; on closer examination, however, they frequently expose the limitations of the knowledge thus produced. Hence, the process of generating and interpreting knowledge is in many ways a challenging if elemental aspect of what constitutes the sustainable city. Consequently, it requires ongoing, critical self-reflection by the various epistemic communities involved in the construction of the sustainable city.

The three ways in which knowledge is central to the conceptualization and practices of the sustainable city, as outlined above, are discussed in more detail in the sections which follow, and some of their key characteristics are summarized in Table 7.1.

Knowledge-based urban development

Sejong is particularly illustrative of the sustainable city conceptualized as knowledge city: the South Korean government, on whose behalf the new 73 km^2 city is being developed, promotes it in equal measure as 'a new growth engine' and 'one of the world's greenest cities' (MACCA, undated: 1–2). This dual strategy is a core element of the government's national growth paradigm, reflected in the *National Strategy for Green Growth* launched in 2009 (UNEP, 2010). The policy seeks to respond to two concurrent needs facing

Table 7.1 *Knowledge and the sustainable city: summary of key dimensions*

	Knowledge-based development	Digital data integration	Management by measurement
Key metaphors	Urban innovation hub, research incubator, business cluster, knowledge networks	Urban operating system, digital nervous system, city dashboard, control centre, self-aware urban infrastructure, digital collaboration	Urban indicators and standards, modelling, performance assessment, frameworks, monitoring, control
Related discourses	Green growth, knowledge society, regional innovation, next-generation infrastructure	'Big data', 'Internet of Things', 'Cyborg Cities', service delivery, digital skills, privacy, security	International comparability, accountability, inter-regional competitiveness
Typical applications	Knowledge city, special economic zones (SEZs), science parks, eco-industrial parks	Smart city, ubiquitous city, Future Cities Demonstrator	Green city index, carbon reporting, ecological footprints

the country: on one hand, addressing various environmental challenges resulting from rapid economic growth and corresponding urbanization since the 1970s, by promoting environmentally sustainable urban development; and on the other, stimulating new economic growth in response not least to the global financial crisis of the late 2000s, through the 'greening' of existing industries and the development of new green technologies (Kamal-Chaoui et al., 2011). The close interplay between Sejong as both 'green' and 'knowledge' city can be seen in relation to the city itself as well as its wider programmatic and spatial positioning: while Sejong is an initiative in its own right, planned and implemented through a specially established governmental agency (the Multifunctional Administrative City Construction Agency), it at the same time forms part of a wider innovation nexus. The latter, dubbed International Science Business Belt (ISBB), is based in the Daejeon metropolitan area close to where the new city of Sejong is in the process of emerging. Launched in 2011 by the Ministry of Education, Science and Technology, the purpose of the ISBB is 'to boost the country's basic science capacity'; within it, Sejong's particular function is to 'house R&D and training centres and commercialise new knowledge' (MACCA, undated: 9).

At the level of the city itself, principles of green–knowledge urbanism translate into the spatial design, with the city centre occupied by a large central park and green space and a restored river system taking up over 50 per cent of the city's overall area. The six distinct functional zones are dotted around the central park and connected with one another through a circular transit system designed to favour public transportation. (The spatial design has a rather striking resemblance with Howard's original garden city plan; see Figure 3.2.) In emphasizing spatial connectivity between the various zones, the integration of knowledge activities is actively sought, with the zones intended to 'facilitate opportunities for collaboration between start-ups, large enterprises, and universities' (ibid.: 6). With its explicit focus on learning networks and related knowledge innovation, the various 'green' elements of Sejong may seem not much more than a desirable setting and convenient backdrop; after all, the official literature (posted online at www.happycity.go.kr) highlights the liveability of the new city: 'The open green space in the center of the city, surrounded by many art facilities, will be used for community activities and relaxation. Bustling with many citizens, the park will be the symbol of the city' (MACCA, 2011: 18). Yet, the connectivity between the 'green' and 'knowledge' city appears to go deeper:

it forms a central element of Korea's current eco-innovation strategy. The *National Strategy for Green Growth* emphasizes the need for an economic transition from 'quantitative growth' to low-carbon 'qualitative growth' with specific policies 'to tackle climate change and enhance energy security, create new engines of growth through investment in environmental sectors, and develop ecological infrastructure' (UNEP, 2010: 8); and it specifies a dozen or so new 'green growth' industries – encompassing renewable energy, green transportation, biomedicine, IT fusion systems, healthcare and education services, among others (Kamal-Chaoui et al., 2011: 48) – all of which Sejong seeks to support. It even explicitly lists 'state-of-the-art green cities' among the new growth industries (ibid.).

Sejong's status as green-knowledge city, then, has not come about by accident; it is part of a concerted strategy on the part of the South Korean government. As such, it is not an isolated case: since the middle of the 2000s, the government has embarked on a programme to develop a dozen or so 'regional innovation cities' aimed at achieving more balanced territorial development and fostering industrial clusters (ibid.: 49). The emphasis, not unlike in the case of Sejong, is on 'promot[ing] networking and collaboration among regional industries, universities and local governments to stimulate local economies and enhance the innovation capacity of local areas' (ibid.). Elsewhere, the government has pushed the development of 'regional environmental technology development centres' aimed at greening the existing regional innovation system. The focus on knowledge is, once again, to the fore through 'analysis and study of local environmental pollution, development of environmental technology, environmental education and technical support to enterprises coping with environmental management problems, dissemination of new environmental technologies, and promotion and education regarding new environmental technologies to local people' (ibid.: 49–50). A further Korean example of the green city as knowledge city is Songdo, a 54 km^2 district situated to the west of Seoul and part of the 209 km^2 large Incheon Free Economic Zone (see Box 3.3). It is promoted as an international centre delivering a 'new business paradigm' – under the slogan 'accelerate your business in Songdo' – and includes among other functions a 'knowledge and information industrial park', a 'bio research complex', an 'advanced IT convergence valley', a 'high-tech industrial cluster', and the 'Songdo Global University Campus' (IFEZ, undated). It boasts Asia's first convention centre accredited under the LEED NC (new construction) certification framework (see Chapter 6); and like Sejong, it is designed as ubiquitous city: 'Experience a city of the future that fully integrates ubiquitous technology and where everyday life, like diverse transportation information and shopping is connected to the internet' (ibid.).

The connectivity of 'green' and 'knowledge' city may be particularly pronounced in the case of South Korea on the basis of its explicit national policy on urban innovation clusters and ubiquitous city technology, but it is by no means unique to that country. Across global regions, the concept of 'green-knowledge city' has found increasing policy appeal and practical application. As discussed in Chapter 3, since the early 2000s a paradigmatic shift has occurred in the discussion of urban sustainability towards a closer, more explicit conceptual linking of environmental sustainability with economic development. The resulting 'ecological modernization', or 'green growth', agenda seeks to reconcile urban development and economic growth with environmental protection mainly by focusing on less resource-intensive, low-carbon technological innovation. Within this paradigm, knowledge occupies a pivotal position in enabling various green technological innovations and information-based urban development.

China's various national eco-city and low-carbon city initiatives are implemented under the guidance of 'ecological modernization' (see Box 3.2), with several projects pursuing explicit knowledge-city strategies. Suzhou Industrial Park, for example, was designated one of the first 'national eco industry demonstration zones' with three-fold support from the Ministry of Environmental Protection, the Ministry of Commerce and the Ministry of Science and Technology (SIP, 2008). Like Tianjin Eco-City (see Chapter 6), this is a bilateral programme developed jointly with Singapore; more recently, an additional co-operation was formed with US partner organizations to implement an 'eco science hub', as demonstration project for low-carbon and related renewable energy technology development. Another Chinese example is Caofeidian International Eco-City (see Chapter 4, Introduction), which is concurrently termed 'eco-city', 'city of innovation' and 'information city'. As the promotional literature exalts, the city-to-be 'lays emphasis on scientific and technological innovation … and gives top priority to constructing an innovative system … The city must be constructed through ceaseless innovation' (Tangshan Bay Eco-City Management Committee, 2011). This 'ceaseless' innovation is illustrated in the following terms:

Make use of the favorable location, scientific resources and coastal resources, preferentially develop knowledge innovation industries such as education, R&D and cultural creativity on the basis of high-tech industries, encourage the development of urban service industries such as coastal vacation tourism and sports leisure, as well as production service industries such as finance consultation [sic] and convention & exhibition, and build an information media industry base ... in the era of informatisation by means of creating a living, working and leisure space ... on the basis of the ubiquitous network coverage (3G network) of the digital city'. (Ibid.: 18)

The planners of Caofeidian International Eco-City call this approach a new concept of 'informatization-based eco-city', which translates as 'a city fully covered by the Internet and a platform for "digital city" sharing' which will be used to design and implement 'public service systems such as education, medical care and finance systems as well as public management systems such as transportation and public security systems' (ibid.: 13). 'This', Caofeidian's promoters declare, 'is a more vigorous eco-city mode, which will become a model and sample [sic] for China and even the whole world' (ibid.).

Elsewhere, cities as the hub for knowledge-based innovation also forms the core argument of *Delivering the Next Economy*, a report published by the Brookings Institution with a mainly American audience in mind (Katz et al., 2010). Its authors propose the 'next economy' for the US as one which is 'driven by exports (to take advantage of rising global demand), powered by low carbon (to lead the clean energy revolution), fuelled by innovation (to spur growth through ideas and deployment) and rich with opportunity ... An economy with these characteristics will necessarily have one additional feature: it will be led by metropolitan areas' (ibid.: 2). The authors then proceed to demonstrate the central role for cities in enabling (sustainable) innovation and the need, therefore, for effective policies and support mechanisms:

The low-carbon economy will be primarily invented, financed, produced, and delivered in the top 100 metros. Fifteen of the 21 national labs overseen by the US Department of Energy are located within the top 100 metropolitan areas, making them hubs of clean energy innovation. And making our old and new homes, office, retail and commercial facilities energy efficient will primarily be a metropolitan act, given where most people live and businesses locate ... the top 100 metros concentrate 85 percent of the jobs in green architecture, building design, and construction. On innovation more broadly, our metropolitan areas are the nation's knowledge and finance centers. (Ibid.: 3)

Portland's EcoDistricts initiative – discussed more fully in Chapter 5 – can be seen as an exemplar of this metropolitan knowledge-based innovation strategy. Not only is this illustrated by the strapline 'accelerating urban innovations' used by the Portland Sustainability Institute, it is also explained by its mission 'to systematically bring together business, higher education non-profit and municipal leaders to drive a set of next-generation initiatives for urban sustainability' (PoSI, 2010a, b). More recently, the EcoDistricts initiative has been expanded to cities outside Oregon, across the US. Under the heading 'fuelling innovation', the fusion of 'green' and 'knowledge' innovation is once again to the fore, with the EcoDistricts framework offered up as facilitating tool to enable such innovation:

cities have to be effectively designed in a way that generates wealth, improves living standards, and protects the environment while simultaneously enabling the interactions necessary to drive creativity, productivity and happiness. No easy trick. However, with the right mix of inspired design, smart planning and skillful execution, cities can be engines of innovation full of talented and creative people who accelerate economic growth, shared prosperity and ecological resiliency. And without the proper planning and development tools, they can't. (EcoDistricts, undated)

The increasing emphasis on cities as hubs of innovation is also reflected in policy debate in the UK. Calling for greater autonomy for municipal governments, the Centre for Cities, a policy research group, urges politicians to pay more attention to cities: 'Cities are home to the most productive parts of the global economy. They are places where new ideas are generated, businesses are started and expanded, wages are higher and people's ambitions can be fulfilled ... Around the world, city economies benefit from sharing information, ideas and amenities, from transport to broadband ... Politicians need to "think cities"' (Jones, 2014: 40). Recognizing this need, the UK government's Technology Strategy Board, the national innovation agency, launched its Future Cities Demonstrator initiative in 2012, as part of which it funded 29 cities to develop proposals for accelerating innovation and addressing various sustainability challenges (Technology Strategy Board, undated). These proposals had to demonstrate how multiple urban infrastructure and services systems would be integrated using information technology, and how platforms would be created to 'allow innovative companies, particularly SMEs [small and medium enterprises] to test their ideas' and thereby 'create a more effective test environment' (ibid.). The city of Glasgow (Scotland) was eventually selected from among the 29 candidates to receive substantial government funding to implement its 'future city' innovation plan. According to the city's authorities, the bid 'outlined how public, private and academic sectors can combine expertise and use cutting-edge technology to enhance day-to-day life in the city. It addressed issues such as public safety, transport, health, and sustainable energy' (Glasgow City Council, undated a). Among the projects to be implemented are: an 'integrated operations centre' to manage 'a new futuristic public space CCTV [close circuit television] network and TRAFFCOM [traffic command] roads management system' (ibid.); the Sustainable Glasgow initiative, including energy conservation and generation and greater use of green technology; the creation of a 'big data store' aimed at 'collecting and analyzing information from previously unconnected databases to influence future city services and developments' (ibid.); and a centralized 'city dashboard' to provide agencies and the public with real-time information on a range of issues, from traffic flow to accident and emergency waiting times.

'Knowledge city' and the related term 'knowledge-based urban development' are recognized categories in the urban policy and planning literature (see, e.g., Arboníes and Moso, 2002; Carrillo, 2005; de Jong et al., 2015; Yigitcanlar et al., 2008; Yigitcanlar and Lönnqvist, 2013). This literature establishes and discusses conceptual and analytical links between, on one hand, knowledge-based economic activity and, on the other, sustainable development and, in turn, relates these to questions of urban policy and design. The literature identifies several interrelated characteristics of what constitutes 'knowledge-based urban development'; these characteristics can be seen clearly mirrored in the aforementioned exemplars of recent 'sustainable city' as 'knowledge city' initiatives. A first characteristic is the promotion of networking and collaboration among industry, universities, social enterprises and local government, with the purpose of developing complementary expertise, encouraging learning and stimulating innovation. Closely related, a second characteristic is the need for integration concerning not just related areas of expertise, but also various urban systems and functions. This underlines the close interrelationship between knowledge as innovation process and urban function and form. A third feature is the focus on innovation in new technology, especially through the combination of various green technologies and information technology. A fourth characteristic is the dissemination of the new knowledge emerging from those technological innovation processes, by implementing and applying technological products and services developed within the 'incubators' and 'hubs' across the wider urban area and beyond. This dissemination, then, also requires education – an additional feature – through both formal establishments (universities, colleges, etc.) and skills training programmes for people employed in the local economy. Finally, a further characteristic of the knowledge city is to provide an urban environment which offers advantageous living standards and a desirable cultural experience, so as to be able to attract the skilled population and international business needed to realize and sustain the knowledge city.

It goes without saying that these ideal-typical, conceptual features of the knowledge city may not be as effortlessly realized in practice as some of the academic literature and much of the promotional materials suggest. The varied, particular local contexts within which knowledge-city initiatives are implemented may well produce contingencies that impact on the initiatives' feasibility. Existing urban innovation systems and infrastructure may be obdurate and, thus, less receptive to alternative modes of knowledge creation and dissemination; the application of new knowledge processes may not yield expected urban sustainability benefits if, for example, wider market conditions or regulatory regimes are stacked against green innovation; and the desired social learning and networking processes may be hampered by adverse social conditions, such as a lack of adequate education and skills training. For example, in its review of Korea's national growth strategy and related innovation cities policy programme, the Organisation for Economic Co-operation and Development (OECD) lists several 'governance gaps' – from fragmented policy regimes to conflicting priorities between economic and environmental aims of green growth, and from slow market response to a lack of expertise and capacity at local level – which pose challenges and obstacles to effective implementation (Kamal-Chaoui et al., 2011: 61ff). The discrepancy between the envisioned green-knowledge city and its practical realization is also brought to the fore in a recent analysis of Songdo (Shwayri, 2013). This shows how existing political and economic conditions and constraints of sustainable urban development can transform original concepts into different urban realities. Over the last decade or so, during the development phase as well as now at the operational stage, Songdo has undergone several adaptations owing to changes, and at times tensions, in the local and national policy landscape. As a result, the rationale has gradually shifted from that of a model 'green growth', internationally planned city aimed at attracting foreign investment and serving as international business and innovation hub, to one focused more on accommodating residential needs and enhancing existing regional urban spaces. In similar vein, Portland's EcoDistricts initiative has undergone significant changes in the space of just a few years, departing from its original vision of 'accelerating urban innovations' across the Portland metropolitan area (see Chapter 5).

Nevertheless, even if the practical experience of knowledge-city initiatives suggests more complex and compromised realities, the conceptualization of 'knowledge-based urban development' has in itself exerted significant influence on the way in which the sustainable city is understood, by focusing on and favouring particular types of knowledge, shaping urban sustainability programmes, even exercising influence over urban form.

Data city

> This is a place where we can bring algorithms and intelligence to bear to help make the world a better place, and in the longer term the opportunity to reshape cities and reduce congestion; we think this is very exciting, too.
>
> (Chris Urmson, BBC Radio, 4 June 2014)

There was palpable exhilaration in the world of technology – and reflected in the wider media – when American Internet giant Google presented its driverless car project in spring 2014. The autonomous car technology includes an on-board light radar system which generates 3D (three-dimensional) maps of the car's environment; these maps are then combined with Google's satellite-generated high-resolution maps of the world, and processed by an integrated software programme that produces instantaneous data models allowing the car to drive itself. The promised benefits of driverless cars – essentially by factoring out human behaviour and error – include congestion-free traffic and accident-free driving. Chris Urmson, the director of Google's driverless car project, clearly sees a bright future for this new technology, with potential not just to transform car travel but, in its course, also to reshape cities and, thus, make the world a better place.

Excitement about the use of advanced technology involving digital data and integrated systems is by no means limited to automobile manufacturing; it is increasingly felt across urban research laboratories and planning offices alike. The prospect of generating, harvesting and modelling urban data on large scales using digital technology has started to have an important bearing on how cities are thought and talked about, and it increasingly shapes sustainable city initiatives, too. The strong surge of 'smart-city' discussion topics in the academic literature – let alone the wider policy discourse – since the late 2000s suggests a paradigmatic shift in the conceptualization and practice of urban sustainability (de Jong et al., 2015). In the digital urban age, knowledge – the creation, integration and dissemination of information and intelligence – takes centre stage in sustainable urban development in ways that only a few decades ago would have been difficult to imagine and predict. Terms and phrases, such as 'advanced IT convergence valley' (Songdo), 'TraffCom roads management system' (Glasgow), 'informatization-based eco-city' (Caofeidian), or even simply 'u-city' (Sejong), have quietly and seemingly effortlessly entered the sustainable city vocabulary.

At a superficial level, the arrival of digital urban technology becomes apparent in the form of various 'smart' applications and gadgets: for example, smart meters installed in homes and offices are designed to send – using wireless technology – automatic electronic meter readings to utility companies, while at the same time providing consumers with real-time feedback on energy usage; in doing so – and especially if they are plugged into wider smart grid systems – they should enable more responsive and flexible management of energy demand and supply and, in turn, contribute to improved energy efficiency and saving. Other examples include a growing array of mobile apps – software applications for mobile devices – that make use of location-based services, such as GPS (Global Positioning System), to provide real-time information on, say, bus or train arrivals, facilitating the use of public transport. The availability of these and similar smart applications, then, requires the systematic integration of multiple components; and it is in this integrative capacity – rather than in individual (mobile) applications – that the deeper significance of digital urban technology lies, with its potential to reshape and transform the city. This becomes apparent, for example, from the focus of the UK's Future Cities Demonstrator Programme which defines urban innovation with reference to the concerted interaction between four components – 'organization', 'infrastructure', 'platform' and 'application' – as part of the development of 'future city' strategies and solutions, as the following example illustrates:

> The organization is the source of the data, for example the local bus service operator providing the GPS location of the local buses, or crowd-sourced data from citizens on the use of the local leisure centre. The infrastructure is any infrastructure required to enable the smart solution, such as environmental sensors, a Wi-Fi network or a central database. The platform is where the data is processed and made available, for example through an online portal. The processed data can then be used in its final application, where it can deliver its planned outcome, for example a transport app displaying live bus locations and arrival times on a smart phone to aid mobility, increase public transport usage and reduce congestion. (Technology Strategy Board, 2013: 20)

In evaluating the feasibility studies of the 29 cities involved in the Future Cities Demonstrator Programme, the UK's national innovation agency makes the case for city-wide, system-based integration not just in terms of the opportunity for technological innovation, but essentially in relation to the need for sustainable urban development:

> To succeed in the future, city governments have to deliver a sustainable local economy, and a good quality of life with a reduced environmental footprint. We need to create city systems that maximise the benefits of city life, whilst managing the downsides. High-quality city infrastructure is essential to meeting this future need, but it is becoming increasingly clear that we cannot progress fast enough by optimising the city's individual components and systems. We need innovation in integrated and city-wide solutions. (Ibid.: 7)

If one way of discussing urban innovation – informed by, and reflecting, the digital knowledge perspective – is in terms of 'organization', 'infrastructure', 'platform' and 'application', another is in terms of 'supply', 'demand' and 'storage'; here again, the emphasis is on co-ordination between various systems, as illustrated by the description of smart cities by Hitachi, the Japanese engineering and electronics conglomerate which is presently involved in several eco-city initiatives in Japan and elsewhere in Asia:

> Common features in this [smart-city] vision are consideration of the aspects of 'supply', 'demand', and 'storage', and a core model that involves using IT to make these operate in harmony ... Advances in the next generation of infrastructure will take place in a way that coordinates the operation of different systems, and it will be built to be sustainable. Systems based on this 'symbiosis autonomous decentralised' concept will have the scalability to keep up with ever-evolving cities. (Hitachi Technology, 2012: 5)

These examples make clear the deep influence that advances in digital knowledge have begun to exert on the way the city is configured – conceptually, spatially and functionally. It is not uncommon to find characterizations of the city as 'digital nervous system' and 'urban operating system' and related discussion of optimizing and integrating system components (e.g. *The Economist*, 2013: 26–7; see also Chapter 2). In its briefing on 'clever cities', *The Economist* magazine, citing urban studies specialist Ricky Burdett, likens the impact of ubiquitous digital information to a 'second electrification' of the city: 'The power cables that penetrated cities in the late 19th century transformed their shape (there are no tall buildings without lifts), their transit systems, their nightlife, their sewerage (cities need a lot of pumps). Ubiquitous data services might have impacts as wide-ranging' (ibid.: 25; see also original source: Burdett and Rode, 2012a: 2). By way of example, the report goes on to discuss the increasing use of open data and 'data dives' by which cities make data sets publicly available and invite activists and data specialists to analyse diverse data sources with a view to increasing analytical capacity and perhaps even 'democratise' digital knowledge. The resulting effect might be that 'the city would become literally a publicly shared domain', quoting sociologist Saskia Sassen (*The Economist*, 2013: 27; original source: Sassen, 2012).

The digital knowledge approach underlying much of the recent, often overlapping 'knowledge city', 'smart city', 'intelligent city' and, of course, 'digital city' discourses might understandably be criticized for its focus on urban infrastructure and related data and systems and, conversely, for its relative neglect of wider social and political dimensions and concerns. The city as 'digital nervous system', or 'operating system', surely must be an incomplete, imperfect – and some would say, undesirable – representation. And yet, it would arguably be missing the point if the digital knowledge city were understood as merely concerned with the urban 'hardware'. Rather, its conceptual – and increasingly practical – aspiration equally reaches into the social and political domains. This is, for example, brought to the fore in the 'smart-city' standard commissioned by the UK government and published in 2014 by the British Standards Institution (see also Chapter 2). It carries the following definition: '"Smart cities" is a term denoting the effective integration of physical, digital and human systems in the built environment to deliver a sustainable, prosperous and inclusive future for its citizens' (BSI, 2014a: 3). The intended outcome of the application of digital urban knowledge is ultimately directed at urban society ('human systems', 'citizens') at large, rather than confined to urban infrastructure systems: 'Smart Cities use digital systems to communicate with citizens and organizational stakeholders, they exploit data and information for planning and service delivery and they nurture the digital skills required to participate in society and be economically successful' (ibid.: 4). The report goes one step further, by suggesting – within the context of the challenge of unprecedented urbanization and unsustainable urban development – that the knowledge city must replace traditional and allegedly 'unresponsive' and 'costly' governance mechanisms:

> By 2050 the global population is forecast to grow to 9+ billion, 80% of which will inhabit cities. The increase in demand for all resources is unsustainable, as are traditional delivery mechanisms, which are unresponsive and too costly. To maintain quality of life expectations in the developed world, and match these in the developing world, we urgently need to identify and implement innovative delivery systems to more effectively manage and control resource use in the built environment – particularly cities. Smart-city systems are emerging as a major response to the joint challenges of resource management and economic recovery in cities – nationally and globally. These systems will displace traditional delivery vehicles for physical and social resources, potentially providing cost effective and innovative delivery channels. (Ibid.: 1)

That the application of digital knowledge systems and processes is increasingly pushing into, and beginning to transform, the urban

governance domain is most explicitly apparent in the form of variously styled 'information control centres' set up to steer and
manage urban functions and services. At the heart of Sejong – both
geographically and functionally – is the Integrated City
Information Center from where the ubiquitous city will be
controlled. It is described in the promotional literature, under the
heading 'u-city with advanced IT technology', as the 'center which
will play the role of the city's brain', designed to 'manage the whole
city including the transportation department, crime and disaster
prevention department, environment monitoring department,
facility management department, and public equipments [sic]
management department' (MACCA, 2008: 31). Similarly, the
plans for Caofedian International Eco-City boast a
Multifunctional Resource Management Center, to be located in the
city's designated service quarter, from where the city's energy,
transport, water, waste and recycling systems will be remotely
guided and controlled. In both cases, as new cities designed and
built from scratch, the application of ubiquitous digital technology
systems – the control centre forming the city's 'brain' and the various urban systems and functions the 'nervous system' – co-deter-
mines the layout of the city and thus contributes to its physical
shape and its functionality.

In the case of Glasgow, too, a new Integrated Operations Centre
is to be built as part of the Future City Glasgow initiative. It will
harvest and analyse information from over 400 'advanced digital
cameras'; these 'are so intelligent they can be programmed to
automatically detect unusual activity, for example if someone
leaves a box or bag unattended. Suspicious instances will trigger
an alarm prompting further investigation by the emergency services' (Glasgow City Council, undated b). The operations centre
will combine with the City Technology Platform which will collect
and analyse a wealth of data (both stored, long-term data and
instantaneous data from real-time events) which can be computed
and related to various city maps and custom-made 'city dash-
boards':

> More than 200 data streams have been identified in Glasgow.
> They include information on everything from bin collections to
> footfall in retail areas. Some of this data is already available to the
> public but often it is held in isolation, difficult to access and even
> harder to understand … The new City Technology Platform will
> integrate the data streams, analyse the information, present it in a

meaningful format and make it open for use by the public, businesses and academics alike. It will be accessed through websites and smartphone apps including a data portal, a mapping portal and the MyGlasgow dashboard. (Glasgow City Council, undated c)

There is an inherent – some would say somewhat ironic – tension at work between, on one hand, the emphasis on the city as autonomous, decentralized network system and, on the other, the predominant place and role given to all-encompassing control centres. Chapter 2 discusses how concepts and metaphors borrowed from biology (the city as metabolism, or nervous system) and complexity science (the city as adaptive network system) have increasingly come to inform and determine thinking about urban sustainability and related governance processes. These suggest an understanding of the (sustainable) city as autonomous, self-evolving system, not unlike an organism perhaps or artificial adaptive system. These conceptual influences can be seen prominently at work in various 'smart', 'intelligent' and 'digital' city initiatives and related literature. (For an example, see Hitachi's description, quoted above, of smart-city concepts as 'symbiosis, autonomous, decentralised'.) And yet, the new (sustainable) knowledge city cannot exist, it appears, without a commanding control centre. As *The Economist* wryly observes in its briefing on 'clever cities': 'Although many such systems are supposed to work automatically, it is a rare smart-city project that does not aspire to a NASA-style control room filled with electronics, earnestness and a sense of the future' (*The Economist*, 2013: 26). It can also not escape observers' attention that one control system – traditional urban planning and management departments, supposedly providing 'delivery mechanisms' that are 'unresponsive' and 'too costly' (see the discussion of smart-city innovation by the British Standards Institution, above) – is replaced with another: in the knowledge city, it would seem, control shifts from the city hall to the new information-stacked command centre.

The application of digital information and knowledge in sustainable city initiatives entails an elaborate, complex process of defining data types and categories, generating and harvesting data, assembling often disparate data sets, and computing and modelling data to provide integrated information and intelligence. This requires sophisticated machinery, systems and software – from super computers to mapping and modelling programmes, and from geospatial information systems to remote sensors. As noted, this can be expected to shape both the physical side of the city – particularly pronounced in new urban developments, where the layout is often designed with the digital technology networks in mind – as well as various urban functions and services. In doing so, it raises a number of important issues concerning sustainable city governance: first, it requires advanced technical skills from those wishing to use digital urban systems and applications. Smart-city enthusiasts like to promote the democratic potential of digital information, with the promise of 'data dives' and 'hackathons' which should make data accessible and encourage the co-production of knowledge between city officials, information specialists and community groups (see e.g. Hill, 2012; Ratti and Townsend, 2012). And yet, the 'digital divide' between those who are expert in handling digital information and those who lack the necessary skills may prevent the effective opening up of the sustainable knowledge city to the broader citizenry. Second, the amassing, processing and storing of large sets of data raises important issues about data security and accountability (see e.g. Margetts, 2011; Future of Privacy Forum, 2013). Accessing various mobile apps may benefit residents in managing their energy use more efficiently and sustainably, as they may assist commuters in using public transport; at the same time, this allows personal data to be centrally tracked and stored and, thus, may harbour a risk of unwanted surveillance. Complex questions arise, then, about how digital information is used, who handles it, and who is given access to it – and these are only likely to multiply as more knowledge-city initiatives of one kind or another are put in place.

A third issue concerns the costs involved in developing and implementing various information technology systems in support of sustainable urban development. In launching the Future Cities Demonstrator Programme, the UK government has sought not only to encourage smart-city innovation in British cities, but also to position British technology, engineering and services companies at the forefront of international business. The Technology Strategy Board (2013: 8) estimates that 'integrated city solutions' could represent a global market worth £200 billion by 2030. While clearly a potentially lucrative opportunity for businesses, it seems likely that the costs involved in urban information technologies may prove prohibitive for towns and cities in developing countries strapped for financial resources. There is some risk, then, that such technologies may serve to widen the 'digital divide' between cities across the developed and developing world.

Knowledge: between measurement and social negotiation

'I've always believed that if you can't measure it, you can't manage it,' states Michael R. Bloomberg, as Mayor of New York City and chair of C40 Cities (Climate Leadership Group), in his foreword to the *Cities 2012 Global Report* published by the Carbon Disclosure Project (CDP, 2012: 2). Sub-titled '*Measurement for Management*', the report brings together data and analyses from over 70 cities, underlining the growing importance of international assessment for sustainable urban development, in this particular case reporting on cities' annual greenhouse gas (GHG) emissions. 'So far,' Bloomberg reflects, 'the results have been very encouraging. With C40 cities leading the way, the number of cities reporting to CPD has increased dramatically ... the quality of the data is better, allowing for a more thorough analysis and a better understanding of what constitutes effective climate change. This is tremendous progress, and we stand to benefit even further if international organisations standardise the carbon-reporting process among all the world's cities' (CPD, 2012: 2).

The last couple of decades have seen an almost explosive increase in various indicators, metrics and systems, all aimed at modelling, measuring and comparing sustainable urban development (for an overview, see e.g. Miller, 2005; Hezri and Dovers, 2006; Keirstead and Leach, 2008; Rydin, 2010; OECD, 2011c; Joss, 2012; Joss et al., 2012; Williams et al., 2012; Zhou and Williams, 2013). This reinforces the centrality of knowledge and the power of data in contemporary sustainable city concepts, methods and practices. 'Carbon reporting', as carried out through CDP by a growing number of cities on a regular annual basis, is therefore just one among numerous tools for measuring and comparing aspects of sustainable city performance. Chapter 6 lists some 43 recent frameworks currently in use internationally; while these may vary in terms of emphases on sustainable urban development and guidance on design and implementation, they all have in common the use of indicators. Behind these frameworks, there is an extended academic and policy hinterland specializing in the study of the sustainable city through indicators and related assessment methodologies. In short, constructing knowledge through measurement has become a central, powerful tool in sustainable urban development. Modelling and assessment are widely accepted as essential for both theoretical and practical reasons: precisely because the sustainable city is conceptually such a complex, multi-dimensional phenomenon, there is demand for robust and tangible analytical knowledge based on indicators and measurement tools, with scope for quantification, comparison and standardization; and precisely because sustainable urban development is practically such a challenging, long-term undertaking, policy-makers and developers alike routinely rely on modelling and assessment methods to guide (and justify) design, planning and performance management. What is more, as part of a global discourse, data comparability plays an increasingly important role in assessing urban sustainability across cities and countries, facilitating knowledge transfer and, not least, driving competitiveness (see Chapter 4 for examples of competitive sustainable city initiatives at both national and international levels). Hence, the adage may well need to be expanded, not least in the case of sustainable urban development: 'if you can't measure it, you can't manage it; and if you can't compare it, you can't compete'.

Knowledge generated through indicators, models and measurements, while such a key focus of contemporary discourses on urban sustainability, is in itself, however, far from unproblematic. At first glance, it may well give the appearance of exactness, objectivity and certainty; on further inspection, it reveals itself as necessarily more limited, contingent and, consequently, open to interpretation, even contestation and conflict. The basic process of defining an indicator and related targets alone entails certain assumptions, normative choices and methodological decisions. After all, indicators essentially consist of reducing complex phenomena – say, sustainable water (management) – to simplified abstractions – here, for example, the amount of water consumed per urban resident per day. This reduction, while necessary in order to allow related measurement, inevitably loses some of the complexity of what the indicator seeks to represent, thereby only ever incompletely managing to capture the full richness of the sustainability dimension in question. Furthermore, assigning a related target – here, the number of litres of water – requires making a choice which might be based on some national policy (which in itself may, or may not, define the sustainability dimension adequately), a generic averaged value derived from international research or, conversely, a relative value arrived at through local decision-making. Consequently, defining indicators for urban sustainability is far from a straightforward undertaking. As an international review of eco-city index systems concludes: 'Although there is wide-spread consensus on high level issue areas [of urban sustainability], little agreement exists regarding specific indicators. Wide variance in indicator systems and their structural choices shows that international consensus on the best indicators may not be possible' (Williams et al., 2012: 12). Apart from challenges to do with normative conceptualizations and methodological elaborations, the authors point to a further reason for the lack of clarity in the definitions of indicators – namely, the relative absence of concrete physical examples of sustainable cities (ibid.: 2). Hence, as sustainable urban development is essentially future-oriented, indicators are defined within a context where knowledge is necessarily evolving and, thus, characterized by ongoing limitation and uncertainty.

In recent years, various attempts have been made to respond to some of these limitations by developing more comprehensive indicator systems (see e.g. Dong, 2013; Joss, 2012). The intention here is to bundle together several complementary indicators, thereby overcoming the disadvantage of the atomistic approach of using single indicators and, consequently, allowing for a more integrative, holistic approach to urban sustainability. For example, by defining indicators for sustainable water management alongside indicators for, say, urban green spaces, biodiversity and building efficiency, these sustainability dimensions become co-related and possible feedback mechanisms and dependencies between them can be considered. Interestingly, if anything, however, this more sophisticated approach to designing indicators has further underlined the complexity of what constitutes sustainable urban development and the continuous limitations to the knowledge generated through indicator systems. Dong (2013: 55–6), for example, points to the multiple, inherent uncertainties involved in the construction and application of even elaborate eco-city indicator systems. These uncertainties involve the unpredictability of future developments: indicators are typically defined based on existing behaviours but to an extent also factor in, necessarily incompletely, future estimates and assumptions. Relatedly, uncertainty can arise from the unpredictability of how individual points within the defined system behave, especially ones that may turn out to be instable with unexpected consequences for the system as whole. A further, important uncertainty arises from what Dong calls the 'ambiguous dualism' between, on one hand, the internal integrity of the eco-city indicator system itself and, on the other, the diversity of urban sustainability beyond what is captured by the system: 'the integrity of a system is difficult to define because system boundaries are often uncertain and ambiguous. An integrated system could also be a subsystem of a larger whole' (Dong, 2013: 55).

According to a detailed policy brief by the OECD on the use of urban system modelling, 'the process of selecting appropriate and specific indicators and data to model the performance of particular urban systems against sustainability criteria is of increasing significance' (OECD, 2011c: 7). The report singles out two main reasons for this growing significance: first, the fact that much of international and national urban policy has steered towards sustainability in recent times elevates indicators and related modelling systems above the sphere of research – from where they mainly evolved – into the sphere of policy, thus placing them more centrally in the decision-making processes and giving greater political salience. The second, concurrent reason lies with the potential for much more sophisticated indicator modelling resulting from digital information technology:

> Recent rapid advances in computer and software capacities have increased the capacity to model complex environmental and urban systems ... aggregated metrics and spreadsheet models that represent urban metabolism and 'carbon footprint' of cities are emerging to make visible the full global impact of urban activities – beyond their geopolitical boundaries ... Data about physical and social phenomena are now largely stored digitally, forming the basis of models that represent not only existing interactions, but also possible future scenarios. (OECD, 2011c: 4–5)

At the same time as highlighting the increasing significance of, and potential for, urban sustainability indicator systems and models, the OECD report, like other reviews, points to several challenges that have yet to be fully addressed. Here, this includes the challenge of urban modelling 'carried out by an extremely diverse and scattered community with few interconnections ... [this] results in difficult scientific and technical challenges when trying to address the complexity of new urban systems' (ibid: 2). Relatedly, another challenge arises from the lack of integration across various methods, metrics, indicators and data, especially in the context of large data sets: 'increasingly complex urban models require vast amounts of physical as well as socio-economic data, which are often incomplete ... this calls for new modelling tools and algorithms that can take into account such data gaps' (ibid.: 2). In turn, these challenges contribute to a situation where 'there is a lack of standardized, accessible and reliable data sources and protocols for urban models' (ibid.: 5).

If arriving at grounded knowledge about sustainable urban development shows itself in many ways as challenging, this need not necessarily be seen as problematic. On the contrary, it can be viewed as an essential part of figuring out the sustainable city – a pluralistic, iterative process of constructing as well as deconstructing, contextualizing as well as decontextualizing, interpreting as well as reinterpreting, the sustainable city through theory and practice. Given the multidisciplinary nature of urban sustainability knowledge – taking in natural sciences, engineering, architecture, planning, economics, social sciences, arts and others – it is only to be expected that the various disciplines each engage with certain aspects of urban sustainability, producing particular, and therefore necessarily partial and incomplete, knowledge. Consequently, this prompts efforts to go beyond individual spheres of knowledge to generate cross-disciplinary knowledge, by bringing together various epistemic communities – groups of professionals with differing knowledge-based expertise and competencies – around questions of the sustainable city. Importantly, however, such cross-boundary engagement also typically takes in various communities of practice, as an essential part of the innovation process connecting theoretical with practice-based knowledge (which is sometimes referred to as 'civic epistemology'). A 'community of practice' is understood as 'a network of practitioners that grows up over time through the sustained pursuit of a shared enterprise. It is task focused but is also concerned with the connection between knowledge and practice, that is, with learning' (Rydin, 2010: 64–5). The significance of the extension of the knowledge process from epistemic communities to wider communities of practice, then, is two-fold: first, it emphasizes 'the engagement with knowledge as an ongoing cultural process embedded in everyday practices' (ibid.: 65), rather than confining it to the scientific and related expert communities; and consequently, second, it underlines the centrality of networking – involving diverse actor groups in collaboration and co-operation – driving the construction, analysis and interpretation of knowledge about the sustainable city.

While many would welcome the extension of the sustainable city as extended knowledge process – even seeing it as essential from the dual governance and innovation perspective – it should not be taken as given that this comes about effortlessly, without difficulties of its own. The OECD policy brief, for example, points to the problem of disconnect between epistemic communities and communities of practice. It argues that, rather paradoxically, the recent application of information and communication technologies in the construction of sustainable city indicators and models, on one hand, facilitates knowledge production through communities of practice:

> urban modelling is now a field where experts (model makers) are challenged by new types of stakeholders. These stakeholders not only include non-experts such as local decision makers and opinion leaders, but also citizens or members of NGOs (model users) who want to use models and the information they provide to challenge decisions and participate in urban local policies. (OECD, 2011c: 12)

On the other, the report identifies the possibility of a growing gap across expert and practitioner communities, considering it a serious limitation to the full exploitation of new modes of knowledge on urban sustainability:

> Model users often identify an issue about which they want to be better informed, but may not know what they are looking for or what models actually do. They do not always understand the limits of models, how data availability influences them, and the amount of time required to create them. Given their exposure to ICT and social networking tools, there is some evidence that users also expect models to present complex information and interactions simply ... rather than as dense technical abstractions. Conversely, model makers make assumptions about how models should be applied and may lack the skills to interact effectively in the socio-cultural and political domains in which models are used. (Ibid.: 15)

Constructing and co-producing knowledge about urban sustainability, then, involve complex processes of translation, negotiation and communication between diverse groups of experts, practitioners and the wider community. What this means is that knowledge is not exclusively anchored in, and owned by, any single group of actors; and the process of generating, managing, validating and warranting is not the preserve of any one knowledge community. Consequently, knowledge is subject to social negotiations, as part of the governance process for sustainable cities. In turn, this lends it an inherently political dimension: it becomes open to interpretation, contestation, even conflict, within the wider public sphere involving a plurality of actors; and it can be – and often is shown to be – deployed instrumentally in pursuit of certain strategies and interests. Again, this need not be seen as problematic as such; however, it requires the recognition of the social and political dynamics involved in the knowledge process, and the multiple and frequently subjective and contingent nature of the knowledge thus produced. Furthermore, this calls for an active stance on how knowledge is considered and fashioned as part of the governance for sustainable cities.

Knowledge through governance?

Developing a socially grounded perspective on, and a more public governance approach to, knowledge in the sustainable city, while arguably essential, should not be expected to come about without substantive challenges of its own. The reason for this lies not least in the concurrence of two inherent features of the emerging new knowledge for urban sustainability: not only does knowledge become intricately knitted into the urban fabric, it also takes on ubiquitous features; together, this tends to render it intangible and elusive and, therefore, difficult to capture and scrutinize as part of the governance process. In turn, this creates something of a dilemma: while knowledge arguably merits closer attention and critical exam-ination owing to the fact that it permeates the sustainable city increasingly deeply, effective engagement through governance may be frustrated for exactly the same reason.

That knowledge is profoundly implicated, in potentially radically new ways, in the sustainable city becomes clear from recent writings on 'future cities' and 'smart cities' – with urban sustainability always implied – and from various practical pioneer initiatives, such as are represented by Sejong, Songdo and Caofeidian International Eco-City. For example, in their essay 'Skewing the City', Calvillo et al. (2012) argue that, from a smart-city perspective, digital information infrastructure and knowledge networks will increasingly transform the physical and social dimensions of the city. Knowledge and infor-mation will become an integral part of the foundation of the city, by closely interacting, and even merging, with the physical infrastruc-ture and the social sphere. Reviewing the case of Songdo, the authors point to the 'steady flow of information that links the physical with the social world and the data cloud' (ibid.: 18), citing innovations trialled in the Korean u-city, such as 'intelligent' lamp-posts equipped with information services and so-called 'telepresence systems' embedded across the city aimed at delivering healthcare, education and other government services. Based on this model initiative, the authors predict the blurring of traditional boundaries, resulting in skewed urban structures and functions, even raising the ambiguous prospect of the city as a cyborg, a man-machine system:

> As modern information infrastructure allows citizens to become enmeshed in a growing number of ever more complex and inter-connected networks, traditional places and boundaries of the social sphere rearrange themselves, or completely disappear. With respect to physical space, the network structures of the city become increasingly skewed ... Long established boundaries, which were once all referenced by physical space ... become blurry. (Ibid.: 18)

> cityspaces will become increasingly dominated by the flexible, personalised, and responsive infrastructures that are a direct consequence of the Internet of Things. All these developments lead to a further merging of the social and technical spheres, eventually realising a cyborg [cybernetic organism] vision of the city as a complex socio-technical network. (Ibid.: 18)

The sustainable city understood as a new kind of socio-technical network of communication and control is echoed by Hill (2012), who uses the phrase 'self-aware urban infrastructure' to highlight the emergent, close interaction between physical urban space and information and communication technology: 'the promise of smart sustainable cities is predicated on the harmonious interplay of three forces: the dynamics of social media, allied to the analytics of Big Data, generated by a "self-aware" urban infrastructure' (ibid.: 19). While recognizing the limitation of the smart, sustainable city mainly conceptualized in technocratic terms, Hill nevertheless holds out for a 'radically different urban condition' based on citizens inter-actively engaged in creating knowledge and sharing practices through 'digital collaboration' (ibid.), as illustrated by numerous urban crowd-sourcing initiatives: 'due to the inherent dynamics and platform characteristics of social media, such tools suggest a new interface with the city that could, potentially, alter the way in which most citizens interact with it' (ibid.). Viewed optimistically, this implies the possibility of a new co-operative style of governance through which citizens and civil society organizations can get involved directly and creatively in generating knowledge and developing strategies in pursuit of urban sustainability. As such, the 'self-aware' urban infrastructure and related information technology could enable the city to become what Sassen (2012: 14) calls a 'heuristic space': a space capable of producing knowledge, by allowing those living in, working in, and travelling through the city to explore, question and interact with, urban structures and processes and, in doing so, continuously to remake the city.

From this perspective, sustainable city initiatives can be viewed as a laboratory: 'a piece of real life that functions as a window, allowing us to learn about an abstract, complex condition (for example, a fully intelligent and green large city) that we cannot replicate in a university laboratory' (Sassen, 2012: 12). With reference this time to Masdar (see Box 4.5) – which, similarly to Songdo, is cited by some, and critiqued by others, as a model of the sustainable knowledge, or smart, city – Sassen illustrates the knowledge process arising from the interaction between urban infrastructure and technology:

> Masdar has the same upper and lower worlds that all cities have, but in this instance the lower world [the infrastructure] includes much more than the usual pipes and tunnels. In Masdar it also includes a hidden trove of advanced technologies for handling all of the basic urban systems: all that flows in and out of the city, whether water or refuse, is measured and monitored and thus produces information. In this sense, everything in Masdar is considered significant. Even refuse is not simply refuse – it is a source for building knowledge. Meanwhile, the upper part of Masdar ... is a showcase for an enormous variety of green technology. (Ibid.: 12)

In making the case for the (sustainable) city as heuristic space – where knowledge is generated by the interaction between people and urban infrastructure and space through which the city is continuously made and remade – Sassen at the same time highlights concerns about the negative effects of the managerial, systematic application of information and communication technology beyond the initial, experimental phase:

> The first phase of intelligent cities is exciting. The city becomes a living laboratory for smart urban technologies that can handle all the major systems a city requires: water, transport, security, waste, green buildings, and clean energy ... But the ensuing phase is what worries me; it is charged with negative potentials. From experimentation, discovery, and open-source urbanism, we could

slide into a managed space where 'sensored becomes censored'. (Ibid.: 12)

Judging by recent policy initiatives, such as the UK's Future Cities Demonstrator programme, as well as practical projects, such as those spearheaded by Glasgow and Sejong, the prospect of the sustainable city as a managed and 'censored' space is already real and present: as noted, variously styled information management and control centres typically loom large in the knowledge city, serving as conceptual and actual 'brain' of the city from where various urban functions can be defined, monitored and regulated. This raises rather obvious concerns about the possibility of information and knowledge being deployed to exercise control in ways which could prove both socially problematic and politically controversial; these concerns are heightened by the increasingly fluid interaction between people, technology and urban infrastructure, which opens up the prospect of unprecedented types of controls being exercised over individuals and communities through digital information and related 'smart' knowledge. In turn, this raises important concerns about how these new forms of control can be made subject to political scrutiny and public accountability, prompting the question of who will monitor the monitors. Significantly, the emergent (sustainable) knowledge-city discourse has remained relatively silent about these concerns; and where they are acknowledged, little seems to be suggested by way of substantive redress. In addition, this discourse may be seen as having failed to address properly the obvious tension – if not contradiction – between, on one hand, the knowledge city realized through new co-operative forms of governance, where citizens become co-creators of knowledge and interface with the city through emerging 'intelligent information infrastructure' and, on the other, the knowledge city achieved through managerial, technical measurement ('if you can't measure it, you can't manage it') and centralizing, technocratic monitoring and control.

One of the reasons why knowledge in the sustainable city has to date been relatively neglected as a governance *problematique* may well be to do with the novelty of the smart-city discourse, with which issues of knowledge are most closely associated. This discourse is still mainly a conceptual one, and as a result often speculative, although it has begun to find increasing favour in the world of policy as well as business. What is more, concrete initiatives are still relatively few and far between, epitomized by 'clean-slate' initiatives – such as Sejong, Songdo and Masdar – that perhaps do not readily translate into sustainable city initiatives within established urban settings. Another, related, reason has to do with the fact that the sustainable city conceptualized as knowledge city has mainly emerged from within the sphere of technology, with specialists in information and communication technology, systems theory and artificial intelligence cheerleading the debate. As noted, some social scientists have begun to inquire more critically into the nature and conditions of the smart sustainable city; however, by positioning the sustainable city, rather unproblematically, as laboratory in which knowledge is created and disseminated through a new kind of co-operative governance, this discussion tends to neglect essential questions about how interests, conflict and power – all key concerns of governance analysis – are negotiated and made accountable. Beyond the social sciences, a more critical stance on the smart sustainable city has yet to be mirrored in wider policy discourse and public debate.

There is, though, a further, more profound, reason why the governance conditions of sustainable urban knowledge, and the contradictions contained therein, are as yet to be analysed in greater depth: the knowledge proposed through the smart sustainable city, while arguably inherently social and socially negotiated as part of sociotechnical network processes, nevertheless proves strangely elusive and, consequently, difficult to bring into governance discourse. Precisely because of the blurring of traditional boundaries, the decentralizing and individualizing of relationships, and the fusing of the social, technological and physical – as illustrated by notions of the sustainable city as cyborg and, less futuristic maybe but just as profound, of emerging 'intelligent' lamp-posts, 'thinking' roads and 'speaking' telepresence systems co-ordinated through distant control centres – the new modes of information and knowledge show themselves in fundamental ways to be intangible, evasive and, therefore, resistant to governance discourse. Knowledge, as the process and outcome of these new socio-technical urban networks, is at the same time proximate yet remote, concrete yet abstract, specific yet ubiquitous and, thus, 'not quite here'. As such, it eludes and arguably avoids accountability.

Conclusions

Knowledge may be abstract and elusive, both theoretically and practically, but in equal measure it proves pervasive and ubiquitous. Altogether, it forms a core dimension of the sustainable city. This chapter has sought to discern and discuss three key facets of knowledge for urban sustainability – namely, sustainable urban development achieved through knowledge-intensive economic activity, through smart technological innovation, and through knowledge-based analysis and modelling. Importantly, these facets should be understood as closely interrelated, thereby underlining the growing centrality of knowledge in the normative and practical conceptualization of the contemporary sustainable city. At its most overt, knowledge presents itself in the form of various applications of information and communication technologies: smart meters for improving energy efficiency, mobile apps for accessing public transport services, telepresence systems for delivering health care, and so on. Significantly, however, these digital applications are not stand-alone; rather, they serve as conduit between, on one hand, urban infrastructure and related services and, on the other, a growing number of users – people living, studying, working and travelling in the city. As such, these applications have the potential to create new kinds of socio-technical networks – knowledge here becomes a part-social, part-technological, process – by digitally interconnecting people and urban infrastructure and services through webs and systems of information and knowledge. From this, some expect radically new relationships and interactions to arise between the physical, technical and social urban spheres, in the course of which the city as space and experience is transformed – city dwellers may literally talk to their city, the city may talk back, and the conversation may well be on sustainability.

Knowledge as a socio-technical process relies on the systematic analysis and modelling of information and data, thus highlighting another facet of the sustainable city. Technical indicators and metrics have now become standard tools in the design, development and management of urban sustainability initiatives. Indicator systems and modelling techniques have grown more elaborate and sophisticated, both benefitting from advances in information technology and responding to the need for more powerful analytical capacity to process ever-increasing data sets. What is more, there has been a push towards greater comparability of sustainable city initiatives through various reporting protocols, thereby internationalizing and further standardizing knowledge about sustainable urban development. This knowledge, however, may stand in tension with a more grounded view of the sustainable city, which sees the process of creating, analysing and interpreting knowledge essentially as locally conditioned and socially constructed and negotiated. In turn, this may pitch the professionalization of sustainable urban planning against embedded local 'lay' expertise, practices and cultures. In response, some consider the co-production of knowledge, as an extended socio-political undertaking, as key to constructive and effective sustainable urban development.

The interrelationship between knowledge and sustainability is ultimately a normative one, just as much as it can be explained by socio-technical innovations. This is highlighted by the third facet discussed here: a programmatic emphasis on knowledge-based urban development. This normative stance sees knowledge-intensive economic and social activity – based upon education, research, innovation and creative engagement – as a core condition for bringing about urban sustainability. Consequently, the sustainable city is structured – spatially, institutionally, functionally – in terms of knowledge production and dissemination; and in turn, the sustainable city becomes the 'hub' and 'incubator' of this new knowledge-based economy and society. This is most explicitly envisaged for, and comes to the fore in, new purpose-built cities, such as Sejong, Songdo and Caofeidian International Eco-City, but it has begun to manifest itself with similar force within existing cities, such as illustrated by Glasgow's 'future city' initiative.

Claims in favour of the sustainable city as knowledge city often come with a fair amount of hyperbole. This is half to be expected, given the futuristic visions and technological optimism (and determinism) frequently at work in this nascent discourse; and, therefore, assertions of the sustainable city as cyborg, or as unprecedented socio-technical system realized through new co-operative self-governance, had better be taken with a pinch of salt. At the same time, however, this discourse needs to be engaged with seriously, for it raises the prospect, not unrealistically, of new modes of knowledge fundamentally influencing, shaping and remaking the sustainable city. In turn, this all raises important questions about what governance responses are needed to bring this knowledge into the open, make it accessible, and render it publicly accountable. Some possible answers are discussed in the concluding Chapter 8.

Chapter 8

Sustainable Cities: Towards a More Public Governance

CHAPTER OVERVIEW

The central theme of the governance of sustainable city innovation is revisited and further developed in this concluding discussion. First, drawing on the theoretical elaborations and empirical case studies from across the book, the chapter summarizes the key arguments for conceptualizing the sustainable city in terms of interrelated innovation and governance processes. Second, based on this integrated review, key strengths as well as weaknesses of the prevailing perspective on the governance of sustainable city innovation are discussed. The analysis points to a certain governance bias, the consequence of which is that important aspects of sustainable urban governance tend to be neglected or underplayed. The third and final task, therefore, entails setting out what a more public governance stance should mean conceptually and analytically for sustainable city innovation. Among the suggestions made is the need for designing more accountable governance structures and processes for sustainable urban development initiatives, as well as the benefit of opening up the sustainable city to pluralistic public discourse.

Introduction: reconsidering sustainable city processes

An attempt to draw comprehensive yet succinct conclusions on the sustainable city may seem like something of a Herculean task. This is not just because of the sheer challenge of encapsulating a fast-growing, diversifying field of policy and practice, reflected in a myriad of initiatives both small and large mushrooming across the globe; and it is not just because of the considerable labour involved in distilling vast amounts of information drawn from across disciplines and spheres of expertise and practice. Above all, it is because of the continuously evolving and inherently contingent nature of the sustainable city: at each turn, while one aspect of urban sustainability is being illuminated and clarified, other aspects crop up and new queries pose themselves; each time some conclusion can be reached about sustainable urban development in one setting, this is immediately put to the test and often called into question when applied elsewhere; and by the time some findings materialize, these are soon superseded by emerging, new developments. Realistically, then, any conclusions need to be treated as necessarily partial and temporary. In nevertheless trying to reach some, albeit tentative, culmination in this chapter, the aim is chiefly to address once more, and take forward, the central theme at the heart of this book – namely, how the sustainable city can be productively understood from a process perspective.

Considering the sustainable city as a process – or, more accurately, a series of processes, following the explorations in this volume – is useful when trying to unpack this fascinating yet complex socio-political phenomenon and consider it both within diverse contemporary settings and in relation to development periods stretching across decades into the future. As such, the process perspective helps to analyse, and generate a critical understanding of, the contingent governance and innovation mechanisms at work within individual sustainable city initiatives, thereby highlighting the shortcomings of reducing the sustainable city to a predominantly technological or routinized design and planning proposition. Beyond a focus on individual sites and practices, the perspective is equally useful for considering the dynamic interactions – in terms of evolving policy discourses, technology and knowledge transfer, shared practice learning, etc. – between emerging and maturing sustainable city initiatives and how, taken together, this may point to more broad-based, future-oriented 'transition pathways' towards more sustainable development. At the same time, the process perspective reminds us that contemporary policy and practice are influenced and shaped by older discourses and that it is, therefore, fruitful to trace past developments and experiences so as to learn about the present situation and contemplate future directions. What is more, and arguably most important, the process perspective reminds us that the sustainable city is not a static, absolute proposition that, once it might be figured out, awaits ready implementation. Instead, it urges us to keep the sustainable city a continuous open, and open-ended, activity and discourse.

Throughout this book, the process perspective is used to interrogate various facets of the sustainable city. This is chiefly done by deploying the twin perspective of governance and innovation. The main argument made is that the governance of innovation is a crucial if relatively under-analysed aspect of sustainable cities. What is meant overall by 'governance of innovation' are the mechanisms and processes of steering, co-ordinating, facilitating and justifying socio-technical development, here applied to the domain of urban sustainability. An analysis of the sustainable city, from this perspective, seeks to understand the dynamics of how ideas of sustainable urban development evolve into strategies and policies; how these are translated into plans, methods and techniques and implemented through projects and initiatives; and, in turn, how this shapes – and is shaped by – wider public discourse and social practices. In doing so, the analysis is concerned with questions about policy making, institutional regimes, networking between multiple actors within and across organizational and institutional boundaries, and the emergence of socio-technical practices.

The focus on the governance of innovation, then, is intended to provide new, critical insights into the longstanding discussion of the sustainable city phenomenon, which traditionally has been shaped by urban planning, architecture and design, engineering, and the environmental sciences. The particular relevance and contribution of this complementary perspective becomes clear from two key observations about recent sustainable city initiatives: first, the resource and time investments required to implement various initiatives – from entirely new cities to national programmes, and from local in-fill projects to large-scale urban retrofitting – are typically substantial, necessitating long-term policy and planning support and complex multi-level and multi-lateral governance efforts and, as such, frequently involve 20–30 year development trajectories. Second, it is not uncommon to see sustainable city initiatives running into difficulties of one kind or another in the course of planning and implementation. Several of the initiatives featured in this book – including high-profile ones trumpeted by governments and business – have stopped in their tracks, been quietly shelved or suffered lengthy delays; and several have undergone significant changes owing to evolving and at times disruptive governance processes. These include, each for distinct reasons, Dongtan (China), Caofeidian International Eco-City (China), the English Eco-Towns, London's Thames Gateway 'eco-region', Portland's EcoDistricts initiatives (US), Songdo (South Korea), and Treasure Island (US), among others. Even comparatively straightforward and supposedly 'successful' initiatives typically experience major changes in the course of development, leading to outcomes that often bear little resemblance to original visions and plans. These observations, then, underline the importance of recognizing the governance of innovation as a key dimension of the sustainable city process, as well as the related need for engaging in critical analysis and reflection.

In drawing together some conclusions, the aim of this chapter is two-fold: first, it summarizes key findings and insights arising from the various theoretical discussions and empirical case studies featured in the preceding chapters. This serves to reflect, and critically comment, on key conceptual and policy discourses, as well as mainstream practice developments, that have come to dominate sustainable urbanism in general, and sustainable city initiatives in particular. Bringing the sustainable city into question in this way, through probing inquiry and nuanced analyses, is a main objective of this volume and, more importantly, should be a core task for all those interested and involved, one way or another, in the contemporary sustainable city debate and practice. Following from this, the second aim of the chapter is to take the discussion of the sustainable city as a process forward a step or two. This is done by sketching the contours of what is posited as a more pronounced public governance mode for the sustainable city. The argument to be made is that a more open, pluralistic and reflexive way of conceptualizing and practising sustainable cities should go some way towards redressing some of the diagnosed problems and challenges of contemporary sustainable urbanism. This should also help ensure that the discourse on sustainable cities retains, and indeed nurtures, capacity for critical and imaginative thinking and innovation in response to emerging developments and evolving circumstances.

From the outset, it is important to emphasize that the governance of sustainable urban development ultimately needs to be analysed and advanced within its own particular contexts. As demonstrated by the various examples featured in this book, sustainable city initiatives are closely intertwined, and exist in a dynamic interrelationship, with their settings (spatial, policy, social, cultural, etc.), resulting in often unique governance constellations and processes. Therefore, while it is possible and necessary to abstract more generally applicable observations on the governance of sustainable city innovation, these should always be considered in relation to, and as conditioned variously by, specific contexts. Furthermore, by focusing on the dominant narratives and leitmotifs propagated in mainstream contemporary sustainable city policy discourse, for the purpose of analysing and critiquing them, one should at the same time look out and make room for possible alternative governance accounts. This is part of the *raison d'être* of this final chapter, intended to help ensure that governance itself – through a more pluralistic, public expression – remains a process of innovative engagement.

Diagnosis: sustainable urban governance and its biases

In advocating the usefulness of governance as a conceptual perspective and emphasizing various governance dimensions at work in sustainable city initiatives, this book at the same time highlights several apparent biases and contradictions. Altogether, the analysis points to something of a governance paradox: on one hand, governance is seen as increasingly to the fore, especially in the conceptualizations of sustainable urban development as innovation and transition processes; and this is increasingly translated into, and reflected in, policy discourses and practical sustainable city frameworks that variously emphasize 'collaborative design', 'co-operative governance' and 'public–private partnerships'. On the other, this particular stance leaves out or even negates certain other important aspects of governance, thus skewing both the conceptualization and practice of sustainable cities. These contradictory tendencies become evident in the dominant discourses which view sustainable city initiatives as innovation niches, complex adaptive systems, knowledge laboratories, and green growth opportunities, respectively. While these discourses can be seen as each having distinct roots and trajectories, they can equally be seen as sharing certain conceptual perspectives and together forming a powerful overarching narrative of the sustainable city which, in turn, influences and shapes the conceptualization and practice of mainstream governance.

Governance through innovation niches

Chapter 2 introduced the notion of sustainable city initiatives as innovation niches, as part of a wider systemic transition process. According to this view, sustainable city initiatives can be seen as relatively protected, often small-scale spaces, from where innovative practices emerge. Through these niches, various actors – from architects to technologists, and from planners to community groups – come together as 'design communities' in joint efforts to develop and trial new socio-technical concepts, methods and practices, such as local food networks or district energy systems. Over time, the innovative ideas and practices emerging from within these niches may come to influence and transform wider 'systems' – for example, the municipal energy grid, and transport network – ultimately, over a period of several decades, effecting a transition to a more sustainable, low-carbon society. Not unlike the 'niche' concept, in Chapter 6 sustainable city initiatives are discussed in terms of 'urban laboratories', in which knowledge about urban sustainability is generated by a diversity of actors in situ – that is, embedded within and relating to particular local settings. Both notions of the sustainable city as 'niche' and 'laboratory' emphasize the socio-technical process: a focus on technological innovation combined with social functions and interests, as exemplified by 'smart' energy grids, integrated transport systems and sustainable food networks. Central to the sustainable city as a socio-technical process is knowledge: both creating new theoretical insights and generating practical solutions, based on the combination of technological innovations and social applications.

Viewed from this perspective, governance plays a central role in the sustainable city, given the emphasis on diverse 'knowledge holders' coming together and co-operating through various kinds of socio-technical networks. It is, then, also in this context that reference to 'collaborative design' and 'co-operative governance' is frequently made. (For an example of the former, see the discussion of the 'expanded platform for collaborative design and decision-making' in Suzuki et al., 2010; for examples of the latter, see Burdett and Rode, 2012b, including the essays by Hill and by Hajer and Huitzing.) Significantly, however, the notion of governance here is different from a more publicly and politically oriented one, to be explored further below. Governance within the 'niche', or 'laboratory', is essentially defined by the processes of creating and producing various kinds of knowledge about urban sustainability. This is by no means restricted to technical expertise; on the contrary, the very purpose is to assemble various types of 'knowledge holders' to facilitate the creation of applied knowledge and, in the course of doing so, introducing new socio-technical systems, methods and practices. Citizens themselves may be encouraged to engage in this process, for example by using their mobile apps to collect data on public transport use or participating in a 'charrette' to help design sustainable neighbourhoods. However, they, alongside the various other actors involved, do so principally as co-producers of knowledge, by contributing social insights and local, practice knowledge. The laboratory, then, is meant to be taken out of the technical facility and set up openly within the city, but it retains its function – albeit in an extended sense – as a laboratory for generating knowledge and trialling products and solutions.

Sustainable city initiatives conceptualized as innovation 'niches' and urban 'laboratories' raise important issues about the governance processes internal to the experimental space. For example, it seems important to question who can access the niche/laboratory; what the networking requirements and rules of engagement are; and whether residents and citizens have the opportunity to get involved on a par with experts and interest groups. These and other questions cannot be expected to answer themselves, but require careful theoretical as well as empirical consideration. Decades of research matched by extensive practical experience in the fields of innovation studies, public participation in science and technology, and indeed urban planning, have amply demonstrated just how complex and frequently problematic socio-technical governance processes, such as those found at work in sustainable city initiatives, can be (see Chapter 2, and also Joss, 2014).

The governance complexity encountered is further illustrated, in Chapter 2, in the discussion of what is termed there as the 'in-between', or 'outside', nature of the space occupied by socio-technical networks underpinning sustainable urban innovation niches and laboratories. This refers to the fact that these spaces typically do not reside within, and are not owned by, any particular organizational structure; rather, they are shared – quite deliberately so – between actors and institutions, and are often co-ordinated by 'intermediary' organizations (such as research organizations, consultancies and social network owners) acting as facilitators and mediators of both processes and knowledge. This applies especially to informal, ad hoc networks, but it can also be seen in more formal governance arrangements, such as public–private partnerships where the organizational structure is shared among governmental and non-governmental parties, with no one single actor fully owning the partnership (for an example of the latter, see the Treasure Island case study, Chapter 5). The supposed benefit of niches/laboratories as 'in-between' or 'outside' spaces is the emphasis on generating new, integrated knowledge and capacity that may otherwise not be readily available within individual organizations. This further underlines the creative and experimental nature of sustainable city initiatives; and it underscores the importance of governance process, especially the dynamics generated through co-operation, negotiation, co-ordination and shared learning among often diverse actors involved.

Governance beyond the niche

Beyond these niche-internal considerations, the relationship between the niche/laboratory (and associated networks) and its surrounding urban space and policy contexts raises another set of important governance questions. This wider relationship is an equally intricate one. From an innovation perspective, cities can be seen as 'critical geographical units' through which to achieve the transition to the green economy and a sustainable, low-carbon society. They embody various socio-technical systems (energy, water, waste, food, transport, communications, etc.) which intertwine with urban space. As a result, cities are considered key sites through which, from the top down, wider systemic transition is enacted; at the same time, they harbour niches through which, from the bottom up, radical innovation is envisaged and developed. The interrelationship between these two levels is not necessarily a straightforward one. In the case where individual sustainable city initiatives – as exemplified by the French ÉcoQuartier and Portland's EcoDistricts initiatives (see Chapters 2 and 5, respectively) – mainly intervene at the niche level, these are nevertheless closely embedded in the wider urban setting and inevitably interact, sometimes uneasily, with established municipal policy and decision processes. This raises relevant governance questions about how, for example, strategies are negotiated and priorities agreed, who controls processes, and where boundaries are drawn.

Alternatively, in some cases sustainable city initiatives may intervene at city-wide level, as illustrated by Tianjin Eco-City and Sejong's 'green metropolis of the future' (see Chapters 6 and 7). In these cases, the city as a whole is conceived of as acting as something of an experimental innovation space, or urban laboratory, again raising governance-related questions and challenges of their own. In the case of Tianjin Eco-City, an elaborate indicator framework is used as a key governing mechanism; this is not only designed to define various environmental, economic and social sustainability dimensions horizontally across policy domains (transport, housing, open space etc), but it is complemented with a vertical, multi-level governance approach that seeks to interrelate and integrate the individual block, district and overall city levels. As such, the framework has a twin function: acting as an innovation tool, through which urban sustainability knowledge is generated and related practices and solutions are developed, as well as a governance mechanism for steering and controlling the innovation process. For its part, Sejong takes the concept of the sustainable city as innovation niche, or laboratory, a significant step further by directly translating it into its functional and spatial design: a series of functional zones are arranged in a radius around the city centre; each zone specializes in a particular area of research and development by assembling related research organizations, technology firms and production companies in cognate clusters, aimed at producing synergies and promoting collaborative working relations. The Integrated City Information Centre, situated within the city's administrative zone, forms the physical and functional hub; from here, the city's various 'integrated information networks' are to be managed. Governance functionality is defined in terms of socio-technical systems based on various 'smart' information and communication technologies.

De-contextualizing governance trends

If the sustainable city as socio-technical innovation niche, or urban laboratory, creates certain distinct governance dynamics, then this is complemented and reinforced by its concurrent conceptualization as economic development hub, or urban economic cluster. The close interconnect between, on one hand, a dominant policy emphasis on 'green growth' and 'ecological modernization' and, on the other, the promotion of 'knowledge' and 'smart' city concepts, significantly determines contemporary sustainable urban development. Not surprisingly, this is reflected in related governance discourse, which emphasizes the centrality of urban sustainability as an economic value proposition and privileges economic actors as core enablers and facilitators of sustainable urban development. As a consequence, this discourse promotes governance mechanisms in which private sector organizations become central partners. Some of the effects of this 'new mode' governance are discussed in detail in Chapter 5, with the examples of San Francisco's Treasure Island and Portland's EcoDistricts initiatives. This analysis shows how the prevailing economic paradigm decisively shapes governance relations, by introducing new actors – international financial institutions, developers, engineering and consultancy firms, among others – in new constellations through elaborate public–private partnerships and creating complex organizational structures and technical processes.

The effect is a tendency to 'de-contextualize' and 'de-politicize' sustainable urban development: the sustainable city initiatives in question become, to an extent, separated from the context from which they originally arise. The de-contextualization manifests itself in physical terms, through a certain spatial dislocation of the sustainable city initiative from its surrounding urban context; programmatically, through the disconnect of the initiative from wider municipal sustainability strategies; financially, through the reliance on external, even international funding; and in organizational terms, through the creation of separate legal entities and project management structures. Relatedly, the aspect of de-politicization can be seen in the pronounced distancing from the notion of traditional government in the narratives used to describe and justify the new types of urban sustainability initiatives. Conventional municipal government is largely posited as hampering effective, integrative governance and, consequently, standing in the way of innovative practices; in its place, a new economic governance paradigm is promoted as core condition for enabling sustainable urban development. The new governance processes thus created are, of course, in themselves inherently political, although the nature and dynamics of governance relations at work become distinctly different.

Adaptive system governance

There is a further characteristic of the contemporary sustainable city, which closely intertwines with the concurrent notion of innovation niche and urban economic cluster and, as such, contributes to the prevailing governance stance at work: this is the system approach increasingly informing and guiding much of the theory and practice of sustainable urbanism. As explored in Chapter 2, the conceptualization of cities as living machines and as self-organizing social organizations is by no means new – it can be traced back to the beginning of modern urban planning theory – but it has gained a more prominent position in recent years in connection with attempts to come to terms with the multiple complexities involved in urban design, planning and governance. From this perspective, the city can be understood as a complex system, which is defined, on one hand, by the internal relationship of its various constituent parts and, on the other, by its dynamic interaction with its surrounding environment. Both internal and external interactions are governed by what are referred to – using language which closely resembles that of electronic system science – as 'closed signalling loops' and 'feedback

dynamics'. The system is adaptive if and when its internal aggregation organizes itself and evolves in response to changes in the
surrounding environment. These adaptive, co-evolutionary
processes rely on the system and its constituent parts – which are
also referred to as 'agents' – to learn, engage in behavioural change
and arrange itself. The resulting agency, then, is a largely endogenous process, emanating from within and taking the form of self-
organizing behaviours.

The practical significance of the conceptualization of the (sustainable) city as complex adaptive system is two-fold: first, it has come
to inform centrally the design of sustainable city initiatives, and it
has started to be translated into various 'smart' technical system
applications. This is especially to the fore in new urban developments and new cities built from scratch, as illustrated by Masdar,
Sejong and Songdo, among many others; but it can also be seen
increasingly within existing cities and relating to 'retrofit' initiatives,
such as Glasgow's Future City project (see Chapter 7). In this
connection, references to cities, and sometimes urban government,
as 'operating system', 'publicly shared domain', even 'cyborg', are
not entirely unheard of. Second, and just as importantly, the notion
of the city as complex adaptive system has begun to influence the
discourse on urban governance: this is increasingly evident in discussions of sustainable urban development as self-similar, self-organizing processes. As such, there is a close kinship with theories of
governance which emphasize decentralized, non-hierarchical and
autonomous interaction, networking and co-ordination among
heterogeneous organizations and social actors. This, once again,
raises critical questions about what the interrelationship is between
such self-organizing governance processes and established decision-
making institutions and mechanisms. Somewhat ironically, as noted
in Chapter 7, even proponents of the sustainable city as adaptive
complex system do not seem able to do without all-encompassing
information management and control centres. Significantly,
however, these new-style command centres nevertheless carry the
potential to impact on governance relations, by shifting governance
functions from more traditional governmental institutions (the city
hall) to new-style information and communication hubs.

A governance paradox?

In summary, major conceptual and policy discourses on sustainable
cities have in recent years come to emphasize the centrality of the

governance of innovation. In doing so, these discourses have the combined effect of promoting a particular, dominant stance on governance which, while strong on some aspects, nevertheless fails to account properly for other salient aspects of governance. This, it is argued, creates a certain bias, perhaps even a paradox, of governance. The strength of the prevailing governance mode lies in its engagement with the sustainable city as diverse, multi-level innovation processes. Important insights can be gained from the dynamics of experimentation and innovation within particular niches, and in particular the knowledge processes and socio-technical practices emerging from the collaborative interaction among different 'design communities'. Additional valuable insights can be gained from the larger-scale dynamics between various niches which, while individually representing different arrangements and constellations, can be understood as cumulatively interacting along evolving innovation paths that across time may lead to more systemic transitions towards urban sustainability. From this perspective, what may look like a failed sustainable city initiative at an individual level may at the same time be appreciated as an important pilot project and learning experience, contributing to an evolving process at a broader, collective level. A further strength of the prevailing governance-of-innovation mode lies in its engagement with socio-technical processes, highlighting not just the interaction among various knowledge holders, but also the diverse interactions between, on one hand, technological developments and applications and, on the other, social interests and functions. This is particularly pertinent, given the central role played by technology in sustainable urban development.

These strengths, however, at the same time harbour some weaknesses. By emphasizing the governance-of-innovation processes, the prevailing discourse neither manages to engage sufficiently clearly with issues of spatial integration and embeddedness, nor properly with broader socio-political issues of governance. Concerning the former, while the innovation perspective usefully relates individual niche processes to wider, systemic transition processes, when applied to the urban context it remains relatively silent about how the sustainable innovation niche, or urban laboratory, is integrated into and interacts with the wider urban realm. The niche is conceptualized more in the abstract, in relation to socio-technical issues and systems, such as energy grids, transport systems and food networks. Furthermore, the focus of analysis and development is more on niche-internal processes, aimed at seeking to understand and advance the self-organizing, creative learning processes around a particular socio-technical issue; in doing so, it tends to blend out wider spatial and functional urban dimensions and issues. Concerning the wider socio-political governance dimensions, these tend to be neglected, too, and occasionally even actively negated. The reason for this can be seen in the emphasis on governance as a self-organizing, autonomous process, derived from an understanding of the (sustainable) city as adaptive complex systems and socio-technical innovation processes, respectively. Conversely, it can be seen in the often negative view taken of more traditional governmental mechanisms and processes (see, for example, the discussion of Portland's EcoDistricts initiative, Chapter 5). Significantly, even the governance literature, as a domain of political science, which has taken a more active interest in sustainable urban development over the last decade or so, has typically been deficient in this respect. It frequently emphasizes the non-hierarchical, heterogeneous (sometimes dubbed 'heterarchical') nature of social networking processes, without necessarily relating this back to traditional government structures and processes corresponding to pertinent questions about public accountability and political power. (As noted in Chapter 2, though, there is a growing literature which has begun to engage critically with these questions.)

It is important from a conceptual perspective to address the governance bias which, it is suggested here, arises from the combination of these strengths and weaknesses in the dominant sustainable city discourse, so as to develop a more comprehensive and sophisticated understanding of sustainable urban governance, identify and analyse gaps, and consider related methodological implications. Just as relevant, however, should be the practical perspective, which suggests the need to enhance sustainable city governance mechanisms to render them more attuned and responsive to spatial dimensions and wider socio-political processes. As noted, many of the challenges involved in getting sustainable city initiatives off the ground in the first instance, and then ensuring their progression across often lengthy periods of development, appear to be closely linked to issues of governance and, in particular, a failure to engage more fully with governance questions. The following section, in keeping with the approach taken so far in this book, seeks to address the governance bias from a conceptual perspective, rather than serving up practical solutions, although the theoretical and analytical considerations offered may well prove relevant for practice, too.

Towards a more pluralistic public governance

It may seem an unpopular move to propose a more explicit political discourse on the sustainable city, and greater public engagement with sustainable urban development. Certainly, much of the conceptual discussion about, and related innovative practices in, sustainable urbanism appear to take place away from the political sphere; some would say sustainable city innovations happen *in spite of* politics and should, therefore, be kept at a healthy distance from political and public interference. In a recent essay entitled 'Who's really driving change?', political scientist David Runciman addresses the challenge for politics in an age transformed by fast-paced technological innovation and change: 'Technology has the power to make politics seem obsolete. The speed of change leaves government looking slow, cumbersome, unwieldy and often irrelevant. It can also make political thinking look tame by comparison, with the big ideas coming out of the tech industry' (Runciman, 2014: 2). He goes on to suggest that while scientific and technological advances do in fact throw up all-important questions for political consideration, these are typically not addressed as such: 'the new answers rarely get expressed in political terms … More often they are expressions of frustration with politics and sometimes of outright contempt for it. Technology isn't seen as a way of doing politics better. It's seen as a way of bypassing politics altogether' (ibid.: 2).

A similar impression can sometimes be gained from reading the literature on urban sustainability, attending international conferences on the topic, and visiting sustainable city projects fêted as 'showcases'. The relative absence here of political discourse may, of course, in part be explained – as would be expected – by the focus on, and preoccupation with, more technical questions of design, technological development, engineering and planning among the specialists involved; alternatively, it may be explained by a lack of engagement on the part of political scientists. Often, however, it seems due in no small part to what appears to be an active bypassing of relevant political perspectives. Both possibilities are aligned with the tendency, noted above, to refer to sustainable city initiatives variously as 'niches', 'urban laboratory', and 'socio-technical processes' – all of which suggests innovative activity taking place away from the political and public spheres. It is in this sense that the discussion here raises the possibility of a governance paradox: while the importance of governing for sustainable urban development is increasingly recognized in research and reflected in policy and practice, key questions and issues concerning governance conditions are frequently left under-analysed or untouched.

The rationale behind the call here for a more pronounced public governance approach, then, is two-fold: first, the aim is to address, and take issue with, the de-politicizing and de-contextualizing tendencies at work in much of mainstream sustainable city discourse and practice; and in response, second, the goal is to suggest an alternative approach – namely, one which more actively and imaginatively attends to, and embraces, public discourses as an integral part of the sustainable city and its processes. Both objectives look to a wider debate, in political theory and policy studies, which concerns itself with the essential yet often problematic role of the public (or 'publics') in modern politics, policy, and planning (e.g. Rhodes, 1997; Weintraub and Kumar, 1997; Pierre and Peters, 2000; Fischer, 2003; Marquand, 2004; Latour, 2005; Parkinson, 2006; Newman and Clarke, 2009). This debate seeks to understand the social and political implications of the transformation of the public sphere – both as concept and practice – resulting from the emergence of new modes, forms and sites of governance. Among other contributions, Newman and Clarke (2009) discuss the ramifications of de-politicized governance (which they characterize as a paradox, in terms of the concurrent decline of a 'politics of the public' and the proliferation of diverse new sites and discourses of governance), concluding that: 'there are contestations that consistently seek to de-politicise things, people, policies and practices, rendering them technical, private or natural' (ibid.: 184). There are clear echoes of these wider findings in mainstream sustainable city discourse and practice: these can be heard in the language of the city as quasi-natural or complex system, in policy discourses emphasizing sustainable urbanism as investment opportunity and market mechanism, and in the increasing calls espousing various 'smart' technological solutions.

Importantly, while in de-politicized forms of governance – and this applies to sustainable city initiatives, too – political and public dimensions may be deliberately rendered less overt, taking the form of various technocratic discourses and procedures, they should certainly not be understood as being absent: they fundamentally shape strategies and exert influence over decision processes and outcomes, although they typically do so with less explicit articulation and reflexivity. In the case of sustainable city initiatives, this may be seen mirrored in, for example: a presupposition about the superiority of market-based governance mechanisms; tacit assumptions about what constitutes the public and public interests; uncritical views of the benefits of public engagement in design processes; and implied expectations of sustainable development producing, as a matter of course, beneficial, 'harmonious' social outcomes. Consequently, if nothing else, a critical public governance perspective serves to make more explicit, and problematize, the presence and influences of these socio-political dimensions.

As noted, however, the purpose of moving towards a more public governance perspective goes deeper: it prompts us to consider what the sustainable city as a re-politicized process should entail, and how a more public-oriented stance could help take the debate forward. According to Newman and Clarke (2009: 184), the process of re-politicization involves making things and people public; and this very process necessarily involves opening up questions and issues of politics and power: 'this means making contestation, conflict, and contradiction visible and debatable, both about the large issues and about the practices of publicness ... What matters is to make the "dilemmas" visible and available for being acted upon, rather than compressing and displacing them into difficult choices of individual actors' (ibid.: 184). From this perspective, sustainable city initiatives can be viewed as sites and spaces of public action where challenging questions and dilemmas – say, concerning the balance between competing environmental, social and economic goals; the choice between investments in new urban developments and existing urban communities; and the reconciliation of local, national and even global priorities – are opened up to debate and scrutiny, rather than being downplayed or buried in technocratic language and procedures. If, however, the impression might arise that the sustainable city as site and space of public action, rather dispiritingly, only brings out and highlights problems and dilemmas then this needs qualifying: just as essentially, it should be recognized for (the potential of) providing a valuable discursive space for sharing and learning about, even celebrating, public interest in the sustainable city and, crucially, connecting this to institutional processes and practices.

On the face of it, the terms 'public', 'publicness' and 'public governance' may seem rather abstract and theoretical. However, as posited here, they are understood as a constitutive part of, and closely interconnected with, the (sustainable) city as site and space. This follows Cowley (2015), whose research on a range of recent eco-city initiatives provides a detailed, probing account of how urban spaces are variously co-constructive of public discourse. The city, as both a physical space and what Cowley terms a 'dynamic nexus of social relations', produces publicness: the processes of making things, ideas, people, relationships and issues public and, as such, rendering visible matters of connective concern (Newman and Clarke, 2009: 2). Cowley (2015) applies the concept of 'assemblage' to analyse how such processes of publicness are produced and constituted in and through particular eco-city sites, and especially through the formation and evolution of public spaces. In doing so, this research identifies an important difference at work between 'civic' and 'emergent' public spaces, in terms of their varying influence on how sustainable urbanism is constructed and comes into being: civic public space represents official norms and, as such, embodies dominant codings of urban space and defines (and restricts) what is permissible use of such space; in contrast, emergent public space is a more fluid, loose space, through which alternative interpretations of the sustainable city may emerge, thereby challenging established civic norms.

The posited shift towards a more public, and hence pluralistic, governance of the sustainable city, then, is a process that one should equally look out for, and consider, in informal, emergent spaces and practices, as much as in established institutional arrangements and public spaces; and, so too, in the numerous 'in-between' spaces, where much of sustainable city innovation occurs. In fact, it is arguably precisely at the interface between formal, institutional arrangements and informal, temporary processes that the consideration of a more public governance is at its most critical and, in turn, potentially also at its most promising. The remaining part of this chapter, therefore, pays particular attention to how three key aspects of public governance – public engagement, accountability, and discourse – relate to sustainable city initiatives played out within various 'in-between' spaces.

Governance through public engagement

Some of the recent literature on urban sustainability brims with palpable excitement about the prospect of community groups, local activists and citizens joining forces with designers and technologists in developing, trialling and implementing sustainable urban solutions. 'Design communities', 'collaborative working groups', 'participatory planning forums' and similarly termed concepts and methods can increasingly be seen at work in sustainable urban development, building on decades of experimentation in urban planning as well as experience in other policy arenas (Joss, 2014). For example, with reference to the concept of 'empowered deliberative democracy', Hajer and Huitzing (2012) extol the potential of the 'energetic society' drawing on the – often untapped – creativity and learning capabilities present among citizens and various stakeholders. Information technology, notably, is a key enabler of citizen involvement: 'The technical possibilities offered by Web 2.0 to create two-way communication, as well as the increase of information available, provide the right circumstances for hands-on involvement of articulate citizens and companies in formulating sustainability and local environmental policies' (ibid.: 22). The explicit socio-technical conceptualization of sustainable city governance is reinforced in the authors' concluding remarks: 'A smart, social and sustainable city creates an attractive image. Cities and the Internet, at both the local and global level, together are the breeding ground for ideas and shared visions of a sustainable society' (ibid.: 23). In similar vein, Ratti and Townsend (2012) place the general public at the centre of sustainable city governance, with the promise that 'citizens could become deeply engaged in environmental monitoring and regulation' (ibid.: 15). Here again, such engagement is to be enabled not so much by the 'centralized dictates' of the municipality, but by urban information technology:

> city governments, technology companies and their urban planning advisers can exploit a more ground-up urban approach to creating even smarter cities, in which people become the agents of change. With proper technical support structures, the populace can tackle problems such as energy use, traffic congestion, health care and education more effectively than centralized dictates can. And residents of wired cities can use their distributed intelligence to fashion new community activities, as well as a new kind of citizen activism. (Ibid.: 15)

> Bottom-up approaches are also leveraging the sociability of cities to change patterns of activity ... connecting local businesses and city dwellers through mobile social networks is a powerful catalyst for action. These new ways of scripting the city can create more lasting kinds of social touch points, too. (Ibid.: 15)

At international level, the World Bank through its Eco2 Cities initiative (see Chapter 3) is a similarly enthusiastic advocate of collaborative design and decision-making, calling it 'a new approach to governance and, perhaps, a new way of living together' (Suzuki et al., 2010: 55). Citing the example of 'design charrette', a participatory method – comparatively traditional, without reliance on wired information systems – which brings together diverse actor groups (technical experts, designers, planners, residents, etc.) in discussion and deliberation, the organization is in no doubt about its benefits: 'More recently, the [charrette] techniques have been applied to entire neighbourhoods, cities, and regions. The results have been excellent' (ibid.: 119). And it is similarly effusive in its assessment of the benefits of using collaborative planning frameworks, such as offered through its Eco2 pathway:

> As cities undertake a more well integrated approach to system design and develop an extended platform for collaboration, the shared framework may help to solve the problems in organizing and communicating complexities ... Everyone involved in the planning is able to follow the transparent, logical connections between, on one hand, intended goals and overall vision, and, on the other, detailed actions and results. This allows all agencies and stakeholders to understand how their work fits within and contributes to the long-term vision and goals. (Ibid.: 57)

Judging by these statements, there certainly seems to be a great deal of enthusiasm about the potential for broad, shared participatory governance in sustainable city innovation. Yet, beyond these optimistic statements, it cannot be taken for granted that in practice the co-production of sustainable urban development is so easily achieved through multi-actor participation, however much wiring of urban infrastructures and systems is made available. It is precisely because of the pervasive, underlying assumption of self-organizing, autonomous governance, on one hand, and strong belief in technological solutions, on the other, that the discussion led by these advocates largely refrains from critical probing into the requirements and conditions for participation. To be clear, this is not to say that there is no potential for broad-based, collaborative engagement in sustainable city innovations; however, this potential needs careful consideration and critical analysis. There is a growing body of evidence justifying a cautious approach, attuned to sensitive issues of what enables, and conversely what hinders, participatory governance. For example, UN-Habitat, in a review of participatory processes and partnerships in its global report *Planning Sustainable Cities*, flags up a range of critical political and social preconditions for effective participation: 'research shows that this [participation] is not a simple solution that can be imposed anywhere and is not a technical process that can be detached from local political culture' (UN-Habitat, 2009b: 65). Expanding on these findings, the agency identifies several critical issues including: the challenge of establishing a common language and achieving understanding between experts and professionals (e.g. technologists, planners) and non-experts (e.g. residents, community groups); the difficulty of giving socially marginalized groups a voice; and the problem of linking participatory governance to formal decision-making. As a result, while seeking to encourage participatory engagement, the agency at the same time calls for close attention to these and other critical issues:

> Potentially, participation in planning can empower communities and build social capital, lead to better design of urban projects and allow for participants' concerns to be incorporated within strategies. Physical planning is often accused of neglecting the social and economic dimensions of projects, and participation is a mechanism for addressing this. The general conclusion is that participation is important and necessary, but that, in practice much of it is consultative or instrumental, providing participants with little real influence over decision-making. Lessons from experiences suggest that successful participation is dependent upon certain preconditions relation to the political context, the legal basis for participation and available resources. (UN-Habitat: 2009b: 65)

If participatory governance proves challenging within organizational settings, then additional challenges can be expected from participatory processes played out in inter-organizational spaces, such as those represented by innovation niches. One of the advantages of an 'in-between' niche space may be that it is perceived as more neutral territory, not wholly owned by any one actor group, as a consequence of which different actors can participate on a more equal footing. Then again, the 'in-between' space may not turn out to be that neutral after all if, for example, the innovation process relies one-sidedly on resources – technical data and methods, expertise, organizational support, finances, etc. – from one or a few participants. Also, an innovation space constituted around a particular socio-technical process – as is typical of innovation niches – can be expected to provide particular thematic framings from the outset and may favour certain socio-technical strategies and solutions. For example, hypothetically, a network formed to develop electric car technology and related urban applications would be unlikely to pay equal attention to a cyclist group advocating the expansion of safe cycling routes, and to a car manufacturer association or electronics firm. Furthermore, the informal, autonomous nature of the hybrid niche space may make it more difficult to establish agreed ground rules of engagement than in the case of participatory governance processes based within organizational settings. Once again, these and other likely issues should not necessarily be considered a deterrent to developing and supporting participatory processes – as one manifestation of a more public governance – for sustainable city innovation; however, they deserve and require closer conceptual attention, analytical investigation and practical elaboration.

Accountable governance

A flip side of public engagement is the issue of accountability, which is equally relevant to the consideration of public governing processes in sustainable urban innovation. Broadly, accountability refers to the publicity, monitoring and scrutiny of decision-making processes and outcomes (e.g. Moncrieffe, 2001; Mulgan, 2003; Bovens, 2005; Parkinson, 2006; Philip, 2009; Joss, 2010). In the modern state, accountability typically takes three overlapping forms: political (relating to governmental institutions), managerial (relating to organizations), and professional (relating to expertise); these often interact in complex interplay in decision-making, including in the arena of urban policy and planning. Apart from its status as normative ideal – accountability is seen in many societies and most national and international organizations as a core commitment, and principle of 'good governance' – it serves particular instrumental purposes, too: namely, to enhance and ensure the transparency and fairness of decision processes as well as the quality and effectiveness of decision outcomes, which is sometimes referred to as 'input legitimacy' and 'output legitimacy', respectively. It should become immediately apparent that accountability matters in sustainable city initiatives given the centrality of the governance process; and it should equally become clear that it involves some complexity given the hybrid socio-technical and multi-actor constellations at work. (Chapter 5 presents a detailed analysis based on the two case studies of Treasure Island and EcoDistricts.) Three facets of accountability relating to the sustainable city are considered below; while each highlights a particular, intricate aspect, it is in their combined interaction that the challenge of accountability involved in sustainable urban development comes fully to the fore.

The first facet concerns the hybrid nature of governance arrangements frequently involved in sustainable city initiatives. Rather than being embedded within singular institutional policy frameworks, jurisdictional competences and organizational structures, sustainable urban development characteristically takes places across boundaries: it draws on, and seeks to correlate and amalgamate, policies from various arenas (environmental, economic, social, planning, etc.); it brings together actors from various professional and practice fields, and sometimes the wider community; and it involves co-ordination of planning and decision-making between organizations. As such, the resulting governance mode may be said to be 'new' not just in that it departs from more bounded, hierarchical decision-making associated with traditional government, but also in that it creates new assemblages of actors for the purpose of co-operating on particular sustainable city initiatives. These networks, then, are often temporary and sometimes fragile; they can be expected to evolve and change as a project progresses, and they may dissolve or evolve further upon completion of the project. Consequently, rather than being permanent or stable, the governance arrangements have to be established involving negotiating and setting up various networking and partnership rules, protocols and mechanisms. In some instances, especially large-scale, long-term urban development projects requiring official institutional commitment and substantive financial support, these arrangements can become heavily formalized through various kinds of public–private and public–public partnership agreements. (Treasure Island is an example of a formal public–private partnership which took almost a decade to negotiate and set up.) In other instances, the governance arrangements remain more informal and flexible, open to ongoing negotiation and development by the actors involved. Even where government, through national or municipal programmes, spearheads sustainable city initiatives, this typically spawns hybrid governance arrangements, given the need to mobilize resources, expertise and interests from across institutions, organization and the community.

Accountability issues crop up concerning, on one hand, the processes and related dynamics within a given urban sustainability governance arrangement and, on the other, its interaction with the wider policy and decision processes. Concerning the former, the heterogeneous, hybrid nature of governance means that accountability processes become complicated and potentially problematic: conventional accountability procedures cannot necessarily be relied upon, as the sphere of influence of established governmental and organizational decision-making is limited; and new procedures may not be readily available, so need to be designed and negotiated to suit the particular sustainable city initiative in question. The challenge here consists not only in setting up appropriate accountability mechanisms within a context of emerging and evolving governance networks, where rules and boundaries may not as yet be established, but also in doing so through negotiation and co-ordination among all actors involved. This challenge is further compounded by the very hybrid nature of governance: accountability essentially relies on clear lines and channels of responsibility, as well as on the transparency of decision-making processes; this may prove particularly difficult to achieve in hybrid organizational arrangements, the very characteristics of which are dynamic, multiple interactions involving diverse actors across institutional and organizational boundaries. The role of intermediary organizations, as facilitators, is often an influential one, though by no means always clear in terms of accountability relations. To add to this, the interrelationship of a given governance arrangement with its wider policy and decision context can pose further accountability hurdles. Opening up a sustainable city initiative to wider political and public scrutiny may be hampered by an arrangement containing strong internal governance dynamics and boundaries, thus making it impenetrable to outside scrutiny; or conversely, by an extensive and diffuse governance network, rendering its discourse and decision-making difficult to capture and encapsulate.

The second, related side of accountability concerns the socio-technical discourse at the heart of much of sustainable city governance. It is, of course, to be expected that urban sustainability as a field of research and innovation is informed by and conducted in technical language and professional discourse, as part of which it is subject to professional accountability mechanisms, such as peer review and professional codes and standards. However, this should not mean that urban sustainability is treated as an exclusively technical debate, from which contestation over the structural causes of unsustainability, and therefore more radical or imaginary solutions, are excluded. Such an outcome would seem indicative of what some commentators have termed a 'post-political' tendency in contemporary society, in reference to 'a politics in which ideological or dissensual contestation and struggles are replaced by techno-managerial planning, expert management and administration' (Swyngedouw, 2010: 225). More optimistically, the principle that this debate should encompass a broader set of questions seems straightforward enough: sustainable city initiatives by definition cross into policy and practice, and they are embedded within particular local settings. The sustainable city as urban laboratory is, therefore, not an exclusively technical, but equally a public, site. Hence, professional, policy and public discourses closely intermingle and jointly contribute to the narrative and rationale of the sustainable city. As a consequence, this requires ongoing translation, especially if governance is supposed to be based on the co-production of knowledge, meaning and practice involving diverse actors. And yet, the reality of sustainable urban development suggests that professional and technical discourses often dominate, with the risk of excluding or marginalizing certain actors, such as community groups and citizens and, consequently, preventing broader public accountability.

Governance is supposed to counteract this tendency, by opening up involvement in sustainable city innovation to a broader range of actors and mobilizing diverse knowledge and expertise. Unintentionally, however, it may compound the situation, by imposing a technical language of its own, as can be seen in the increasing use of various urban sustainability 'indicators' and 'frameworks', which in themselves require expert knowledge and skills and only add to the abundance of technical information and data. In practice, rather than facilitating governance processes and empowering community involvement, such technical governance discourse has been shown to have the opposite effect of increasing contestation, conflict and resistance (see e.g. Rydin, 2007; Joss, 2010). Furthermore, the close kinship of governance discourse with the language of 'systems' and 'complexity' – whereby governance processes respond to complexity by providing increased co-ordinative capacity – may additionally distance it from public discourse and accountability by highlighting the technical governance of the sustainable city as a 'complex adaptive system'.

There is a further, third facet to the accountability *problematique* of the sustainable city, and possibly its most complex and abstract yet: this relates to the discussion in Chapter 7 of the increasingly ubiquitous application of information and communication technology in a way which creates 'self-aware urban infrastructure', and even raises the prospect of the sustainable city as a cyborg (man-machine) vision. While still some way off from full realization, and as such usually accompanied by a fair amount of hyperbole, this notion of the sustainable city nevertheless hints at a new kind of blended and fluid interrelationship of urban infrastructure and systems, social media and digital data, and citizens (residents, workers, commuters, visitors, etc.). Hybridity here not only relates to the governance processes and networks of sustainable urban development in the classical sense, but also more profoundly to a novel virtual interface between the city and its people, facilitated by digital media: urban systems and the built environment become more individually responsive to citizens, and citizens interact more directly – or indirectly? – with urban space: individuals talk to the city, and the city talks back to them, via social media and through big data. As such, the (sustainable) city creates and embodies new hybrid spaces of variable reality. Quite apart from the potentially profound wider consequences, this scenario raises important questions for accountability: for example, whether, positively, accountability is rendered a more immediate process by creating new direct relationships between citizens and their city; or conversely, whether public and political accountability as a collective process becomes disabled, as decisions and actions escape into the virtual, individualized realm. Meanwhile, at a more pragmatic level, as the applications of digital technology through various 'smart sustainable city' initiatives start to take hold, important questions need to be asked about how the processes of generating, analysing and storing digital information and data can be made properly accountable.

The issues of accountability, as well as participation, have been raised here as essential components of the conceptualization of the sustainable city as a more public governance process. As the discussion makes clear, neither of them can be taken for granted easily, given that sustainable urban development, on one hand, increasingly occurs at the interface between institutional governance settings and multiple informal, temporary governance arrangements and, consequently, on the other, produces complex new knowledge discourses and socio-technical practices. Instead, they need actively figuring out, experimenting and practising as a fundamental part of the process of governing for sustainable city innovation. It is, then, also not simply a matter of looking to established forms of public accountability and engagement – such as can be found represented in traditional accounts of government – in the expectation of being able to borrow and apply these readily to the new hybrid governance processes involved in the sustainable city. Rather, in setting about developing new public accountability and engagement strategies, salient questions need to be asked and carefully addressed, including: how urban sustainability issues are framed, and what are related knowledge processes; how actors gain access to, and develop agency; how interests and conflicts are recognized and negotiated in networking processes; what power relations and asymmetries come into play; and how governance is controlled and rendered transparent.

The sustainable city as public discourse

Beyond these more instrumental considerations, there is a further – less immediately tangible perhaps, but just as important – dimension to the sustainable city as public governance stance, to be explored in the remaining pages of this book. The suggestion here is that governance should open up the sustainable city, beyond its particular niches and spaces, to wider public discourse. Such an opening up could not only bring with it the potential to broaden the range of people getting involved in debate – from local publics to global communities, and from special interest groups to general audiences – but at the same time the possibility of inviting and welcoming more open-ended exploration, contestation, even unorthodox and radical thinking. Together, this should help engender social and political voice, engagement, and critical reflexivity. This may seem counterproductive to some. Sceptics might argue that there is not the luxury of time; that sustainable urban development is such a pressing matter for the present, let alone for the future, that the time for debate has passed and instead time for action is now. (There are some who argue seriously that democratic governance might even need to be suspended, and instead government by diktat introduced, if the radical transition to a sustainable global society is to be realized in good time.) Other sceptics might quip that public and political debate only adds more hot air to the already disturbing levels of atmospheric GHG emissions, pointing – perhaps not entirely without justification – to failed international negotiations, such as the Copenhagen Summit (the 2009 UN Climate Change Conference), and lacklustre domestic political commitment and waning public interest. Again others could point to the already considerable technical complexities and laborious governance processes involved in trying to get sustainable city initiatives off the ground, which might only be further hampered by additional public intrusion and political meddling.

Yet, while noting these reservations, the opening up of the sustainable city to more pluralistic, unrestricted and unbounded public discourse is nevertheless suggested here as what could, and arguably should be, a fundamental aspect of the sustainable city. This is not done looking at public discourse through rose-tinted glasses, seeing it as a pleasant and unproblematic pastime. Rather, it is proposed seriously, as a way of both adding much-needed critical analytical capacity, and contributing to public understanding and political awareness, concerning this important topic of our times. Apart from the more instrumental reasons for public engagement and accountability, discussed above, the wider rationale for public discourse lies in the (potentially) inherently radical nature of the sustainable city: unless one reduces urban sustainability to certain facts, technical fixes, and obvious solutions, the sustainable city entails a proposition for, and the prospect of, a fundamental transition towards a future which differs from the present in profound ways. This, in turn, provokes unavoidable fundamental and perplexing questions. How is this transition to be understood – if indeed there is agreement about it – and how should it be brought about? What should the sustainable city look like in the present, and what is it expected to look like in 20, 30, or 50 years' time? And, all importantly, how are individuals, communities and societies implicated in this process of transitioning towards the sustainable city? How are they, and how will they be, affected by, and engaged in, sustainable urban development? What is their individual and collective agency; and what is their individual and collective responsibility?

These questions suggest that the sustainable city is as much a discourse as a matter of technological innovation, bureaucratic planning and real-estate development; and it is as much an idea, an ideal and an imaginary, as it involves facts, certainty and consensus. This, then, also implies that it cannot be reduced to a technocratic proposition, to be determined solely by scientific experts, planners and technologists, and neatly encapsulated through technical indicator schemes, frameworks and projects. The questions further imply that the sustainable city cannot be captured exclusively with reference to local settings, as much as it cannot be fully grasped with reference to the global context alone. Above all, these questions suggest that trying to impose and cement consensus is likely to prove unrealistic, and ultimately even counterproductive. Rather than producing action, an insistence on certitude and agreement may well have a stupefying effect on public discourse and unwittingly provoke disengagement. Instead, the sustainable city as public discourse recognizes the manifold open and continuously evolving questions involved; it acknowledges the plurality of interests – and frequently also conflicts – at stake; and, consequently, it makes space for partial answers, differences of approach and opinion, and contingent and conflictual knowledge about what is and should be sustainable urban development.

In a thoughtful and thought-provoking analysis on climate change discourse, political theorist Amanda Machin (2013) suggests that, far from hampering progress on climate change negotiations and delaying collective action, opening up this dominant challenge of the age to critical public discourse and political debate is necessary for society to be able to come to terms with and find answers to the challenges of climate change. While Machin does not directly address the question of the (un)sustainable city, her analysis of climate change discourse nevertheless provides valuable, parallel insights for the discussion here. She forcefully argues that a central aspect of coming to grips with the *problematique* of climate change is 'to look at climate change by looking at ourselves' (Machin, 2013: 1). Calling climate change the 'silhouette of our own self-image' (ibid.: 1), she suggests that instead of treating this phenomenon as an external *problematique*, to be referred to and understood by science and tackled by imposed consensus, it would be more productively approached by acknowledging its inherently political nature. This does not exclude the application of science and the development of technological solutions, but it makes clear that science and technology are no substitute for considering climate change as a political question. Otherwise, attempting to shift what are ultimately political considerations and public interests onto science would risk depoliticizing climate change to the detriment of political debate and engagement. In the course of her analysis, which looks at the issue from various political theoretical perspectives, Machin reaches the conclusion that opening up what is often presented as a closed discussion and, in doing so, acknowledging differences and even disagreement are key to unlocking the challenge of climate change and encouraging public engagement and political action.

It would go well beyond the scope of this concluding section to outline in detail what a more public governance of the sustainable city in the form of open(-ended) public discourse could and should in practice look like. Indeed, it would probably prove quite impossible to provide any in-depth account and prescriptive guidance, beyond some broad principles and analytical criteria as highlighted above. After all, public discourse can be expected to be multifaceted and pluralistic, involving various publics engaged in diverse, overlapping public spheres across a multitude of different spatial settings and policy contexts. As such, public discourse may come in many forms and shapes and may take several directions, some unexpected and unpredictable. What is more, rather than being prescribed, the nature of public discourse essentially is, and ought to be, fashioned and co-determined by the actors involved themselves.

Coda

There remain, though, a couple of final observations to be made. First, the suggestion in these concluding remarks is not just that open, and open-minded, public debate *about* the sustainable city should be encouraged and facilitated. Instead, more profoundly perhaps, the suggestion is that the sustainable city *is* a public discourse – that is, exploring, analysing, talking about, debating and contesting should be an elemental part of, and have a firm place in, sustainable city initiatives; and this not only as a means of achieving effective and prudent sustainable urban development, but equally as an intrinsic aspect of governing for sustainable cities. Viewing a sustainable city plan, visiting a sustainable city initiative, or even living in a sustainable urban environment, one should ideally be able to expect as much attention to detail on how the city caters for and encourages open, public discourse, as one can expect elaborate technical information and instructions on the built environment and various urban systems. Relatedly, second, if the sustainable city can be usefully conceptualized as a series of interconnected sociotechnical niches, from which new experimental knowledge, creative design ideas and technological innovations emerge, then it could equally productively be conceptualized as a series of interrelating public spheres, through which new ideas, proposals and actions arise concerning how to govern and engage in the sustainable city. And just as the technological innovation path may take different turns and can, therefore, not be fully predicted, so the course of public discussion within and around the sustainable city may lead in various unexpected directions. If the sustainable city is to be part of a radical transition towards a more sustainable future, then it should itself entail the possibility for radical social and political thinking, debate and action.

References

Abbott, C. (1997). The Portland Region: Where City and Suburbs Talk to Each Other – and Often Agree. *Housing Policy Debate*, 8 (1): 11–51.

Adams, B. (1997). The Portland Way, in Adams B. and Parr J. (eds) *Boundary Crossers: Case Studies of How Ten of America's Metropolitan Regions Work*. College Park, MD: Burns Academy of Leadership, University of Maryland.

Adger, W.N. and Jordan, A. (eds) (2009). *Governing Sustainability*. Cambridge: Cambridge University Press.

Administrative Committee of Tangshan Caofeidian International Eco-City (2009). *City of the Future 2009. Guide to Investment of Caofeidian International Eco-City*. Caofeidian, Tangshan: Administrative Committee of Tangshan Caofeidian International Eco-City.

Akintoye, A., Beck, M. and Hardcastle, C. (eds) (2003). *Public–Private Partnerships: Managing Risks and Opportunities*. Oxford: Wiley-Blackwell.

Allen, P.M. (1997). *Cities and Regions as Self-organizing Systems: Models of Complexity*. Amsterdam: Gordon and Breach Science Publishers.

Anderson, S. (2011) EcoDistricts tap into neighborhood energy. *Sustainable Business Oregon*, 24 Oct. Online source: http://www.sustainable businessoregon.com (home page), accessed 22 May 2014.

Arboníes, A.L. and Moso, M. (2002). Basque Country: The Knowledge Cluster. *Journal of Knowledge Management*, 6 (4): 347–55.

Archer, K. (2012). Rescaling Global Governance: Imagining the Demise of the Nation-State. *Globalizations*, 9 (2): 241–56.

Arcosanti (undated). *Introduction to Arcology*. Online source: http://www.arcosanti.org/arcology, accessed 30 August 2013.

Audubon International (undated a). *Audubon International: Sustainable Communities Program*. Online source: http://www.auduboninternational.org (home page), accessed 29 June 2014.

Audubon International (undated b). *Sustainable Communities Program: Frequently Asked Questions*. Online source: http://www.auduboninternational.org (home page), accessed 27 June 2014.

Barles, S. (2009). Urban Metabolism of Paris and Its Region. *Journal of Industrial Ecology*, 13 (6): 898–913.

Barles, S. (2010). Society, Energy and Materials: The Contribution of Urban Metabolism Studies to Sustainable Urban Development Issues. *Journal of Environmental Planning and Management*, 53 (4): 439–55.

Barton, H. (2000a). Conflicting Perceptions of Neighbourhood, in Barton, H. (ed.) *Sustainable Communities: The Potential for Eco-Neighbourhoods*. London: Earthscan, pp. 3–18.

Barton, H. (ed.) (2000b). *Sustainable Communities: The Potential for Eco-Neighbourhoods*. London: Earthscan.

Batty, M. (2013). *The New Science of Cities*. Boston MA: MIT Press.

Bay City News Service (2011). Initial Vote is Unanimous; Critics Say Plan is 'a Triumph of Politics Over Policy'. *The Bay Citizen*, 8 June. Online source: https://www.baycitizen.org (home page), accessed 22 May 2014.

BBC (2005). Changing Planet Revealed in Atlas. *BBC News*, 4 June. Online source: http://news.bbc.co.uk (home page), accessed 3 March 2014.

BBC Focus (2008). 197. Bristol: Immediate Media Company.

Berkhout, F., Smith, A. and Stirling, A. (2003). *Socio-technological Regimes and Transition Contexts*. SPRU Electronic Working Paper Series, Paper 106. SPRU – Science and Technology Policy Research. Online source: http://www.sussex.ac.uk/Units/spru/publications/imprint/sewps/sewp106/sewp106.pdf, accessed 30 March 2014.

Bernstein, S. (2001). *The Compromise of Liberal Environmentalism*. New York: Columbia University Press.

Bettencourt, L.M.A., Lobo, J., Helbing, D., Kühner, C. and West, G.B. (2007). Growth, Innovation, Scaling, and the Pace of Life in Cities. *PNAS (Proceedings of the National Academy of Sciences)*, 104 (17): 7301–6.

Bexell, M. and Mörth, U. (eds) (2010). *Democracy and Public–Private Partnerships in Global Governance*. Basingstoke: Palgrave Macmillan.

BioRegional (2011a). *Common International Targets*. BioRegional Development Group. Online source: http://www.oneplanetcommunities.org (home page), accessed 27 June 2014.

BioRegional (2011b). *One Planet Regions: UK Targets*. BioRegional Development Group. Online source: http://www.brighton-hove.gov.uk (home page), accessed 27 June 2014.

BioRegional (2013). *The Communities*. BioRegional Development Group. Online source: http://www.oneplanetcommunities.org. (home page), accessed 20 August 2013.

BioRegional (2014). *Annual Review 2012/2013*. BioRegional Development Group. Online source: http://www.bioregional.com (home page), accessed 27 June 2014.

BioRegional (undated). *What is One Planet Living?* BioRegional Development Group. Online source: http://www.bioregional.com (home page), accessed 25 January 2012.

Birch, E. (2002). Five Generations of the Garden City, in Parsons, K. and Schuyler, D. (eds) *From Garden City to Green City: The Legacy of Ebenezer Howard*. Baltimore, MD: Johns Hopkins University Press, pp. 171–200.

Book, K., Eskilsson, L. and Khan, J. (2010). Governing the Balance between Sustainability and Competitiveness in Urban Planning: the Case of the Orestad Model. *Environmental Policy and Governance*, 20: 382–96.

Bovens, E. (2005). Public Accountability, in Ferlie, E., Lynne, L. and Pollitt, C. (eds) *The Oxford Handbook of Public Management*. Oxford: Oxford University Press, pp. 103–16.

Boyd, E., and Folke, C. (eds) (2011). *Adapting Institutions. Governance, Complexity and Socio-Ecological Resilience*. Cambridge: Cambridge University Press.

BRE Global (2013). *BREEAM Communities: Integrating Sustainable Design into Masterplanning*. Online source: http://www.breeam.org (home page), accessed 29 June 2014.

Brenner, N. (2004). *New State Spaces, Urban Governance and the Rescaling of Statehood*. Oxford: Oxford University Press.

Bretagnolle, A., Daudé, E. and Pumain, D. (2006). From Theory to Modelling: Urban Systems as Complex Systems / La Complexité dans les Systèmes Urbains: de la Théorie au Modèle. *Cybergeo european journal of geography*, Article 335. Online source: http://spi.cybergeo.revues.org/2420, accessed 22 March 2014.

Bruegmann, R. (2006). *Sprawl: A Compact History*. Chicago, IL: University of Chicago Press.

BSI (2014a). *PAS 180:2014 Smart Cities: Vocabulary*. London: British Standards Institute.

BSI (2014b). *PAS 181:2014 Smart City Framework – Guide to Establishing Strategies for Smart Cities and Communities*. London: British Standards Institute.

Buchwald, E. (ed.) (2003). *Toward the Livable City*. Minneapolis, MN: Milkweed Editions.

Bueren, E.M., Klijn, E.H. and Koppenjan J.F.M. (2003). Dealing with Wicked Problems in Networks: Analyzing an Environmental Debate from a Network Perspective. *Journal of Public Administration Research and Theory*, 13 (2):193 – 212.

Bulkeley, H. and Castán Broto, V. (2013). Government by experiment? Global Cities and the Governing of Climate Change. *Transactions of the Institute of British Geographers*, 38 (3): 361–75.

Bulkeley, H., Castán Broto, V., Hodson, M. and Marvin, S. (eds) (2013). *Cities and Low Carbon Transitions*. Abingdon: Routledge.

Bulkeley, H. and Marvin, S. (2014). Urban Governance and Eco-cities: Dynamics, Drivers and Emerging Lessons, in Hofmeister, W., Rueppel P. and Lye, L.F. (eds) *Eco-Cities: Sharing European and Asian Best Practices and Experiences*. Singapore: EU-Asia Dialogue, pp. 19–34.

Burdett, R. and Rode, P. (2012a). The Electric City, in Burdett, R. and Rode, P. (eds) *Urban Age Electric City Conference: London 6–7 December 2012*. London: LSE Cities, p. 2.

Burdett, R. and Rode, P. (eds) (2012b). *Urban Age Electric City Conference: London 6–7 December 2012*. London: LSE Cities.

Calvillo, N., Halpern, O., LeCavalier, J. and Pietsch, W. (2012). Skewing the City, in Burdett, R. and Rode, P. (eds) *Urban Age Electric City Conference: London 6–7 December 2012*. London: LSE Cities, pp. 18–19.

Caprotti, F. (2015). *Eco-Cities and the Transition to Low Carbon Economies*. Basingstoke: Palgrave Macmillan.

Caragliu, A., Del Bo, C. and Nijkamp, P. (2011). Smart Cities in Europe. *Journal of Urban Technology*, 18(2): 65–82.

Carrillo, F. (2005). *Knowledge Cities: Approaches, Experiences, and Perspectives*. Oxford: Butterworth-Heinemann.

Carson, R. (1962). *Silent Spring*. Boston, MA: Houghton Mifflin.

CBD (2010). *User's Manual for the City Biodiversity Index*. Online source: http://www.cbd.int (home page), accessed 28 June 2014.

CCI (2011). *Climate+ Development Program: Framework for Climate Positive Communities*. Clinton Climate Initiative. Online source: http://climatepositivedevelopment.org (home page), accessed 27 June 2014.

CCI (undated). *Clinton Climate Initiative: Programs*. Online source: http://www.clintonfoundation.org (home page), accessed 27 June 2014.

CCICED (2009). *China Announces Targets on Carbon Dioxide Emission Cuts*. China Council for International Cooperation on Environment and Development. Online source: http://www.gov.cn/ldhd/2009-11/26/content_1474016.htm, accessed 1 September 2013.

CCSM (2009). *The Copenhagen Climate Communiqué*. Online source: http://www.nyc.gov/html/planyc2030/downloads/pdf/cities_act_copenhagen_communique.pdf, accessed 21 August 2013.

CDP (2012). *Cities 2012 Global Report: Measurement for Management*. Online source: https://www.cdp.net (home page), accessed 2 July 2014.

CDP (2013). *Wealthier, Healthier Cities: How Climate Change is Giving us Wealthier, Healthier Cities*. London: CDP. Online source: https://www.cdp.net (home page), accessed 1 March 2013.

CEC (1990). *Green Paper on the Urban Environment: Communication from the Commission to the Council and the Parliament. Brussels: Commission of the European Communities*. COM(90) 218, Brussels 27 June.

CEC (1992). *Towards Sustainability: A European Community Programme of Policy and Action in Relation to the Environment and Sustainable Development*. COM(92) 23, Brussels 27 March.

CEC (1996). *European Sustainable Cities. Report of the Expert Group on the Urban Environment*. Commission of the European Communities. Luxembourg: Office for Official Publications of the European Commission.

Centre for Cities (2013). *Cities Outlook 2013*. London: Centre for Cities. Online source: http://www.centreforcities.org (home page), accessed 20 February 2014.

Centre for Liveable Cities (2014). *New Lenses on Future Cities: A New Lens Scenarios Supplement*. Online source: http://s05.static-shell.com/content/dam/shell-new/local/country/sgp/downloads/pdf/new-lenses-on-future-cities.pdf, accessed 30 March 2014.

China (Binhai Tianjin) International Eco-City Forum Journal (2010). Tianjin, 28 September.

Chang, I-C. and Sheppard, E. (2013). China's Eco-Cities as Variegated Urban Sustainability: Dongtan Eco-City and Chongming Eco-Island. *Journal of Urban Technology*, 20 (1): 57–75.

Chourabi, H., Nam, T., Walker, S., Gil-Garcia, J.R., Mellouli, S., Nahon, K., Pardo, T.A. and Scholl, H.J. (2012). Understanding Smart Cities: An Integrative Framework, in *Proceedings of the Forty-Fifth Annual Hawaii International Conference on System Sciences*. Wailea, HI: IEEE Computer Society, pp. 2289–97.

City of Portland (2009). *City of Portland and Multnomah County Climate Action Plan 2009*. Portland, OR: City of Portland Bureau of Planning and Sustainability. Online source: http://www.portlandoregon.gov (home page), accessed 22 May 2014.

City of Portland (2012). *Resolution No. 36974 As Amended*. Online source: http://assets.sustainablebusinessoregon.com/pdf/Ecodistrict_resolution_1031.pdf, accessed 5 January 2013.

City of Portland, Oregon (undated). *Neighborhood Involvement: Building Inclusive, Safe and Livable Neighborhoods and Communities*. Online source: https://www.portlandoregon.gov (home page), accessed 27 May 2014.

City of Vancouver (2012). *A Bright Green Future. An Action Plan for Becoming the Greenest City by 2020*. Vancouver: City of Vancouver. Online source: http://www.vancouver.ca (home page), accessed 26 March 2012.

Climate Positive (2013). *Climate + Development Program: Framework for Climate Positive Communities. Version 1.1*. Online source: http://climatepositivedevelopment.org (home page), accessed 12 July 2014.

Coaffee, J. (2008). Risk, Resilience, and Environmentally Sustainable Cities. *Energy Policy*, 36: 4633–8.

Cochrane, A. (2010). Exploring the Regional Politics of 'Sustainability': Making up Sustainable Communities in the South-East of England. *Environmental Policy and Governance*, 20 (6): 370–81.

Connelly, S. (2007). Mapping Sustainable Development as a Contested Concept. *Local Environment*, 12 (3): 259–78.

Cowley, R. (2015). *Eco-Cities: Technological Showcases or Public Spaces?* PhD thesis. London: University of Westminster.

CPRE London (2014). *Towards a Liveable London.* Online source: www.cprelondon.org.uk (home page), accessed 30 June 2014.

CPRE London (undated). Our Vision for London. Online source: http://www.cprelondon.org.uk (home page), accessed 12 July 2014.

Crot, L. (2003). Planning for Sustainability in Non-democratic Polities: The Case of Masdar City. *Urban Studies.* 50 (13): 2809–25

CSUS (2011a). *Eco-City Assessment and Best Practice: Annual Achievements 2010–11.* Beijing: Chinese Society for Urban Studies.

CSUS (2011b). *Proposed Eco-city Development Index System: Eco-City Assessment and Best Practices.* Beijing: Chinese Society for Urban Studies.

Cugurullo, F. (2013). How to Build a Sandcastle: An Analysis of the Genesis and Development of Masdar City. *Journal of Urban Technology,* 20 (1): 23–37.

Curwell, S., Yates, A., Howard, N., Bordass, B. and Doggart, J. (1999). The Green Building Challenge in the UK. *Building Research and Information,* 27 (4–5): 286–93.

C40 (2011). 'Carbon Disclosure Project Invites Most Populated Cities to Report Water.' Press Release, 1 November 2011. Online source: http://www.c40cities.org (home page), accessed 21 August 2013.

Dale, A., Dushenko, W. and Robinson, P.J. (2012). *Urban Sustainability: Reconnecting Space and Place.* Toronto: University of Toronto Press.

de Jong, M., Joss, S., Schraven, D., Zhan, C. and Weijnen, M. (2015). Sustainable-Smart-Resilient-Low-Carbon-Eco-Knowledge Cities: Making Sense of a Multitude of Concepts Promoting Sustainable Urbanization. *Journal of Cleaner Production* (doi: 10.106/j.jclepro.2015.02.004)

de Jong, M., Yu, C., Chen, X., Wang, D. and Weijnen, M. (2013). Developing Robust Organizational Frameworks for Sino-foreign Eco-cities: comparing Sino-Dutch Shenzhen Low Carbon City with other initiatives. *Journal of Cleaner Production,* 57: 209–20.

Dieleman, F. and Wegener, M. (2004) Compact City and Urban Sprawl. *Built Environment,* 30 (4): 308–23.

Dille, I. (2012). America's Best Bike City: 1. Portland, OR. *Bicycling.* Online source: http://www.bicycling.com (home page), accessed 22 May 2014.

Dobson, A. (ed.) (1991). *The Green Economy: Environment, Sustainable Development and the Politics of the Future.* London: Pluto Press.

Dong, S. (2013). *Beautiful China: Eco-City Indicators Guidebook.* Beijing: Tongxin Press.

Dong-Hee, S. (2009). Ubiquitous City: Urban Technologies, Urban Infrastructure and Urban Informatics. *Journal of Information Science,* 35 (5): 515–26.

Donnelly, M. (2012). Cameron Reaffirms Garden Cities Ambition. *Planning.* 19 March. Online source: http://www.planningresource.co.uk (home page), accessed 30 July 2013.

Dryzek, J.S. (2005). *The Politics of the Earth: Environmental Discourses.* Oxford: OUP.

Duany, A., Speck, J. and Lydon, M. (2010). *The Smart Growth Manual.* New York: McGraw-Hill.

Ecocity (2009). Introducing Eco City Hamburg-Harburg, cited in Welch, A. (2014) Eco-City Hamburg: Architecture Information + Images. Online source: http://www.e-architect.co.uk/hamburg/eco_city.htm, accessed March 26, 2012.

Ecocity Builders (2011). *International Ecocity Framework and Standards.* Online source: http://www.ecocitybuilders.org (home page), accessed 12 July 2014.

EcoDistricts (2012). *EcoDistricts Institute: The Building Blocks of Sustainable Cities.* Portland Sustainability Institute. Online source: http://ecodistricts.org (home page), accessed 22 May 2014.

EcoDistricts (2013). *The EcoDistricts Framework: Building Blocks of Sustainability.* Portland, OR: EcoDistricts.

EcoDistricts (undated). Online source: http://ecodistricts.org/projects (home page), accessed 3 June 2014.

Economist, The (2013). The Multiplexed Metropolis. 7 September, pp. 25–7.

Eco-quartiers.fr (undated). Online source: http://www.eco-quartiers.fr (home page), accessed 14 July 2014.

Ekins, P., Simon, S., Deutsch, L., Folke, C. and De Groot, R. (2003). A Framework for the Practical Application of the Concepts of Critical Natural Capital and Strong Sustainability. *Ecological Economics*, 44 (2–3): 165–85.

Embassy of Switzerland in the UK (2010). *A Swiss-UK Dialogue: Urban Sustainability, a Contradiction in Terms?* London: Embassy of Switzerland in the UK. Online source: http://www.minergie.ch/tl_files/download_en/Swiss_UK_Dialogue_1006-03_final.pdf, accessed 12 July 2014.

Engels, F. (1987) [originally published in German in 1845]. *The Condition of the Working Class in England.* London: Penguin.

Engwicht, D. (1993). *Reclaiming Our Cities and Towns: Better Living with Less Traffic.* Gabriola Island, B.C., Canada: New Society Publishers.

EPA (2013). *Sustainable Design and Green Building Toolkit for Local Governments.* Washington DC: United States Environmental Protection Agency.

European Commission (1994). *Charter of European Cities and Towns Towards Sustainability.* Aalborg: Aalborg Municipality. Online source: http://ec.europa.eu (home page), accessed 20 August 2013.

Ewing, B., Moore, D., Goldfinger, S., Oursler, A., Reed, A. and Wackernagel, M. (2010). *Ecological Footprint Atlas 2010.* Oakland, CA: Global Footprint Network.

Farrell, K.N., Kemp, R., Hinterberger, F., Rammel, C. and Ziegler, R. (2005). From *For* to Governance for Sustainable Development in Europe: What is at Stake for Further Research? *International Journal of Sustainable Development*, 8 (1–2): 127–50.

Featherstone, M. (1994). City Cultures and Post-modern Lifestyles, in A. Amin (ed.) *Post-Fordism: A Reader*. Oxford: Blackwell, pp. 387–408.

Fischer, F. (2003). *Reframing Public Policy: Discursive Politics and Deliberative Practices*. Oxford: Oxford University Press.

Fisher, D.R., and Freudenburg, W.R. (2001). Ecological Modernization and its Critics: Assessing the Past and Looking Toward the Future. *Society and Natural Resources*, 14: 701–9.

Forum for the Future (undated). *Sustainable Cities Index*. Online source: http://www.forumforthefuture.org (home page), accessed 28 June 2014.

Freilich, R. and Peshoff, B. (1997). The Social Costs of Sprawl. *The Urban Lawyer*, 29 (2): 183–98.

Frumkin, H. (2002). Urban Sprawl and Public Health. *Public Health Reports*. 117 (3): 201–17.

Future of Privacy Forum (2013). *Big Data and Privacy: Making Ends Meet*. Stanford Law School Center for Internet and Society. Online source: http://www.futureofprivacy.org (home page), accessed 3 July 2014.

GCIF (undated). *Global City Indicators Facility*. Online source: http://www.cityindicators.org, accessed 28 June 2014.

GEC (2005). *Eco-Towns in Japan: Implications and Lessons for Developing Countries and Cities*. Global Environment Centre Foundation research paper. Online source: http://www.unep.org/ietc/Portals/136/Publications/Waste%20Management/Eco_Towns_in_Japan.pdf, accessed 12 July 2014.

Geels, F.W. (2002). Technological Transitions as Evolutionary Reconfiguration Processes: a Multi-level Perspective. *Research Policy*, 31 (8): 1257–74.

Geels, F.W. (2010). Ontologies, Socio-Technical Transitions (to Sustainability), and the multi-level perspective. *Research Policy*, 39 (4): 495–510.

Geels, F.W. (2011). *Strategic Niche Management for Eco-cities*. Conference paper. ESCR-seminar on Eco-city innovation: integrated systems management on policy co-ordination, University of Westminster, London, 11 October.

Geels, F.W. and Schot, J. (2007). Typology of Sociotechnical Transition Pathways. *Research Policy*, 36 (3): 399–417.

Gerdes, J. (2013). Copenhagen's Ambitious Push to be Carbon-neutral by 2025. *The Guardian*, 12 April. Online source: http://www.theguardian.com (home page), accessed 1 March 2014.

German Sustainable Building Council (undated). *DGNB System*. Online source: http://www.dgnb-system.de/en, accessed 29 June 2014.

Giddings, B., Hopwood, B. and O'Brien, G. (2002). Environment, Economy and Society: Fitting them together into Sustainable Development. *Sustainable Development*, 10: 187–96.

Gill, S. (1995). Globalisation, Market Civilisation, and Disciplinary Neoliberalism. *Millennium – Journal of International Studies*, 24 (3): 399–423.

Gillham, O. (2002). *The Limitless City: A Primer on the Urban Sprawl Debate*. Washington, DC: Island Press.

Girardet, H. (1996). *The Gaia Atlas of Cities: New Directions for Sustainable Urban Living*. 2nd edn. London: Gaia.

Girardet, H. (1999). *Creating Sustainable Cities*. Totnes: Green Books.

Glasgow City Council (undated a). *Future City Glasgow*. Online source: http://www.glasgow.gov.uk/FutureCities, accessed 14 November 2014.

Glasgow City Council (undated b). *Operations* Centre. Future City Glasgow. Online source: http://futurecity.glasgow.gov.uk/index.aspx?articleid=10252, accessed 14 November 2014.

Glasgow City Council (undated c). *City Technology Platform*. Future City Glasgow. Online source: http://futurecity.glasgow.gov.uk/index.aspx?articleid=10255, accessed 19 January 2015.

Global Commission on the Economy and Climate (2014). *Better Growth, Better Climate: The New Climate Economy Report*. Synthesis report. Online source: http://www.newclimateeconomy.report, accessed 16 November 2014.

Goodland, R. and Daly, H. (1996). Environmental Sustainability: Universal and Non-Negotiable. *Ecological Applications*, 6 (4): 1002–17.

Greenwood, D. and Newman, P. (2010). Markets, Large Projects and Sustainable Development: Traditional and New Planning in the Thames Gateway. *Urban Studies*, 47 (1): 105–19.

Griffin, L. (ed.) (2010). Special Issue: Governance Innovation for Sustainability: Exploring the Tensions and Dilemmas. *Environmental Policy and Governance*, 20 (6): 365–421.

Grober, U. (2012). *Sustainability: A Cultural History*. Totnes: Green Books.

Gudmundsson, H. and Fukuda, D. (2012). Towards Sustainable Transport in Japan? The use of Indicators in the Governance of Japanese Urban Transport Policy. Paper presented at *WCTRS SIG10 Workshop*, Vienna, 14–16 March. Online source: http://orbit.dtu.dk/fedora/objects/orbit: 110470/datastreams/file_7702879/content, accessed 20 March 2014.

Guy, S., Marvin, S., Medd, W. and Moss, T. (eds) (2011). *Shaping Urban Infrastructures: Intermediaries and the Governance of Socio-technical Networks*. London: Earthscan.

Hackworth, J. (2007). *The Neoliberal City: Governance, Ideology, and Development in American Urbanism*. Ithaca, NY: Cornell University Press.

Hajer, M. and Huitzing, H. (2012). Energetic Society, in Burdett, R. and Rode, P. (eds) *Urban Age Electric City Conference: London 6–7 December 2012*. London: LSE Cities, pp. 22–23.

Hall, P. (2002). *Cities of Tomorrow: An Intellectual History of Urban Planning and Design in the Twentieth Century*. Oxford: Blackwell.

Hall, P. and Ward, C. (1998). *Sociable Cities: The Legacy of Ebenezer Howard*. Chichester: John Wiley & Sons.

Hammer, S., Kamal-Chaoui, L., Robert, A. and Plouin, M. (2011). *Cities and Green Growth: A Conceptual Framework*. OECD Regional Development Working Papers, 2011/08. OECD Publishing. Online source: http://www.oecd.org (home page), accessed 21 August 2013.

Harvey, D. (1989). From Managerialism to Entrepreneurialism: the Transformation of Urban Governance in Late Capitalism. *Geografiska Annaler: Series B, Human Geography*, 71 (1): 3–17.

Harvey, D. (2006). The Political Economy of Public Space, in Low, S. and Smith, N. (eds) *The Politics of Public Space*. London: Routledge, pp.17–34.

Haughton, G. (1999). Environmental Justice and the Sustainable City. *Journal of Planning Education and Research*, 18: 233–43.

Heinberg, R. and Lerch, D. (eds) (2010). *The Post Carbon Reader: Making Sense of the 21st Century's Sustainability Crises*. Healdsburg, CA: Watershed Media.

Herrschel, T. (2014). *Cities, State and Globalization: City-Regional Governance in Europe and North America*. Abingdon: Routledge.

Heynen, N., Kaika, M. and Swyngedouw, E. (2006). Urban Political Ecology: Politicizing the Production of Urban Natures, in Heynen, N., Kaika, M. and Swyngedouw, E. (eds) *In the Nature of Cities: Urban Political Ecology and the Politics of Urban Metabolism*. Abingdon: Routledge, pp. 1–20.

Hezri, A.A. and Dovers, S.R. (2006). Sustainability Indicators, Policy and Governance: Issues for Ecological Economics. *Ecological Economics*, 60: 86-99.

Hill, D. (2012). Digital Collaboration, in Burdett, R. and Rode, P. (eds) *Urban Age Electric City Conference: London 6–7 December 2012*. London: LSE Cities, pp. 19–22.

Hill, M. (1997) *The Policy Process in the Modern State*. 3rd edition. Hemel Hempstead: Prentice Hall/Harvester Wheatsheaf.

Hitachi Technology (2012). *Building Liveable Cities: Emerging Worldwide Concept of Smart Cities*. Online source: http://www.hitachi.com (home page), accessed 12 June 2014.

Hodge, G.A. and Greve, C. (2007). Public–Private Partnerships: An International Performance Review. *Public Administration Review*, 67 (3): 545–58.

Hodson, M. and Marvin, S. (2010a). Can Cities Shape Socio-technical Transitions and How Would We Know if They Were? *Research Policy*, 39 (4): 477–85.

Hodson, M. and Marvin, S. (2010b). Urbanism in the Anthropocene: Ecological Urbanism or Premium Ecological Enclaves? *Cities*, 14 (3): 298–313.

Hodson, M., and Marvin, S. (2010c). *World Cities and Climate Change: Producing Urban Ecological Security*. Maidenhead: Open University Press.

Hogue, K. (2014). Lloyd EcoDistrict gets Stable Financing. *Portland Tribune*, 13 February. Online source: http://portlandtribune.com (home page), accessed 27 May 2014.

Hollands, R.G. (2008). Will the Real Smart City Please Stand Up? *City: Analysis of Urban Trends, Culture, Theory, Policy, Action*, 12 (3): 303–20.

Holling, C.S. (1973). Resilience and Stability of Ecological Systems. *Annual Review of Ecology and Systematics*, 4: 1–23.

Hopwood, B., Mellor, M. and O'Brien, G. (2005). Sustainable Development: Mapping Different Approaches. *Sustainable Development*, 13: 38–52.

Howard, E. (1965) [1902]. *Garden Cities of To-morrow*. Cambridge, MA: MIT Press.

Howard, E. (2003) [1898]. *To-morrow: A Peaceful Path to Real Reform*. London: Routledge

Hult, A. (2013). Swedish Production of Sustainable Urban Imaginaries in China. *Journal of Urban Technology*, 20 (1): 77–94.

IFEZ (undated). *Incheon, Economic capital of Korea: New Business Paradigm*. Incheon: Incheon Free Economic Zone Authority.

IHS Global Insight (2013). *US Metro Economies: Outlook – Gross Metropolitan Product, with Metro Employment Projections*. Lexington, MA: IHS Global Insight (USA).

IPCC (2001). *Climate Change 2001: The Scientific Basis*. Cambridge: Cambridge University Press.

IPCC (2007). *Climate Change 2007: The Physical Science Basis*. Cambridge: Cambridge University Press.

IPCC (2013). *Climate Change 2013: The Physical Science Basis*. Cambridge: Cambridge University Press.

ISO (2013). *Draft International Standard ISO/DIS 37120: Sustainable development and resilience of communities — Indicators for City Services and Quality of Life*. Geneva: International Organization for Standardization.

Jacobs, M. (1999). Sustainable Development as a Contested Concept, in A. Dobson (ed.) *Fairness and Futurity: Essays on Environmental Sustainability and Social Justice*. Oxford: Oxford University Press, pp. 21–45.

Japan GreenBuild Council (undated). *CASBEE: Comprehensive Assessment System for Built Environment Efficiency*. Online source:

http://www.ibec.or.jp/CASBEE/english/index.htm, accessed 29 June 2014.

Jessop, B. (1994). Post-Fordism and the State, in Amin, A. (ed.) *Post-Fordism: a reader*. Oxford: Blackwell, pp. 251–79.

Jessop, B. (2002). *The Future of the Capitalist State*. Cambridge: Polity Press.

Jessop, B. (2004). Multi-level Governance and Multi-level Metagovernance Changes in the European Union as Integral Moments in the Transformation and Reorientation of Contemporary Statehood, in Bache, I. and Flinders, M. (eds) *Multi-level Governance*. Oxford: Oxford University Press, pp. 49–74.

Jones, A. (2014). Give UK Cities More Autonomy. *Political Insight*, 5(1): 40.

Jörby, S. (2002). Local Agenda 21 in four Swedish Municipalities: a Tool Towards Sustainability. *Journal of Environmental Planning and Management*. 45 (2): 219–44.

Joss, S. (2010). Accountable Governance, Accountable Sustainability? A Case Study of Accountability in the Governance for Sustainability. *Environmental Policy and Governance*, 20(6): 408–21.

Joss, S. (2011a). Eco-City Governance: A Case Study of Treasure Island and Sonoma Mountain Village. *Journal of Environmental Policy and Planning*, 13(4): 331–48.

Joss, S. (2011b). Eco-Cities: The Mainstreaming of Urban Sustainability: Key Characteristics and Driving Factors. *International Journal of Sustainable Development Planning*. 6 (2): 1–18.

Joss, S. (ed.) (2012). *Tomorrow's City Today: Eco-City Indicators, Standards and Frameworks. Bellagio Conference Report*. London: University of Westminster International Eco-Cities Initiative.

Joss, S. (2014). Rising to the Challenge: Public Participation in Sustainable Urban Development, in Hofmeister, W., Rueppel P. and Lye, L.F. (eds) *Eco-Cities: Sharing European and Asian Best Practices and Experiences*. Singapore: EU–Asia Dialogue, pp. 35–51.

Joss, S., Tomozeiu, D. and Cowley, R. (2011). *Eco-Cities: A Global Survey 2011*. London: University of Westminster International Eco-Cities Initiative.

Joss, S., Tomozeiu, D. and Cowley, R. (2012). Eco-city Indicators: Governance Challenges. *WIT Transactions on Ecology and the Environment*, 155:109–20.

Joss, S., Cowley, R. and Tomozeiu, D. (2013). Towards the 'Ubiquitous Eco-City': An Analysis of the Internationalisation of Eco-city Policy and Practice. *Urban Research and Practice*. 6 (1): 54–74.

Joss, S. and Molella, A. (2013). The Eco-City as Urban Technology: Perspectives on Caofeidian International Eco-City (China). *Journal of Urban Technology*. 20 (1): 115–37.

Joss, S. and Tomozeiu, D. (2013). 'Eco-City' Frameworks: A Global Overview. London: University of Westminster International Eco-Cities

Initiative. Online source: http://www.westminster.ac.uk/ecocities/projects/leverhulme-international-indicators, accessed 27 June 2014.

Kamal-Chaoui, L., Grazi, F., Joo, J. and Plouin, M. (2011). *The Implementation of the Korean Green Growth Strategy in Urban Areas.* OECD Regional Development Working Papers 2011/02. Online source: http://www.oecd.org (home page), accessed 13 July 2014.

Kargon, R. and Molella, A. (2008). *Invented Edens: Techno-Cities of the 20th Century.* Boston, MA: MIT Press.

Karlenzig, W. (2010). The Death of Sprawl: Designing Urban Resilience for the Twenty-First-Century Resource and Urban Crises, in Heinberg, R. and Lerch, D. (eds). *The Post Carbon Reader. Managing the 21st Century Sustainability Crisis.* Healdsburg, CA: Watershed Media, pp. 295–313.

Kates, R., Parris, T. and Leiserowitz, A. (2005). What is Sustainable Development? Goals, Indicators, Values, and Practice? *Environment,* 47(3): 8–21.

Katz, B., Bradley, J. and Liu, A. (2010). *Delivering the Next Economy: The States Step Up.* Brookings-Rockefeller Project on State and Metropolitan Innovation. Washington DC: Brookings Institution.

Katz, P., Scully, V. and Bressi, T.W. (1994). *The New Urbanism: Toward an Architecture of Community.* New York: McGraw-Hill.

Keil, R. and Boudreau, J.-A. (2006). Metropolitics and Metabolics: Rolling out Environmentalism in Toronto, in Heynen, N., Kaika, M. and Swyngedouw, E. (eds) *In the Nature of Cities: Urban Political Ecology and the Politics of Urban Metabolism.* Abingdon: Routledge, pp. 41–62.

Keirstead, J. and Leach, M. (2008). Bridging the Gaps Between Theory and Practice: a Service Niche Approach to Urban Sustainability Indicators. *Sustainable Development,* 16 (5): 329–40.

Kennedy, C., Cuddihy, J. and Engel-Yan, J. (2007). The Changing Metabolism of Cities. *Journal of Industrial Ecology,* 11(2): 43–59.

Kenworthy, J.R. (2006). The Eco-city: Ten Key Transport and Planning Dimensions for Sustainable City Development. *Environment and Urbanization,* 18(1): 67 –85.

Kibert, C.J. (2013). *Sustainable Construction: Green Building Design and Construction.* Hoboken, NJ: John Wiley and Sons.

Kim, Y., Kim, H., Moon, S. and Bae, S. (2009). *Ubiquitous Eco-City Planning in Korea: A Project for the Realization of Ecological City Planning and Ubiquitous Network Society.* REAL CORP Proceedings, Sitges, 22–25 April 2009. Online source: http://www.corp.at/archive/CORP2009_174.pdf, accessed 21 August 2013.

Lachman, D.A. (2013). A Survey and Review of Approaches to Study Transitions. *Energy Policy,* 58: 269–76.

La Fabrique de la Cité (2013). *Overview: How Can we Create Value for Cities?* Online source: http://www.thecityfactory.com (home page), accessed 19 May 2014.

Laituri, M. (1996) Cross-Cultural Dynamics in the Eco-city: Waitakere City, New Zealand. *Cities*, 13 (5): 329–37.

Lang, R.E. and Hornburg, S.P. (1997). Planning Portland style: Pitfalls and Possibilities. *Housing Policy Debate*, 8 (1): 1–10.

Latour, B. (2005). *From Realpolitik to Dingpolitik or How to Make Things Public*. Karlsruhe: Center for Art and Media.

Lehmann, S. (2010). *The Principles of Green Urbanism: Transforming the City for Sustainability*. London: Earthscan.

Leichenko, R. (2011). Climate Change and Urban Resilience. *Current Opinion in Environmental Sustainability 2011*, 3: 164–68.

Lélé, S. (1991). Sustainable Development: A Critical Review. *World Development*, 19: 607–21.

Li, H., Bao, W., Xiu, C., Zhang, Y. and Xu, H. (2010). Energy Conservation and Circular Economy in China's Process Industries. *Energy*, 35 (11): 4273–4281.

Li, X., Li, X., Woetzel, J., Gengtian, Z. and Zhang, Y. (2014). *The China Urban Sustainability Index 2013*. The Urban China Initiative. Online source: http://www.urbanchinainitiative.org/en (home page), accessed 1 July 2014.

Living PlanIT (undated). *PlanIT Valley: The Living Laboratory and Benchmark for Future Urban Communities*. Online source: http://living-planit.com/design_wins.htm, accessed 22 August 2013.

Loftman, P. and Nevin, B. (1994). Prestige Projects and Urban Regeneration in the 1980s and 1990s: A Review of Benefits and Limitations. *Planning Practice and Research*, 10: 299–315.

Low, M. (2013). Eco-Cities in Japan: Past and Future. *Journal of Urban Technology*, 20 (1): 7–22.

MACCA (2008). *The World's Exemplary City Where Everyone Has Ever Dreamt to Live: Multifunctional Administrative City Sejong*. Geumnam-myeon, Yeongi-gun: Multifunctional Administrative City Construction Agency.

MACCA (2011). *Sejong: Multifunctional Administrative City*. Geumnam-myeon, Yeongi-gun: Multifunctional Administrative City Construction Agency.

MACCA (undated). *Sejong: Asia's Green Metropolis of the Future*. Geumnam-myeon, Yeongi-gun: Multifunctional Administrative City Construction Agency.

Machin, A. (2013). *Negotiating Climate Change: Radical Democracy and the Illusion of Consensus*. London: Zed Books.

MacLeod, G. (2011). Urban Politics Reconsidered: Growth Machine to Post-democratic City? *Urban Studies*, 48 (12): 2629–60.

Margetts, H. (2011). The Internet and Transparency. *The Political Quarterly*, 82 (4): 518–521.

Marquand, D. (2004). *Decline of the Public*. Cambridge: Polity Press.

Masdar City (undated). *What Is Masdar City?* Online source: http://www.
masdarcity.ae/en/27/what-is-masdar-city- (accessed 25 March 2012).

Massey, D. (2007). *World City*. Cambridge: Polity Press.

Matier, P. and Ross, A. (2013). S.F.–China Development Deal Falls Apart.
SFGate, 11 April. Online source: http://www.sfgate.com (home page),
accessed 20 May 2014.

Mayor of London (2010). *Mayor Unveils £30m Plans to Kick-start
London's 'Green Enterprise District*. Press Release. Online source:
http://www.london.gov.uk (home page), accessed 21 August 2013.

McCann, E. (2010). Urban Policy Mobilities and Global Circuits of
Knowledge: Toward a Research Agenda. *Annals of the Association of
American Geographers*, 101 (1): 107–30.

McHarg, I. (1969). *Design With Nature*. New York: Natural History Press.

Meadowcroft, J. (2000). Sustainable Development: A New(ish) Idea for a
New Century. *Political Studies*, 48: 370–87.

Meadows, D., Meadows, D., Randers, J. and Behrens, W. (1972). *The
Limits to Growth: a Report for the Club of Rome's Project on the
Predicament of Mankind*. London: Earth Island.

Mega, V. (2000). Cities inventing the Civilisation of Sustainability: An Odyssey
in the Urban Archipelago of the European Union. *Cities*, 17 (3): 227–36.

METL (2012). *La Charte des ÉcoQuartiers*. Ministère de l'Égalité des
Territoires et du Logement. Online source: http://www.developpement-
durable.gouv.fr (home page), accessed 20 March 2014.

METL (2013). *ÉcoCité la démarche*. Ministère de l'Égalité des Territoires et
du Logement. Online source: http://www.territoires.gouv.fr (home page),
accessed 14 July 2014.

Metro (undated). *2040 Growth Concept*. Online source: http://www.
oregonmetro.gov (home page), accessed 22 May 2014.

Mieszkowski, K. and Smith, M. (2012). Condominium Project Moves
Forward Despite Radiation Cleanup Concerns. *The Bay Citizen*,
December 19. Online source: https://www.baycitizen.org (home page),
accessed 22 May 2014.

Miller, B. (2007). Modes of Governance, Modes of Resistance: Contesting
Neoliberalism in Calgary, in Leitner, H., Peck, J. and Sheppard, E. (eds)
Contesting Neoliberalism. New York: Guilford Press, pp. 223–49.

Miller, C.A. (2005). New Civic Epistemologies of Quantification: Making
Sense of Indicators of Local and Global Sustainability. *Science,
Technology and Human Values*, 30 (3): 403–32.

Miller, M. (2002). Garden Cities and Suburbs: At Home and Abroad.
Journal of Planning History, 1 (1): 6–28.

Ministry of the Environment Government of Japan (undated). *Minamata
Disease: The History and Measures*. Government of Japan. Online
source: http://www.env.go.jp/en/chemi/hs/minamata2002, accessed 4
August 2013.

Ministry of Foreign Affairs of Denmark (undated). *Copenhagen - The First Carbon Neutral Capital in the World*. Online source: http://denmark. dk/en/green-living/copenhagen, accessed 1 March 2014.

Mitchell, K. (2008). Portland Mayor-elect Announces Bureau Changes, Council Duties. *The Oregonian*, 16 December. Online source: http://www.oregonlive.com (home page), accessed 22 May 2014.

MNRE (undated). *Solar/Green Cities*. Ministry of New and Renewable Energy. Online source: http://www.mnre.gov.in/schemes/decentralized-systems/solar-cities, accessed 30 August 2013.

Moffatt, S., Suzuki, H., and Iizuka, R. (2012). *Eco2 Cities Guide. Ecological Cities as Economic Cities*. Washington DC: World Bank.

Mol, A.P.J., Sonnenfeld, D.A., and Spaargaren, G. (eds) 2009. *The Ecological Modernisation Reader: Environmental Reform in Theory and Practice*. London: Routledge.

Moncrieffe, J.M. (2001). Accountability: idea, ideals, constraints. *Democratisation*, 8 (3): 26–50.

Mulgan, R. (2003). *Holding Power to Account: Accountability in Modern Democracies*. Basingstoke: Palgrave Macmillan.

Mumford, L. (1938). *The Culture of Cities*. San Diego: Harcourt Brace Jovanovich.

Mumford, L. (1961). *The City in History: Its Origins, its Transformations, and its Prospects*. New York: Harcourt Brace Jovanovich.

Murakami, S. (2011). Eco-Model-City Program and Performance Assessment by CASBEE-City. Paper presented at *2nd High Level Seminar on Environmentally Sustainable Cities*. Vienna, 15–16 March. Online source: http://www.hls-esc.org (home page), accessed 20 March 2014.

Murshed, M.S., Goulart, P. and Serino, L.A. (eds) (2011). *South-South Globalization: Challenges and Opportunities for Development*. London: Routledge.

Myllylä, S. and Kuvaja, K. (2005). Societal Premises for Sustainable Development in Large Southern Cities. *Global Environmental Change*, 15 (3): 224–37.

Nasr, J. and Volait, M. (eds) (2003). *Urbanism: Imported or Exported?* Chichester: John Wiley and Sons.

Newman, J. and Clarke, J. (2009). *Publics, Politics and Power: Remaking the Public in Public Services*. London: Sage.

Newman, P., Beatley, T. and Boyer, H. (2009). *Resilient Cities: Responding to Peak Oil and Climate Change*. London: Island Press.

Oatley, N. (ed.) (1998). *Cities, Economic Competition and Urban Policy*. London: Paul Chapman Publishing.

OECD (2006). *OECD Territorial Reviews: Competitive Cities in the Global Economy. Summary in English*. Organisation for Economic Co-operation and Development. Online source: http://www.oecd.org (home page), accessed 28 February 2014.

OECD (2009). *Declaration on Green Growth Adopted at the Meeting of the Council at Ministerial Level on 25 June [C/MIN(2009)5/ADD1/FINAL].* Organisation for Economic Co-operation and Development. Online source: http://www.oecd.org (home page), accessed 10 August 2013.

OECD (2011a). *Green Cities Programme.* Organisation for Economic Co-operation and Development. Online source: http://www.oecd.org (home page), accessed 21 August 2013.

OECD (2011b). *Towards Green Growth.* Organisation for Economic Co-operation and Development. Online source: http://www.oecd.org (home page), accessed 10 August 2013.

OECD (2011c). *Effective Modelling of Urban Systems to Address the Challenges of Climate Change and Sustainability.* Organisation for Economic Co-operation and Development Global Science Forum. Online source: http://www.oecd.org (home page), accessed 3 July 2014.

Ottawa Biosphere Eco-City Initiative (undated). *The Biosphere Eco-City Model.* Online source: http://obec-evbo.ca/background/the-biosphere-eco-city-model, accessed 27 June 2014.

Otto-Zimmermann, K. (ed.) (2011). *Resilient Cities and Adaptation to Climate Change: Proceedings of the Global Forum 2010.* New York, NY: Springer.

OUP (2006). Carbon Neutral: Oxford Word of the Year. *OUPblog*, 13 November. Online source: http://blog.oup.com (home page), accessed 28 February 2014.

Parkinson, J. (2006). *Deliberating in the Real World: Problems of Legitimacy in Deliberative Democracy.* Oxford: Oxford University Press

Parsons, K.C. and Schuyler, D. (eds) (2002). *From Garden City to Green City: The Legacy of Ebenezer Howard.* Baltimore: Johns Hopkins University Press.

Pattberg, P.H., Biermann, F., Chan, S. and Mert, A. (eds) (2012). *Public-Private Partnerships for Sustainable Development: Emergence, Influence and Legitimacy.* Cheltenham: Edward Elgar.

Pearce, D. (2002). An Intellectual History of Environmental Economics. *Annual Review of Energy Environments*, 27: 57–81.

Pearce, D. and Barbier, E. (2000). *Blueprint for a Sustainable Economy.* London: Earthscan.

Pearce, D.W. and Turner, R.K. (1990). *Economics of Natural Resources and the Environment.* New York: Harvester Wheatsheaf.

Peck, J. and Theodore, N. (2001). Exporting Workfare/Importing Welfare-to-Work: Exploring the Politics of Third Way Policy Transfer. *Political Geography*, 20 (4): 427–60.

Peck, J. and Tickell, A. (1994). Searching for a New Institutional Fix, in Amin, A. (ed.) *Post-Fordism: A Reader.* Oxford: Blackwell, pp. 280–315.

Pezzey, J. (1992). *Sustainable Development Concepts: An Economic Analysis*. World Bank Environment Paper Number 2. Washington DC: World Bank.

Philip, M. (2009). Delimiting Democratic Accountability. *Political Studies*, 57 (1): 28–53.

Pierre, J. and Peters, G. (2000). *Governance, Politics and the State*. London: Palgrave Macmillan.

Pisano, U., Lepuschitz, K., and Berger, G (2014). *Sustainability Transitions at the International, European and National Level: Approaches, Objectives and Tools for Sustainable Development Governance*. ESDN Quarterly Report 33. European Sustainable Development Network. Online source: http://www.sd-network.eu (home page), accessed 16 November 2014.

Poracsky, J. and Houck, M.C. (1994). The Metropolitan Portland Urban Natural Resource Program, in Platt, R.H., Rowntree, R.A. and Muick, P.C. (eds) *The Ecological City: Preserving and Restoring Urban Biodiversity*. Amherst, MA: University of Massachusetts Press, pp. 251–67.

Porritt, J. (2004). Sustainable Development Past and Present. Sir Patrick Geddes Commemorative Lecture, Royal Museum of Scotland, Edinburgh, 1 October. Sustainable Development Commission. Online source: http://www.sd-commission.org.uk (home page), accessed 30 August 2013.

Portland City Council (2012). *The Portland Plan*. Portland, OR: Portland City Council.

Portugali, J., Meyer, H., Stolk, E. and Tan, E. (eds) (2012). *Complexity Theories of Cities Have Come of Age: An Overview with Implications to Urban Planning and Design*. Berlin: Springer.

PoSI (2010a). *Accelerating Urban Innovations*. Portland, OR: Portland Sustainability Institute.

PoSI (2010b). *Getting to Next Generation Neighborhoods*. Portland, OR: Portland Sustainability Institute.

PoSI (2012). *Lloyd EcoDistrict Roadmap*. Portland, OR: Portland Sustainability Institute.

Power, M., Mohan, G. and Tan-Mullins, M. (2012). *China's Resource Diplomacy in Africa: Powering Deveopment?* Basingstoke: Palgrave Macmillan.

PRC-UN (2012). *China's National Report on Sustainable Development*. Permanent Mission of the People's Republic of China to the UN. Online source: http://www.china-un.org/eng/zt/sdreng/P020120608816288649663.pdf, accessed 10 August 2013.

PSU ISS (undated). *EcoDistricts*. Portland State University Institute for Sustainable Solutions. Online source: http://www.pdx.edu/sustainability/ecodistricts, accessed 10 August 2013.

Pugh, C.D.J. (ed.) (2000). *Sustainable Cities in Developing Countries: Theory and Practice at the Millennium.* London: Earthscan.

Pulselli, R.M., Magnoli, G.C. and Tiezzi, E.B.P. (2004). Energy Flows and Sustainable Indicators: The Strategic Environmental Assessment for a Master Plan. *WIT Transactions on Ecology and The Environment*, 72: 3–10.

Purcell, M. (2008). *Recapturing Democracy: Neoliberalization and the Struggle for Alternative Urban Futures.* Abingdon: Routledge.

Qiang, M. (2009). Eco-City and Eco-Planning in China: Taking An Example for Caofeidian Eco-City, in Qu, L., Yang, C., Hui, X. and Sepúlveda, D. (eds) (2009). *The New Urban Question: Urbanism Beyond Neoliberalism.* 4th Conference of International Forum on Urbanism: Conference Proceedings. Amsterdam/Delft: International Forum on Urbanism [IFoU]: 511–20.

Rapoport, E. (2014). Globalising Sustainable Urbanism: The Role of International Masterplanners. *Area.* Advance online publication. DOI: 10.1111/area.12079.

Ratti, C. and Townsend, A. (2012). The Social Nexus, in Burdett, R. and Rode, P. (eds) *Urban Age Electric City Conference: London 6–7 December 2012.* London: LSE Cities, p. 15.

Redclift, M. (2005). Sustainable Development (1987–2005): An Oxymoron Comes of Age. *Sustainable Development*, 13: 212–27.

Rees, W.E. (1992). Ecological Footprints and Appropriated Carrying Capacity: What Urban Economics Leaves Out. *Environment and Urbanization*, 4 (2): 121–30.

Rees, W. and Wackernagel, M. (1996). *Our Ecological Footprint: Reducing Human Impact on the Earth.* Gabriola Island, BC: New Society Publishers.

Register, R. (1987/1996). *Ecocity Berkeley: Building Cities for a Healthy Future.* Berkeley, CA: North Atlantic Books.

Revue Urbanisme (2010). La démarche ÉcoCité: Villes durables en projet. 36 (special edition).

Rhodes, R.A.W. (1997). *Understanding Governance: Networks, Governance, Reflexivity and Accountability.* Buckingham: Open University Press.

Rip, A. and Kemp, R. (1998). Technological Change, in S. Rayner and E. L. Malone (eds) *Human Choice and Climate Change: An International Assessment, Volume 3.* Columbus, OH: Batelle Press, pp. 329–99.

Rittel, H.W.J. and Webber, M.M. (1973). Dilemmas in a General Theory of Planning. *Policy Sciences*, 4: 155–69.

Rockefeller Foundation (2013). *Rebound: Building a More Resilient World.* New York, NY: Rockefeller Foundation.

Roseland, M. (1997a). Dimensions of the Eco-city. *Cities*, 14 (4): 197–202.

Roseland, M. (ed.) (1997b). *Eco-City Dimensions: Healthy Communities, Healthy Planet.* Gabriola Island, BC: New Society Publishers.

Roseland, M. (2012). *Toward Sustainable Communities: Solutions for Citizens and their Governments*. 4th edn. Gabriola Island, BC: New Society Publishers.

Rosenau, P. (ed.) (2000). *Public–Private Policy Partnerships*. Cambridge, MA: MIT Press.

Runciman, D. (2014). Who's Really Driving Change? *The Guardian*. 24 May: Review, p. 2–4.

Rydin, Y. (2007). Indicators as a Governmental Technology? The Lessons of Community-based Sustainability Indicator Projects. *Environment and Planning D: Society and Space*, 25: 610–24.

Rydin, Y. (2010). *Governing for Sustainable Urban Development*. London: Earthscan.

Rydin, Y., Bleahu, A., Davies, M., Dávila, J.D., Friel, S., De Grandis, G., Groce, N., Hallal, P.C., Hamilton, I., Howden-Chapman, P., Lai, K.-M., Lim, C., Martins, J., Osrin, D., Ridley, I., Scott, I., Taylor, M., Wilkinson, P. and Wilson, J. (2012a). Shaping Cities for Health: Complexity and the Planning of Urban Environments in the 21st Century. *The Lancet*, 379 (9831): 2079–108.

Rydin, Y., Davies, M., Dávila, J.D., Hallal, P.C., Hamilton, I., Lai, K.-M. and Wilkinson, P. (2012b). Healthy Communities. *Local Environment: The International Journal of Justice and Sustainability*, 17 (5): 553–60.

Rydin, Y. and Thornley, A. (eds) (2002). *Planning in a Global Era*. Aldershot: Ashgate.

San Francisco Office of Economic and Workforce Development (2010). *Treasure Island Development Project. Summary Project Description*. Online source: www.oewd.org (home page), accessed 19 November 2013.

San Francisco Planning Department (undated). *Sustainable Development: Program Overview*. Online source: http://www.sf-planning.org (home page), accessed 10 April 2014.

San Francisco Public Press (2010). Special Report: Treasure Island. *San Francisco Public Press*, 22 June. Online source: http://sfpublicpress.org (home page), accessed 22 May 2015.

Sassen, S. (2012). Urbanising Technology, in Burdett, R. and Rode, P. (eds) *Urban Age Electric City Conference: London 6–7 December 2012*. London: LSE Cities, pp. 12–14.

Schneider, V. (2012). Governance and Complexity, in Levi-Faur, D. (ed.) *The Oxford Handbook of Governance*. Oxford: Oxford University Press, pp. 129–42.

Scott, A.J., Allen, J., Soja, E.W. and Storper, M. (2001). Global City-Regions, in Scott, A.J. (ed.) *Global City-Regions: Trends, Theory, Policy*. Oxford: Oxford University Press, pp. 11–32.

Seghezzo, L. (2009). The Five Dimensions of Sustainability. *Environmental Politics*, 18(4): 539–56.

Shatkin, G. (2008). The City and the Bottom Line: Urban Megaprojects and the Privatization of Planning in Southeast Asia. *Environment and Planning A*, 40 (2): 383 – 401.

Shwayri, S. (2013). A Model Korean Ubiquitous Eco-City? The Politics of Making Songdo. *Journal of Urban Technology*, 20 (1): 39–55.

Siemens (2012). *The Green City Index: A Summary of the Green City Index Research Series*. Online source: http://www.siemens.com (home page), accessed 28 June 2014.

Singapore Government (2012). *Introduction*. Online source: http://www.tianjinecocity.gov.sg/bg_intro.htm, accessed 27 June 2014.

Singapore Government (2013). *KPIs*. Online source: http://www.tian-jinecocity.gov.sg/bg_kpis.htm, accessed 27 June 2014.

SIP (2008). *SIP Listed Among the First National Ecological Demonstration Industrial Parks*. Suzhou Industrial Park. Online source: http://www.sipac.gov.cn/english/2008y/200805/t20080526_28187.htm, accessed 3 July 2014.

Smardon, R.C. (2008). A Comparison of Local Agenda 21 implementation in North American, European and Indian Cities. *Management of Environmental Quality: An International Journal*. 19 (1): 118–37.

SmartCities (undated). *What is the European Innovation Partnership for Smart Cities and Communities?* Online source: http://www.eu-smart cities.eu/faqs#Smart_Cities, accessed 1 September 2013.

Smith, A., Voß, J.-P. and Grin, J. (2010). Innovation Studies and Sustainability Transitions: The Allure of the Multi-level Perspective and its Challenges. *Research Policy*, 39: 435–48.

Smith, M. and Miezskowsk, K. (2014). Treasure Island cleanup exposes Navy's mishandling of its nuclear past. *Bulletin of the Atomic Scientists,* 24 February. Online source: http://thebulletin.org (home page), accessed 20 May 2014.

Smith, R., Simard, C. and Sharpe, A. (2001). *A Proposed Approach to Environment and Sustainable Development Indicators Based on Capital*. Report prepared for The National Round Table on the Environment and the Economy's Environment and Sustainable Development Indicators Initiative. Online source: http://www.oecd.org (home page), accessed 26 February 2014.

Star Communities (2014). *Star Community Rating System: Version 1.1.* Online source: http://www.starcommunities.org (home page), accessed 28 June 2014.

Stephenson, B. (2002). The Roots of the New Urbanism: John Nolen's Garden City Ethic. *Journal of Planning History*, 1: 99.

Stern, D.I. (1997). The Capital Theory Approach to Sustainability: A Critical Appraisal. *Journal of Economic Issues*, XXXI (1): 145–173.

STRN (2010). *A Mission Statement and Research Agenda for the Sustainability Transitions Research Network*. Online source:

http://www.transitionsnetwork.org (home page), accessed 30 March 2014.

Sustainable Cities International (2012). *Indicators for Sustainability: How Cities are Monitoring and Evaluating their Success*. Vancouver, BC: Sustainable Cities International.

Suutari, A. (2006). *USA – Oregon (Portland) – Sustainable City*. The EcoTipping Points Project.

Online source: http://www.ecotippingpoints.org (home page), accessed 22 May 2014.

Suzuki, H. (2013). Foreword V., in Dong, S. *Beautiful China: Eco-City Indicators Guidebook*. Beijing: Tongxin Press.

Suzuki, H., Dastur, A., Moffatt, S., Yabuki, N. and Maruyama, H. (2010). *Eco2 Cities: Ecological Cities as Economic Cities*. Washington, DC: World Bank.

SWCR (undated). *South Waterfront Community Relations: Sustainability*. Online source: http://www.southwaterfront.com (home page), accessed 24 May 2014.

Swilling, M., Robinson, B., Marvin, S. and Hodson, M. (2013). *City-Level Decoupling: Urban Resource Flows and the Governance of Infrastructure Transitions. A Report of the Working Group on Cities of the International Resource Panel*. United Nations Environment Programme. Online source: http://www.unep.org (home page), accessed 30 March 2014.

Swyngedouw, E. (2006). Metabolic Urbanization: The Making of Cyborg Cities, in Heynen, N., Kaika, M. and Swyngedouw, E. (eds) *In the Nature of Cities: Urban Political Ecology and the Politics of Urban Metabolism*. Abingdon: Routledge, pp. 21–40.

Swyngedouw, E. (2010). Apocalypse Forever? Post-Political Populism and the Spectre of Climate Change. *Theory, Culture and Society*, 27 (2–3): 213–32.

Talen, E. (1999). Sense of Community and Neighbourhood Form: An Assessment of the Social Doctrine of New Urbanism. *Urban Studies*, 36 (8): 1361–79.

Tangshan Bay Eco-City Management Committee (2011). *Tangshan Bay Eco-City*. Caofeidian, Tangshan: Tangshan Bay Eco-City Management Committee.

Taylor, I. (2008). ECO-CITY: The Green City of Tomorrow Being Built Today. *BBC Focus*, 197: 44–52.

TCPA (2011). *Re-imagining Garden Cities for the 21st Century: Benefits and Lessons in Bringing forward Comprehensively Planned New Communities*. London: Town and Country Planning Association.

Technology Strategy Board (undated). *Future Cities Special Interest Group: Demonstrator Programme*. Online source: https://connect.innovateuk.

org/web/future-cities-special-interest-group/demonstrator, accessed 1 July 2014.

Technology Strategy Board (2013). *Solutions for Cities. An Analysis of the Feasibility Studies from the Future Cities Demonstrator Programme.* Report T13/55. London: Technology Strategy Board.

Telos (undated). *Comprehensive Manual for the Community Capital Scan.* Online source: http://www.ccscan-ca.cscd.sfu.ca/ccs-project-group-manual, accessed 29 June 2014.

Termeer, C.J.A.M., Dewulf, A., Breeman, G. and Stiller, S.J. (2013). Governance Capabilities for Dealing Wisely With Wicked Problems. *Administration and Society,* published online before print. DOI: 10.1177/0095399712469195.

TICD (2006). *A Sustainable Future for Treasure Island. Exhibit K: Sustainability Plan.* October 2006. Treasure Island Community Development. Online source: http://www.sftreasureisland.org (home page), accessed 15 November 2013.

TIDA (undated). *Approved Plans and Documents.* Treasure Island Development Authority. Online source: http://sftreasureisland.org (home page), accessed 25 May 2014.

TIDA (undated). *Sustainability: Sustainable Design at its Best.* Treasure Island Development Authority. Online source: http://sftreasureisland. org/sustainability, accessed 10 April 2014.

TIDA (2011). *Treasure Island/Yerba Buena Island Sustainability Plan. Final, June 28, 2011.* Treasure Island Development Authority. Online source: http://sftreasureisland.org (home page), accessed 20 May 2014.

TIDA and TICD (2011). *Disposition and Development Agreement (Treasure Island/Yerba Buena Island).* Treasure Island Development Authority. Online source: http://sftreasureisland.org (home page), accessed 20 May 2014.

Tomozeiu, D. and Joss, S. (2014). Adapting Adaptation: The English Eco-town Initiative as Governance Process. *Ecology and Society,* 19 (2): 20.

UK Green Building Council (2013). *Pinpointing: One Planet Living Framework.* Online source: http://pinpoint.ukgbc.org/resource/8187-pinpointing-one-planet-living-framework.php, accessed 27 June 2014.

UK Parliament (undated). *New Towns.* Online source: http://www. parliament.uk/about/living-heritage/transformingsociety/towncountry/towns/overview/newtowns, accessed 25 July 2013.

UN (1972). *Stockholm 1972 Report of the United Nations Conference on the Human Environment.* United Nations Conference on the Human Environment. Online source: http://www.un-documents.net/unche.htm, accessed 13 July 2014.

UN (1976). *The Vancouver Declaration on Human Settlements.* United Nations Conference on Human Settlements A/CONF.70/15. Online source: http://www.un-documents.net/van-dec.htm, accessed 13 July 2014.

UN (2001). *Declaration on Cities and Other Human Settlements in the New Millennium*. United Nations General Assembly Resolution A/RES/S-25/2. Online source: http://www.un-documents.net/k-002281.htm, accessed 13 July 2014.

UN (2002). *Johannesburg Declaration on Sustainable Development*. United Nations World Summit on Sustainable Development A/CONF.199/20. Online source: http://www.un-documents.net/jburgdec.htm (accessed 21 August 2013).

UN Johannesburg Earth Summit (2002). *Local Government Declaration to the 2002 UN Johannesburg Earth Summit*, cited in Girardet, H. (2008). *Cities People Planet*. Chichester: John Wiley and Sons, p. 11.

UNDESA (1992a). *Earth Summit Agenda 21: The United Nations Programme of Action from Rio*. UN Department of Economic and Social Affairs, Division for Sustainable Development. Online source: http://sustainable development.un.org (home page), accessed 18 December 2011.

UNDESA (1992b). *Agenda 21*. United Nations Conference on Environment and Development, Rio de Janeiro, 3–14 June. Online source: http://sustainabledevelopment.un.org/content/documents/Agenda21.pdf, accessed 15 August 2013.

UNEP (2009). *Cities and Green Buildings: In the Transition to a Green Economy: A UNEP Brief*. United Nations Environment Programme. Online source: http://www.unep.org (home page), accessed 20 March 2014.

UNEP (2010). *Overview of the Republic of Korea's National Strategy for Green Growth*. United Nations Environment Programme. Online source: http://www.unep.org (home page), accessed 1 July 2014.

UNEP (2012a). *21 Issues for the 21st Century: Results of the UNEP Foresight Process on Emerging Environmental Issues*. Nairobi: United Nations Environment Programme.

UNEP (2012b). *Working Paper: Framework Elements for Assessing Urban Environmental Performance*. United Nations Environment Programme. Online source: http://www.unep.org (home page), accessed 27 June 2014.

UNFCCC (1998). *Kyoto Protocol to the United Nations Framework Convention on Climate Change*. United Nations Framework Convention on Climate Change. Online source: http://unfccc.int (home page), accessed 28 February 2014.

UNFCCC (2008). *Kyoto Protocol Reference Manual*. Bonn: United Nations Framework Convention on Climate Change.

UN-Habitat (1996). *The Habitat Agenda: Istanbul Declaration on Human Settlements*. Online source: http://www.unhabitat.org/downloads/docs/2072_61331_ist-dec.pdf (accessed 30 July 2013).

UN-Habitat (2003a). Sustainable Local Government, Sustainable Development: Involving the Private Sector and NGOs. Opening Keynote

Speech, 4 March. United Nations Human Settlements Programme UN-Habitat. Online source: http://www.unhabitat.org (home page), accessed 20 February 2014.

UN-Habitat (2003b). *The Habitat Agenda Goals and Principles, Commitments and the Global Plan of Action.* United Nations Human Settlements Programme UN-Habitat. Online source: http://mirror.unhabitat.org/downloads/docs/The Habitat Agenda.pdf, accessed 13 July 2014.

UN-Habitat (2004). *Urban Indicator Guidelines: Monitoring the Habitat Agenda and the Millennium Development Goals.* United Nations Human Settlements Programme UN-Habitat. Online source: http://ww2.unhabitat.org/programmes/guo/documents/urban_indicators_guidelines.pdf, accessed 28 June 2014.

UN-Habitat (2006a). *Report of the Third Session of the World Urban Forum.* Vancouver, Canada, June 19-23 2006. United Nations Human Settlements Programme UN-Habitat. Online source: http://ww2.unhabitat.org/wuf/2006/WUF3-Report.pdf, accessed 13 July 2014.

UN-Habitat (2006b). *World Urban Forum III: Introduction.* Online source: http://mirror.unhabitat.org/content.asp?cid=3157andcatid=41andtypeid=24andsubMenuId=0, accessed 13 July 2014.

UN-Habitat (2007). *The Medium Term Strategic and Institutional Plan (MTSIP) at a Glance: UN-Habitat's Institutional Response to Meeting the Urban Challenge.* UN-Habitat Donors Meeting, Norway, 8–9 March 2007. Online source: http://www.finland.or.ke/public/download.aspx?ID=29127andGUID={48872F8B-5D51-4017-BB81-683B3F02992B}, accessed 13 July 2014.

UN-Habitat (2009a). *Climate Change Strategy 2010–2013.* Nairobi: United Nations Human Settlements Programme UN-Habitat.

UN-Habitat (2009b). *Global Report on Human Settlements 2009: Planning Sustainable Cities.* London: Earthscan.

UN-Habitat (2010). *State of the World's Cities 2010–2011: Bridging the Urban Divide – Overview and Key Findings.* Nairobi: United Nations Human Settlements Programme UN-Habitat.

UN-Habitat (2011a). *Global Report on Human Settlements 2011: Cities and Climate Change.* London: Earthscan.

UN-Habitat (2011b). *Global Report on Human Settlements 2011: Cities and Climate Change: Policy Directions.* Abridged Report. London: Earthscan.

UNISDR (2012). *How To Make Cities More Resilient: A Handbook For Local Government Leaders.* UNISDR United Nations Office for Disaster Risk Reduction. Online source: http://www.unisdr.org (home page), accessed 13 July 2014.

Urmson, C. (2014). Interviewed on *Frontiers.* BBC Radio 4, 4 June.

USEPA (2013). *Green Communities: Indicators.* US Environmental Protection Agency. Online source: http://www.epa.gov/greenkit/indicator.htm, accessed 27 June 2014.

USGBC (undated). *Getting to know LEED: Neighborhood Development.* US Green Building Council. Online source: http://www.usgbc.org (home page), accessed 29 June 2014.

van Berkel, R., Fujita, T., Hashimoto, S. and Geng, Y. (2009). Industrial and Urban Symbiosis in Japan: Analysis of the Eco-Town Program 1997–2006. *Journal of Environmental Management,* 90 (3): 1544–56.

van Bueren, E.M., Klijn, E.-H. and Koppenjan, J.F.M. (2003). Dealing with Wicked Problems in Networks: Analyzing an Environmental Debate from a Network Perspective. *Journal of Public Administration Research and Theory,* 13 (2): 193–212.

Wackernagel, M. and Rees, W.E. (1997). Perceptual and Structural Barriers to Investing in Natural Capital: Economics from an Ecological Footprint Perspective. *Ecological Economics,* 20: 3-24.

Walker, J. and Cooper, M. (2011). Genealogies of Resilience: From Systems Ecology to the Political Economy of Crisis Adaptation. *Security Dialogue,* 42 (2): 143–60.

Wang, G. (ed.) (2010). *The State of China's Cities 2010/2011. Better City, Better Life.* Beijing: Foreign Languages Press.

Watson, V. (2009). Seeing from the South: Refocusing Urban Planning on the Globe's Central Urban Issues. *Urban Studies,* 46 (11): 2259–75.

WCED (World Commission on Environment and Development) (1987). *Our Common Future.* Oxford: Oxford University Press.

WEF (2009). SlimCity Facilitation Guide. World Economic Forum. Online source: http://www3.weforum.org/docs/WEF_SlimCity_Facilitation Guide_2009.pdf, accessed 19 August 2013.

Wei, J. (2013). Foreword I., in Dong, S. *Beautiful China: Eco-City Indicators Guidebook.* Beijing: Tongxin Press.

Weintraub, J.A. and Kumar, K. (eds) (1997). *Public and Private in Thought and Practice.* Chicago: University of Chicago Press.

Weisz, H. and Steinberger, J.K. (2010). Reducing Energy and Material Flows in Cities. *Current Opinion in Environmental Sustainability,* 2 (3): 185–92.

Weskamp, A.S. (2013). *Ecological Modernization in China's Settlement Development. Dongtan Eco-city and Chongming Eco-Island.* (Masters Dissertation). Tongji University/Technical University of Berlin.

Wheeler, S. (2000). Planning for Metropolitan Sustainability. *Journal of Planning Education and Research,* 20: 133–45.

Wheeler, S. (2009). Regions, Megaregions, and Sustainability. *Regional Studies,* 43 (6): 863–76.

Wheeler, S. and Beatley, T. (eds) (2009). *The Sustainable Urban Development Reader.* 2nd edn. London: Routledge.

While, A., Jonas, A. and Gibbs, D. (2010). From Sustainable Development to Carbon Control: Eco-state Restructuring and the Politics of Urban and Regional Development. *Transactions of the Institute of British Geographers*, 35: 76–93.

WHO (2009). *Zagreb Declaration for Healthy Cities: Health and Health Equity in all Local Policies*. International Healthy Cities Conference, Zagreb, 15-18 October 2008. Online source: http://www.euro.who.int (home page), accessed 17 July 2014.

WHO (undated). *Healthy Cities*. World Health Organization. Online source: http://www.euro.who.int/en/health-topics/environment-and-health/urban-health/activities/healthy-cities, accessed 17 July 2014.

Wiedmann, T. and Minx, J. (2008). A Definition of 'Carbon Footprint', in Pertsova, C.C. (ed.) *Ecological Economics Research Trends*. Hauppauge, NY: Nova Science, pp. 1–11.

Williams, C. (2012). Portland Ecodistricts Move Ahead Under City Guidance. *Sustainable Business Oregon*, December 18. Online source: http://www.sustainablebusinessoregon.com/articles/2012/12/portland-ecodistricts-move-ahead-under.html, accessed 5 January 2013.

Williams, C., Zhou, N., He, G. and Levine, M. (2012). *Measuring in All the Right Places: Themes in International Municipal Eco-City Index Systems*. Pacific Grove, CA: American Council for an Energy-Efficient Economy.

Wolman, A. (1965). The Metabolism of Cities. *Scientific American*, 213 (3): 179–90.

World Bank (2009). *Sino-Singapore Tianjin Eco-City: A Case Study of an Emerging Eco-City in China*. (Technical Assistance Report No 59012/2009). The World Bank Infrastructure Department East Asia and Pacific Region. Online source: http://www.worldbank.org (home page), accessed 20 December 2011.

World Bank (2010a). *Eco2 Cities Brochure*. Online source: http://siteresources.worldbank.org/INTEASTASIAPACIFIC/Resources/Eco2_Cities_Brochure.pdf, accessed 9 January 2014.

World Bank (2010b). *Eco2 Cities: Ecological Cities as Economic Cities: Synopsis*. Washington, DC: World Bank.

World Bank (2011). Eco2 Cities: a Guide for Developing Ecologically Sustainable and Economically Viable Cities. Press Release 8 November. Online source: http://www.worldbank.org (home page), accessed 20 February 2014.

Yanitsky, O. (1982). Towards an Eco-City: Problems of Integrating Knowledge with Practice. *International Social Science Journal*. 24 (3): 469–80.

Yigitcanlar, T. and Lönnqvist, A. (2013). Benchmarking Knowledge-based Urban Development Performance: Results from the International Comparison of Helsinki. *Cities*, 31: 357–69.

Yigitcanlar, T., O'Connor, K. and Westerman, C. (2008). The Making of Knowledge Cities: Melbourne's Knowledge-based Urban Development Experience. *Cities*, 25 (2): 63–72.

Young, S.C. (2000). *The Emergence of Ecological Modernisation: Integrating the Environment and the Economy?* London: Routledge.

Yu, L. (2014). *Chinese City and Regional Planning Systems.* Farnham: Ashgate.

Yudelson, J. (2008). *The Green Building Revolution.* Washington: Island Press.

Zhang, X., Wu, Y. and Shen, L. (2011). An Evaluation Framework for the Sustainability of Urban Land Use: A Study of Capital Cities and Municipalities in China. *Habitat International,* 35 (1): 141–49.

Zhang, Y., Yang, Z., Fath, B.D. and Li, S. (2010). Ecological Network Analysis of an Urban Energy Metabolic System: Model Development, and a Case Study of Four Chinese Cities. *Ecological Modelling,* 221 (16): 1865–79.

Zhou, N. and Williams, C. (2013). *An International Review of Eco-City Theory, Indicators, and Case Studies.* Berkeley, CA: Ernest Orlando Lawrence Berkeley National Laboratory.

Zhou, N., He, G. and Williams, C. (2012). *China's Development of Low-Carbon Eco-Cities and Associated Indicator Systems.* Berkeley, CA: Ernest Orlando Lawrence Berkeley National Laboratory. Online source: http://eetd.lbl.gov/sites/all/files/china_eco-cities_indicator_systems.pdf, accessed 1 September 2013.

Zukin, S. (2010). *Naked City: The Death and Life of Authentic Urban Places.* Oxford; New York: Oxford University Press.

Index